India, GCC and the Global Energy Regime

Published in association with
Observer Research Foundation
New Delhi

Dr. Samir Ranjan Pradhan is currently Senior Researcher at the Gulf Research Centre (GRC); a Dubai based premier independent policy research and consultancy organisation. He is a trained economist and obtained his M.Phil and Ph.D degrees from the School of International Studies, Jawaharlal Nehru University, New Delhi. His main areas of research interests include: energy security in the perspective of international relations; national, regional and global dimension of India's energy security; developments and changes in the global oil and gas market with special focus on India, Gulf and China; regional cooperation and energy security in Asia, and India's economic relations with West Asia in general and GCC in particular. He has important national and international publications to his credit.

India, GCC and the Global Energy Regime

Exploring Interdependence and Outlook for Collaboration

SAMIR RANJAN PRADHAN

ACADEMIC FOUNDATION
NEW DELHI

ACADEMIC FOUNDATION

First published in 2008
by

ACADEMIC FOUNDATION
4772-73 / 23 Bharat Ram Road, (23 Ansari Road),
Darya Ganj, New Delhi - 110 002 (India).
Phones : 23245001 / 02 / 03 / 04.
Fax : +91-11-23245005.
E-mail : academic@vsnl.com
www. academicfoundation.com

in association with the

Observer Research Foundation, New Delhi

Cataloging in Publication Data--DK
Courtesy: D.K. Agencies (P) Ltd. <docinfo@dkagencies.com>

Pradhan, Samir Ranjan.
India, GCC and the global energy regime : exploring interdependence and outlook for collaboration / by Samir Ranjan Pradhan.
p. cm.
Includes bibliographical references (p.)
ISBN 9788171886333

1. Energy policy--India. 2. Energy policy--Persian Gulf States. 3. India--Commerce--Persian Gulf States. 4. Persian Gulf States--Commerce--India. 5. Gulf Cooperation Council. I. Title. II. Title: India and Gulf Cooperation Council.

DDC 382.095 405 36 22

Typeset by Italics India, New Delhi.
Printed and bound in India.

Contents

List of Tables, Figures and Boxes 7

Acknowledgements 13

Notes, Definitions and Abbreviations 15

Preface 23

Introduction 31

1. The Global Oil and Gas Regime: Analytical Overview of Structural Transition 37
2. Changing Pattern of the Global Energy Trade: India, A Destination for the GCC Countries Oil and Gas Exports 87
3. India and GCC Countries: An Emerging Pattern of Energy Interdependence 149
4. Interdependence and Mutual Vulnerability: Issues in Energy Security 251
5. The Interdependence Framework: A Catalyst to Augment Economic Relations 307
6. Competition-Interdependence Dilemma in Asia: Implications for India's Gulf Strategy 345
7. Conclusion: Towards an Asian Energy Charter 363

Annexures 375

References 413

Index 423

List of Tables, Figures and Boxes

Tables

1.1 The Main Consortia in the Middle East, 1953-1970 (Ownership Distribution of Capital in Percentages) 44

1.2 Key Oil Discoveries in the Middle East 47

1.3 Rates of Growth of World Oil Consumption 48

1.4 Posted Price Cuts in the Late 1950s 52

1.5 Crude Oil Discoveries, 1944-1974 53

1.6 Size of Private Companies in 1998 and Impact of Mergers 67

1.7 Crude Oil Production of Major Companies, 1950-2005 68

2.1 The Trends of Oil Production by Area in the World 89

2.2 The Trends of Oil Consumption by Area in the World 89

2.3 The Trends of Natural Gas Production by Area in the World 92

2.4 The Trends of Natural Gas Consumption by Area in the World 93

2.5 The Trends of Oil Imports by Area in the World 95

2.6 The Trends of Oil Exports by Area in the World 96

2.7 Trends of Natural Gas Imports (Shares) by Area in the World 98

2.8 Trends of Natural Gas Exports (Shares) by Area in the World 99

2.9 World Oil Demand Outlook in the Reference Case 102

2.10 Total World Primary Supply of Gas 103

2.11 Asia Pacific Primary Energy Consumption by Fuel Type 106

2.12 Oil and Gas Fundamentals in Asia Pacific, 2005 109

2.13 Oil and Energy Use in Asia, 2003 110

2.14 Energy Efficiency in Different Countries 111

2.15 Oil Demand-Supply Balance in Asia, 2005-2025 114

2.16 Asia's Heavy Dependence on Middle East Oil 115

2.17 Historical Energy Consumption Growth Rates in India 120

2.18 Production of Primary Energy in India 121

2.19 AAGR of Consumption of Petroleum Products 123

2.20 India's Net Imports of Crude Oil and Products 125

2.21 Share of Future Energy Supply in India 125

2.22 GCC Macroeconomic Indicators 2006 134

2.23 GCC's Real GDP Growth Rate 1980-2005 138

2.24 Population Statistics for GCC Countries 144

3.1 Important Oil-Gas Discoveries of 1960s and 1970s in India 152

3.2 Important Oil-Gas Discoveries of 1980s 154

3.3 Basin-wise Hydrocarbon Resources of India 163

3.4 Performance of Various E&P Companies in India 165

3.5 Discoveries made by Pvt/JVs in NELP and Pre-NELP Blocks and Fields 169

3.6 Oil & Gas Industry Structure in India, 2004-05 174

3.7 Trend of Crude Oil Production and Demand in India 1990-91–2005-2006 175

3.8 Installed Capacity and Refinery Throughput 176

3.9 Sale of Petroleum Products in India, 1997-98 to 2005-06 177

3.10 Area-wise and Sector-wise Gas Consumption in India, 1999-2000 180

3.11 Sectoral Consumption of Natural Gas 181

3.12 Projections of Supply/Demand—Petroleum Products 1999-2000–2024-2025 183

3.13 Sectoral Oil Demand (MTS) Projections: The Base Case Scenario 183

3.14 Projected Demand and Supply of Crude Oil: The Base Case Scenario 184

3.15 Short-term Gas Demand Outlook 186

3.16 Various Gas Demand Projections 187

3.17 Projected Domestic Gas Production 187

3.18 The Oil Demand of Investment in Indian Oil-Gas Sector till 2010 196

3.19 Global, Middle East and GCC Oil Production, 1965-2005 198

3.20 Middle East's Share in World Oil Exports 199

3.21 Major Increases in Non-OPEC Productions, 2007 208

3.22 OPEC Oil Export Revenue 209

3.23 IMF Estimate of Oil Revenue Dependence for Selected Major Exporters, 2001 211

3.24 OPEC Members' Value of Petroleum Exports 212

3.25 OPEC Members' Current Account Balance 213

3.26 Total GCC Countries' Energy Consumption 1995-2000 214

3.27 GCC Countries' Estimates of Consumption of Oil Products for the Period 2001-2015 215

3.28 Projected Financial Requirements for Maintenance and Expansion of GCC Oil Sector, 2002-06 223

3.29 Projected Investments in GCC Gas, Refining and Petrochemical Projects, 2002-06 223

3.30 Major LNG Projects of India with Qatar & other GCC Countries 236

4.1 World Oil Supply Disruptions 261

4.2 Greatest Oil and Natural Gas Reserves by Country, 2006 271

4.3 Idle Capacities of OPEC Countries in the First Half of 2001 272

4.4 World Oil Production by Region and Country, Reference Case, 1990-2025 273
4.5 Saudi Oil Production and its Share of Total of OPEC ('000b/d, 1980-2005) 274
4.6 Adherents to the Forum of Gas Exporting Countries: Reserves, Production and Exports (2001, bcm) 283
4.7 World Oil Consumption, Production and Imports 291
4.8 India's Imports and Exports of Crude Oil and Products 293
4.9 Sources of India's Import of Crude Petroleum and Products 294
4.10 GCC Countries' Share in India's Total Imports of Crude Oil and Products 295
5.1 India and GCC: Relative Mutual Importance in Trade Profile 311
5.2 India's Major Export Items to Bahrain 315
5.3 India's Major Import Items from Bahrain 316
5.4 India's Major Export Items from Kuwait 318
5.5 India's Major Import Items from Kuwait 319
5.6 India's Major Export Items to Oman 321
5.7 India's Major Import Items from Oman 321
5.8 India's Major Export Items to Qatar 323
5.9 India's Major Import Items from Kuwait 323
5.10 India's Major Export Items to Saudi Arabia 325
5.11 India's Major Import Items from Saudi Arabia 325
5.12 India's Major Export Items to UAE 327
5.13 India's Major Import Items from UAE 327
5.14 Project Exports to GCC Countries 329
5.15 FDI Flows to India from GCC 330
5.16 India's Approved ODI in GCC 331
5.17 Indian JVs and WOS Approved in GCC Countries 332
6.1 Qualitative Comparison of Production Characteristics of Asian Countries 359

Figures

2.1 World Primary Energy Consumption by Fuel (Share in per cent), 1972 and 2005 88

2.2 World Oil Production Shares by Area 90

2.3 World Oil Consumption Shares by Area 91

2.4 World Natural Gas Production Shares by Area 92

2.5 World Natural Gas Consumption Shares by Area 94

2.6 World Oil Imports Shares by Area 95

2.7 World Oil Export Shares by Region 97

2.8 Shares of Various Fuels in Asia-Pacific's TPEC 107

2.9 Asia Pacific Energy Balance, 2006 108

2.10 Asia Pacific's Oil Import Outlook 115

2.11 India's Commercial and Non-Commercial Energy Consumption Trends (Trend of % Share of Commercial *Vs* Non-Commercial Energy) 119

2.12 India's Oil Product Consumption and Domestic Production (Widening Gap between Demand and Domestic Supply) 124

2.13 India's Demand and Domestic Production of Natural Gas, BCM 126

2.14 Oil Import Outlook in Asia, mb/d 127

2.15 Share of Main Asian Countries in Total Asian Oil Imports (Oil-Import Shares of Countries in Asia Pacific) 128

2.16 OPEC Crude Oil Export Market Share by Region 131

3.1 New Significant Discoveries 167

3.2 Product-wise Share in Total Sale of Petroleum Products, 2005-06 178

3.3 India—External Oil Dependency Outlook 185

4.1 Top Net Oil Imports, 2006 292

4.2 Share of Regions in India's Crude Oil Imports 295

4.3 India's Energy Diplomacy 301
4.4 Asian Premium: Average Price Differentials for Arab Light Crude (fob), between Asia and EU, US 305
5.1 India's Trade with GCC: Various Indicators 308
5.2 India's Exports to GCC Countries, 2004-05 309
5.3 GCC's Trade with India: Various Indicators 310
5.4 Country Shares in India's Total Project Exports to GCC 329
6.1 The Energy Security Strategy Quadrant Model (ESSQM) 349

Boxes

3.1 GCC Countries: Recent Key Structural Reforms 242
4.1 Development of Oil/Gas Supply and Demand Security Issues in the Global Oil and Gas Regime 264
4.2 Effects of Oil Shock on Indian Economy 297
6.1 India's Energy Sector: Major Issues and Challenges 346
6.2 Recent Developments in Energy Security Policies in Asia 353
6.3 Sub-Regional Energy Cooperation in Asia: Trends and Patterns 354

Acknowledgements

This academic endeavour would not have been possible without the help of a number of people who with their kind cooperation, benign supervision and able support have made this work a reality. Above all, I must single out Prof. Girijesh Pant who kindled my interest in the subject during my stint as M.Phil and Ph.D. scholar at the School of International Studies, Jawaharlal Nehru University from 1997 to 2004.

Ms. Lydia Powell, Director, Centre for Resources Management and Mr. Baljit Kapoor, Honorary Secretary of the Observer Research Foundation (ORF), New Delhi, astutely facilitated the logical culmination of my research endeavour in the form of this book. I shall remain ever grateful to them and ORF for giving me this privileged opportunity to showcase my research output for expert supervision and suggestions. I sincerely acknowledge the expert comments and suggestions provided by Mr. Najeeb Jung, Ambassador Hamid Ansari and anonymous experts which enabled the updation and fine-tuning of this work. I also appreciate the sincere support of Ms. Anshu John, editor ORF and administrative help of Mr. Akhilesh and Mr. Janardhan of ORF.

My association with the Research and Information System for Developing Countries (RIS) was a great learning experience. Dr. Nagesh Kumar (DG), all senior colleagues at RIS and their scholarly accomplishments continuously motivate me in my own area of research.

I owe a lot to the numerous leading experts and analysts and their thought provoking and path breaking scholastic contributions that enabled me to look at the subject comprehensively. In this work, I have been influenced by numerous sources and tried to acknowledge each and every contribution, if by default anyone is missing or wrongly incorporated, then the responsibility rests with me.

Finally, this book is dedicated to the unflagging support and steadfast appreciation of my family members (especially my parents and my lovely wife, Bharti) and friends. My friend circle is the greatest source of personal pleasure, emotional support, and professional respect in their capacity as my toughest critic. I hope this book elicits their approval.

Samir Ranjan Pradhan

Notes, Definitions and Abbreviations

'000 b/d	Thousand Barrels per Day.
ABC	Assam, Bombay and Cambay.
ACC	Associated Cement Companies Limited.
ADNOC	Abu Dhabi National Oil Co.
AHDR	Arab Human Development Report.
APM	Administered Pricing Mechanism.
ASEAN	The members of the Association of South East Asian Nations are Brunei Darussalam, Cambodia, Indonesia, Laos PDR, Malaysia, Myanmar, Philippines, Singapore, Thailand, and Vietnam.
Aramco	Arabian American Oil Company.
ASSOCHAM	Associated Chambers of Commerce and Industry of India.
ATF	Aviation Turbine Fuel.
B	Barrels.
b/d	Barrels per day.
BATC	Bahrain Asian Trading Committee.
BBA	Bahrain Businessmen's Association.
bcf	Billion Cubic Feet.
bcm	Billion Cubic Metre.
BEC	Bhilai Engineering Corporation Limited.
BHEL	Bharat Heavy Electricals Limited.
BIPA	Bilateral Investment Promotion Agreement.

BIPPA	Bilateral Investment Protection and Promotion Agreement.
Bn	Billion.
BOC	Burma Oil Co.
BP	British Petroleum.
BPO	Business Process Outsourcing.
Btoe	Billion Tonne Oil Equivalent.
CSO	Central Statistical Organisation.
CES	Consultancy Engineering Services.
Cif	Cost, Insurance, Freight.
CII	Confederation of Indian Industry.
CSCCI	Council of Saudi Chambers of Commerce and Industry.
DBEC	Dakshin Bharat Energy Consortium.
DGCIS	Directorate General of Foreign Commercial Intelligence and Statistics.
DME	Dimethyl Ether.
DTAA	Avoidance of Double Taxation Agreement.
EIA	Energy Information Administration.
ENI	Ente Nazionale Idrocarburi.
ESCWA	Economic and Social Commission for Western Asia.
ETG	Expert Technical Group.
FDI	Foreign Direct Investment.
FICCI	Federation of Indian Chamber of Commerce and Industry.
Fob	Free on Board.
FSU	Former Soviet Union, comprising Russia, Georgia, Armenia, Azerbaijan, Kazakhstan, Kyrgyzstan, Tajikistan, Turkmenistan, and Uzbekistan.
GAIL	GAIL (India) Ltd.
GATS	General Agreement on Trade in Services.

GCC	The Cooperation Council for the Arab States of the Gulf, known as the Gulf Cooperation Council, was founded in 1981 by Bahrain, Kuwait, Oman, Qatar, Saudi Arabia and the United Arab Emirates. In 1982, it issued an agreement covering the freedom of movement of people and capital, the abolition of customs duties, technical cooperation, harmonisation of banking regulations, and financial and monetary coordination. A common, minimum customs levy of between 4 per cent and 20 per cent was imposed in 1986 and in 1992. GCC ministers agreed to set up a custom union by 2010 but, as of the time of writing, a five per cent of united external tariff has been agreed upon.
GDP	Gross Domestic Product.
GIDG	GDP Indexed Demand Growth.
GNP	Gross National Product.
GoI	Government of India.
HBJ	Haldia-Bijapur-Jagdishpur.
HSD	High Speed Diesel.
ICSIR	Indian Council for Scientific and Industrial Research.
ICT	Information and Communication and Technology.
IEA	The International Energy Agency, located in Paris, was founded in 1974 as an autonomous body within the OECD. It carries out an energy cooperation programme among 24 of the 29 countries in the OECD. Its main aims are to reduce excessive dependence on oil; to provide information on the international oil market; to cooperate with oil producing and consuming countries in order to ensure stabile conditions on international energy markets; to prepare plans to help member states avoid the risks of major disruption of oil supplies; and to share supplies in the event of an emergency. Its members are Australia, Austria, Belgium, Canada, Denmark, Finland, France, Germany, Greece, Hungary, Ireland, Italy, Japan, Luxembourg, the Netherlands, New

	Zealand, Norway, Portugal, Spain, Sweden, Switzerland, Turkey, the United Kingdom and the United States. The Commission of the European Union also takes part in the work of the IEA.
IKCC	India-Kuwait Chamber of Commerce.
IOC	Indian Oil Corporation Ltd.
IOCs	International Oil Companies.
IOP	Iran Oil Participants Ltd.
IPC	Iraq Petroleum Company.
IPCL	Indian Petrochemical Corporation Limited.
ISPP	Indo-Stanvac Petroleum Project.
ITES	Information Technology Enabled Services.
JBC	Joint Business Council.
JCM	Joint Commission for Economic, Trade, Scientific, Technical and Cultural Cooperation.
KACST	King Abdul Aziz City for Science and Technology.
KISR	Kuwait Institute of Scientific Research.
Km	Kilometres.
KOC	Kuwait Oil Company.
LDPE	Low-density Polyethylene.
LNG	Liquefied Natural Gas.
LPG	Liquid Petroleum Gas.
mb/d	Million Barrels per Day.
mboe/d	Million Barrels of Oil Equivalent per Day.
mcmd	Million Cubic Metres per Day.
MFN	Most Favoured Nation.
MMSCMD	Million Metric Standard Cubic Metres per Day.
Mmt	Million Metric Tonnes.
Mn	Million.
MoPNG	Ministry of Petroleum & Natural Gas.

MoU	Memorandum of Understanding.
Mtoe	Million Tonnes Oil Equivalent.
Mtpa	Million Metric Tonnes per Annum.
NASSCOM	National Association of Software and Services Companies.
NEDC	Near East Development Corporation.
NELP	New Exploration Licensing Policy.
NGLs	Natural Gas Liquids.
NIOC	National Iranian Oil Company.
NOC	National Oil Companies.
NODCO	National Oil Distribution Company (Qatar).
NSIC	National Small Industries Corporation.
OAPEC	The Organization of Arab Petroleum Exporting Countries was established in 1968 by Saudi Arabia, Kuwait and Libya. Members of OAPEC now include the Arab members of OPEC and Egypt, Syria, Bahrain, Oman, Tunisia and Morocco.
OCCI	Oman Chamber of Commerce and Industry.
OCIPED	Omani Centre for Investment Promotion and Export Development.
OECD	The Organisation for Economic Co-operation and Development, located in Paris, was founded in 1960. Its aim is to promote economic growth, employment and financial stability in member states and to contribute to the development of the international trade and the world economy. Its members are Australia, Austria, Belgium, Canada, the Czech Republic, Denmark, Finland, France, Germany, Greece, Hungary, Iceland, Ireland, Italy, Japan, Korea, Luxembourg, Mexico, the Netherlands, New Zealand, Norway, Poland, Portugal, Spain, Sweden, Switzerland, Turkey, the United Kingdom and the United States. The Commission of the European Union also takes part in the work of the IEA.

OIL	Oil India Limited.
ONGC	Oil and Natural Gas Commission Ltd.
OPA	Oil Pool Account.
OPEC	The Organization of the Petroleum Exporting Countries (OPEC) is a permanent, intergovernmental organisation, created at the Baghdad Conference on September 10-14, 1960, by Iran, Kuwait, Saudi Arabia and Venezuela. The five Founding Members were later joined by nine other Members: Qatar (1961); Indonesia (1962); Socialist Peoples Libyan Arab Jamahiriya (1962); United Arab Emirates (1967); Algeria (1969); Nigeria (1971); Eucador (1973-1992); Gabon (1975-1994) and Angola (2007). OPEC had its headquarters in Geneva, Switzerland, in the first five years of its existence. This was moved to Vienna, Austria, on September 1, 1965. The new OPEC Reference Basket (ORB), implemented as of 16 June 2005, is made up of the following: Saharan Blend (Algeria), Minas (Indonesia), Iran Heavy (Islamic Republic of Iran), Basra Light (Iraq), Kuwait Export (Kuwait), Es Sider (Libya), Bonny Light (Nigeria), Qatar Marine (Qatar), Arab Light (Suadi Arabia), Murban (UAE) and BCF 17 (Venezuela).
ORB	OPEC Reference Basket.
PDEXCIL	Power Loom Development & Export Promotion Council
PDO	Petroleum Development Oman.
PSUs	Public Sector Undertakings.
QAFCO	Qatar Fertiliser Company.
QAPCO	Qatar Petrochemical Company.
Q-Chem	Qatar Chemical Company.
QIMCO	Qatar Industrial Manufacturing Company.
R/P Ratio	Reserve to Production Ratio. It shows the longevity of reserves at the current rate of production.
SAGIA	Saudi Arabian General Investment Authority.

SASO	Saudi Arabian Standards Organization.
SFD	Saudi Fund for Development.
SKO	Superior Kerosene Oil.
SOCAL	Standard Oil of California.
SONJ	Standard Oil of New Jersey.
SPA	Sales and Purchase Agreement.
SPIC	Southern Petrochemicals Industries Corporation Limited.
Tcf	Trillion Cubic Feet.
TEESE	TERI Energy Economy Simulation and Evaluation.
TISSCO	Teyseer Industrial Supplies and Services.
TPC	Turkish Petroleum Company.
Transition Economies	Non-OECD Europe (excluding Poland), the FSU, Cyprus, Gibraltar and Malta.
UNDP	United Nations Development Programme.
Unocal	Union Oil of California.
VSA	Valued Stock Account.
WSIS	World Summit on the Information Society.
WTO	World Trade Organization.

Preface

The global oil and gas regime has transformed fundamentally over the years, primarily influenced by the cyclical and seasonality trends of the world economy. In contrast to the earlier regimes of the 60s and 70s, the present regime exhibits an emerging pattern of interdependence between the world's traditional oil supplier—the Gulf Cooperation Council (GCC) countries namely, Bahrain, Kuwait, Oman, Qatar, Saudi Arabia and the United Arab Emirates (UAE)—and the major oil importing emerging economies of Asia in general and India in particular. The evolving oil sector interdependence centering on the demand and supply imperatives of the current energy security dynamics is poised to transcend India's economic engagement with the GCC countries to new trajectories.

The current world oil market fundamentals no more conforms to to the patterns of the past oil eras when the seller was the price setter, be it the 'Majors' (the big international oil companies, IOCs) popularly known as the 'Seven Sisters' or the national government collectivity under the aegis of the Organization of Petroleum Exporting Countries (OPEC). A number of players have entered into the field since the late 70s, so much so that in the 90s the oil price is no more set by the seller alone; rather, it is not only influenced by assorted factors, but also determined by the actions of varied market participants. In fact, the supply-demand balances and trade patterns are starkly in contrast to that of the Cold War era. The traditional rule of thumb of the 'OPEC *versus* non-OPEC' way of thinking about crude oil supplies, though persists, has lost relevance in understanding both current supply and future potential. The conventional 'OECD *versus* non-OECD' consideration regarding the world oil demand has also become irrelevant. Instead, it has become trendy now to focus on the actual patterns of trade among key exporting and importing geographic regions and on the main centres of world economic growth, regardless of their allegiance and/or membership to/of any group or organisation. In such a global energy setting, changes can also be discerned in the location of the market demand. Asia, not the Atlantic has become the major destination of oil exports, particularly that from the Persian Gulf. In recent years, the Asian region in general and India and China, in particular, have raised worldwide interests due to their highly sustainable economic growth rate and consequent gigantic volume of energy consumption. Most notable is their explosive demand for every commercial form of energy, that of oil and gas in particular, which in fact is the highest in comparison to any other region in the world in recent years.

Thus, the present oil regime configuration points to the emergence of a 'demand heartland'—comprising the main Asian drivers such as Japan, China, India, South Korea and ASEAN member countries, coinciding with the 'resource periphery' spanning from the Siberian region, Russia, Central Asia and Iran to the Arabian Gulf region. The main objective of this book is to unravel this emerging pattern of interdependence between the consumers and producers. More specifically, the book explores the evolving pattern of interdependence between India, a giant consumer and importer of oil and gas and the GCC, world's major oil supplier, and the ensuing energy-related tendencies and their implications for bilateral relations along with their regional connotations.

India's economic miracle in the late 1990s succeeded the *dramatis personae* of development success in the main Asian economies—the centre of gravity of world economy. Like other Asian economies, this development miracle in India resulted in voluminous increase in every form of energy consumption, especially that of oil and gas. As the pattern of development and consequent production process became more and more oil reliant the consumption and demand for oil gathered momentum over the years. It is not the availability of domestic oil resources but rather the cheap oil imports and the misallocation of other energy resources such as abundant domestic coal reserves that have made the Indian economy oil-reliant over the years. The result is the heavy reliance on oil imports from the Gulf region as the domestic as well as the regional reserves and production of oil did not match the ever-expanding demand.

Though the Government over the years has not emphasised its focus on the vital energy front, the post-liberalisation period of the late 1990s witnessed renewed vigour and sharpened focus on this sector in plans and policy making. The government with its policy of liberalising various sectors of the Indian economy started the liberalisation of the petroleum industry, albeit slowly due to its sensitiveness to the society as a whole. Several key decisions were taken and a vision document, *Hydrocarbon Vision 2025,* was prepared for future course of action. The recent years have witnessed some achievements in the vital energy front, as large fields of oil and gas were discovered by private and public sector joint ventures, acquisition of equity oil abroad, and a vibrant downstream sector, etc. However, there is unanimity in the policy planning level that despite the efforts to be secured on the vital energy front through accelerating domestic reserve accretion and production of oil and gas, diversifying import sources from the Gulf, cooperating with major oil consuming countries and their blocks such as the IEA, engaging the regional energy consumers in the Asian region to have a joint framework of cooperation in the hydrocarbon sector, etc; there are clear indications based on the present trends that India is and will rely heavily on the Gulf region for its ever expanding energy needs.

On the supply side perspective of the global regime, lots of changes can be witnessed, especially the declining western market share of the Gulf countries in the global oil industry. As the fundamentals of the oil and gas regime have altered over the years, and the Gulf countries under the aegis of OPEC resorted to faulty policies in order to maximise revenues at any cost, causing major oil crises having pernicious effects in the global economy, compelled the major oil consuming industrialised countries to develop alternate energy sources and destinations through technological breakthroughs and financial concessions, the Gulf's share in the world oil supply declined, thereby affecting revenue flows. The declining revenue flows combined with the financial profligacy of the governments in the Gulf region made the matters worse for them to take key decisions in the oil and gas sector in order to make these sectors adaptable to global trends. In addition, the policy failure in diversifying their narrow depleted-resource based economies made them highly vulnerable to adapt to the changing global economic regime configurations. The result is domestic instability and resentment, making these countries as laggards in the globalised world of today. However, despite the internal as well as external rigidities facing the Gulf economies, there are clear indications that the Gulf is going to regain its lost position in the world economy, mainly due to its vast reserves of oil and gas, spare production capacity, etc. Moreover, studies show that the non-OPEC production is uncertain and volatile and the most appropriate example of this is the hype about the Caspian Basin as an alternative to the Gulf. The reality is radically different from the initial hypes, as the trend shows that the total exports of oil and gas from the Caspian Basin is meagre in comparison to the Gulf. Thus, the Gulf countries are going to play prominent role as suppliers in the coming global regime centering on the Asian energy consumption growth.

Therefore, in such a global energy setting, a pattern is emerging in which Asia in general and India in particular and the GCC countries have a larger role to play. It can also be visualised that the countries of the GCC and India have convergence of interests in the present global oil and gas regime. The strategic positioning of the GCC and the Asian drivers in general and India in particular in the global oil and gas regime has led to the emergence of a pattern of interdependence, as witnessed in previous regimes between Gulf countries such as Saudi Arabia and developed western countries such as the United States. The pattern of interdependence based on the oil and gas fundamentals have compelled both India and GCC countries to interact aggressively in the oil and gas sector. This can be substantiated from the various projects and operations of both India and GCC countries in their respective oil and gas sectors, both in downstream and upstream. However, the pattern of interdependence has also its vulnerabilities in the ambit of energy security, i.e., demand security for the Gulf oil suppliers and supply security for India.

In fact, the changes and transformations in the global oil and gas business have reaffirmed the contours of the present day's energy security debate. The global oil and gas game of today is categorically different from the early oil eras when the producers/exporters used to dictate the terms for the consumers/importers, who were the ultimate bearers of these cartel's business misadventures. This can be substantiated from the fact that the major oil importers—the OECD and other European developed countries—suffered heavily and which had in fact ripples flown across the globe, thereby led to recession in the world economy. But nowadays the consumers/importers are considerably influencing every aspects of the global oil and gas business such as pricing, trading, and financing major oil and gas projects either through their national energy companies or their multinational counterparts. Besides, the suppliers/exporters have now become highly vulnerable to any eventual demand disruptions in the major consuming and importing countries either due to any economic crisis or other reasons, which analysts are referring to the 'reversal oil boom'. In addition, the major industrial countries who till recent years were the main importers and consumers of oil and gas have adopted advanced technologies to switch over to cleaner and viable energy options such as nuclear energy and others such as new hydrocarbon sources, etc. It is here worth mentioning that the Asian financial crisis in the year 1998, have taken its toll not only on the world oil and gas business but more importantly on the major oil producing and exporting countries of the Gulf region, as this region is presently the most energy consuming and importing region in the world and Gulf is the major energy supplier of this region. Thus, in the present day global energy scenario, the oil and gas producers/suppliers and the oil and gas consumers/importers are both vulnerable in the wake up of any possible demand as well as supply disruptions. In addition, it can be contended that though the industrialised West has, somehow, leveraged from the energy security point of view, the newly developing countries of the East, especially in Asia, like India are highly vulnerable. And in such transition, the oil and gas producers and consumers, especially the Gulf countries have become vulnerable in the sense that their previous market has shrunk and now dependent on some newly industrialising countries of Asia.

However, given the fact that India and GCC countries have traditional trading affinity, they will come closer to take pragmatic steps in order to mitigate the apprehensions regarding energy security.

They will be tempted to extend their interdependence in the energy front to wider and diversified economic relations to absorb the periodical bottlenecks that may emerge in the global oil and gas regime. This can be witnessed from the initiatives taken by both India and GCC countries in the global regime to consolidate and assert them in order to survive.

Moreover, given that the Asian countries in general and India in particular are poised to depend overwhelmingly on the GCC countries for their energy needs, a situation of keen competition among the Asian countries for securing energy needs in the Gulf is ensuing, which may have multifarious strategic implications. The most potent factor in such conflict can be identified as to the possible conflict in transit point of transportation—the Strait of Hormuz—the potential global choke point. The increasing penetration of China into the energy sectors of almost all GCC countries through crisscross investment deals is being viewed by other Asian countries as a cause of concern. However, the pattern of interdependence among the consumers and producers can be used as a tool to transform the vulnerabilities thereof into co-prosperity of all through the mechanism of an Energy Charter comprising India, the other Asian countries and the GCC countries. This framework of 'Asian Energy Charter' will also be the platform to address the issues and policies relating to global oil and gas business in the ambit of 'Consumer-Producer Dialogue'—the most debated issue in the global oil and gas regime of present times.

In the current environment, this study bears utmost importance for both India and GCC's evolving energy and economic diplomacy. Despite India's unrelenting efforts to diversify its oil and gas imports and reduce the dependence on the Gulf, the trends and predictions clearly point to continued overwhelming dependence on Gulf that makes a strong case for pragmatic approach towards the region. On the other hand, with the continuously declining market share of GCC countries in the exports to the industrialised West, Asian market in general and India in particular is of crucial importance for GCC. GCC region is not only important from India's energy security front but also from other vital economic, geopolitical and strategic fronts. With China as a competitor and the complexity of the emerging geopolitical equations, India has to tread a cautious and renewed approach towards the region by concentrating on its core economic strengths pertaining to the region in order to leverage its position. There are enormous scopes for interaction between India and GCC countries in the oil and gas sector. If one looks at the China-Saudi Arabia cross investment, this makes a case for India to assert its stand while it is discussing Free Trade Agreement (FTA) with the GCC countries. Moreover, in comparison to China, India has competitive advantage in the downstream operation, that may give space for Indian companies to enter the booming GCC market presently reliant on optimising operation across the oil value chain. Moreover, the GCC can be persuaded to make India a regional trading hub for their oil exports meant for the other emerging and huge markets in the Asian region, purely due to the strategic location of India, making the transportation costs competitive. Therefore, the GCC countries could pump oil and investment in the Indian refining sector and then pump their exports to other destinations. That in way can also give scope for joint stockpiling of oil and products in India with the investment support by the GCC countries.

However to sum up, oil, as analysts put, has remained a key vector of rivalry or cooperation in transnational relations. Institutions created in response to various challenges posed by the oil and gas sector will have to evolve by adapting their (India as an emerging consumer and GCC countries as suppliers) functions and operations to the changing realities—if they are to survive and develop. The essence of sustained cooperation is, therefore, adaptability.

Introduction

Corollary to the placid march of multilateralism in the ambit of globalisation, economic configurations are witnessing a qualitative change in the throes of open regionalism. Asian region has gained new prominence as the nerve centre of the world economy, primarily due to the superlative performance of two leading economies namely India and China, ably supplemented by the forward looking economies of the members of the Association of Southeast Asian Nations (ASEAN). In the global energy market, the regional shift is quite visible.

Over the last few decades, the global oil market has witnessed significant transformations. The market fundamentals across the oil value chain have radically altered, signifying consequent changes in the world demand as well as supply matrices. Short-to-medium term decision making has clearly gained precedence in the current oil market dynamics, in contrast to long-term decision making of the sellers' market scenario witnessed during the OPEC heydays of the 1970s. Importantly, the increasing integration of the world oil market with the world financial market has reshaped the operational dynamics and is considerably contributing to the highly fluctuating business cycle of the oil industry. The daily market trends, trade patterns, short-term price determinations set the present day global oil game as a commercial exercise. Notwithstanding, the spectre of geopolitics still continues to considerably influence the indicators and barometres of world oil trade.

From the supply side, market trends of the past two and a half decade or so indicate cut down of production in the lowest cost producing areas on the one hand, and raising production of full capacity in the relatively high cost producing areas on the other hand. As a result, the relatively high cost producers have become the main incremental suppliers eating away the market share of the lowest cost producers who were until recently the main marginal suppliers (residual suppliers). It is argued that the proximate factors responsible for such eventualities are, first the vast revenue needs of the lowest cost producers which has created a huge gap between 'the price level at which the national oil companies cover all their costs and the price level that balances their overall government budgets', and, second the technological revolution that have driven down the production cost in the high cost producing areas. Thus, these factors have made vulnerable the lowest cost producers and the traditional energy suppliers to the world, especially, the energy producing countries of the Arabian Gulf, the sense that it led to their loss of market share and strengthen their inability further to meet their overall revenue needs in the scenario of low world oil prices.

Coinciding with such supply-side transformations, the centre of gravity of world oil demand has shifted to Asia and importantly for the oil exporting Gulf region. This indicates the most significant geopolitical regime shift where a virtual demand heartland (Asian region) has emerged in geographical vicinity of the world traditional energy supply periphery (Gulf region). In other words, the Asian region in general and large countries like India in particular and the Gulf countries are strategically positioned as vital stakeholders in the global oil regime. The emerging pattern of energy interdependence between India and the Asian countries with the Gulf region in general and the six-member GCC countries in particular has taken centre stage in the contemporary discourse on the geopolitics of global energy security. Analysis runs from alarmist projections of tectonic geopolitical shifts making the current global superpowers upside down as a result of the increasing Islamic-Confucian bonhomie to more benign cooperative interdependent engagement between producers and consumers in their efforts to address mutual energy security sensitivities and vulnerabilities.

Moreover, the current market dynamics reaffirm the contours of the energy security debate signifying the importance of demand security for exporters and supply security for importers. While the GCC oil producers have witnessed continuous decline of the export market share, in particular, the westernised industralised region, they have also become vulnerable to cyclical economic fluctuations of the main importing countries. As a result, they are no more flexible enough to meet ever increasing domestic financial requirements simultaneously with the adequate oil sector capital investment in order to make these sectors adapt to the changing global fundamentals. However, the GCC region is poised to regain their lost status in the global energy regime solely on the basis of abundant reserve-based low cost production profile and importantly increasing call on exports due to the overwhelming import dependence of the Asian region. On the other hand, the Asian countries in general and large emerging markets like India are highly vulnerable to supply disruptions in comparison to somehow insulated western industralised importers who have not only minimised their oil intensity effectively but also developed alternate energy sources and expedited energy conservation measures effectively.

As a result, both producers and consumers are increasingly seeking an interdependent relationship to insulate against possible demand as well as supply disruptions. This can be substantiated from the various (proposed as well as coming) cooperative joint ventures between Asian consumers in general and India in particular, and the GCC countries in the energy sector. However, energy interdependence involves both short-term sensitivities and long-term vulnerabilities affecting both the producers as well as consumers. Therefore, energy interdependence framework needs to be broadened across economy sectors in order to absorb cyclical fluctuations and to foster stability.

This book aims at analysing the trends in the global market especially oil and gas with reference to the regional shift pointing to the emergence of India as a major energy consuming and importing country and the resilience of the GCC countries as world's major supplier. The analysis highlights how a pattern of interdependence is emerging between India and the GCC countries due to their strategic positioning and centripetal role in the current global energy security discourse and argues a strong case for synergising policy decision making in the producer-consumer framework It is argued that the emerging trends of energy related links and tendencies have the potential to ascend India-GCC bilateral economic relations to new trajectory. In other words, the main objective is to analyse the intricacies of the unfolding potentials and emerging opportunities of the Indian oil and gas sector in the liberalised phase and its implications for the oil and gas exporting countries of the GCC who are struggling to reposition themselves in global energy scene. The focus of analysis is on the emerging rationale of the relations between India and GCC countries in the present global oil and gas regime, which is to be strategically embedded in the framework of interdependence in order to augment mutually beneficial long-term economic relations. The emerging deficits in the framework of a symmetry in the knowledge sector of the GCC countries and energy sector of India is perceived as the appropriate tool to synergise policies in order to usher in an era of sustained multi-pronged economic interaction.

This book comprises six chapters. Chapter 1 delves into the historical moorings of the world oil market since the discovery of oil and the integration of the Middle East with the global economy till the present phase of liberalisation and integration of the oil market with the global financial market. The main focus is on the role of major players in the global oil regimes over the years, and their role in the power hierarchy in influencing the pattern of production, distribution, pricing and trade of oil. Importantly, the role of international oil companies (IOCs) or super majors and their relationship with the national oil companies (NOCs) in the Middle East has been thoroughly examined to delineate the pattern of transition of the global oil regime over the years.

In Chapter 2, an attempt has been made to analyse the pattern of world oil trade since the 1970s till today to show that how the Asian countries in general and India in particular are becoming the major consumers and importers of oil, and especially, are the main destination of oil and gas exports from the GCC countries.

In Chapter 3, a SWOT analysis has been carried out to analyse the various fundamentals of the oil and gas market in India and GCC countries vis-à-vis the global trends and it has been shown that how a pattern of interdependence is emerging between the two in the present regime. This pattern of interdependence clearly points out the transitions in the global oil and gas market and thereby substantiating the resilience of the GCC as a major factor in the world oil market and the emergence of India as a power to reckon with.

Chapter 4 explains the mutual vulnerabilities of India and GCC countries in the energy interdependence framework having relevance to their energy security. An attempt has been made to identify and explore various issues pertaining to energy security and the imperatives of expanding the pattern of energy interdependence in order to take care of the vulnerabilities has been emphasised.

After overviewing the existing pattern of economic engagement between India and GCC over the years, Chapter 5 explores the potential avenues for expanding the energy sector interdependence in order to usher in sustained and heightened bilateral economic relations.

Chapter 6 analyses the existing energy strategies of major Asian countries such as China, Japan and South Korea in the GCC countries and their implications for India. It has been pointed out that the energy security approach of the major Asian countries is in a state of flux, envisaging a dilemma between interdependence and competition. This state of affairs complicates and somehow constrains India's enhanced engagement with the GCC economies. Therefore, India should re-strategise its approach towards the GCC in a proactive manner and adopt a judicious mix of astute bilateralism and prudent regionalism in its foreign policy space in order to absorb the costs of the quest security and ascertain the benefits of multidirectional spillovers thereof.

In the concluding part, it has been asserted that India, other Asian countries and the GCC countries should strive to institutionalise a cooperative framework in the energy sector in order to take care of their energy vulnerabilities. An Asian Energy Charter to promote transparent pricing, trade, and investment in the energy sector has been proposed. Particularly, energy as a major factor in enhancing bilateral economic relations between India and the GCC has been envisaged as a possible platform for regional economic integration in Asia.

1

The Global Oil and Gas Regime

Analytical Overview of Structural Transition

Introduction

Since the days of the 'liquid revolution' in the late 1800s, the oil and gas industry has undergone multiple structural changes and transformations that have not only altered its global competitive landscape, but also the strategic *modus operandi* of its major stakeholders. One significant aspect of the transition as witnessed in the present day global oil regime is the market forces' determination of each and every aspect of world oil and gas trade. Though the market seemed to have stabilised for a brief period (last quarter of the 20th century to the first quarter of the present century), yet, the past few years have witnessed high volatility and a state of flux supplemented by increasing demand, tightening supply, low spare production capacity and an unprecedented increase in oil prices; sending shock waves across the globe.

The post-war oil era saw a lengthy period of stability under the Seven Sisters, followed by a somewhat shorter, but much more exciting period of transition and turmoil in the 1970s, primarily due to the nationalisation of the local assets of foreign companies, and also in some cases through greater participation and/or regulation. Therefore, it can be argued that there was virtually no international oil market prior to the mid-70s, as the great majority of crude oil and products trade remained within the systems of the Majors or went directly to third party customers such as Japanese Refiners. Moreover, the spot trading which in fact dominates today's world oil market was minimal in the 1960s and access to oil was primarily through the Majors who produced it. In the present oil regime, the market has undergone a revolutionary shift reflecting spectacular changes and transformations. These changes and transformations include an enormous increase in market freedom and revolutionary shift in the type of market actors leading to a complete reorganisation of these actors in terms of ownership and behaviour, thereby reshaping the global oil regime that is radically in contrast to the 60s and 70s. The most astounding aspect of the present regime has been the integration of the world oil trade with the global financial market and the so-called 'terror premium', considerably affecting the pricing of oil.

Against this backdrop, this chapter attempts to analyse the veracity of structural changes in the world oil industry as well as the regime transformations over the years, having considerable influence on the pattern of production, consumption, trade and pricing of oil over the years. The main focus will be on the role of major stakeholders and their power struggle to appropriate a major share of the pie, from a historical perspective, that will enable to base the main argument of this book in subsequent chapters.

Global Oil and Gas Regime: An International Political Economy Approach

Oil is an ambivalent commodity, i.e., strategic and economic. World oil history evinces that oil in terms of international political economy is to be viewed simultaneously as a potential object of inter-state confrontation and of economic competition. These twin dimensions have considerably influenced the global oil dynamics over the years and have restructured the "regime" configurations. Less schematically, it could be said that the degree of transnationalisation of the oil industry has fluctuated according to the changes in the international system, the interests of the great powers, and market conditions.

The concept 'regime' in international political jargon[1] refers to 'the process or the procedure that is born of a treaty that the treaty signatories agree to follow'. The treaty usually sets up a goal, a time-line and some kind of permanent organisational framework to monitor

1. Regime theory developed by Oran Young holds that international cooperation depends on well-designed regimes. If a treaty promotes a well-designed regime, the chance of the treaty being implemented is much greater than if it designates a flawed regime. However, research continues as to what factors constitute a well-designed regime and what motivates states to implement treaties, see Duncan, W. Raymond *et al.* (2002). *World Politics in the 21st Century.* New York: Longman. pp.22 and 606.

progress. In other words, regime refers to 'a particular process of interaction among groups within the framework of certain rules, norms and institutions, thrive to achieve certain designed goals'. In this way, the global oil and gas regime can be defined as, 'the interaction among major players in the international oil and gas industry within the framework of certain rules, norms and institutions (OPEC for oil exporters and IEA for oil and gas importers) to achieve certain designed goals (demand security for the oil and gas producing/ exporting states and supply security for the oil and gas importing countries)'. Thus, by global oil and gas regime,[2] it is generally meant the whole processes making the world oil and gas market and its different aspects, which include:

- Pattern of interaction among major players in the oil and gas industry—the international oil companies (IOCs) and the national governments possessing vast reserves of oil and gas—and their struggle for control of the strategic economic commodity.
- The pattern of world oil and gas trade—the key producing and consuming countries, the pricing system, and production/quota, etc.
- The linkages of the Middle East oil industry with the world.
- The strategic interventions to 'control oil', to achieve certain economic, political and other objectives, by the major players in the game.
- The process of energy transition—'the shifting balance' from coal to oil to natural gas.

In order to analyse the changes and transformations in the global oil regime, it is prudent to distinguish four different periods in the history of the world oil industry. First, was the era of early oil concessions during which the existing international oil companies (IOCs) made an early attempt to penetrate and expand into the underdeveloped economies of the Middle Eastern societies.[3] This was

2. The global oil and gas regime here can be referred to the various aspects of international oil trade, given the fact that natural gas is a new entrant and its trade though is different from the international trade in oil, yet gas trade is yet to take the concrete shape of a regime.
3. Mikdashi, Zuhayr (1966). *A Financial Analysis of Middle East Oil Concessions*: 1901-1965. New York: Praeger Publishers. p.64.

done by way of obtaining oil concessions, which means gaining exclusive property rights for exploration, development and production of crude oil in these areas. Second, was the period of transition from early concessions up to 1970, during which the global oil industry transformed into today's modern industry. Third, was the period in which the oil industry in the Middle East became a full-fledged capitalist entity, integrated in the world market. In this period, due to the internationalisation of all circuits of capital in the oil industry, market values, prices and oil rents were being determined within the international arena, as opposed to the regional markets.[4] Finally, the period of market domination due to liberalisation and globalisation after 1980, whereby, there is flagitious increase in market freedom, periodical shift in the type of market actors and the reorganisation of the global oil regime.[5] More recently there are debates by bringing the issues in the world oil and gas market in the ambit of the World Trade Organization (WTO) guidelines. There are issues and concerns regarding the linking up of 'energy services' under the General Agreement on Trade in Services (GATS) as per the WTO guidelines. It can be seen from the so called Mexico Energy Debate:

> NAFTA failed to open up Mexico's state-owned oil company (PEMEX), but "energy services" negotiations under GATS is a strategic initiative by the Bush/Cheney White House to reduce dependence on oil from the Middle East by increasing access to and control over energy supplies via the break-up of state-owned oil and gas enterprises. Privatisations of PEMEX and electricity delivery services are highly controversial issues, and a global trade summit advancing the privatisation of "energy services" could attract much attention. Connecting GATS to Mexico's energy debate and its key constituencies can raise the profile of the WTO Ministerial as well as elevate domestic voices on the global stage. Southern Mexico's rich petroleum resources are also at stake, as energy services liberalisation would allow US companies to access more exploration and drilling opportunities in the region. There is currently no organised effort to monitor or influence WTO negotiations on Energy Services.[6]

---

4. Cyrus, Bina (1985). *The Economics of the Oil Crisis.* New York: Merlin Press Ltd. p.22.
5. For details see Lynch, Micheal C. (2000-2001). "Oil Market Structure and Oil Market Behaviour", *MEES* 43(52), 25th December 2000/*MEES* 44(1), 1st January 2001, p.D1-D11.
6. *http://www.ifg.org/analysis/wto/cancun/plan_cancun.htm*

The above periods can be historically identified as the early period of 1901-1950, the transitional period of 1950-1970, the period from 1970 up to 1980s, and the period since 1980, after the onset of privatisation and globalisation in the world economy. The changes and transformations of the global oil regime in the first three phases can be attributed to the struggle between the players of the global oil game at two levels: among the foreign companies themselves in their struggles for concessions or Majors against Majors, and between the oil companies and the local rulers over shares in profits. The last phase reveals the vicissitudes of the changing commercials and fundamentals of world oil trade as a result of transformations and paradigm shifts in the global economic thinking.

Emergence of the Global Regime (First Regime)

The real start of the modern oil industry began when Colonel Edwin Drake discovered the first underground oil well of 70 feet deep near Titusville in Pennsylvania on 27th August 1859.[7] Although the main use of oil at that time was for lamp lighting, it did not take long to discover other machines and engines which opened the new opportunities for the use of oil and its products. The expansion of the market was quick and sudden, as oil became the fuel for railways, ships and electrical generators. Consequently, the demand increased rapidly and oil companies were quickly formed and no effort was spared to find new oil sources and produce more oil to meet the growing market.

The oil resources of the world are unevenly distributed over the earth's surface and the concentration of reserves is usually not geographically coincident with the concentration of consumption. It was inevitable therefore, that the industry would become internationally oriented and dominated by international trade, which would assume greater importance, as the uses of oil in manufacturing and transport expanded as industrial development spread throughout the world, especially in the Northern Hemisphere. Another facet of the internationalisation of the oil industry was the fact that the

---

7. Colonel Edward Drake was an adventurer who used to go on expeditions in search for oil using the hand pump technology. For details see Adelman, M.A. (1995). *The Genie Out of the Bottle: World Oil since 1970*. London: MIT Press.

capital, technical and manpower resources required to discover and develop reserves were, at the dawn of the 'modern' age of oil industry in the middle of the 19th century, also very unequally distributed among the countries of the world and again, were geographically unmatched with the distribution of potential oil reserves. Thus, the physical development of the world's oil resources required the international movement of capital and specialised skills.[8]

Although Southeast Asia and Southern Europe including Russia, were important oil producers in the later part of the 19th century, their resources were not only limited than those of the United States but had been developed with foreign capital, technology and manpower, partly, American. Of the countries with extensive oil reserves only the United States was substantially endowed with the requisite capital, technology and manpower to exploit them in the production of oil. With these advantages and a large domestic market United States soon became pre-eminent in the modern technology of drilling and refining and quickly became the world's largest exporter of oil products. Except for a brief period towards the end of the century, it remained so until the Second World War.[9] In fact, the Standard Oil Trust, established by Rockefeller in 1970 had monopoly in the crude sector and controlled 40,000 miles of pipeline in the United States. The Trust was divided into more than 30 companies, among them, the Standard oil Company of New Jersey, later became Exxon, Standard Oil of California (SOCAL), Standard Oil of New York later Mobil, Standard Oil of Indiana and Continental Oil Company.[10] The Standard Oil Trust dominated the petroleum market and the petroleum transportation facilities not only in the United States but also internationally which can be observed from the trends of the then world oil trade. Moreover, five of the seven companies, which are known, as the 'International Majors' are American oil companies whose origins can be traced to

8. In fact, the problem of oil production since the early days of the industry has always been the high sum of capital, technology and skilled manpower. For details, see Penrose, Edith T. (1968). *The Large International Firm in Developing Countries: The International Petroleum Industry*. Chapter IV. London: Allen and Unwin.

9. Ferrier, R.W. and A. Fursenko (eds.) (1989). *Oil in the World Economy*. Chapter I. New York and London: Routledge.

10. For details see, Wilkins, Mira (1970). *The Emergence of Multinational Enterprise: American Business Abroad from the Colonial Era To 1914*. Mass., Cambridge: Harvard University Press.

that period of American oil history.[11] Thus, United States was the world's most advanced country with respect to large business organisation and its large oil companies were capable of following up their success in export markets, not only with the successful acquisition of foreign crude oil resources to serve their foreign product market, but also with the construction of refineries, transport and distribution systems.

The emergence of the Middle East in the world petroleum scene dates back to 1911, when the Turkish petroleum company was established with the purpose of exploring oil in Iraq by the Turkish National Bank owned by the British companies who were already in a semi-monopolistic position in the Middle East, which immediately prompted the American 'majors' to react. The American group led by Standard oil Company of New Jersey established a company named the Near East Development Corporation (NEDC),[12] which in fact sparked off the struggle for existence among the major players of the global oil regime in later years.

Most of the oil concessions concluded during the period, 1901-1950 in the Middle East had the following features as summarised by Bina Cyrus:[13]

- They all covered the entire or a substantial part of a country for significantly long period of time.
- The number of oil companies involved was fairly small.
- Concession terms were often uniform and simple.
- Royalty payment was the principal financial transaction.
- The financial terms were extremely moderate.
- There was little change in the terms and conditions of the concessionary agreements during this period, thereby indicating minimal conflict between parties involved.

The uniformity of the terms associated with such concessionary contracts was the result of the monopolisation and financial domination of a small number of oil companies in their successful

11. See Annexure 1.1 for the history of major oil companies in the Gulf Region.

12. Shukri, Ghanem (1988). *OPEC: The Rise and Fall of an Exclusive Club.* London: KPI. p.7.

13. Cyrus *op. cit.*, No. 4, pp.23-24.

attempt to impose a set of general terms on all territories. In addition, the royalty rates of the early period were exclusively geared to the extent of political clout of international oil companies and their governments with respect to a particular oil region, the Middle East. Since the economies of the Middle Eastern societies in general, and their realm of oil production in particular, were not yet integrated into the global economy, there was no objective mechanism for joint determination of oil prices and oil royalty rates at the international level during this period. In fact, the system of control of oil production in the Middle East was at the heart of the organisation of the international oil industry. This system was based on a network of consortia, linking all the international majors, which were present in the network in a variety of combinations. There were originally four consortia in the Middle East (Table 1.1).

Table 1.1

The Main Consortia in the Middle East, 1953-1970

(Ownership Distribution of Capital in Percentages)

	*IPC**	*KOC*	*Aramco*	*Iranian*
BP	23.75	50	–	40
Shell	23.75	–	–	14
Exxon	11.875	–	30	7
Texaco	–	–	30	7
Chevron	–	–	30	7
Mobil	11.875	–	10	7
Gulf	–	50	–	7
CFP	23.75	–	–	6
Others	5.0	–	–	5
Total	100	100	100	100

Note: *–The same combination was found in Mosul Petroleum Company, Bharat Petroleum Corporation Ltd., Abu Dhabi Petroleum Company Ltd. and Qatar Petroleum Company.

Source: Luciani, Giacomo (1984). *The Oil Companies and the Arab World*. London: Croom Helm. p.18.

The first Consortium and historically the most important in determining the shape of global oil regime was the Iraq Petroleum Company (IPC). It was formed in 1928, comprising five out of the Seven Sisters of the 1950s and 1960s. The second type of Consortium was found in Kuwait, which was not included within the Red Line. Its territory was covered by a concession granted in 1934 to the Kuwait Oil

Company (KOC) in which Gulf and BP each held a 50 per cent share.[14] The third pattern of Consortium was established in Saudi Arabia. It was started by Chevron (on the basis of an exclusive concession), Texaco, and later by the Aramco on the basis of the Saudi Arabian concession. The fourth Consortium was the Iranian, which took control over the Iranian oil after the defeat of Mossadeq's government in 1953.

It has been argued[15] that, these consortiums served many things in the oil regime such as the integration of the world oil industry both horizontally and vertically, which gave birth to the vibrant industry of today, somehow stability in terms of pegging supply of oil to the ever-increasing demand, development of rational oil pricing system, etc. Despite these contributions of the consortiums and their allied contributions in shaping the various oil regimes, they have also contributed equally to the oil power game in later years. The proximate factors for this inevitability were the terms of arrangements of the various Consortiums having multiple effects:

> The Consortiums were not organised primarily as profit making institutions which would try to maximise profits and then distribute it among their shareholders; rather, they were conceived as agencies that would make crude oil available to the shareholders at cost in proportion to their respective shares. Therefore, the crucial point of decision making was only regarding the level of production and programmes of investment, as the basis of future level of production. Moreover, at any moment in time a company was allowed to lift more crude oil than the share to which it was entitled, but had to pay a premium above cost. Thus, the most obvious effect of these arrangements was that they discouraged downstream competition, because a company that was successful in increasing its share of the market downstream would be faced by an obvious tendency of all others to restrict crude production and would probably have to accept a competitive disadvantage, which means pay crude at a higher price. Another effect was to slow down the development of the Middle East oil especially in the case of Iraq. However, this would not have been the case if the same Consortium had controlled all the oil supplies of the parent companies.[16]

14. Luciani, Giacomo (1984). *The Oil Companies and the Arab World.* London: Croom Helm. p.19.

15. Ibid.: 21.

16. See Adelman *op. cit.*, No. 7, pp.25-36.

Competition among the Majors

The period during 1920s and 1930s witnessed an intense competition for the control of oil in Iraq among the major oil companies themselves—first between the British Anglo-Persian Oil Company and British Royal-Dutch Shell, and then between these two companies and the American Majors, principally Standard Oil of New Jersey (SONJ).[17] During the pre-First World War period, it had been widely believed that Iraq was rich in oil, especially in its northern province. A concession granted by the Ottoman Sultan led to the establishment of the Turkish Petroleum Company (TPC) in 1914, controlled by the British. The Anglo-Persian Oil Company held 50 per cent of its shares, the Anglo-Saxon Petroleum Company (represented Shell) held 25 per cent, and a German investor, the Deutsche Bank, acquired the remaining 25 per cent.[18] The collapse of the Ottoman Empire in the First World War, the British conquest of Iraq and the consequent establishment of the British mandatory regime in Iraq strengthened the British government and companies' domination over Iraqi oil. The British government divulged the Deutsche Bank's holdings in TPC, which in 1920 were transferred to the French Government as part of the 'Sam Reno Peace Conference Agreement', and TPC thereby entirely came under British-French control.[19]

These developments in the oil regime prompted the several American oil companies to expand their production capacity outside the United States and thus found Iraq's potential most attractive. It can be mentioned that this period in particular and its aftermath witnessed key oil discoveries in the Middle East (Table 1.2). These companies succeeded in conjuring up and then exploiting an atmosphere of supply threat in the US, managed to impress upon the administration and State Department to interfere and thereby help them in achieving a share of Iraqi Oil.[20] After a series of drawn out negotiations, the British Government agreed upon to transfer 25 per

17. Blair, John (1976). *The Control of Oil*. New York: Pantheon Books. p.157.
18. Gilbar, Gad G. (1997). *The Middle East Oil Decade and Beyond*. Frank Cass. p.18.
19. Kent, Marian (1976). *Oil and Empire, British Policy and Mesopotamian Oil 1900-1920*. London: Macmillan Press. pp.103-12, 137-55.
20. Randell, Stephen J. (1976). *United States Foreign Oil Policy, 1919-1948*. Kingston and Montreal: McGill—Queen's University Press. pp.10-14.

cent of TPC shares owned by Anglo-Persian to a group of five American oil companies organised as the Near East Development Corporation, dominated by SONJ and Socony-Vacuum. TPC changed its name to Iraq Petroleum Company (IPC) and became a production Joint Venture Company under the multi-ownership of British (47.5 per cent), American (23.75 per cent) and French (23.75 per cent) firms. The remaining 5 per cent was offered to an American geologist and businessman, Calouste Gulbenkian (popularly know as, "Mr. Five-Per Cent") for his service in the establishment of the Turkish–Iraqi Oil Company.[21]

Table 1.2

Key Oil Discoveries in the Middle East

Country	*Initial Oil Discovery Year*	*First Oil Field*
Iran	1908	Masjid-I-Sulayman
Iraq	1927	Kirkuk
Bahrain	1932	Awali
Saudi Arabia	1936	Damman
Kuwait	1938	Burgan
Qatar	1939	Durkhan
UAE	1958	Murban
Oman	1962	Yibal

Source: *Oil & Gas Journal* (OGJ), July 9, 2001. p.23.

Thus, until the early 1930s, most areas of production in the Middle East were in the hands of European Companies, especially, Anglo-Persian, which controlled oil production in Iraq exclusively and which together with Shell, held about half the shares of IPC. The American oil companies had obtained only a small share of Iraqi oil, along with control of the Bahrain Petroleum Company. However, a major thrust was given to the status of American involvement in the Middle East oil industry and thereby, initiating the struggle among the Majors in 1933; when the ruler of Saudi Arabia, 'Abd al-Aziz Ibn Saud' awarded SOCAL, an American Company, a concession to produce oil in an area

21. In fact, the State Department of US insisted that British and French should apply the "Open Door Policy"—which envisages non-discrimination in economic activity within the mandated areas—to which they had committed themselves.

of 728,000 square kilometres in the country's eastern province.[22] SOCAL hurriedly divested the ownership of the Saudi concession with another American Company, Texaco, in order to actualise the vast potentials of oil. The two established a joint production company, Caltex in 1936 and in 1938, produced oil in commercial quantities. This joint venture later came to be known as Aramco (Arabian American Oil Company), in 1944.

The growing global oil demand after the Second World War, (Table 1.3) and the immense production potential in Saudi Arabia tempted two other American Majors; SONJ and Mobil, to join Aramco, which increased total investment in Saudi oil industry and opened up new channels of marketing. The four Majors owned the company jointly, with SOCAL, Texaco and SONJ holding 30 per cent of shares each, and Mobil holding 10 per cent. Within the next two decades, Aramco had become the biggest oil producing company in the World and Saudi Arabia, the largest oil exporter in the Middle East and the third largest oil exporting country in the world, together with the United States and the Soviet Union.

Table 1.3

Growth Rates of World Oil Consumption

(Per Cent)

Year	*World*	*WECC**	*OECD*	*Asia Pacific*
1950-1960	8.2	7.6	7.4	—
1960-1970	8.1	7.9	7.9	—
1970-1973	6.9	6.5	6.6	—
1950-1973	8.0	7.6	7.5	—
1960-1973	7.8	7.2	7.6	—
1970-1980	3.2	2.7	1.7	5.2
1980-1990	0.6	0.7	-0.2	2.8
1990-2000	1.3	2.4	1.4	5.0
2000-2006	1.6	1.6	0.4	2.7

Source: Calculated from *BP Annual Statistical Bulletin*, Historical Series Data.

22. Mikdashi, Zuhayr (1972). *The Community of Oil Exporting Countries.* New York: Ithaca Press, Cornell University Press. pp.21-35.

It is here worth mentioning that, Saudi oil came under American domination at a time when Britain enjoyed undisputed control in the Persian Gulf area and considerable influence among the rulers of Saudi Arabia and when European oil companies still controlled most of the concession area and thereby most of the production area. Surprisingly, while an intense and prolonged struggle had been waged over the control of the Iraqi oil concessions, the American companies did not have to exhaust themselves in order to win Saudi concessions. In contrast to TPC, Saudi Arabia dropped like a 'ripe plum'.[23]

Majors' Confrontation with Most Governments: Nationalisation of Oil in Iran

The aftermath of the long conflict among the Majors witnessed a new contest for control of oil between a domestic government and one of the Majors, although it indirectly involved all Majors operating in the Middle East. In 1944, the Iranian Government approved a proposal by the Anglo-Iranian Oil Company to increase the company's royalty to the Government on the basis of the famous 'fifty-fifty' agreements, adopted by the Governments' of Venezuela and Saudi Arabia.[24] And after a month of debate in the *Majlis*, a special Majlis Oil Commission was appointed in 1950 and it decided to reject the oil agreement and recommended that the Anglo-Iranian Oil Company be nationalised. All installations of the Anglo-Iranian Oil Company were earmarked to be requisitioned by the newly founded National Iranian Oil Company (NIOC). The British Company did not recognise the nationalisation law as valid and a bitter dispute was carried on between the Iranian Government on the one hand, and Anglo-Iranian, the British Government and other Majors on the other. This conflict lasted until the military coup of 1953, which derailed the nationalisation attempts of the Iranian Government, and as a consequence, production of Iranian oil retained under the control of foreign companies for many years.

The reason for the failure was that the NIOC could not market the oil it produced, which led to steep fall in foreign currency revenues and consequent deficits in the balance of payments. The inability of

23. Gilbar *op. cit.*, No. 18, p.21.
24. Mikdashi *op. cit.*, No. 3, pp.135-45 and 148-51.

NIOC to export oil reflected the prevailing condition in the global oil market in the early 1950s. First, the oil shortfall on the global market resulting from Iran's efforts at nationalisation was easily redressed by other sources. Some of the producing states having vast unexploited reserves of oil, far from demonstrating solidarity with the Iranian Government, took advantage of the situation. Secondly, the Majors backed the Anglo Iranian, being aware of the fact that the struggle of the British Company against the nationalisation was of their own. If Iran succeeded in its attempts, it would be repeated in all Middle Eastern oil producing states. Moreover, the Majors still controlled the most of the means of transporting and refining oil (the downstream operations in the 1950s), which enabled them to block the marketing of Iranian oil. They also threatened legal and economic sanctions in the form of an embargo against any purchaser of Iranian oil.[25]

However, the formation of a consortium of foreign oil companies known as 'Iran Oil Participants' (IOP), which replaced the Anglo-Iranian Oil Company, essentially settled the oil dispute in Iran. The consortium consisted of Anglo-Iranian, later known as British Petroleum (BP) holding 40 per cent shares; Shell with 14 per cent, the American Majors with 7 per cent each; the Compagnie Francaise des Petroles (CFP) with 6 per cent and a group of six American Independents organised as the Iricon Agency with 5 per cent. The major consequence of the Iranian attempts to nationalise, then, was the loss of exclusive control by the Anglo-Iranian Oil Company and the acquisition of a share in Iran's oil production by all the Majors, both European and American, as well as by a group of Independents. Moreover, not a single oil state of the region attempted the process of nationalisation during the rest of the 1950s and 1960s, thereby strengthening the position of the Majors in the global oil regime.

Competition between the Majors and non-Majors or Independents

Changing market conditions in the later part of the 1950s and 1960s and again in the early 1970s precipitated a phenomenon that became evident in the global oil regime. The sizeable increase in oil

25. Katouzian, Homa (1981). *The Political Economy of Modern Iran.* New York and London: NY University Press. pp.164-87, as cited in Gilbar *op. cit.*, p.24.

consumption in industrialised economies that lacked abundant energy resources, such as Italy and Japan, forced these countries to seek ways of reducing their dependency on the Majors, which were their chief oil suppliers and thereby reduce rising outlays in foreign currency on oil imports. This led to the formation of a public holding company, ENI, in Italy along with another exploration and production company called AGIP, which made vigorous attempts to win production concessions in the Middle East. However, its attempts to secure holding shares in the IOP consortium did not materialise. Moreover, the Majors, which had been pressurised by the US administration and congress to grant holding shares to the American Independents, did not feel compelled to respond in a similar fashion to AGIP's pleas for a share in Iranian oil. This compelled the AGIP to acquire production rights in areas outside the concessions granted to the Majors, through new agreements based on cooperation in control of production between the foreign company and the domestic oil company.[26]

The outcome of the ENI agreements was the introduction of the principle of joint control, which became the cornerstone of all new accords between foreign and national oil production companies in the Middle East. These agreements conflicted with what the Majors regarded as the optimal format of the relationship between the foreign companies and domestic government. In fact, the signing of agreements as well as the expansion of operations by non-Majors—American, European and Japanese Oil Companies—in the joint venture framework presaged the end of the era of exclusive control by foreign companies over oil production. Moreover, these developments also undermined the status of the Majors in their negotiations with the local governments over both old and new concessions. The emergence of a joint venture framework thus contributed to the reversal that took place in the global oil regime to control oil production in the Middle East at the start of the 1970s.

Emergence of OPEC in the World Oil Regime

Towards the end of the 1950s, competition in product markets began to force down the prices of products especially in Europe, which

26. ENI's director, Enrico Mattei set himself the task of breaking the nearly absolute control by the Majors over Middle East oil; through new agreements.

led to the reduction of revenues of the integrated oil companies while the tax price of oil was maintained. The companies cut posted prices in 1959 and 1960, arguing that the reduction was necessary to bring the prices of oil in line with the lower product prices (Table 1.4). The consequent reduction in tax revenues was unacceptable to the oil producing states.

Table 1.4

Posted Price Cuts in the Late 1950s

		1957	*February 1959*	*August 1960*
Iranian heavy	31°	1.80	1.62	–
Iraqi Basra	34°	1.98	1.80	1.68
Banias	34°	2.59	2.31	2.15
Kuwait	31°	1.85	1.67	1.59
Saudi Arabia light Ras Tanura	34°	2.08	1.90	1.80
Venezuela Bachaquero	16.5°	2.23	1.85	–

Source: *Economist*, 1960, p.1017, as cited in Shukri *op. cit.*, p.19.

These new developments witnessed during the 1950s eventually led to the formation of the Organization of Petroleum Exporting Countries (OPEC), which took control of the global oil regime afterwards. The nationalisation of the Mexican oil industry in 1948, followed by the Iranian oil nationalisation of 1951 provided the impetus to other oil states in the Middle East to act in the same direction, which in fact reflected the serious concern for political and economic sovereignty which could be found in most of the oil producing countries. At the same time, the production of oil gained tremendous momentum, thereby shaping the growth of a modern oil industry in the region. Moreover, as the oil industry developed further, the conditions for the surrender of oil property rights—the fundamental basis of oil exploration—became much more complex. And also the usage of 'posted price'[27] came into circulation in the global oil regime.

As a result, OPEC was founded in order to organise the efforts of the principal oil exporting countries to challenge the international oil

27. Posted Price is the price that is "devised for long term oil transactions and contracts and, that is connected with the determination of oil royalties." It is usually a, "measure primarily used by oil companies to value crude oil as it was transferred from one subsidiary to another within their own international framework."

companies in a collective manner. During this period, due to the discovery of large oil fields in the Middle East, the centre of gravity of proven world oil reserves has sharply shifted to the Middle East (Table 1.5). Another important development was the emergence of spot markets,[28] which arguably altered the set up of the global oil regime in the decades to follow.

Table 1.5

Crude Oil Discoveries, 1944-1974

Year	*World Total*	*OPEC*	*Middle East*	*Centrally Planned Economies*	*Capitalist Countries*	*Others*
			Billions of Barrels			
1974	115	75	64	18	14	8
1973-1969	51	28	22	11	9	3
1968-1964	38	24	17	8	4	2
1963-1959	19	13	9	2	3	1
1958-1954	34	25	21	4	4	1
1953-1949	16	11	10	1	4	—
1948-1944	7	5	4	—	2	—
			As Percentages			
1974	100	65.2	55.6	15.6	12.2	7.0
1973-1969	100	54.9	43.1	21.6	17.6	5.9
1968-1964	100	63.1	44.7	21.0	10.5	5.4
1963-1959	100	68.4	47.4	10.5	15.8	5.2
1958-1954	100	73.5	61.8	11.8	11.8	2.9
1953-1949	100	68.7	62.5	6.2	25.0	—
1948-1944	100	71.4	57.1	—	28.6	—

Source: Cyrus, Bina (1985). *The Economics of the Oil Crisis*. Table No. 4. New York: Merlin Press Ltd. p.29.

The formation of the oil cartel marked the erosion of integration witnessed in the global oil regime. During the 1960s, some financial

28. The spot market is evolved in one time transaction in crude oil, as opposed to the usual long-term contracts between OPEC and the oil companies. In fact, there was no spot market prior to 1970. As a result, the spot market prices themselves have had an impact on the terms of the long-term contracts since the time of their development.

concessions were obtained from the companies as OPEC organised itself and formulated its demands.[29] Although the companies were fully aware of the radical movements in the Middle East, they apparently did not realise fully the extent to which the post-war spirit of 'resource nationalism' and resentment of 'neo-imperialism' had spread even to the conservative countries of the Middle East, such as Saudi Arabia and Kuwait, whose governments were traditionally friendly towards the West, but who could not ignore the popular sentiments of the Arab world in general. Consequently, the companies did not fully understand the effectiveness of OPEC in achieving their objectives.

In 1968, OPEC issued a declaratory statement of petroleum policy in which its objectives were clearly stated.[30] These included the demand that governments should participate in the equity of the oil producing companies and be able to operate directly in exploration and production, and that they should control posted prices. The assumption of ownership and/or control of their crude oil operations by the governments of the oil producing states thus broke a major link in the integration that had characterised the operations of the international companies. This in itself, however was not a shock to the international oil economy or for the companies and in fact, the companies continued to lift most of the crude oil produced by their old operating companies.[31]

In addition, during 1971-1979, the Majors lost control of oil production in areas where they had enjoyed exclusive rights since the 1920s and 1930s, with control of production passing to domestic national companies. In the early 1970s, both Libya and Iraq unilaterally nationalised production concession and rights that had been granted to foreign companies. The other oil producing states in the Middle East avoided unilateral nationalisation of foreign companies, bringing production in their areas under their complete control through an exhaustive sequence of negotiations that lasted throughout most of the 1970s and was called the "participation

29. For details see, Shurki *op. cit.*, No. 12, Part II.

30. Ibid.

31. Penrose *op. cit.*, No. 8, pp.122-4.

process"[32] under the auspices of OPEC. The Majors accepted the proposal and the bargaining power of the local governments in the process got enhanced. The main thrust to the bargaining power of local governments was given in October 1973, when OPEC began fixing the posted price of oil in the world oil market without prior negotiations with the Majors. And consequently, the control of every aspect of the global oil regime shifted in favour of the oil producing states.

It can be argued that the success of oil states in the 1970s, where the Iranian Government had failed two decades earlier was the outcome of a change in the basic structure of the world oil industry.[33] First, a situation of excess demand prevailed in the world oil market during most of the 1970s, which implied that the capacity for unexploited production in the short and medium term was reduced. Had there been a fall in production and exports from any of the countries as a result of confrontation with the local governments, the foreign oil companies could not have delivered the supply shortages from alternative sources. The fact that disruptions in production, which did, in fact, occur in the winter of 1973[34] could cause tremors in strategy of the local governments with the foreign oil companies. Secondly, the oil industry was incomparably more complex and multi-faceted in the 1970s than it had been in the early 1950s. As OPEC was beginning to claim control in the late 1960s, the majors' small world of oil had already begun to disintegrate. Not only had national oil companies (e.g., Agip/ENI, Total) and American independents (ARCO, Amoco) encroached upon their traditional turf (e.g., Iran), but Japanese 'trading houses' had asked for their share of exploration rights (getting the Neutral zone's offshore) and international traders (among others, Marc Rich, Marimpex and Phibro) had entered the oil

32. The 'participation process' involved the producer governments buying a share in their concessionaire companies, and getting a direct say in such matters as the relinquishment of concession acreage, the employment of nationals, production rates, and investment in new capacity. For details see, Field, Micheal (1975). *A Hundred Million Dollars a Day.* London: Sidgwick and Jackson.

33. For details see Al-Chalabi, F.J. (1980). *OPEC and the International Oil Industry: A Changing Structure.* Chapter 2. Oxford: OUP.

34. In October 1973, there was a double jump in the posted prices, which culminated in the four-fold increase by Arab and non-Arab members of OPEC; thereby led to a major oil crisis in the global oil scenario.

fray. Thus, by the early 1970s, the Majors' resilient structure, which had dominated and managed the world of oil for half a century, was in the process of falling apart. The rule of the industry by a handful of select global companies was coming to an end. The transition from the 'old system' to the 'new system' was bound to be explosive. In the mean time, the industry was in a crisis, because the 'old' was not dead yet and the 'new' was yet to be born.[35] The Majors lost their oligopolistic status, as a number of new companies entered this industry. Their share in refining apart from the United States and the Communist block fell from 73 per cent in 1953 to 49 per cent in 1972, and their share in marketing distillates decreased from 72 per cent to 54 per cent in the same period.[36] As a result, the Majors no longer had the power to prevent a local government that had resolved to nationalise the foreign companies operating in its territory from marketing the oil the company produced. The third factor that had not existed in the 1950s, which affected the power balance in favour of the oil producing countries, was the 'participation principle' under the auspices of OPEC.

Moreover, decisions by individual members of the organisation to nationalise oil production in their territory were backed by the rest of the members—a markedly different policy from that in the 1950s, when the oil producing countries exploited Iran's aborted marketing to increase their market share in the world market. Thus, the local government had not only acquired total oil production revenues, but also, their control of oil production provided them with a weapon of enormous political and economic power at the regional as well as global level.

The OPEC Era and the Second Regime

The brief period since the late summer of 1970, 'Tripoli', 'Caracas', 'Teheran', and then 'Tripoli'[37] again, had witnessed unprecedented demands upon the international oil industry by major oil producing

35. Levy, Walter J. (1982). *Oil Strategy and Politics, 1941-1981*. West View Press. p.181.
36. Mikdashi, *op. cit.* No. 22, p.37.
37. Tripoli, Teheran and Caracas are the venues of negotiations between the oil companies and national governments, under the auspices of OPEC. For details see Ahrari, Mohd. E. (1986). *OPEC: The Falling Giant*. The University Press of Kentucky. p.130.

countries, dramatic confrontations with threat to withhold essential oil supplies and far reaching 'settlements'.[38] As a result, the economic terms of the oil trade had been radically altered. The balance among oil producing and oil exporting countries, and among oil consuming and importing countries, and oil companies themselves appeared to have shifted decisively in favour of the oil producing countries. The winds of change that had been stirring the oil industry throughout the decade since the 1950s rose to hurricane proportions. The aim of the major oil producing countries in this vortex was to maximise their governments' 'take out' of the value of their oil production and to obtain substantial control over oil production. The countries thus organised effectively under OPEC to wield the economic and political power of an oil monopoly.

For their part, consuming countries were faced with appreciably higher prices for their oil imports, which for most countries constitute by far the major part of their total energy supplies and energy costs. Foreign exchange outlays were thus mounting rapidly. And the traumatic experience of confrontation between the industry and producing governments against interruptions, clearly, a very real challenge to the historical structure and operation of the internationally integrated oil industry emerged at a time when demand for oil was increasing swiftly. The relevant figures reveal dramatic upheaval in the global oil regime. Oil consumption in the non-communist world increased from 10 million barrels daily (mb/d) in 1950 to 39 mb/d in 1970 and 67 mb/d in 1980; US oil consumption increased from 7 mb/d in 1950 to 15 mb/d in 1970 and 21 mb/d in 1980; Europe's consumption shot up from only 1.2 mb/d in 1950 to 12 mb/d in 1970, close to that of United States, and in 1980 it was expected to reach around 23 mb/d exceeding that of the US; while Japan's consumption zoomed from 100,000 b/d in 1950 to 3.7 million b/d in 1970 and was expected to reach 10 mb/d in 1980.[39]

As for the supply of oil, world production paralleled consumption. Western Hemispheres production doubled, from 8 mb/d in 1950 to 18 mb/d in 1970, whereas Eastern Hemispheres production increased

38. Bakhtiari, A.M. Samsam (1999). "The Price of Oil", *OPEC Review* 23(1): 5. March.

39. Levy *op. cit.*, No. 35, pp.183-88.

about ten-fold, to 2.1 mb/d in 1970. The output of OPEC members was 22 mb/d in 1970 and their oil exports accounted for nearly 90 per cent of total free world oil trade. Despite discoveries in the North Sea, Far East and elsewhere, it was clear that the world would continue to depend heavily on OPEC to meet mounting oil requirements. Thus, the economic terms of the global oil regime radically shifted in favour of oil producing states and the occasion had also been marked by an equally dramatic shift in the institutional and political positions of the industry and of producing and consuming countries.

The second oil regime witnessed an unprecedented increase in the price of crude oil in the scenario of burgeoning world oil demand, thus contributing to the first oil crisis which had ripples flown across the world economy. It was in the late 1960s[40] that forecasts of an imbalance between supply and demand for oil in the 1980s, assuming no radical change in prices, began to influence policy formulation in the developed industrialised countries. By the early 1970s, a spectacular increase in American demand for imported oil had created a seller's market. But calculations about the future were upset by the unilateral action of the Arab oil producing countries in October 1973 when, with the outbreak of the War of Yom Kippur, they announced an immediate cut in their production and an increase in the prices of crude oil. The quantitative restrictions on oil supplies were firmly tied to political objectives. Countries 'friendly' towards Israel, chiefly the United States and the Netherlands were formally boycotted while those 'friendly' to the Arab cause were promised preferential treatment. The rest of the world was to receive reduced supplies, which were to be tightened every month until a settlement with Israel—on Arab conditions—was reached.[41] The period witnessed almost 70 per cent increase in the posted prices of crude oil, with special premia for oil of low sulphur content. On 16th December 1973, the new price was doubled again, thus, at the beginning of 1974, the importing countries were faced with crude oil prices that were three and half to four times more than what they had been three months earlier. The strength of the OPEC countries waxed

---

40. It was in the United States, in the late 1960s that the nature of the impending 'energy crisis' was generally first appreciated. For details see Rybczynski, T.M. (1976). *The Economics of the Oil Crisis*. London: Macmillan.

41. Ibid.: 2.

even greater over the ensuing year, when they became able to increase the posted prices as well as royalties and greater participation. This raised considerably the income of the OPEC countries, since it means that the original concessionaire's equity, now belonging to the producing government has to be bought back at a price significantly higher than the equity price.[42]

Apart from the role of oil as a political weapon which precipitated the energy crisis of 1973, there are two other important contributing factors, such as, first was the determination of the oil producing countries to appropriate control over the extraction and disposition of their major natural resources rather than delegate that power to others. The formation of OPEC as a result of the wave of 'resource nationalism' in the aftermath of the Second World War substantiates the above assertions. Secondly, towards the end of the 1960s there was a shift in the balance between supply and demand, largely as a result of the US becoming the largest importer and the Japanese market growing out of all recognition.

However, in the Second Oil Regime, the demand supply vortex altered the regime configuration and in fact had a stronger impact than it did in the first oil regime. From 1974 to 1977, the real price of oil fell about 20 per cent. Much of this decline was due to demand slackness and the fact that the spot market for oil showed lower prices than the OPEC price. With the partial elimination of vertical integration through the nationalisation of oil production in the Middle East, a large number of mutually interdependent buyers, sellers and intermediaries came to the field, which created intense competition and hence, stronger price fluctuations. In this phase, the spot market and short-term transactions covered a greater proportion of international oil trade than the previous phase. As OPEC countries diversified into downstream operations, such as refining, transportation and even marketing, stronger competition emerged and this moved the prices of production and even crude oil downwards. It should be noted that this might have been caused by OPEC apprehensions about the market, but concern over the long-run health

42. For example the participation of the producing country's government increased to 60 per cent in Kuwait and Abu Dhabi, to 55 per cent in Nigeria and to 51 per cent in Libya.

of the OECD economies could also have played a role. However, since 1974, there has been a greater diversification of oil prices according to quality, with particularly low sulphur oil getting a high price.[43]

The years 1979 and 1980 witnessed two consecutive rounds of price increases, which pushed the price from $12.00 to $36.00 per barrel. First, a strike by oil workers at the fall of 1978 reduced the Iranian supply and by December, Iranian exports had completely stopped as production fell below domestic demand.[44] As percentage of the world output, this reduction in production was nearly twice as large as the worldwide shortfall due to the embargo and cutbacks of 1973 at their worst scenario. However, spot prices rose only moderately because other producers made up all but 1.5 mb/d of the loss. By spring 1979 Iranian production had resumed, but prices reached a high of $38 later that year. As in 1973, during this crisis also OPEC's actions lagged behind the market requirements. At the December 1978 meeting OPEC decided to increase the market price by only 10 per cent. By June, while the spot price had risen to $38, OPEC announced a ceiling of $23.50 for the official price. Saudi Arabia kept its price even lower at $18. However as the crisis worsened, several countries increased their prices without consulting the agreements, charging up to $38. Successive OPEC meetings aiming at unification of the price structure could not materialise until October 1981.

The first supply disruption was quickly followed by another in the aftermath of the Iran-Iraq War in September 1980. The aggregate cut in supply due to the war was to the tune of 9 mb/d in 1980 compared to 1978. Prices that had declined during the early part of 1980 to about $36 jumped back to $38. OPEC set its price at $36, while Saudi Arabia sold its oil for $32 per barrel.

Whereas OPEC output remained constant for two years after the 1973 price increase, after 1979 it declined continuously, and never regained its all time high of 32 mb/d in mid-1979. In this period also, production shares changed drastically. Virtually all the decrease in the shares of Iran and Iraq was picked up by Saudi Arabia, who produced

---

43. For details see Adelman *op. cit.*, No. 7.

44. Cremer, Jacques and Djavad Salehi-Isfahani (eds.) (1991). *Models of the Oil Market*. Switzerland: Harwood Publishers. p.13.

less than 30 per cent of OPEC output in 1978 and more than 47 per cent in mid-1981 and its output reached a record 10.6 mb/d in the last quarter of the year 1980 after Iraq and Iran had ceased to export.[45] The proximate cause for the expansive Saudi oil production was lower Saudi oil prices than its competitors. It is remarkable that, except for Iraq, all other major OPEC members reduced production, choosing a strategy opposite to that of Saudi Arabia.

The 1980s have been marked by a continuous decline in demand for OPEC oil, a decline in the oil production in Saudi Arabia both in volume and as a share of OPEC, the introduction of output rationing by OPEC, and by a drastic fall in the real prices of oil. This development has been attributed to the repercussions of the oil crisis. This period also witnessed the importance of natural gas in the global energy scene.[46] In fact, the share of natural gas in the world's primary energy consumption recorded impressive growth in this period. It has been argued that the environment movements of the 1970s and the 1980s pioneered by non-government organisations (NGOs) highlighted the importance of natural gas as a fuel compared with coal and oil products when levels of pollution emissions is considered.[47] These developments in fact changed the determinants of global energy consumption in the succeeding years. This has been aptly described through two imperatives[48] such as the self-sufficiency imperative (conservation, domestic energy production, and diversification), and the environmental imperative.

Thus, so long as the oil industry experienced conditions of excess demand and was a sellers' market, the ability to determine the volume of oil produced, influence prices, fix marketing destinations and dictate terms of supply; all imparted political power to the oil state governments. But this political leverage became greatly attenuated when over supply conditions—a buyers' market—began to prevail,

45. Ibid.: 15.
46. This aspect will be explained descriptively in Chapter 2.
47. Clegg, Michael W., in ECSSR (ed.) (2001). *The Future of Natural Gas in the World Energy Market*. UAE, Abu Dhabi: ECSSR. p.1.
48. Dowling, Edward T. and F.G. Hilton (1995). "The Changing Determinants of Global Energy Consumption", in Siamack, Shojai (ed.), *The New Global Oil Market: Understanding Energy Issues in the World Economy*. Chapter 3. London: Praeger. pp.27-40.

from 1983 until the end of the decade, as can be reflected in the succeeding analysis. In these circumstances the producer governments no longer had the freedom of manoeuvre to fix supply destinations and conditions of sale. 'All buyers are welcome' became the axiom in the oil market after 1983.[49]

Before analysing the changed scenario after the 1980s, it may be worth mentioning that the Majors played a pivotal role in sustaining oil prices during the 1970s and stabilised the global oil market to a great extent. Although the Majors lost their economic, political and strategic power in the Middle East, they found ways of sustaining the high level of profits from their operations in the oil industry. The attitude of the industrialised countries towards these companies also changed. After a long period in which policymakers, economists and large sectors of the public censured the concentration of such enormous economic power in the hands of a small group of private enterprises, a revisionist view emerged in 1980s which held that these companies had acted as a stabilising factor for a period of decades in a highly complex system. According to this view, low and stable oil prices until the 1970s had constituted one of the major contributing factors towards the creation of an affluent society in the West following the Second World War.[50]

Market Forces Domination in the Global Oil Regime (the Third Regime)

This phase of the regime witnessed the development of the international oil industry and trade in a geopolitical environment in which the governments of major oil-importing and consuming countries, and of many oil producers (including Russia since 1993) generally reduced their attempts to manage economic affairs, including trade and prices across a wide range of subjects, besides energy. Information and communication technology has facilitated instant communication of pricing information and contact offers and acceptances across the world's trading screens. The expertise of other commodity markets, including financial and exchange markets, has

49. Al-Chalabi *op. cit.*, No. 33.

50. For details see, Gilbar *op. cit.*, No. 8, p.30.

been brought to the oil trade. It has been argued that the open international commodity market for oil was not driven by the developments in the importing countries only. It would not have advanced so rapidly if many OPEC governments had not destroyed the trading channels, which previously existed between and within a few major international integrated companies.[51] This can be substantiated from the fact that most of the OPEC countries nationalised or took over by participation, the upstream operations of integrated international private sector companies in their territories during the 1970s. And then during the second oil shock they destroyed the 'long-term contacts' which maintained special relationships with those companies. Moreover, as a result of two developments such as marketisation and deregulation in much of the world, and de-integration of most OPEC oil exports from the international chain, the world oil market is the central feature of the relationship between producers and consumers in the new geopolitics. Idea of a producer-consumer dialogue at the government level, or special favourable bilateral relationships between individual producer and consumer countries, are inevitably marginalised when, on the consumer side, markets are open, the state has withdrawn and as a result competition prevails.

The primary change in the global oil regime after 1980 till today is the increased freedom of operations in a variety of ways due to market liberalisation. Before the first oil price shock of 1973, nearly all oil moved in the channels of a handful of companies, with the Seven Sisters producing 22 mb/d of oil outside the US in 1972, which was 67 per cent of the non-Communist total. Although there were a number of traders in the business, most dealt in the regional product market. All the Majors used to sell to independent refiners and did not put oil into the open market. After the crisis of 1973, many oil products were subject to government price controls set by fiat or arcane regulations, even throughout the OECD countries—the major consuming countries. But, now a few of the major-consuming countries' government are in a position to influence product prices, in fact they are rarely doing so.[52]

51. Mitchell, John *et al.* (1996). *The New Geopolitics of Energy*. Chapter 2. London: The Royal Institute of International Affairs. p.8.

52. The product price spikes in the later half of 1990s in the global oil market vindicate the above assertion.

The crude pricing mechanism also has become highly flexible and the great majority of crude is no longer under any control. During the market upheaval of the 1970s most OECD oil producers placed price controls on their own production, OPEC posted its official sales prices, which were typically changed twice a year; Soviet Union which was market responsive set its prices through a centrally marketed organisation. Therefore, the outcome was that even on a monthly basis, prices were fairly stable when there was no major market disruption.

However nowadays, the above scenario of stable price regime has become a thing of the past. Now OPEC countries index their sales to the prices in the open market, the OECD countries have almost abolished price controls and the Russians like everyone else index their sales to spot markets. As a result, the lengthy periods of relatively stable oil prices of the mid-1970s and early 1980s have disappeared. In other words, before 1986, prices were set and the market cleared as OPEC nations allowed production to fluctuate, whereas since 1986, OPEC nations set production and allow prices to fluctuate to clear the market. Additionally, the movement of oil as an internationally traded commodity has changed considerably, partly reflecting the greater number of actors and partly reflecting dispersion of oil production due to a combination of the drop in FSU production and the rise of a number of oil producers (though of moderate size) from Angola to Yemen.[53] The spot trade in crude oil and products has also expanded enormously in recent years. According to one estimate, world spot trade in crude oil had grown from 2.5 mb/d in 1978 to over 5 mb/d in the early 1990s.[54] Another important development is the emergence of 'future markets', which is technically a 'paper market', although delivery sometimes occurs.

Another change in the global oil regime earmarked in recent years is the growing importance of both smaller economies and their oil companies. In the 1960s, the Majors were challenged by the small Independents but most of them were Americans. Today, not only the vortex of global oil consumption has shifted to the developing

---

53. *Petroleum Intelligence Weekly*, 18th September 2000. p.10.

54. *MEES*, 25th December 2000. p.D2.

countries but also the number of companies operating in these countries has soared. In 1972, the US alone accounted for 30 per cent of world oil consumption and India for less than 1 per cent; now, the respective figures are 25 per cent and nearly 4 per cent.[55] It is a fact that, many developing countries reserved their markets for domestic companies was not a major concern three decades ago; but now these markets are not only large, they are the primary source of volume sales growth and much sought after in the global oil regime. Domestic companies—private or state owned—in developing countries are often avidly courted as partners. It has therefore been rightly remarked that, "where Texaco was once bigger than the Indian market, now the situations are reversed."[56]

Simultaneously, these developments reflect a shift in the global oil production from the least cost producing areas to the high cost producing areas like, Malaysia, Brazil, etc. where national oil companies are either the operators or partners. Moreover, downstream operations in somehow closed markets like Korea and India[57] has meant that the domestic companies dominated there and as their demand have become important on a global scale, as a result the companies have come to have a greater presence in the global oil regime. Recently, these companies have begun to invest overseas for the first time.[58] The possible reasons for this development are market oriented policies induced by reforms, technology and innovation leading to cost reduction and geographic diversion in oil production in areas hitherto inaccessible in a number of countries, especially in the USA.

The other major transformation discernible in recent years is the reorganisation of the oil sector, whereby, several largest companies are downsizing their operations and a number of others transforming on a wider scale. The underlying factors responsible for such

55. Ibid.

56. *The Economist*, 21st March 2000. London.

57. India has the largest grass-roots state-of-the-art oil refinery in the world—owned by Reliance Company at Jamnagar, Gujarat.

58. Some of the initiatives by such companies are: Malaysian Petronas in Africa and the Middle East, Chinese CNPC in Iran and India's ONGC Videsh Ltd, Oil and IOC are operating in the Middle East, Africa, Latin America, far East Asia and Russia.

transformations in the global oil industry are reform (privatisation), globalisation and consolidation/mergers.

During the 70s, it was widely held that national oil companies (NOC) provided substantial benefits, including greater attention to social objectives including the environment and workforce upgrading. Moreover, oil-importing countries thought having a NOC would ease relations with oil exporting NOCs and therefore many countries, which did not have their own NOCs, established them. However since the 1970s, a combination of theoretical change and growing experience has resulted in the assertion that NOCs do not deliver many of the expected benefits and that the resulting economic and operational inefficiencies are such that they outweigh any benefits. This led to privatisation of NOCs in greater pace. In fact BP, the first national company was also the first to be privatised. Among the developing nations, Argentina's YPF is the most prominent to be privatised and recently the Indian oil industry is joining the ranks of the private sector. Another approach prevalent in reforming is the phase of 'commercialisation', whereby a Government owned company is ordered to behave as a Private Sector Company without changing its ownership status.[59]

Another important aspect of transformation is the impact of globalisation, which has had one particular thrust in the global oil regime. Companies in the phase of globalisation have increasingly focused on their strategic operational objectives: profitability, economic success and sustainability measured in terms of market share, size, and strategic investments, etc., and so on.[60] In response to this realisation, companies have become much more sceptical in their analysis of operations. Such companies had no natural constituents for terminating an operation and began to exit regions or sectors, selling of or closing assets to both terminate poorly

59. In fact, BP was the first example having effectively become a commercial entity long before it was privatised. Other companies including, Petroleos De Venezuela, SA, Pemex and Kuwait Petroleum Corporation can be said to have moved at least partly down this path.

60. For example, in the early 1980s US companies were forced to rethink their approaches in response to intense Japanese competition, which compelled them to send executives to Japan to have a thorough look at the Japanese success story.

Table 1.6

Size of Private Companies in 1998 and Impact of Mergers

('000 b/d)

Pre–Mergers			*Post-Mergers*		
Company	*Liquid Output*	*Refining Capacity*	*Company*	*Liquid Output*	*Refining Capacity*
Shell	2,354	4,007	Shell	2,354	4,007
Exxon	1,567	4,372	ExxonMobil	2,502	6,549
BP	1,251	1,874	BP Amoco	2,707	3,377
Amoco	635	1,010	Chevron	1,107	1,585
Mobil	935	2,177	Texaco	930	1,506
Chevron	1,107	1,585	TotalFinaElf	1,503	2,430
Texaco	930	1,506	Repsol/Ypf	722	1,242
Total	564	891	ENI	653	859
Petro Fina	140	716	Conoco	348	807
Elf	799	823	Marathon	196	935
Ypf	518	370	Phillips	235	414
Repsol	204	872			
ENI	653	859			
Conoco	348	807			
Marathon	196	935			
Phillips	235	414			
Amereda Hess	206	495			
Petro-Canada	101	308			
Unocal	203	0			

Source : Petroleum Intelligence Weekly, 20th December, 1999.

performing operations but also to help bring the sectors back to equilibrium. The best example is the refinery sector.[61]

The other aspect of transformation is the biggest ever deals in the global oil industry through mergers and acquisitions (approximately 300 billion dollars). Table 1.6 shows the size of the private companies in 1998, which is aptly due to the process of mergers and acquisitions in the world oil industry.

As the Table shows, the merger moved ExxonMobil up to be the biggest privately owned crude oil producer and refiner, BP closes

61. For instance, Japanese companies have closed thousands of service stations. Moreover, OPEC countries cut back their investment in export refineries whose profitability has been questionable; even now they are showing resistance to down stream investment overseas, where the returns did not appear attractive.

Table 1.7

Crude Oil Production by Major Oil Companies, 1950-2005

('000 b/d)

Year	*Shell*	*Exxon*	*Mobil*	*Chevron*	*Texaco*	*BP*
			History			
1950	459	1,015	129	205	190	877
1957	1,215	1,583	350	526	479	1,000
1966	2,093	2,831	854	1,110	1,154	2,612
1972	3,531	4,299	1,575	2,690	2,912	4,664
1986	–	1,715	649	948	1,047	–
1991	2,082	1,600	753	833	685	1,356
1995	2,254	1,622	767	822	644	1,213

Year	*BP*	*ExxonMobil*	*Total*	*RoyalDutch/Shell*	*Chevron*
			Recent		
2000	2,800	2,600	-	2,400	2,080
2001	1,931	2,542	1,454	2,211	1,959
2002	2,018	2,496	1,589	2,359	1,897
2003	2,121	2,516	1,661	2,333	1,808
2004	2,531	2,571	1,695	2,173	1,710
2005	2,562	2,523	2,489	1,998	1669

Notes : BP and Amoco, and Exxon and Mobil merged to create BP Amoco and ExxonMobil in December 1998 and November 1999, respectively. In 2003, BP Amoco was renamed BP. Both data series have been adjusted to include the new companies. TotalFina merged with Elf Acquitaine in February 2000 to create TotalFinaElf, which was renamed Total in 2003. The data series has been adjusted to include data for the new company from 1999. Chevron and Texaco merged to create ChevronTexaco in October 2001. The name was further changed to Chevron in May 2005. Chevron merged with Unocal in August 2005.

Source : Compiled from BP, *Annual Statistical Bulletin*, Historical Series and *OPEC Annual Statistical Bulletin*, 2005.

behind. Moreover, it can be seen from the table that the super Majors remained a shadow of their former selves. None has even regained their former production levels and most are below half. Shell, in terms of crude oil production has done the best because its upstream operation were not as heavily concentrated in the Middle Eastern countries, which nationalised their foreign operators. However, the majors have not been able to increase production substantially after the merger and acquisition. In fact, production by Chevron, ExxonMobil, and RoyalDutch/Shell has declined consistently, and Total has managed to increase since then, see Table 1.7.

Another aspect of the third regime is the integrated pattern of the world energy system evidenced by the rising share of energy crossing borders before reaching final consumers. Energy trade slipped to 40 per cent of primary energy use in 1985 (down from 50 per cent in 1970) but rebounded after the collapse in oil prices in 1986. By the end of the 20th century this share was approaching 55 per cent. The fast growing Asian economies contributed significantly to this increase. Their energy imports tripled between 1985 and 1997, reaching 13 per cent of world energy imports. The share of OECD countries in global energy trade dropped 6 percentage points due to stepped up intra-regional trade and increased domestic oil production (accounting for 13 per cent of domestic oil production in 1990, up from 6 per cent in 1985) and gas production (30 per cent of domestic gas production in 1985). OECD countries in Europe cut their share of global imports from 25 per cent in 1985 to 16 per cent in 1997, while North America doubled its share to 8 per cent over the same period. In fact, the energy self-sufficiency rating[62] increased impressively in the OECD countries, though it declined in the early 1990s. It has been remarked that,

> The two oil shocks traumatised the global economy and drove most nations to pursue greater energy self-sufficiency. Market forces and ambitious government policies forced entire nations to undertake unprecedented and sometimes painful measures to achieve greater energy self reliance. The 24 members of the Organisation for Economic Cooperation and Development (OECD), the world's leading industrialised economies, made particularly strong efforts in this regard. Between 1973 and 1979, OECD's energy self-sufficiency rating increased modestly from 63.2 per cent to 65.4 per cent. Stimulated by the second oil crisis, the ratio jumped to 68.8 per cent in 1980 and then increased steadily, to an all time high of 75.8 per cent in 1985. Thus the self-sufficiency imperative evidently peaked in 1985. [63]

Global energy trade remains dominated by crude oil and oil products. Despite the steady growth in coal trade and accelerated penetration of natural gas in the 1990s, the share of crude oil and oil products in trade only fell from 90 per cent in 1971 to 77 per cent in 1997. While trade in coal, natural gas and even oil products expanded largely unaffected by world oil market prices, trade in crude oil definitely responds—though with a lag—to market price changes.

62. It is measured by the ratio of energy production to energy requirements.

63. Shojai, Siamack (ed.) (1995). *The New Global Oil Market: Understanding Energy Issues in the World Economy.* Chapter 3. London: Praeger. pp.27-40.

Thus, crude oil remains the world's swing fuel, with the Middle East as the swing supplier despite the fact that the region has the lowest production cost.

Developing countries have almost doubled their share of crude oil and oil product imports since 1979. While other major importers such as Western Europe and Japan have reduced their share of the global oil trade, the US thirst for oil has reached an all time high, accounting for 25 per cent of global oil trade in 1999 and declined to 23.61 per cent in the year 2002. In 2002, some 46.27 per cent of the oil trade originated in the Middle East—up from 38 per cent in 1985. This implies the region is back on track to regain market shares of well above 50 per cent.[64] Its low production costs (on average, less than $5 a barrel) expose investments in oil production capacity elsewhere to above average risks. It appears in a sense that the OPEC countries have regained their market share lost in 1986, and can control oil prices in either direction.

For oil importing countries, concerns about oil import dependence and supply security appear to have given way to market forces and high expectations that new exploration and development will bring new oil to the market at a rate commensurate with demand. Moreover, in the wake of globalisation and non-polarisation, quasi-open access to OPEC oil has accelerated the shift of oil from a strategic good to a commodity, further lowering supply security concerns.

Still the world oil market has remained fragile in the recent years. In March 1999, OPEC countries cut production by 85 million tonnes a year, or 2.5 per cent of world oil production. This was in addition to an earlier cut of 125 MT. As a result of strong world oil demand, mostly from the rebounding Asian economies and the surging US economy, market prices almost tripled within about a year.[65]

Unlike oil, natural gas has yet to play a significant role in the global market. Some 20 per cent of global gas crosses borders before reaching final consumers. About 75 per cent of that gas is traded through

64. United Nations (2001). *World Energy Assessment: Energy and the Challenges of Sustainability.* Chapter 1. p.34 and *BP Statistical Review of World Energy.* BP. June 2003. London. p.18.

65. World Market Prices for API Gravity 2 oil were $9.39 per barrel in December 1998 and $27.55 a barrel in March 2000. For details see, *MEES*, 23rd January 2001, p.D11.

pipelines between essentially neighbouring countries. Hence, natural gas trade has developed primarily at the regional level or between adjacent trading regions. Pipeline transaction is highly capital intensive and allows little flexibility in the choice of buyers and sellers. However, pipeline gas is traded between production and consumption sites more than 4,000 kilometres apart. The three major regional gas trade markets which have emerged recently are: the almost fully integrated North American market characterised by accelerated growth of Canadian exports to the US market (from 26 Mtoe in 1990 to 79 Mtoe in 1999). There has also been minor exchange between Mexico and the US. The European market, with the following principal suppliers: the former Soviet Union (with a pipeline producing 108 Mtoe in 1999), Norway (pipeline producing 38 Mtoe), and the Netherlands (pipeline producing 33 Mtoe), and Algeria with minor liquefied natural gas supplies from Libya (pipeline and LNG producing 74 Mtoe).[66] Overall, natural gas trade expanded by 2.7 per cent a year in the period 1990-1998. A gas market is also emerging to take stride in Latin America, with exports from Bolivia to Argentina and Argentina to Chile. The Asian gas market is dominated by LNG trade, which increased from 47 Mtoe in 1990 to 77 Mtoe in 1999. The main suppliers in Asia are Indonesia, Qatar, United Arab Emirates, Malaysia, Australia and Brunei. Japan, the Republic of Korea, China, India and Taiwan are the main consumers of natural gas in the region.

Thus, as is evident from the above analysis, the domination of market forces led to an overall changed scenario in the global oil regime. The commercial and economic fundamentals of the global oil industry have undergone substantial changes and transformations over the years. The daily market trends, trade patterns and short-term price determination set the present day global oil game as purely commercial. No more do the supply-demand balances conform to the boundaries fashioned by the Cold War mindset. The traditional rule of thumb of the 'OPEC *vis-à-vis* non-OPEC' way of thinking about crude oil supplies, though persists, has lost considerable relevance in understanding either current supply trends or future supply potentials. The conventional 'OECD *vis-à-vis* non-OECD' way of thinking about

66. For details see, IEA/OECD (2000). *Natural Gas Information 2000*. Paris: IEA/OECD.

demand has also become irrelevant. It has now become fashionable to focus on the actual patterns of trade among key oil exporting and oil importing geographic regions and on the main economic growth centres of the world, regardless of their allegiance to or membership of the OPEC or OECD camps. Thus, the global oil market no more resembles the late 60s or early 70s, when the seller was the price setter, be they oil companies or national government collectively under the aegis of the OPEC. A number of players have entered into the field and now the buyers set oil prices. It is a buyer's market and is likely to be so in the coming years. The location of the market has also changed. Asia Pacific,[67] not the Atlantic, has become the major destination of oil, particularly oil from the Gulf Cooperation Council countries.

From the supply side, the oil market trends in the last part of the 1980s and throughout the 1990s indicate a cut down of production in the lowest cost producing areas on the one hand and rising production to full capacity in relatively high cost producing areas on the other hand. There has been a clear trend that the relatively high cost producers have become the main incremental supply of crude oil, thereby posing a fundamental challenge to the lowest cost producers, who were traditionally the residual suppliers. This can be attributed to factors such as, first, the vast revenue needs of the lowest cost producers, which have created a huge gap between the price level at which the national oil companies cover all their costs and the price level that balances the overall government budgets;[68] and second, the technological revolution that have driven down production costs in the high producing areas. These factors made vulnerable the lowest cost producers, especially those in the Gulf in the sense that it led to the much-publicised loss of market share and strengthened their inability further to meet overall revenue needs. However, the period after the OPEC decision of 1999 to cut production, particularly the year 2002 witnessed higher prices of oil in the world economy in a scenario of global recession and weakening oil demand. Moreover, the production decline in the non-OPEC high-cost producing areas due to low oil

67. Defined as East Asia, Southeast Asia and South Asia.

68. Steevens, Paul (1994). "Middle East Oil", *MEED Special Report*, MEED. January 16. pp.3-8.

prices and low investment in these areas made matters easy for the OPEC to cut down production and regain market share.

Characteristics of the Regimes

The First Oil Regime can be characterised by an integrated pattern of organisation, based in the major consuming countries and a lower price of oil. These two characteristics have been explained in terms of the structure of the world oil industry itself. During the First Oil Regime, the centre of world oil production gradually shifted from North America to the Middle East. Decreasing exploitation costs and the political dominance of the major industrialised and the then oil producing countries through their oil companies in the fields of investment, technology and skilled manpower made this shift possible. The industrial consuming countries became increasingly dependent on a limited number of developing countries for oil. Within the First Oil Regime the basis of the regime's existence was eventually eroded because power shifted to countries whose interests the regime did not serve. The combination of rapidly growing demand and rising exploitation costs (especially in areas like Alaska and the North Sea) transformed the First Oil Regime because it led the way for a price increase and institutional change through OPEC control of oil production. This loss of the economic and political basis of the regime explains the abruptness of the transition, once the catalyst of the Middle East dispute set it off.

The First Oil Regime was thus a private oligopoly with close ties to the governments of the major consuming countries—mostly the industrialised western countries, the economic giants in the world at that point of time, about the year 1940. Oil at that time sold for about two dollars a barrel and the Seven Sisters (seven large transnational companies) determined the amount of oil that would be produced. The price of oil depended on how much the large companies produced and on the demand in the rich countries where most of the oil was sold. Thus, transnational companies set the rate of production and prices were determined by the conditions in the rich countries. The strongest powers in the international system in traditionally military

---

69. Nye Jr., Joseph S. (2000). *Understanding International Conflicts: An Introduction to Theory and History.* 3rd edition. New York: Longman. p.189.

terms occasionally intervened to keep the system going.[69] For instance, in 1953, when a nationalist movement tried to overthrow the Shah of Iran, Britain and the United States covertly intervened to return the Shah to his throne. The oil regime was in fact largely unchanged.

The Second Oil Regime witnessed major changes after the 1970s. The producing countries set the rate of production and therefore had a strong effect on price, rather than the price being determined solely by the market in the rich countries. There was an enormous shift of power and wealth from the rich to relatively poor countries. A frequently offered explanation is that the oil producing countries banded together and formed the Organization of Petroleum Exporting Countries (OPEC). However, it can be argued that OPEC was formed in 1960 and the dramatic changes did not occur until 1973.[70] Moreover oil prices fell despite OPEC, so there is much more than this explanation.

The Second Oil Regime can be characterised by a fragmented pattern of organisation and a much higher price of oil. The centre of world oil production was the Middle East, but for physical and most importantly political reasons, supplies of oil did not match the growing demand and the result is the energy crisis affecting all aspects of the global economy. In the Second Oil Regime efforts were made to diversify oil supply sources and to find oil elsewhere other than the Middle East. Also the need for developing alternate energy sources, such as, natural gas, nuclear energy, and hydropower, gathered momentum. The Second Oil Regime like the first eroded the basis of its own existence through its inability—for physical and political reasons—to guarantee sufficient supplies of oil. The Second Oil Regime also witnessed the major oil crises, because of the structural bottlenecks of the world oil market, apart from the political situation in the major producing areas. The definite sources of instability in the second oil regime are: the discrepancy between the technical horizon and the market horizon of alternative sources of energy increased because of the combination of the growing pressure on low cost oil and escalating costs of alternative energy; the discrepancy between the demand for oil from the oil producing countries having production

70. Ibid.: 190.

expanding potential and their economic need to do so grew; the discrepancy between the economic requirements of the oil producing countries and their actual income became a real problem; and there was burden on the balance of payments position of the major oil importing countries because of the substantial volumes of oil imports and conversely the accumulation of large currency surpluses in some of the oil exporting countries which with rising oil prices fuelled the crisis.

The Second Oil Regime also witnessed a pattern of interdependence between the consumers, especially the industrialised OECD countries and the producers.[71] The pattern of interdependence can be witnessed at different levels: there was mutual dependence based upon the oil trade. The two sides, OPEC and OECD respectively represented more than 90 per cent of oil exports and imports; there was mutual dependence based upon trade outside oil. The OECD countries were the major suppliers of food, consumer goods, capital goods, arms, technology, etc. to the OPEC nations and thus the OPEC countries especially those in the Gulf, provided important export markets to the industrialised OECD; there was mutual financial dependence. The OECD countries were dependent on the recycling of OPEC financial surpluses, and several of the most important OPEC countries had increasing financial interests in the OECD region, implying that the economic health of the OECD area determined the returns on the OPEC financial investments; there was also mutual political dependence created by the geopolitical situation in the Middle East. This particularly concerned the US, which has leverage over Israel, and Saudi Arabia, which has some leverage over the other Arab countries.

The changes as enunciated in the Second Oil Regime can be explained in three ways through the dynamics of international political economy. The three mechanisms to explain the changes in the second oil regime are the overall balance of power, the balance of power in the oil issue, and international institutions.

One way of explaining is the realistic changes in the balance of power resting primarily on military force, particularly with regard to

71. For details see Adelman *op. cit.*, No. 7.

the Persian Gulf, the major oil exporting region of the world. Two factors affected the changes in the balance: the rise of nationalism and decolonisation witnessed in the world.[72] In 1960, half of the OPEC countries were colonies of Europe; by 1973, they were all independent. Along with the wake of nationalism, military intervention had become a costly affair. For example, when the British and the Americans had tried to keep the Shah of Iran on his throne in 1953, it was not a very costly affair, but if the Americans had tried to keep the Shah on his throne in 1979, the costs would have been prohibitive. It is to be noted that the rich countries did not go in and colonise the oil producing countries in 1973 because of the staggering cost of using force against nationalistically awakened people. The change in British and US power also affected the balance of power in the Persian Gulf. Before and during the formation of OPEC, Britain was to a larger extent the policeman of the Persian Gulf. In 1961, it prevented an earlier Iraqi effort to annex Kuwait. But by the year 1971, Britain was insisting on lowering its international defence commitments due to domestic economic difficulties. In 1971, Britain ended what used to be called its role 'east of Suez' and at that time the US stepped in to support Greece and Turkey and formulated the 'Truman Doctrine'. But in 1971, the US was not well equipped to step in and replace the British in the hot seat as it did in 1947.[73]

A second way of explaining the changes focuses solely on the distribution of power within the world oil industry. The US used to be the largest oil producer in the world, but American production peaked in 1971. American imports began to grow thereafter and the US no longer had any surplus oil. During the two Middle East wars of 1965 and 1967 the Arab countries relied on the principle of an 'oil embargo', but to no avail, as the market was flooded with American oil to meet demands from Europe and elsewhere. Once the American production peaked in 1971 and the US began to import oil, the power to balance the world oil regime switched to countries like Saudi

72. Yergin, Daniel (1991). *The Prize: The Epic Quest for Oil, Money and Power.* New York: Simon & Schuster. pp.588-632.

73. The US was deeply embroiled in Vietnam and was not prepared enough to penetrate in to the Persian Gulf. The American strategy was relying on influencing the regional powers, by projecting Iran as the regional power.

Arabia. The US's role as the supplier of the last resort in the wake of any supply glut in the oil regime got diluted.

Another explanation for changes in the global oil regime is the changes in the role of international institutions, particularly the multinational corporations *vis-à-vis* the OPEC. The Seven Sisters gradually lost power over this period due to their obsolescing bargains with the host countries. At the early stages of the regime the multinational corporations had the monopoly on capital, technology and access to international markets, which fetched them the lion's share in the negotiations with the host resource rich countries. But over time with the transfer of huge resources in the form of capital to the resource based countries, these countries made substantial development, which was out of normal business practices, and not the proverbial 'international aid politics'. In the course of interaction the multinational corporations trained the locals and as a result the locals such as the Saudis, Kuwaitis and others developed expertise in the field. These factors eventually led to the loss of the 'obsolescing bargaining' power of the multinationals with the host countries. Moreover over the course of the period from the 1960s to 1973, the multinationals inadvertently transferred technology and skills that developed the host countries' capacity to undertake oil operations by themselves. As mentioned earlier, further 'little cousins' joined the Seven Sisters who began negotiations with the host countries whenever the major multinationals failed to reach a negotiation. Thus, when an oil producing country wanted to free itself from the clutches of the Seven Sisters, it could strike a deal with a smaller independent multinational. That again reduced the bargaining strength of the largest multinationals.

Institutionally, there was a modest increase in the effectiveness of OPEC as a cartel. Cartels restricting supply had long been typical in the oil regime, but in the past they had been private arrangements of the Seven Sisters. Cartels generally have a problem because there was the tendency of cheating among the members, when there was surplus oil in the market. Usually cartel behaviour used to be smooth in the scenario of scarce oil supply. However, with time market forces eroded the significance of the cartel in the global regime. OPEC represented an effort to shift from a private to a government cartel of the oil producing countries. In its early years, OPEC had trouble exercising power because there was plenty of oil in the market. As long as oil was in surplus, the OPEC had incentives to cheat to get a larger share of the world oil market. OPEC was unable to enforce price discipline from the year it was founded, 1960, until the early 1970s. But after oil became short in supply, OPEC's role in coordinating the bargaining powers of the producing countries increased. The Middle East War of 1973 provided the impetus to OPEC to use the power it has wielded thereof. Though it is a fact that the Arab nations collectively withdrew oil supplies for obvious political reasons, yet the action itself reflects the situations where OPEC could become effective. Over the long term as discussed earlier, OPEC was not able to keep oil prices permanently up because of market forces, but there was stickiness on the downside that was an effect of the OPEC coalition.

A crucial factor was the role of the oil majors in 'smoothing the pain' during times of crises. At one point during the crisis, Henry Kissinger, the then US Secretary of State had opined that "if the US faced 'strangulation', force might have to be used." That was the period when there was a cut in traded oil by almost 15 per cent and the Arab embargo reduced oil exports to the US by almost 25 per cent. However, the oil companies made sure that no one country should suffer much more than the other by redistributing the global supply trade. When the US supply was cut by 25 per cent due to the Arab embargo the companies pumped up more Venezuelan or Indonesian crude to the US market, thus reducing the US vulnerabilities. And it can therefore be argued that the oil majors averted the consolidation of a military conflict ignited by the economic conflict. It is to be noted that the multinationals acted in the interests of the rich nations neither on account of any political pressure nor charity, but on pragmatic commercial purposes of stabilising their market share in the longer term.

In short, changes in three dimensions—the overall balance of power, the issue structure of power and the institutions within the oil regime—explains the dramatic difference between the First Global Regime of the 1960s and the Second Global Regime after 1973.

The Third Oil Regime witnessed the reorganisation of the world oil industry. The international trade in oil became transparent. The past dominant position of either the importing nations or exporting nations got weakened by the emergence of market forces, which dictated all rules of the game. This regime also witnessed the paradigm of energy transformation, which gave space to natural gas as the preferred form of energy, though the share of oil in world primary energy consumption remained stagnant.

This regime witnessed the emergence of a number of players in the oil game as the majors gradually lost their grip on the global oil industry. Remaining first and foremost, amongst the players in the game is the US—the country that had pioneered in almost every aspect of the industry, dominated it for a whole century and was still able to produce no less than a quarter of global output as late as 1970: with an all time high of 11.3 mb/d. In 1999, the US still dwarfed all other consumers, by using more than 25 per cent of planetary requirements and importing more than 8 mb/d of crude oil. Therefore, it has been said that since the days of 'Colonel' Drake, not only were the destinies of the oil industry and the USA closely interlinked, but, moreover, "the rise of oil coincided with the rise of the American Empire and with the attempts by the USA to establish hegemony over the rest of the world."[74] The second player is the group of major international oil and gas companies, especially the Big Three, which still dominate the lot—as shown in table. Thirdly, there is OPEC heavily influenced by Saudi Arabia, which is incidentally the world's largest oil producer and exporter, the Saudis control a quarter of proven global oil reserves and at the end of 2001 produced 30 per cent of OPEC's output. Major non-OPEC producers (outside the USA) make up the fourth major group. Prominent among them are (in order of their output) Russia, Norway, Mexico, China, Great Britain and Canada. These six major non-OPEC producers accounted for no less than 21 mb/d of world output in the year 2000. Fifthly, there are the governments and institutions of the major oil importing countries—Japan, Germany, France, Italy and the booming Asian Economies

74. For the dominant position of the USA in the global oil regime over the years, see Shaffer, Ed (1983). *The United States and the Control of World Oil*. New York: St. Martin's Press.

especially India. The sixth player is the amalgam of the multinational banks, financial institutions, and the international futures and forward exchanges. The next position is occupied by the oil and gas industry's 'independent grey cells'—that is, the global 'think-tanks' (the Club of Rome), the specialised consultancies (Cambridge Energy Research Associates, Centre for Global Energy Studies, Tata Energy Research Institute, etc.), the various fora and institutes, the oil and gas press (Oil and Gas Journals, Middle East Economic Digest and Petroleum Intelligence Weekly, etc.), and independent market observers such as Dr. Paul H. Frankel. Finally, the last major player consists of the aggressive environmental organisations (led by Greenpeace) and the ecological non-governmental organisation, which put pressure on their respective governments and the major oil and gas companies through mobilising public opinion.

Summing Up

Thus, the basic structure and transformations of the global oil and gas regime as described above can be visualised at three stages:

The Formative Phase

This phase includes the origin and development of the modern world oil industry. In this phase the major oil companies completely monopolised the industry until 1960; right from drilling, producing and refining the crude, distributing the products and finally retailing them to the consumer. As the oil potentialities of the Middle East became apparent, the companies formed a series of consortia to negotiate with the local governments and rules in order to arrange production deals. The Middle East States at that time had no complaints, but were very eager to increase their incomes.

The Dominant Phase

This phase includes the emergence of OPEC and its impact on the whole regime. The event that led to the formation of OPEC was the reduction in price of marker OPEC crude (Arab Light) from US $2.08/b to US $1.80/b in less than two years by the majors. During the 1960s, OPEC patiently formulated the principles of strategy that later enabled them to assume the role of leader of the world oil market.

The consolidation and strengthening of OPEC by the end of the 1960s was held first by the extension of its membership from 5 in 1960 to 10 by the end of 1970 and secondly, by the phenomenal growth of world oil demand during that decade which inevitably resulted in increased world dependence on OPEC oil. The Algerian nationalisation of 51 per cent of French oil interests in February 1971 followed by the measures taken by Libya against the operating companies including the British Petroleum in December 1971 and the full nationalisation of Iraq in June 1972 led to the liquidation of the Majors' stronghold on Middle East oil production. The pace of the changes was set by the Gulf members, who during 1971-72, succeeded in forcing the oil companies to accept, firstly, the principle that crude prices would no longer be set unilaterally by the companies without consulting the governments of producing countries and, secondly, the inflation and the fluctuation in the value of the US dollar were the factors which would be accommodated in crude oil prices.

The next important event was the Iranian nationalisation attempts in 1951 followed by the Western boycott of Iranian oil and the Suez Crisis of 1956 which resulted in an Arab oil embargo being imposed on the West. Although total world oil supply was hardly affected because production increased elsewhere, irreparable damage was caused to the relationship between the companies and the host governments, and it became evident that the producers could act together. Another event that led to the end of the Majors' monopoly was the decision of the six Gulf members on 16th October 1973, regarding the determination of crude prices as the exclusive right of the oil producing states. Three months later the same six members decided to set the governments' royalty on Arab Light at US $7/b with effect from the beginning of 1974, thereby raising the posted price of the marker crude to US $11.65/b. This action was soon identified as OPEC policy action and by 1974 OPEC began to act as a unified authority in settling the level of world crude prices. Both in absolute and relative terms, the price assessments of 1974 and 1975 were modest. At the end of 1978 and amid signs of an imminent short term supply disruption, OPEC worked to put an elaborate quarterly price assessment, resulting in an average price increase of 10 per cent in 1979 in relation to 1978. The carefully prepared scheme of price escalation was reduced to shambles by the widespread chaos that prevailed in the world oil market during the first week of 1979. The chaos of 1979 was unprecedented and OPEC efforts to cope with the deteriorating situation proved futile, not because there was an actual supply shortage but because that served primarily the interests of oil companies and the major oil consuming and importing countries. In fact in 1979, OPEC export of crude and products was nearly 1 mb/d higher than in 1978 and the total world production was up by nearly 2.5 mb/d. With the production of OPEC countries at maximum capacity, they neither increased production nor were willing to acquire oil prices two to three times higher. By the end of 1979, OPEC had not only lost its control over the world oil regime, but also, weakened the cohesion within its organisation.

This phase witnessed the consolidation of the major oil importing and consuming countries to confront the oil producing and exporting countries in a concerted manner in order to cope with the short-term repercussions of supply disruptions. The importing countries became conscious that they should consolidate themselves through an international multilateral agency to deal with supply disruptions. The major companies through established markets managed the oil sharing that took place during the embargo. As a consequence, in December 1973, US Secretary Kissinger proposed that the US, Japan and the nations of Western Europe should form an international organisation of consumer countries in order to promote united actions in energy problems. This resulted in the formation of the International Energy Agency (IEA) on November 1974 as an autonomous agency within the Organisation for Economic Co-operation and Development (OECD).

The Transformation Phase

This phase witnessed the declining importance of OPEC as an influencing factor in the world oil trade to some extent. This accompanied by the built-in rigidities of the industry itself and the paradigm shift of global economic thinking led to various structural changes in the global regime. It was not until October 1981 that OPEC managed to restore its cohesion to uniform its pricing structure on the basis of a price of US $34/b for the marker crude. The achievement was too late to correct the imbalance in the market. The oil companies and the consuming countries had accumulated very substantial oil inventories, the market had been fragmented, and the role of speculators and mediators had increased. The most important factor was the impetus provided by higher oil prices to the conservation efforts on the one hand and the development of other energy sources, especially non-OPEC oil on the other.

Thus, the organisation was faced with the classical dilemma of declining world oil demand and increased non-OPEC supplies, which left the OPEC members, particularly the Gulf members with two options: to reduce its overall production in order to confirm its official price structure or to reduce prices in order to discourage the development of high cost non-OPEC crude. This implied a drastic reduction of total OPEC oil revenues. In March 1982, OPEC decided to reduce its total production to 18 mb/d. One year later it decided to reduce prices by US $5/b. But with world oil consumption remaining virtually unchanged, the price reduction could not arrest the declining trend of OPEC's share in world oil production. In fact by 1985, OPEC's share had dropped to as low as 40 per cent. Even though OPEC had reduced its overall production ceiling to 16 mb/d at the beginning of November 1984 in an attempt to cause a destabilising impact on North Sea production. The member countries found it difficult to market their reduced production quota at official prices. Consequently, a variety of marketing practices which involved direct or indirect discount on official prices, were offered. At this point of time there was general impression in the market that OPEC had given up its policy of defending prices and bent upon initiating a price war on outside producers. As a result, prices continued to drift downward and by July 1985 the price was below US $10/b, a level that, in nominal terms were lower than that of 1974. These factors culminated in what is known as 'reverse oil shock'. As noted by El-Beblawi:[75]

> On January 24, 1983, almost a decade after the first oil shock, Ahmad Zaki Yamani, the Saudi oil superstar declared at the end of a Geneva OPEC meeting, "There has been a complete failure", "I do not see a bright future." On March 14, 1983, OPEC could finally

75. El-Beblawi, Hazem (1983). "The Oil Decade: An Appraisal in Perspective", *The IBK Papers*, Series No. 10. Kuwait: The Industrial Bank of Kuwait K.S.C. September. p.42.

> agree on quota production and a new marker price for the Arabian Light, cutting it from $34 to $29—the first such cut in OPEC history. The 'oil glut' took over from 'energy and oil crisis' as catchwords in headlines and news media. From a seller market with all sorts of premiums, oil is becoming a buyer market also asserted with all kinds of discounts. OPEC production declined from its peak of about 31 mb/d in 1979 to less than 17 mb/d in 1983, thus reducing its share in oil trade from about two thirds in the mid-seventies to less than 45 per cent in the early eighties. All this sounds new and strange; the "New Oil Order" seems to be threatened with a different oil shock, a 'reverse oil shock' this time.

However, though stability ensured in 1987, yet OPEC members pledged to defend fixed prices.

On the demand side of the global oil and gas regime, the Eastern Countries or the developing world, especially the Asian countries took centre stage on the consumption front, replacing the industrialised West. Though the US is still the world's largest oil consumer till today, yet the newly industrialising and mature economies of the Asian region such as India, China, and Korea, etc. are becoming prominent on the energy consumption front due to their economic performance and future potentials. The important aspect of the transition is that these new consuming and importing countries are poised to replace the industrialised countries such as North America and Europe as the only market for the world's only producing and exportin region—the Gulf region. And somehow the contours of the present regime have made the Gulf region dependent on these emerging consuming and importing regions for a secure stable outlet for their energy exports.

Thus, the global oil regime has undergone substantial changes and transformations over the years. The structural changes identified above suggest two fundamental criteria for the evaluation and historical comparison of global oil regimes. In terms of ideal types,[76] the oil regime dominated by the oligopoly of the Majors or 'the order of the Majors'[77] was 'hierarchical-transnational' at least until the beginning

76. Noel, Pierre, "Transnational Anew, Competitive at Last: The Oil Market in the Globalisation Era". On the site, *www.upmfgrenoble.fr*.

77. The concept of oil order is developed by Bergson, Bjork and Claes (1990). *The World Oil Market in the 1990s: Is a New Order Possible?*. Norway: Fridtjof Nansen Institute.

of the 1960s. Hierarchical, because the regulation of the market by the firms relied on a complex and relatively formalised administrative system which allowed them to restrain competitive pressure. Transnational, because the large internationalised western companies had direct access to resources, and they operated under concessions giving them almost unlimited freedom to manage reserves. The integration of oil reserves into the world economy did not therefore proceed from a sovereign-state philosophy. The OPEC order was that of a 'sovereign-hierarchical' order. Although the setting of the price remains essentially administrative, this period is marked by the real revolution constituted by nationalisation on the one hand and by the progressive takeover of all the upstream operations by national companies of the producer countries, on the other. The global oil regime in this order is *a priori* more natural than the cohabitation of the administrative and transnational dimensions: one can readily imagine that the market is not the dominant mode of regulating an industry in which the bulk of the supply is controlled by producer states bound to cooperate with each other in a cartel like structure. One would have expected that these states would have had more success in their task of limiting competitive pressure than an oligopoly of firms. Historically it was nothing of the sort, the sovereignty principle proving to be a powerful barrier to the introduction of collective restraining mechanisms within the oligopoly.

The next global regime—after the 1980s till today—is 'transnational-competitive', implying the affirmation of market over authority as a mode of coordination, and re-transnationalisation of the oil industry. These two dimensions explain the intricacies of the present day oil dynamics. The affirmation of the market as a mode of regulation and coordination was structurally destructive of any oligopolistic and centralised management. It multiplied the number of operators at all stages of the oil chain. At the same time, once introduced into the process of price setting, market mechanisms spread inexorably into the whole sector: the expansion of market regulation is a self-enforcing mechanism. Also, it affects the relationship between the IOCs and resource-owner states, encouraging the extension of the transnational principle at the expense of the sovereign one.

2

Changing Pattern of the Global Energy Trade

India, A Destination for the GCC Countries Oil and Gas Exports

As discussed in the last chapter, the most significant aspects of the present global oil and gas regime are: the pattern of energy transformation, whereby natural gas's share in the world's primary energy mix is increasing and that of oil is somehow stagnant; the increasing importance of the major Asian economies in global oil and gas consumption on account of their burgeoning economies; and the penetration of a number of non-OPEC oil and gas producers to the global oil and gas market, which in fact has posed severe threats to the OPEC producers, especially those in the Gulf. This chapter will focus on the implications of these aspects of the present regime. It will highlight how India along with other Asian countries is becoming the destination for the oil and gas exports of the Gulf Cooperation Council (GCC) countries.[1]

World Primary Energy Consumption Trends

Since the first oil crisis, the world's energy map has changed drastically with response to global economic growth pattern and distribution. In 1972, immediately before the first oil crisis, the world's primary energy mix was composed of oil (47.3 per cent), natural gas (18.0 per cent), coal (32.5 per cent), hydro (2.0 per cent) and nuclear (0.2 per cent). In 2005, the respective shares of oil, natural gas, coal, hydro and nuclear stood out to be 36.4 per cent, 23.5 per cent, 27.8 per cent, 6.3 per cent and 6 per cent, thus showing the declining share of oil and coal, while that of natural gas, nuclear and hydro-electricity rose (Figure 2.1).

1. Gulf Cooperation Council (GCC) Countries are Bahrain, Kuwait, Oman, Qatar, Saudi Arabia and UAE.

Figure 2.1

World Primary Energy Consumption by Fuel
(Share in per cent), 1972 and 2005

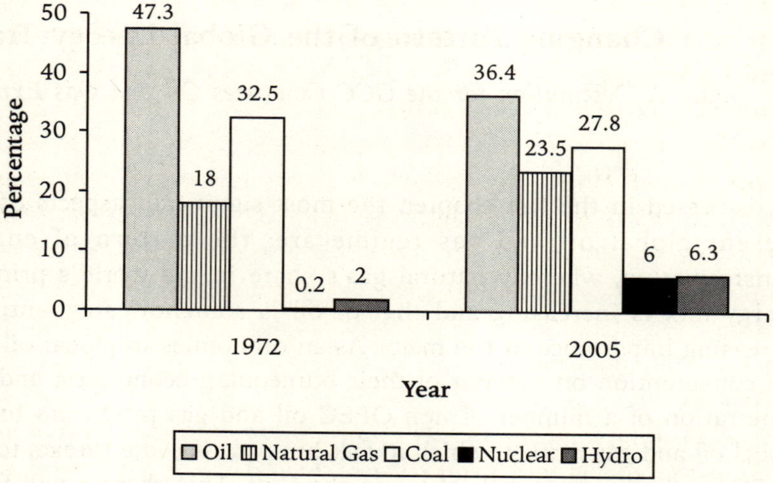

Source: Prepared from BP *Annual Statistical Review of World Energy, 2006*.

North America and Europe together accounted for 52.2 per cent of the world's primary energy consumption in 1972, but their share shrank to 42.4 per cent by 2005. Over the same period the share held by the Asia Pacific region swelled from 16.4 per cent to 32.5 per cent. The world's primary energy consumption increased at an average of 1.9 per year during the past 33 years. A closer examination unveils that, aside from the two oil crises, a crucial point of the changing energy scenario was the sharp economic plunge resulting from the break up of the Soviet Union in the year 1990.[2] With 1990 taken as a peak, primary energy consumption of the FSU/East Europe has slumped to about two-thirds. This region had accounted for 22.2 per cent of the world's primary energy consumption in 1990, which contracted to 12.3 per cent by 2002 and has recently picked up.

2. Fujime, Kazuya (2003). *How the World's Energy Supply-demand/Trade Structure Haves Changed during 30 years since the Oil Crisis?*. Japan: The Institute of Energy Economics (IEE). October.

Oil: Trends in Production, Supply and Demand

The world's oil output grew at an annual average of 1.9 per cent during the period 1972-2005. The North American oil production, accounting for 24.2 per cent of the world's output in 1972, had its share falling to 20.8 per cent in 1992, 18.5 per cent in 2002 and further to 16.5 per cent by the year 2005. During 1972-1982, as a reaction to the price hikes during the oil crises, oil production in the Middle East plunged by about 30 per cent over the 10 years, and its share in the world's oil production shrank from 34.4 per cent to 23.6 per cent as well. With 1982 as a border, as a result of lower prices, Middle Eastern oil production increased by $1/6^{th}$ fold by the year 2002 and its share increased to 31 per cent by the year 2005. Likewise, the African oil production, down by about 20 per cent in 10 years with the share shrinking from 10.4 per cent to 8.2 per cent, rebounded 1.7 times by 2002. It is South and Central America, Europe & Eurasia, and Asia Pacific (this region alone marked a slower growth in the 1990s) that have been on the constant rise in the 30 years. Their shares in the world's total production, 6.0 per cent, 0.8 per cent and 5.1 per cent respectively, expanded to 9.4 per cent, 10.2 per cent and 10.7 per cent each 33 years later. Table 2.1 and Figure 2.2 shows the trends of oil production and their shares by area in the world.

Table 2.1

The Trends of Oil Production by Area in the World

(Million Tonnes)

Area	*1972*	*1982*	*1992*	*2002*	*2005*
North America	639.7	706.3	663.7	660.2	642.5
South & Central America	232.0	182.1	246.5	335.3	350.6
Europe & Eurasia	443.5	780.7	695.6	785.0	845.0
Middle East	907.5	660.1	913.8	1033.0	1208.1
Africa	275.1	230.5	335.3	379.6	467.1
Asia Pacific	138.8	235.9	334.7	378.0	381.7
World Total	**2636.6**	**2795.6**	**3189.6**	**3572.1**	**3895.0**

Source: BP Statistical Review of World Energy. London: Pauffley for BP.

Figure 2.2

World Oil Production Shares by Area (%)

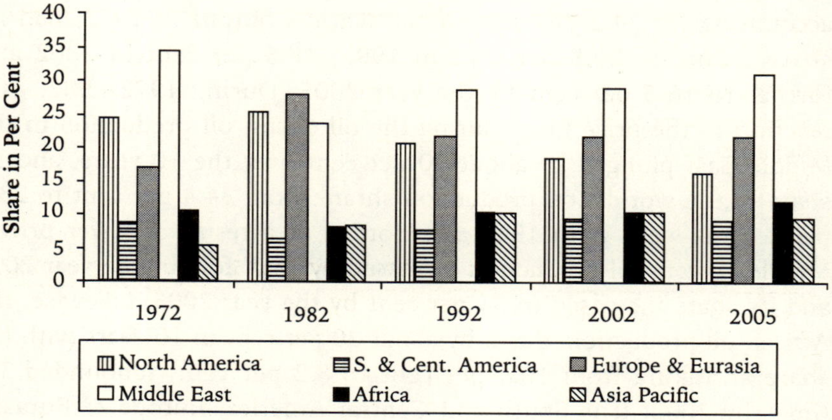

Oil Consumption

The world's oil consumption grew at an average of 1.5 per cent annually during the period, 1972-2005. The two oil crises during the 1970s had the gravest impacts on the advanced industrialised countries, such as oil consumption in North America dropped by about 10 per cent in 10 years of 1972-1982 and that in West Europe down by 15 per cent or so, with their shares in the world shrinking from 34.3 per cent and 27.1 per cent each to 30.07 per cent and 21.6 per cent respectively. On the other hand, during 1972-1982, South and Central America, the Middle East, Africa and developing areas in the Asia Pacific had not been oil-dependent so much as severely hit by the oil crises. In the 33 years of 1972-2005, these regions all had their shares swelling from 4.6 per cent, 2.6 per cent, 1.6 per cent and 15.8 per cent (a total of 24.6 per cent) to 5.8 per cent, 7.1 per cent, 3.4 per cent and 29.1 per cent (a total of 45.4 per cent). The trends can be seen from Table 2.2 and Figure 2.3.

Table 2.2

The Trends of Oil Consumption by Area in the World

(Million Tonnes)

Area	*1972*	*1982*	*1992*	*2002*	*2005*
North America	876.4	834.6	930.2	1071.1	1132.6
South & Central America	119.5	155.6	175.6	219	223.3
Europe & Eurasia	1049.6	1109.6	1063	933	963.3
Middle East	65.4	118.1	177.5	239.9	271.3
Africa	40.8	76.5	97	117.5	129.3
Asia Pacific	403.4	481.1	731.8	1008.5	1116.9
World Total	**2555.1**	**2775.4**	**3175.2**	**3589**	**3836.8**

Source: *BP Statistical Review of World Energy*. London: Pauffley for BP.

Figure 2.3

World Oil Consumption Shares by Area (%)

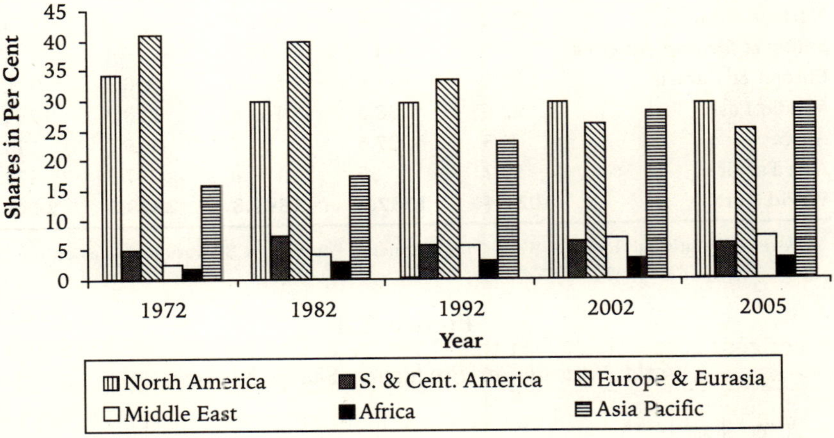

Source: Same as Table 2.2.

Natural Gas: Trends in Production, Supply and Demand

The world's natural gas production grew at an annual average of 4.3 per cent during the period 1972-2005, thus, growing at nearly three-fold faster than the world's oil production growth. However, just like oil production, the North American natural gas production entered the resource depletion period and its world share kept falling from 62.1 per cent in 1972 to 27.2 per cent in 2005. It is the share of the developing countries of South and Central America, the Middle East, Africa and Asia Pacific that have been on the constant increase during 1972-2005 with their shares up from 1.7 per cent, 2.2 per cent, 0.6 per cent and 1.9 per cent to 4.9 per cent, 10.6 per cent, 5.9 per cent and 13.0 per cent, respectively.

The share of Europe and Eurasia though surged from 31.5 per cent in 1972 to 45.9 per cent in 1982 and further to 46.5 per cent in 1992, which, however, slumped to 39.1 per cent in 2002 and further to 38.4 per cent in 2005. The trends can be seen from Table 2.3 and Figure 2.4.

Table 2.3

The Trends of Natural Gas Production by Area in the World

(Mtoe)

Area	*1972*	*1982*	*1992*	*2002*	*2005*
North America	634.2	558.4	601.6	690.7	675.6
South & Central America	17.5	34.5	54.9	94	122
Europe & Eurasia	321.5	613.9	857.2	890.5	955
Middle East	22.6	38.3	102.6	220.2	263.3
Africa	6.5	27.6	67.7	116.7	146.7
Asia Pacific	19.2	65	157.8	267.3	324.1
World Total	**1021.4**	**1337.7**	**1841.8**	**2279.3**	**2486.7**

Source: *BP Statistical Review of World Energy*. London: Pauffley for BP, Various issues on the site, *http://www.bpamoco.com/worldenergy/*

Figure 2.4

World Natural Gas Production Shares by Area (%)

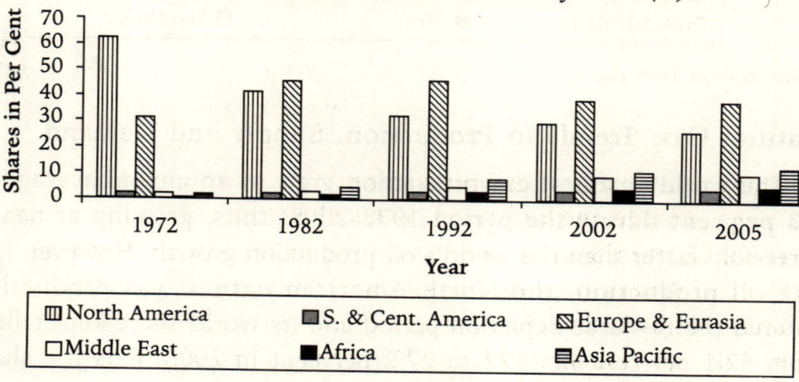

Natural Gas Consumption

Because natural gas is produced nearer to consuming areas (i.e., lesser trade) than oil, natural gas production trends are akin to its consumption moves. The share of North America in the world's natural gas consumption, which was 61.8 per cent in 1972, fell drastically to 28.2 per cent in 2005, or registered a decline of more than half of the 1972 level. On the other hand, in reflection to advancing oil-to-gas shifts, etc., Europe and Eurasia boosted its share in the world's natural gas consumption from 33 per cent in 1972 to 40.8 per cent by 2005. Developing countries of South and Central America, the Middle East, Africa and Asia Pacific which held 1.7 per cent, 1.6 per cent, 0.2 per cent and 1.8 per cent in 1972, respectively expanded to 4.5 per cent, 9.1 per cent, 2.6 per cent and 14.8 per cent by the year 2005. The trends can be seen from Table 2.4 and Figure 2.5.

Table 2.4

The Trends of Natural Gas Consumption by Area in the World

(Mtoe)

Area	*1972*	*1982*	*1992*	*2002*	*2005*
North America	637.2	537	615.6	710.9	697.1
South & Central America	17.6	35.8	54.9	90.7	111.7
Europe & Eurasia	340.2	627.9	869.3	940.7	1009.7
Middle East	16.1	35.5	99.5	193.6	225.9
Africa	2.2	22.1	36.3	54.1	64.1
Asia Pacific	18.1	68.5	161.6	296.1	366.2
World Total	**1031.5**	**1326.9**	**1837.3**	**2286.0**	**2474.7**

Source: *BP Statistical Review of World Energy* (Various issues). London: Pauffley for BP.

Energy Trade

Among primary energy sources, those subject to cross-border transactions (trade) include oil, natural gas and coal. Energy trade no doubt occupies a considerable portion of traded goods both in value and in volume. Particularly, oil is traded in huge quantities because its producing centres are located far from consuming areas.

Oil Trade

About 60 per cent of oil output is exported. In other words, about 60 per cent of oil consumption is covered with imports. Of oil

Figure 2.5

World Natural Gas Consumption Shares by Area (%)

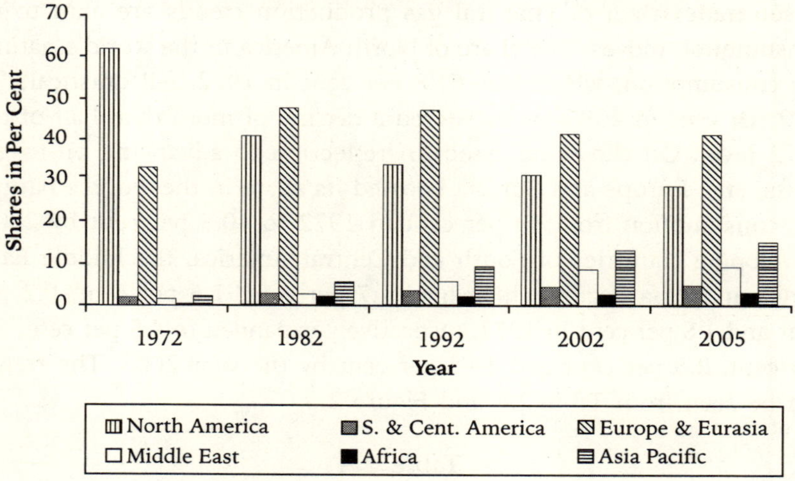

imports/exports, crude oil accounts for 76.7 per cent and petroleum products the remaining 23.3 per cent (2005). It is the US and the rest of the consuming areas, largely consisting of such developing countries as China and India, that recorded growing oil imports in terms of both volume and world share. The US's oil imports increased by an annual average of 4.03 per cent during the last 25 years, 1980-2005, with its world share rising from 20.8 per cent in 1980 to 27.1 per cent in 2005. Oil imports by the rest of the world (RoW) consuming areas increased by an average 4.56 per cent per year during 1980-2005, and its share went up from 25.9 per cent to 35.85 per cent over the same period. Oil imports by these two areas kept swelling even during 1972-1982, the period of the two oil crises. Oil imports by Europe and Japan declined by 30.9 per cent and 13.2 per cent respectively during 1972-1982. On top of economic stagnation, energy conservation and oil substitution, the sharp decline in Europe's oil imports reflected rising self-sufficiency thanks to the start of full-scale crude oil production in the North Sea. The world shares held by the two (Europe and Japan) alike contracted from 46.7 per cent and 15.9 per cent respectively in 1972 to 27.3 per cent in 1982 and to 11.6 per cent in 2002. With these imports-growing and imports-falling areas combined, the world's oil imports dropped 13.8 per cent during 1972-

1982. But, having boosted later, the growth averaged 1.2 per cent per year throughout the period 1972-2002, but the growth rate increased to 4.03 per cent per year during the period 1980-2005 due to phenomenal growth in imports by developing emerging economies of Asia and a pick up in imports by other regions. These trends are shown in Table 2.5 and Figure 2.6.

Table 2.5

The Trends of Oil Imports by Area in the World

('000 b/d)

Area	*1980*	*1985*	*1990*	*1995*	*2000*	*2005*
USA	6735	5065	8026	8831	11092	13525.24
Europe#	12244	8768	9801	10436	11070	13260.93
Japan	4985	4045	4802	5581	5329	5224.51
Rest of the World*	8350	6610	8812	11562	14911	17895.31
World Total	**32324**	**24488**	**31441**	**36410**	**42402**	**49905.99**

Notes: * Includes unidentified trade,
\# Prior to 1993, excludes Central Europe (Albania, Bulgaria, Czech Republic, Former Republic of Yugoslavia, Hungary, Poland, Romania, Slovakia),

Source: *BP Statistical Review of World Energy, 2006*. London: Pauffley for BP.

Figure 2.6

World Oil Imports Shares by Area (%)

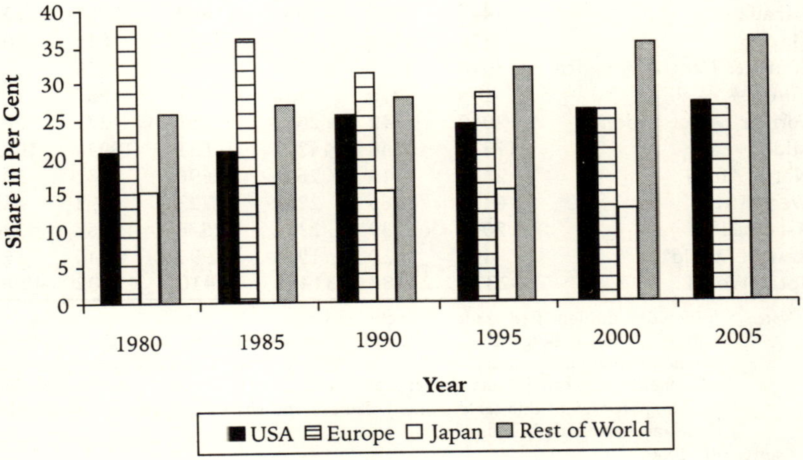

Analysing oil trade from the oil-exporting side, the world's total oil imports equal the world's total oil exports, in statistical terms. As a result of consuming countries' responses to the oil crises, combined with the policy of production curtailments taken by the OPEC, the Middle East and African oil producing countries, especially the Gulf OPEC countries, came to hold lesser weight in the world's oil exports than before. Exports from the former Soviet Union temporarily declined due to the economic collapse. But, reflecting subsequent developments, like shrinking domestic consumption and a stronger will to earn hard currency by boosting exports, exports from this area have been on a sharp rise in recent years.

Exports from the Middle East plunged by 31.2 per cent during the period 1972-1982, and in fact registered a sharp decline of almost 47 per cent during 1980-1985 but later rebounded to almost 112.3 per cent during 1980-2005. Its world share slumped from 56.3 per cent in 1972 to 54.17 per cent in 1980 and further to 39.7 per cent in 2005. The most important fact is the continuous growth of exports from the FSU region over the period (see Table 2.6 and Figure 2.7).

Table 2.6

The Trends of Oil Exports by Area in the World

Area	*1980*	*1985*	*1990*	*1995*	*2000*	*2005*
USA	555	780	889	949	890	1129.4
Canada	445	685	955	1402	1703	2200.9
Mexico	875	1580	1387	1422	1814	2064.7
South & Central America	3010	1985	2367	2797	3079	3528.4
Europe#	n/a	n/a	n/a	1472	1967	2149.0
Former Soviet Union@	2040	2549	2659	2731	4273	7075.6
Middle East	17510	9340	14212	16651	18944	19820.7
North Africa	2820	2415	2604	2696	2732	3070.4
West Africa	2475	1765	2248	2723	3293	4358.4
Asia Pacific£	2099	2339	2182	2576	2767	2967.0
Rest of World*	495	1050	1938	991	940	1541.6
Total World	**32324**	**24488**	**31441**	**36410**	**42402**	**49906.0**

Notes: *–Includes unidentified trade; £–Excludes Japan; #–Prior to 1993, excludes Central Europe (Albania, Bulgaria, Czech Republic, Former Republic of Yugoslavia, Hungary, Poland, Romania, Slovakia); @–Prior to 1993 includes Central Europe and excludes movements between Former Soviet Union and Central Europe; n/a–not available.

For the purposes of this table, annual changes and shares of total are calculated using thousand barrels daily figures.

Source: BP, 2006.

Figure 2.7

World Oil Export Shares by Region (%)

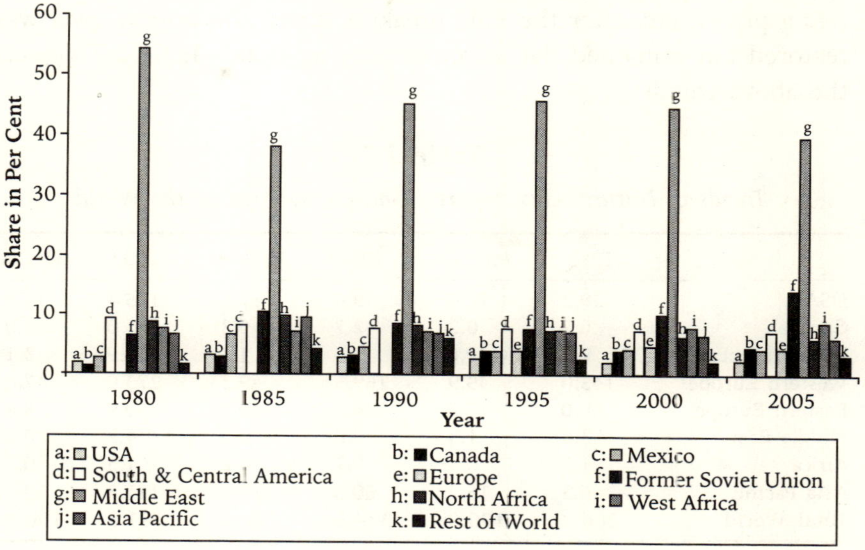

Natural Gas Trade

Natural gas is traded in two ways, that is, through pipelines and by LNG tanker after liquification. As of 2005, pipeline-based trade accounts for three-fourths of total trade in natural gas, and LNG tanker-based the remaining one-fourth. Of total world natural gas produced in 2005, about 26.1 per cent was exported. During the period 1989-2002, natural gas trade[3] (exports/imports) expanded by 5~6 per cent per year on average. Imports expanded particularly at a faster pace in America and the Asia Pacific, where imports surged by an average 8.7 per cent and 7.0 per cent per year respectively during 1989-2002. Their world shares increased from 13.7 per cent and 16.2 per cent each in 1989 to 17.3 per cent and 17.6 per cent in 1992 and further to 19.8 per cent and 19.2 per cent in 2002. Natural gas imports by West Europe grew 5.3 per cent per year on an average during the last 13 years, with its world share falling mildly from 49.9 per cent in 1989 to 49.2 per cent in 1992 and to 47.0 per cent

3. Natural gas trade statistics are available only from 1989 onward.

in 2002. The moderate fall can be attributed to increasing self-sufficiency of the North Sea natural gas production. Natural gas imports by East Europe from the former Soviet Union dropped due to rising prices, etc. after the FSU breakup. Later, the import level was restored but remained flat as an underlying trend. Table 2.7 depicts the above trends.

Table 2.7

Trends of Natural Gas Imports (Shares) by Area in the World

	1989	*Per Cent*	*1992*	*Per Cent*	*2002*	*Per Cent*
USA	39.2	13.4	59.6	17.3	115.4	19.8
Canada	0.7	0.2	2.7	0.8	6.0	1.0
Latin America	2.3	0.8	5.0	1.5	17.9	3.1
Western Europe	143.0	49.9	169.5	49.2	273.0	47.0
Eastern Europe	50.0	17.5	36.4	10.6	50.9	8.8
Middle East	3.6	1.3	0.0	0.0	4.9	0.8
Africa	1.2	0.4	0.7	0.2	1.5	0.3
Asia Pacific	46.3	16.2	60.6	17.6	111.8	19.2
Total World	**286.3**	**100.0**	**334.5**	**100.0**	**581.3**	**100.0**

Source: *BP Statistical Review of World Energy*. London: Pauffley for BP.

The world's total natural gas imports have expanded at the same rate as the world's total natural gas exports. Natural gas exports from Canada grew by 8.9 per cent per year on an average during 1989-2002. It was in a reverse direction in relation to the soaring natural gas imports by America. Canada's share in the world's total exports jumped from 13.2 per cent in 1989 to 18.7 per cent in 2002. Natural gas exports from Asia Pacific swelled 5.4 per cent per year on average during 1989-2002. Its world share expanded from 14.5 per cent in 1989 to 16.7 per cent in 1992, but reversed to the 14 per cent mark, or 14.1 per cent by 2002. Natural gas exports from West Europe increased by an average 6.5 per cent per year during 1989-2002, but its world share levelled off at 22 per cent. The growth of natural gas exports from the FSU remained at 2.2 per cent per year on average during 1989-2002, with its world share declining from 34.9 per cent in 1989 to 22.9 per cent by 2002. When combined, developing countries of Latin America, the Middle East and Africa had their world shares rising from 13.9 per cent in 1989 to 19.9 per cent in 2002, Table 2.8.

Table 2.8

Trends of Natural Gas Exports (Shares) by Area in the World

	1989	*Per Cent*	*1992*	*Per Cent*	*2002*	*Per Cent*
USA	2.0	0.7	6.9	2.1	15.1	2.6
Canada	37.9	13.2	58.3	17.4	108.8	18.7
Latin America	2.3	0.8	2.2	0.7	15.2	2.6
Western Europe	64.9	22.7	71.8	21.5	126.6	21.8
Eastern Europe	100.0	34.9	99.1	29.6	133.1	22.9
Middle East	6.7	2.3	3.4	1.0	34.1	5.9
Africa	30.9	10.8	37.0	11.1	66.2	11.4
Asia Pacific	41.6	14.5	55.8	16.7	82.2	14.1
Total World	**286.3**	**100.0**	**334.5**	**100.0**	**581.3**	**100.0**

Source: *BP Statistical Review of World Energy*. London: Pauffley for BP.

Thus in almost all the countries of the world, oil is consumed. Until 1990, the degree of concentration in demand and supply were indeed quite similar. The top five consumers and producers account for more than half of each world total, and the top 10 of each for around two-thirds of world consumption and production. These patterns of demand and supply overlap, mainly because the US and the FSU were until 1990, the world's largest oil consumer and producer. More than half the world's oil is consumed by the 24 member countries of the organisation for economic cooperation and development (OECD), the rich countries club of the post-war generation, which account for only about 15 per cent of the world population. In 1990, oil represented about 43 per cent of these countries total energy consumption. By the end of the year 2005, it was around 36 per cent. The interesting fact is that these countries have levelled off their oil consumption throughout the 1990s and increased the use of other energy sources, especially the use of natural gas. Natural gas accounts for more than 27 per cent of their total energy consumption. These countries also account for nearly 62.9 per cent and 54.6 per cent of the world oil and natural gas consumption respectively (at the end of 2001). Comparably the FSU was consuming only 13 per cent of world oil and 0.33 per cent of gas. China with four times more population was using only 3 per cent of oil at that time. And at that time, India with a population next to China was using a negligible percentage of world oil and gas. Soviet oil consumption levelled off during the 1980s, with its command economy pushing through a determined switch to natural gas. Indeed the whole communist block managed to stabilise oil consumption. But none of the countries then levelled as 'centrally planned economies' has achieved nearly as much energy conservation as most of the OECD members. With far lower per-capita national income, these countries used energy much less efficiently. These countries, comprising 75 per cent of the world population consumed only 24 per cent of the world's commercial energy in the year 1990. Their per-capita energy consumption varying from only about 125 kg to 1 tonne of oil equivalent annually, was tiny compared with over 5 tonne per head in the OECD countries. But these poor countries' energy consumption went on growing rapidly during a decade and a half of sharply increased and then unstable oil prices, while the OECD's levelled off in the early 1980s, fell and has recovered only slowly.

Thus as discussed above, oil and to some extent gas has remained the form of energy that nearly all developing countries have mainly relied on to achieve and maintain high rates of economic growth. These countries generally use so little per head that they can hardly achieve any energy saving. Also, economic growth is their main priority, well above the world environment that the richer countries urge upon them. So most of the continuing growth in world energy, particularly oil and gas demand during the 90s occurred in these economies.

Moreover, the dynamics of world energy consumption as discussed reveals that from 1990 onwards, OECD is not where the growth of oil consumption took place. What have begun to become more important are the patterns of oil demand outside the OECD—in the developing countries, especially in the Asia Pacific region, the centre of the world economy. Besides, much of oil's contribution to world energy supply nowadays is as a family of specialised transport fuels outside the general fuel market where it competes with other forms of primary energy such as, natural gas. From the last two decades, it looks as if this specialised market sector might be the main element of continuing growth.[4] This primarily constituted a substantial

4. This trend can be witnessed in the world energy consumption patterns. As per estimates, for everything except transport, oil demand in the world's richest countries (OECD) is nearly down by 30 in the 1990s in comparison to the previous decade.

proportion of global oil demand during the 1990s and thereby accounted for the world oil demand trend in this period. This period therefore witnessed a sharp increase in gas consumption in the OECD. It is to be mentioned that, though the nations of the industrialised world continue to consume more of the world's petroleum products than the developing world, yet the gap is projected to narrow considerably by the year 2020,[5] see Table 2.9. In 2001, oil consumption in developing nations was 58 per cent of the amount used in the industrialised world, but by the year 2020 this is expected to increase to 90 per cent. The increase in oil use in the industrialised world is expected to occur in the transportation sector, where there are presently few economically competitive alternatives to oil. In the developing world, oil demand is projected to grow in all end-use sectors. As the energy infrastructures of these emerging economies improve, people are turning from traditional fuels like wood burning to electricity and additional petrochemical feedstock are being used for industry. Moreover, natural gas is expected to take the greatest share of incremental energy consumption in the industrialised world. In the developing world increments in gas use are expected to supply both power generation and industrial uses. As per the projections natural gas will experience robust growth in the developing world, averaging 5.3 per cent per year between 2000 and 2020, reflecting the popularity of the fuel, as well as the expectation that the relatively immature gas markets of emerging countries will develop quickly over the coming years.[6] Moreover as per the projections the developing regions will account for 29 mb/d of the 45 mb/d increase in global oil demand between 2002 and 2030. Developing Asia will take the largest share. Oil demand in China and India will register the highest growth. Other East Asian countries oil demand will double, to 9.4 mb/d. Oil consumption in the OECD and North America will rise strongly too, from 22 mb/d to almost 31 mb/d in that period. Demand in other OECD regions will increase only modestly. North America remains by far the largest single market for oil.

5. As projected by the Energy Information Administration (EIA), Department of Energy (DOE), USA; see, *MEES*, 1st April 2002, p.A9.

6. Ibid.

Table 2.9

World Oil Demand Outlook in the Reference Case

(mb/d)

Year/Region	*2000*	*2005*	*2010*	*2015*	*2020*
North America	24.1	25.0	26.1	27.2	28.2
Western Europe	15.1	15.6	16.3	16.8	17.1
OECD Pacific	8.7	8.9	9.2	9.4	9.6
Total OECD	47.9	49.5	51.6	53.4	55.0
Developing Countries Oil Importers					
Southeast Asia	3.0	3.4	4.1	4.9	5.8
South Asia	2.6	3.2	4.1	5.1	6.3
Africa and Middle East	1.5	1.7	2.0	2.3	2.6
Latin America	3.2	3.8	4.7	5.7	6.9
Total Oil Importing DCs	10.3	12.1	15.0	18.0	21.6
Oil Exporters					
OPEC	5.6	6.2	7.1	8.1	9.1
Other Exporting DCs	2.6	2.9	3.4	3.8	4.3
OPEC + Other Exporting DCs	8.3	9.2	10.5	11.9	13.4
DCs excl. OPEC	13.0	15.1	18.3	21.8	26.0
Dcs incl. OPEC	18.7	21.3	25.5	29.9	35.0
Former Soviet Union	3.8	4.2	4.7	5.1	5.6
China	4.7	5.5	6.7	8.2	9.8
Other Europe	0.8	0.8	1.0	1.0	1.2
Total World	**75.7**	**81.3**	**89.4**	**97.6**	**106.5**

Source: *MEES*, Vol. 45(29), 22 July 2002, p.D3.

Regarding gas, its share in the primary fuel mix is expected to increase in every region, but in volume terms the greatest increases will be in OECD North America and OECD Europe. But the fastest rates of growth will occur in China and India, where gas consumption is currently low. World primary consumption of gas is projected to grow at an average annual 2.7 per cent from 1997 to 2020, as shown in Table 2.10. Demand is strongest in the non-OECD regions, growing by 3.5 per cent, while OECD consumption increases by 1.9 per cent. The non-OECD region's share of total world gas demand is projected to reach 56 per cent by 2020, as against 48 per cent in 1997. Demand growth is particularly strong in non-OECD Asia, although its share of global demand remains below that of Europe and North America in the year 2020. Gas use in the transition economies expands more slowly than in any other region except North America, but these countries remain the second largest consuming and the largest outside the OECD in 2020, Table 2.10.

Table 2.10

Total World Primary Supply of Gas

(Mtoe)

	1997	*2010*	*2020*	*1997-2020**
OECD	999	1349	1549	1.9
North America	579	721	778	1.3
Europe	344	522	650	2.8
Pacific	77	107	121	2.0
Non-OECD	912	1376	2002	3.5
Transition Economies	484	572	714	1.7
Africa	41	73	108	4.3
China	21	56	111	7.5
East Asia	88	176	286	5.2
South Asia	37	87	163	6.6
Latin America	108	205	313	4.7
Middle East	132	207	307	3.8
World	1911.3	2724.4	3551.0	2.7

Note: * Average annual growth rate in per cent.
Source: IEA/OECD, *Natural Gas Information 2002*, (Paris: IEA/OECD, 2003).

Asian Economic Growth Miracle and Energy Demand Pattern

The phenomenon of the Asian economic boom can be analysed in the light of two schools of economic thought. A broadly neoclassical economic view sees it as the result of getting markets right, with governments' interventions normally not only unhelpful, but also adverse, as they leave open the possibility of policy failure and structural rigidities. The second school of thought advocates a more positive function for state intervention and provision of incentives, beyond the conscious policy of improving market performance, and hence a longer-term historical context of mercantilism within a country.[7] This school of thought also refers to what the World Bank

7. See Lall, Sanjaya (1996). *Learning from the Asian Tigers, Studies in Technology and Industrial Policy*. Basingstoke and Laos: Macmillan Press.

designates as the 'market friendly view',[8] which explains growth as the result of a set of central policy prescriptions; macroeconomic stability, trade and capital market openness, an emphasis on education and training, and a policy encouraging private sector development and capital growth. The *dramatis personae* of development success in Asia have been ever expanding. After the takeoff of the Japanese economy in the 1950s and 1960s came the success of the 'four little dragons or four tigers', namely Singapore, Taiwan, Hong Kong, and Korea. In the last two decades, the focus was shifted to the newly industrialised countries of Malaysia and Thailand. More recently, in terms of absolute GDP increments more significantly, the giant economies of China and India have shown their economic potential.

Economic growth has been maintained at high rates in the majority of the Asian countries throughout the 1980s and into the 1990s. Its key feature is, despite widespread growth most Asian countries are still low-income economies, with considerable disparities in economic performance across the continent. It is to be noted that, only some economies in the Asian region had a GNP per capita in 2001 of above $1000.[9] These countries contain less than 7 per cent of the population of Asia, with the remaining 2.9 billion living in low-income economies, 2.1 billion in China and India alone. This implies that for Asia as a whole the development process is still in an early stage, with most of the potential for economic growth still unrealised. Moreover, among the lower income economies, starting later from a lower base means that many years of very strong growth need to be sustained to even reach a position comparable to the current level of development of the 'Tigers'.

Economic growth provides the backdrop to and often the motivating force behind the growth of energy demand. The structural change and market development as a result of the sustained growth rate has tremendous implications for the energy sector in the Asian countries. The implications of economic growth for energy demand is reinforced by growth induced structural changes that have important

8. See World Bank (1993). *The East Asian Miracle: Economic Growth and Public Policy.* Oxford: Oxford University Press (OUP). This view has also been described in World Bank (1991). *World Development Report 1991.* Oxford: OUP.

9. Asian Development Bank, 2002.

resources implications,[10] such as: first, there is the move towards urbanisation manifest in the rapid expansion of the Asian mega-cities, with their implications for power and transport infrastructure and demand; second, there is the changing balance between the economic importance of internal and external markets with the growth in the former leading to further implications for the transport sector; third, there is the change in private aspirations backed by increasing purchasing power, leading to realisation of pent-up demands for private transport and the use of commercial rather than traditional non-commercial energy in the domestic sector; and finally, particularly for countries at early stages of development, such as India and China, there is the sectoral balance shift towards energy intensive manufacturing and heavy industries.

Asian Primary Energy Demand Pattern

The structural change and market development as a result of sustained economic growth has substantially affected regional energy fundamentals in Asia. The implications of economic growth for energy demand is reinforced by growth induced structural changes that have important resource implications, such as; first, there is a move towards urbanisation manifest in the rapid expansion of the Asian mega-cities with their implications for power and transport infrastructure and demand; second, there is the changing balance between the economic importance of internal and external markets with the growth in the former leading to further implications for the transport sector; third, there is the change in the private aspirations backed by increasing purchasing power, leading to realisation of pent-up demands for private transport and the use of commercial rather than traditional non-commercial energy in the domestic sector; and finally, particularly for countries at early stages of development, such as India and China, there is the sectoral balance shift towards energy intensive manufacturing and heavy industries. In short, the direct impact of higher economic growth is reflected through surging consumption of commercial energy such as oil and natural gas in Asia.

---

10. Paul, Horsnell (1997). *Oil in Asia: Markets, Trading, Refining, and Deregulation*. Oxford: OUP for Oxford Institute for Energy Studies. p.16.

A detailed breakdown of energy use trends highlights the increasing proportion of oil and gas use in Asia, as countries such as China, India, Thailand and the Philippines have achieved higher levels of economic development. At present, the more developed Asian economies like Japan, South Korea, Taiwan, Hong Kong, and Singapore consume nearly half of the oil used in Asia, even though they account for only 7 per cent of the regional population. Oil accounts for about 55 per cent of the total energy use in these economies. Table 2.11 and Figure 2.8 show the pattern of primary commercial energy demand across fuels in the Asia Pacific.

Table 2.11

Asia Pacific Primary Energy Consumption by Fuel Type

(Mtoe)

Year	*Oil*	*Natural Gas*	*Coal*	*Hydro-Electricity*	*Nuclear*	*TPEC*
1985	471.7	100.4	664.7	73.8	45.8	1383.5
1990	625.3	142.3	835.7	92.1	65.2	1792.4
1995	818.7	195.8	1056.1	112.2	93	2311.2
1996	854.8	213.5	1112.4	110.2	97.8	2424.7
1997	899.9	225.4	1100	110.2	104.1	2476.7
1998	876.3	228.9	1054.3	120.9	108.5	2426
1999	912.9	243.8	1068.2	117.2	110.2	2490.2
2000	939.1	267	1112.2	120.2	113.3	2589.5
2001	941.8	284.2	1146.5	132.1	114.8	2657.4
2002	970.8	296.1	1203.2	134.1	117.7	2759.5
2003	1004.4	318.4	1361.5	137.7	104.6	2964.8
2004	1065	340.6	1526.2	156.5	119	3245.9
2005	1077.4	366.2	1648.1	167.4	125	3423.7

Source: *BP Statistical Review of World Energy*, Historical Series, 2006.

As evident from the Table, the total primary energy consumption in Asia which was 2311.2 million tonnes oil equivalent (Mtoe) in the year 1995 has increased to 3423.7 Mtoe in 2005, signifying an increase by 50 per cent. The consumption of different energy sources such as oil, natural gas, coal, nuclear and hydro has increased by 35 per cent, 80 per cent, 58 per cent, 41 per cent and 48 per cent respectively during the same period.

Figure 2.8

Shares of Various Fuels in Asia Pacific's TPEC

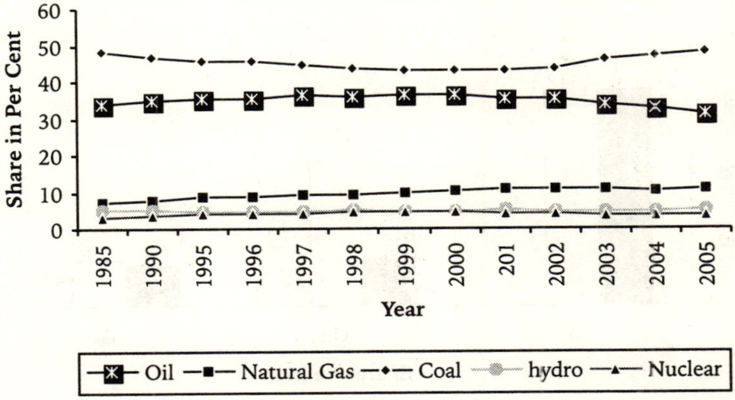

As can be seen, oil and natural gas account for 42.2 per cent of TPEC in Asia, coal accounting for 48.1 per cent and the remaining 8.5 per cent is shared by hydro and nuclear energy. It is evident that, the share of oil has decreased while that of coal and natural gas has increased. The main factors seem to be the Asian financial crisis; low growth in Japan in particular has negatively affected oil consumption. This implies that the prevailing situation has changed considerably since then and most of the countries such as China, India, and other ASEAN countries in particular can propel the oil demand in the coming years, as their economies are fast moving starting from a low energy consumption base. Moreover, the combined annual average growth rate (CAAGR) of total primary energy consumption in Asia during the period, 1995-2005 stands out to be 3.8 per cent. The CAAGR of consumption of oil, natural gas, coal, nuclear and hydro are 2.8 per cent, 5.4 per cent, 4.6 per cent, 3.3 per cent and 3.6 per cent respectively. It is to be noted that the combined annual average growth rate of consumption of oil and natural gas in Asia is substantial in comparison to the world average and that of other regions.

The phenomenal increase in the consumption of energy in Asia over the last decade can also be evident from the region's current supply-demand balance. It is evident that all fossil fuels such as coal, oil and natural gas are short in supply and resulted in increasing imports especially oil and gas (Figure 2.9).

Figure 2.9

Asia Pacific Energy Balance, 2006

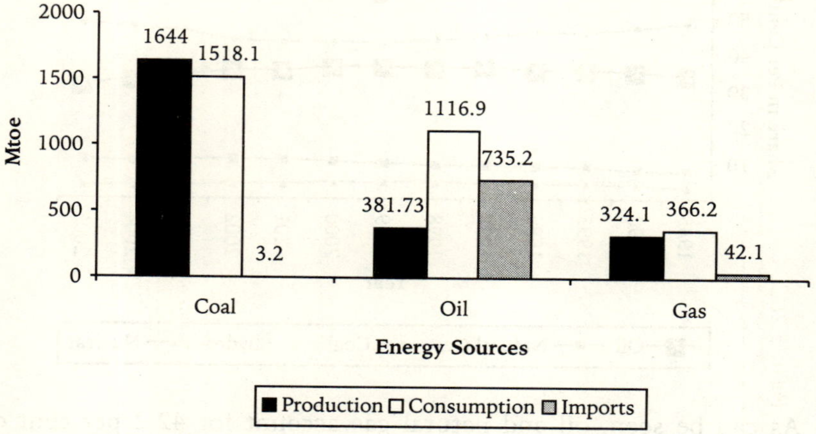

Source: Prepared from BP 2006.

The regional oil and gas market in Asia is relatively dynamic, exhibiting the features of strong consumption growth, declining regional production, an intensely competitive refining sector, and overwhelming import dependence on outside regions. The region's key players are China, India, Indonesia, Japan, Singapore and South Korea, which dominate most aspects of the oil market. The countries of the region include the region's top five consumers and several of its major and minor producers.

As can be seen there is diversity in oil and gas self-sufficiency in Asia. Asia has proven reserves of oil and natural gas to the tune of 40.2 thousand million barrels and 14.8 trillion cubic feet respectively. Importantly, the R/P ratios for oil and gas in Asia stand out to be 14 years and 44 years respectively (Table 2.12).

Several countries are net oil exporters especially Indonesia, Malaysia and Vietnam, but many more are totally reliant on imports. At the country level, India is the most reliant on imports followed by Japan, China and Korea; ASEAN has also become a net importer as Indonesia's production has failed to keep pace with consumption. This

Table 2.12

Oil and Gas Fundamentals in Asia Pacific, 2005

Country	Oil				Natural Gas			
	Reserve ('000 million tonnes)	Prodn. (million tonnes)	Consump. (million tonnes)	Self-sufficiency Index	Reserve (trillion cubic feet)	Prodn. (bcm)	Consump. (bcm)	Self-sufficiency Index
India	0.7 (18.6)	38.0	119.3	-2.13	32.6 (31.3)	29.4	32.1	-0.09
China	2.3 (13.4)	174.5	308.6	-0.76	78.7 (54.7)	40.8	39.0	0.04
Japan	—	—	241.5	-1.0	—	—	72.2	-1.0
S. Korea	—	—	104.8	-1.0	—	—	31.6	-1.0
Indonesia	0.7 (11.5)	55.1	54.7	0.007	90.3 (34.9)	73.3	33.7	0.54
Taiwan	—	—	41.5	-1.0	—	—	10.1	-0.1
Singapore	—	—	38.1	-1.0	—	—	7.8	-1.0
Malaysia	0.6 (12.9)	40.3	23.3	0.42	87.0 (45.7)	53.9	33.2	0.38
Philippines	—	—	15.8	-1.0		—	2.5	-1.0
Thailand	0.1 (6.3)	9.0	43.6	-3.84	15.1(21.1)	20.3	28.7	-0.41
Vietnam	0.4 (19.0)	20.8	—	0.63	8.3 (56.5)	4.2	—	—
Hong Kong	—	—	15.3	-1.0	—	—	2.2	-1.0
Asia Pacific	5.5 (14.2)	379.5	1090.5	-1.87	501.5 (43.9)	323.2	367.7	-0.13
World	**161.9 (40.5)**	**3867.9**	**3767.1**	**0.02**	**6337.4 (66.7)**	**2691.6**	**2689.3**	**8.54**

Notes: 1) Figures in the parentheses denotes the R/P ratio. This implies that if the reserves remaining at the end of any year are divided by the production in that year, the result is the length of time that those remaining reserves would last if production were to continue at that level.

2) Self-sufficiency index is domestic production less consumption, divided by consumption; a positive number indicates self sufficient. No domestic oil and gas production is equal to -1.0.

3) The total figure for Asia includes Australia, Brunei, Pakistan, Bangladesh and other countries.

Source: *BP Statistical Review of World Energy*, 2006.

implies that there is likelihood of large deficits of oil and to an extent natural gas in the coming years based on the expected higher consumption levels. This can be substantiated from the future sectoral trends as envisaged by various estimates.

An important feature of the pattern of primary energy consumption in Asia is the generally low level of energy use in the region compared to developed countries. Three indicators such as the intensity of oil use in energy consumption,[11] energy intensity of GDP, both at the market rate and at purchasing power parity exchange rates and per capita oil consumption reveal diversified trends about the regional oil and energy use pattern in the Asia Pacific (Table 2.13).

Table 2.13

Oil and Energy Use in Asia, 2003

Country	*Oil Intensity*	*Energy Intensity of GDP*		*Oil Consumption Percapita (Barrels)*
		Nominal	*PPP*	
East Asia	0.310	3.188	0.907	2.4
China	0.250	4.259	0.877	1.6
Hong Kong	0.628	0.739	0.573	13.9
Korea	0.520	1.891	1.138	16.5
Mongolia	0.257	10.453	2.677	1.8
Southeast Asia	0.546	2.684	0.821	2.6
Cambodia	0.932	0.263	0.039	0.1
Indonesia	0.507	2.624	0.801	2.0
Lao PDR	0.117	3.149	0.608	0.2
Malaysia	0.445	2.959	1.205	7.5
Myanmar	0.364	2.496	0.332	0.2
Philippines	0.550	2.125	0.446	1.5
Singapore	0.888	2.523	2.143	60.5
Thailand	0.529	2.898	0.840	4.8
Vietnam	0.460	3.304	0.648	1.0
South Asia	0.352	3.072	0.573	0.7
Bangladesh	0.288	1.553	0.301	0.2
Bhutan	0.121	3.866	0.972	0.5
India	**0.343**	**3.230**	**0.588**	**0.8**
Maldives	1.000	1.610	0.480	5.0
Pakistan	0.383	3.439	0.729	0.8
Sri Lanka	0.846	1.425	0.338	1.5
G7	0.403	1.000	1.000	18.6
Japan	0.505	0.692	0.796	16.0
United States	0.395	1.192	1.153	25.1

Source: ADB, 2005.

11. The intensity of oil use in energy consumption index measures the share of oil in an economy's primary energy consumption. If a country relies only on oil to produce energy, the value of the index is 1; if no oil is used in producing its energy, the value is zero.

The oil intensity of energy consumption is much more pronounced in some countries than others. A notable feature is that oil intensity is highest in the ASEAN, Japan, Korea and lowest in China and India, due to their use of alternatives such as coal, natural gas, and hydro power.

The trends of energy intensity of GDP in Asia show that East Asia has become less energy intensive over time but the energy inputs into GDP have risen in Southeast Asia, while South Asia has been on a flat to slightly declining trend. Comparing developing Asia's energy intensity with other countries, it is evident that developing Asia consumes over three times as much energy as the G7 in nominal market terms. But in purchasing power terms, developing Asia is less energy intensive than the G7. Only countries that are major oil producers or refiners, or which have very cold winters, are more energy intensive than the G7 average. However, developing Asia is less energy efficient than industrial countries in activities like power generation, in particular.

Besides the pattern of overall energy use, the potential for energy efficiency merits some considerations. For example, primary energy use is very limited in China and India in per capita terms. However when this is analysed in GDP units, a radically different trend emerges. While China and India use very little energy given their size of population, they use a lot given the size of their economies. Table

Table 2.14

Energy Efficiency in Different Countries

Country	*Kgoe/$ 1000 GDP*	*Index (Taking World as 1)*
India	**631**	**2.2**
China	807	2.8
Malaysia	544	1.9
Japan	128	0.4
UK	142	0.5
USA	220	0.8
World	**292**	**1.0**

Source: Chaturvedi, B.K. (2004). "Domestic Resourcing of Energy, Gulf and Future of Global Energy", Paper Presented at the *National Seminar on India's Energy Security*. New Delhi: GSP, JNU. February 19-20.

2.14 shows the total primary energy used expressed in kilograms of oil equivalent, per thousand dollars of GDP, for selected Asian countries together with the UK and USA for comparison.[12]

As shown in the Table, China and India are shown to have extremely high levels of energy use per unit of GDP, especially when compared to the extremely energy efficient Japanese economy. However, it is to be mentioned that India and China are still at an early sage of development where peasant agriculture is far more important than in most other Asian countries

Future Sectoral Trends

The potential for growth in oil and natural gas use can be illustrated by developmental comparisons. China's per capita oil consumption is nearly 22 times less than that of the United States and 13 times less than that of South Korea. Per capita electricity use in China is about 5 per cent of the OECD average; in India, it is just over 3 per cent. Still the level of energy efficiency is less and since the economies like India and China are starting from a lower base, there is every likelihood of the consumption growth of energy moving upwards.

According to the IEA (2001), Asian oil demand is expected to grow to three times faster than in the industrialised West, reaching around 29 million barrels per day by 2010 in the business-as-usual scenario. In fact, in the period from 1972 to 2004 Asia's energy demand quadrupled in absolute terms and Asia's staggering growth promoted a 274 per cent increase in the amount of oil used over the period, *versus* an average of 63 per cent for the rest of the world. Asia's share in World's oil consumption has increased from 15.8 per cent in 1972 to 28.9 per cent in 2004, an increase of nearly 83 per cent. Similar trends can also be observed in the consumption of natural gas. Consumption of natural gas in Asia was only 2 per cent of the world total in 1972, which increased to 13.7 per cent in the year 2004 (an increase of 585 per cent).

The various forecasts as summarised by Paul Horsnell[13] suggest a range of expected demand increment by the year 2000 of 4.1 mb/d to 6.1 mb/d. This then implies an average annual increment of between

12. This measure is affected by a number of factors such as; balance between energy intensive and traditional sectors; technology of energy use; the relative price of labour to capital; and a set of other economic, social factors.
13. Horsnell *op. cit.*, p.28.

about 600 thousand b/d and 900 thousand b/d. For 2010, the range for the total increment from 1993 is between 9.4 mb/d and 14.7 mb/d (these two extremes being the low and high case from the same forecast), implying average annual increments between 2000 and 2010 within the range of 500 thousand b/d and 900 thousand b/d. The IEA (2001), in addition predicts the global totals in 2010 of about 92 mb/d and 97 mb/d for its two cases, implying that over 40 per cent of increment world oil demand will come from the Asian region.

On the basis of the above forecasts, three main features are evident. The first is the assumption of a declining growth rate of oil demand (the forecasts tend to have near constancy in the average absolute growth in demand). The second feature is that growth in China is forecast to be the highest in the region, with Chinese oil demand in absolute terms reaching about 4 mb/d in 2000, and surpassing 6 mb/d in 2010. The strong forecast rate of growth in India represents the third feature (from 1.3 mb/d in 2000 to nearly 3 mb/d in 2010). Thus, all forecasts give a central role to China and India. In the oil products market that role is in fact even more central, as oil refining surpluses of other countries will look to China and India to take the role of a 'demand sink'.[14]

A sharp difference in the pattern of oil use can be witnessed among countries in Asia. In Asia, oil demand growth has been relatively flat over the last decade in matured economies like Japan, and Korea; in contrast, in developing Asia comprising countries such as China, India and other big economies of the ASEAN, oil demand growth has registered a brisk pace. It is expected that developing Asia will play an increasing role in the global oil market. In 2030, its oil demand is expected to exceed that of the United States and Canada combined and will account for 26 per cent of the world total. Moreover, it is expected that the region will account for 21 per cent of world incremental gas demand by 2030 and 80 per cent of the growth in world coal demand over the same period (IEA, 2005). The transport sector has been and will be the main driver of Asian incremental oil demand. The correlation between oil demand in transport and GDP growth in Asia is striking. Moreover, pricing subsidies on oil products in most of the developing Asian countries provide further

14. Ibid.

encouragement for consumption and thereby aggravate energy security challenges. The current and projected oil demand-supply balance scenario in Asia points to the growing deficits, which will result in increasing imports (Table 2.15).

Table 2.15

Oil Demand-Supply Balance in Asia, 2005-2025

(mb/d)

Year	*Consumption*	*Production*	*Deficit*
2005	22.4	7.3	15.1
2010	27.2	6.6	20.6
2015	32.2	6.1	27.1
2020	38.1	6.1	32
2025	44.6	6.6	38

Note: 2005 figure is actual, based on BP statistical Review of World Energy. The figures for other years are based on high economic growth and high oil price scenario projections.

Source: Calculated from the projections made by the Energy Information Administration (EIA), *International Energy Outlook* 2005, Department of Energy.

While Asian oil consumption is expected to increase from 22.4 mb/d to 32.2 mb/d in the coming decade (2005-2015), regional supplies are expected to decline from 7.3 mb/d to 6.1 mb/d in the same period. Another forecast by the International Energy Agency (IEA) also shows similar trends. As per the projection, Asian oil production is expected to fall to 6.4 mb/d by 2010 from the current level of 7.3 mb/d (2005). Another important spin off of the emerging supply deficits is the expected direction of regional oil import which exhibits considerable concentration in one single region, i.e., the Middle East (Figure 2.10).

Moreover, unlike the US and Europe whose oil imports are sourced from diverse regions such as, South America, the Middle East, Africa, Europe and Russia, where arbitrage provides an economic window for traders; regional oil import in Asia is substantially concentrated in a single producing region, i.e., the Gulf region. This is partly due to geographical location and partly due to slower development of regional oil markets in Asia. In 2004, nearly 70 per cent or 12 mb/d of Asia's oil imports were sourced from the Gulf region, with only a small portion (2 mb/d) from Africa. As per IEA forecasts to the year 2030, the volume of traded oil from the Gulf to Asia will increase to 28 mb/d, with some limited diversity of supply from Eastern Russia/

Figure 2.10

Asia-Pacific's Oil Import Outlook

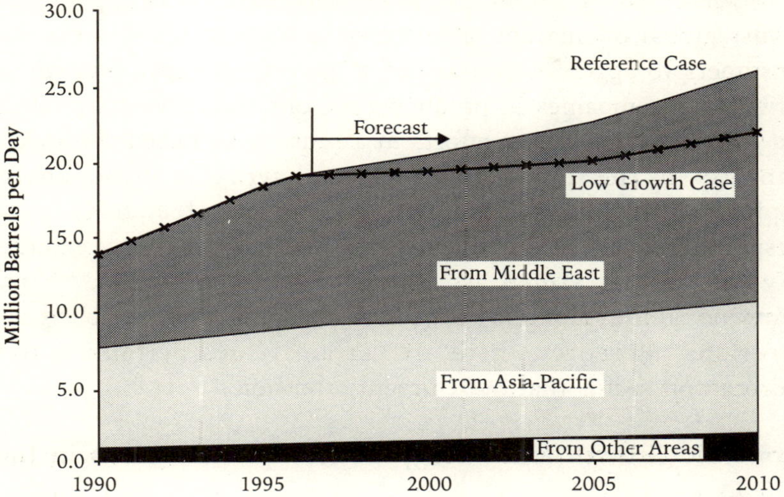

Source: Energy Information Administration (EIA). *Asia-Pacific Factsheet*. US, DoE, 2001.

FSU into North East Asia. This implies that as a consequence of higher oil imports from the Gulf, Asian countries once shielded geographically from the turbulence of the Middle East will no longer be able to leave it on the margins of their geopolitical agenda. This, in other words, envisages that there may be greater common cause in the search for regional stability. Table 2.16 depicts the future dependence of the Asia-Pacific on Middle East oil.

Table 2.16

Asia's Heavy Dependence on Middle East Oil

	2001	*2020*	*Change*
Total ME Exports	16.2	25.2	9
Asia	9.4	16.8	7.4
North America	2.8	3.2	0.4
Western Europe	3.1	3.9	0.8
Other	0.9	1.3	0.4
Asia Share (%)	58	67	

Source: IEA. *World Energy Outlook, 2004*.

Thus, relatively lower reserve base, lack of discovery, except some important discovery of natural gas fields, and pervasive resource scarcity has led many major consuming countries such as Japan, China, Korea and India to bring oil import policies to greater prominence among national strategic concerns. These apprehensions amidst global oil market developments have tempted these Asian consumers to aggressively pursued a 'go out strategy' through their national oil companies in producing regions through equity oil deals and joint ventures. These efforts in a sense have raised the stakes of stability in the producing regions having multidimensional implications, thereby, centering the regional energy security perspective in the global mainstream. This has led to the emergence of what can be termed as "energy security dilemma,"[15] which commends to be minutely analysed in order to devise enabling policy directions. Moreover, there are certain issues pertaining to the hydrocarbon sector that need urgent attention.

Economic Growth and Energy Consumption Pattern in India

India has become an important element in Asian and indeed the world energy markets over the last decade. Its high rate of economic growth has swiftly made it one of the prominent energy consumers in the region as well as in the world. India accounted for nearly 14 per cent of total primary energy consumption in the Asia-Pacific region and four per cent of world primary energy consumption in the year 2005.[16] The Indian economic boom is the byproduct of the reform policies adopted in the year 1991, as a reactionary policy prescription to counteract the crisis ridden economy as per the IMF and World Bank guidelines. The structural changes in the Indian economy resulted in higher growth rates over the last decade that had implications percolating to all the sectors including the energy sector.

In the last decade and a half, significant structural reforms helped India become one of the world's fastest growing economies, boosting living standards and reducing poverty. Economic liberalisation and

15. In recent years, there are a number of studies pertaining to the dynamics of Asian energy security. While some of them foresaw a competitive environment based on the energy security imperatives, that portend to ignite conflict and rivalry, others have pointed towards the emergence of a pattern of interdependence based on sectoral complementarities that may enhance cooperation in Asia. Some of the studies are Caldor, Kent (1996). *Asia's Deadly Triangle*. London: NB Publishing; Manning, Robert A. (2000). *The Asian Energy Factor*. New York: Palgrave. Manning; and Yergin, Daniel (1991). "The Prize". New York: Simon & Schuster.

16. *BP Amoco Statistical Review of World Energy*, 2002.

rising income also stimulated a rapid growth in trade, FDI inflow, and expansion of a high income middle class.

Since the mid-1990s, Indian economic growth pattern has exhibited the features of a 'dual economy'. While, highest growth has been concentrated in the 'new economy' services sectors like information technology, telecommunications and finance; productivity growth and output growth in many 'old economy' sectors such as agriculture, infrastructure, mining and to some extent manufacturing has not been so strong. However, recent years have witnessed growth in manufacturing and other positive developments in the old economy sectors such as agriculture and mining, thereby promising a resilient growth in the future. In fact during the last year 2004-05, the manufacturing sector has registered an impressive growth rate of 9.2 per cent. The Indian economy has achieved the highest ever average growth rate of over 6 per cent per annum, during the 90s and sustained higher growth rates during 2001-2005. The spectacular growth rate has been achieved in services and it is now contributing more than 50 per cent of the country's gross domestic product (GDP). The rate of inflation has been controlled and brought down from a high of 13 per cent in 1991-92 to 4 to 5 per cent on an average in 2004-05. External debt indicators have been substantially brought down in the last decade showing the stability of the Indian economy. The balance of payment (BoP) situation has improved and the current account has become surplus for the first time in 2002-03. A market determined exchange rate has been accomplished with considerable finesse and it is reflected in a gradual but stable exchange rate depreciation. Exports and imports have been increasing more than 20 per cent per annum reflecting the growing Indian economy and its competitiveness in the international market. The financial market, particularly the capital market has remained bullish leading to huge FII inflows into India. The growing Indian economy started attracting FDI at higher scale in recent years (on an average 4 to 5 billion dollars for the last four years). Moreover, as per the trends of huge forex reserves and a positive BoP position, recent years have also witnessed increasing outward flow of FDI from India. Thus, in a nutshell, almost all macroeconomic fundamentals are looking strong, thanks to continuous efforts of the government towards liberalisation.

Thus, a favourable demographic transition, large surpluses on the services and transfer balances, reasonably favourable monsoons, high foreign exchange reserves, increased capital inflows, and improved international factors, etc. are the positive developments that help India to achieve higher economic growth. On the whole, India has the inherent strength and the potential to sustain high economic growth and emerge as a leading economy in the world along with China in the near future. In fact, India has the potential to show the fastest growth over the next 30 and 50 years and could emerge among the top three economies in the world by 2041.[17]

The overall impressive growth rate and its composition have significant structural implications for all other sub-sectors of the Indian economy. One of the most prominent aspects of the growth induced structural changes can be witnessed in the energy sector. The growth induced forward and backward linkages have resulted in excess demand and supply constraints in the energy sector as domestic reserves and production continue to lag behind the demand growth. This has further exacerbated, in a sense, due to the realisation of pent-up demands of the vast middle class consumers owing to their increasing standard of living.

Economic development results in both qualitative and quantitative increases in the use of energy. The growth of energy consumption is, therefore, a function of the growth in the economy and changes in the lifestyle of households as a result of changes in the income levels enjoyed by them. Economic growth, based on rapid structural change and increased urbanisation, is an important factor, which contributed to the increase in energy consumption in India. During the period 1980-1995, the commercial energy used increased at an annual average growth rate of 6.5 per cent. In India, energy consumption reflects the energy demand pattern to the extent it is constrained by supply shortages. Although past experience shows that availability consideration rather than price levels are important determinants of energy demand, the energy-GDP elasticity is often used as an indicator for mapping the energy consumption response. The declining trend of energy-GDP elasticity during the period 1953-1995 is partly due to the

17. Goldman, Sachs (2003). "Dreaming with BRICs: The Path to 2050", *Global Economics Paper*, No. 99.

structural changes in the economy, the changing pattern of demand, and also the penetration of efficient technology. This elasticity is, however, very high when compared to developed countries, reflecting the fact that India's per capita commercial energy consumption levels are still very low, and the use of traditional fuels is still being substituted by commercial energy forms.

The significant structural changes in the economy and population growth led to large increases in the consumption of commercial energy. However, the rural population in the country, despite various interventionist policies, continues to depend on traditional fuels (biomass fuels). Even today, these fuels are estimated to account for around 40 per cent of the total energy consumption in rural areas[18] and nearly 30 per cent of total energy supply in India. However, the role of commercial fuels have increased over the years as they are substituting traditional fuels in the energy mix, due to the stage of energy transition, which is determined by the level of economic development in the country. Figure 2.11 depicts the trend in growth of commercial energy. As shown in the figure the non-commercial

Figure 2.11

India's Commercial and Non-Commercial Energy Consumption Trends

Trend of per cent Share of Commercial *versus* Non-Commercial Energy

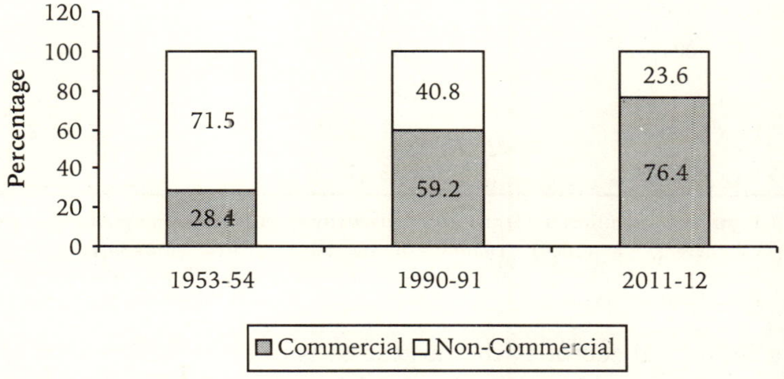

Note: Total Energy: 1953-54=89.61 Mtoe; 1990-91=299.68 Mtoe; 2011-12=723.93 Mtoe

Source: *Ninth and Tenth Plan Documents*

18. The Energy and Resources Institute (TERI) (2001-02). *TERI Energy Data* and *Directory Year Book*. New Delhi.

energy consumption is being replaced with various commercial sources of energy. Use of increasing quantities of LPG, and Kerosene for fuel and lighting in rural areas is reflective of the above trend.

India ranks fifth in the world in terms of energy demand, accounting for nearly 4 per cent of the world's primary commercial energy demand in 2005. Although, the commercial energy consumption has grown rapidly over the last two decades, a large part of India's population does not have access to these sources. At 317 kg of oil equivalent (kgoe), the per capita energy consumption is also low even compared to some of the developing countries. Primary commercial energy demand in India has grown almost three-fold at an annual rate of 6 per cent per year between 1971 and 2001, to reach 314.7 mtoe with corresponding energy elasticity as against a GDP of 1.12. Table 2.17 shows the historical trend in energy consumption growth rates in India.

Table 2.17

Historical Energy Consumption Growth Rates in India

	Primary Commercial Energy	*GDP Growth Rate*
	Decadal Growth (in Per Cent)	
1970-71 to 1980-81	4.89 (1.55)	3.15
1980-81 to 1990-91	6.36 (1.13)	5.61
1990-91 to 2001-02	5.33 (0.96)	5.53
	Rolling Growth	
1970-71 to 1990-91	5.63 (1.28)	4.38
1970-71 to 2001-02	5.35 (1.12)	4.76

Note: Figures in parentheses are the actual elasticity of energy consumption.

Source: Chaturvedi, B.K. (2004). "Domestic Resourcing of Energy, Gulf and Future of Global Energy", paper presented at the *National seminar on India's Energy Security*. New Delhi: JNU. February 19-20,

The industrial sector is the largest consumer of commercial energy in India followed by the transport sector. Together they now account for two-third of the commercial energy consumed in the country. However there has been a marginal fall in their share of the total commercial energy consumption. Their share was as high as 84 per cent in 1953-54; it declined to 64 per cent in 1996-97. The agricultural sector has, however, registered a sharp increase in the consumption of commercial energy, i.e., from 3 per cent in 1970-71 to 9 per cent in 1996-97. During the same period, the share of the household sector in commercial energy consumption has risen to 12 percent. Moreover, it may be observed that the share of coal in total commercial energy consumption has declined steadily over the years; and the share of oil and gas and electricity has steadily increased.

The share of commercial fuels in the total energy supply in India has risen from 41 per cent in the year 1970-71 to approximately 70 per cent in 2003-04, despite the dominance of the traditional fuels in the Indian energy sector. The total domestic primary commercial energy supply in India has risen from 147.05 mtoe in 1970-71 to 248 mtoe in 2005. Table 2.18 gives the break up of primary energy supply for various fuels from 1970 onwards.

Table 2.18

Production of Primary Energy in India

Source	*1970/71*	*1980/81*	*1990/91*	*2001/02*	*2002/03*
Coal and lignite (MT)	76.34	119.02	228.13	352.60	367.29
Crude oil (MT)	6.82	10.51	33.02	32.03	33.04
Natural gas (BCM)	1.45	2.36	18.00	29.71	31.40
Nuclear power (BkWh)	2.42	3.00	6.14	19.48	19.30
Hydro power (BkWh)	25.25	46.54	71.66	73.70	64.10
Wind power (BkWh)	–	–	0.03	1.97	2.1

Note: MT—million tonnes; BCM—billion cubic metre; BkWh—billion kilowatt hour.
Source: TERI. *TEDDY, 2004-05*.

Despite large coal reserves, it is the share of oil and gas in total primary energy consumption that is increasing. The reasons for this are manifold; the most obvious being that the persistent shortages of coal and power supplies in the past decades have resulted in a switch to petroleum product consumption.[19] This switch took place not as a result of the large supply of petroleum products available domestically,

19. Srivastava, Leena and R. Goswami (1999). "The Indian Oil Experience: A Case Study", in ECSSR (ed.), *Privatisation and Deregulation in the Gulf Energy Industry*. UAE: ECSSR. pp.55-68.

but of the relative ease in importing them. This energy transition is also consonant with universal energy pattern of transition witnessed in the industrial countries, as the economy tries to improve the production base on advanced technology to augment growth and instill efficiency in production.

Oil and Natural Gas: Sectoral Growth Picture

In India, commercial fuels constitute about 68 per cent of the total energy consumed. Crude oil is the second largest commercial fuel (accounting for 32 per cent), after coal (51 per cent), and followed by natural gas (9 per cent). Oil and now natural gas are critical inputs to every sector of the Indian economy. India is emerging as a leading consumer of petroleum products with consumption rising at 6.4 per cent annually. In fact, the annual growth rate of oil and gas consumption in India was 4.4 per cent in comparison to the world average of 3.4 per cent in the year 2005. Moreover, per capita oil and gas consumption in India was only 136 kgoe in comparison to the world average of 967 kgoe in the same year. This implies that starting from a lower base the per capita consumption of oil and gas is bound to surge upwards with the economic growth marching forward. In fact as per the *Draft Integrated Energy Policy 2005*, of the Planning Commission, sustenance of 8 per cent growth of India's GDP warrants an annual growth of 6 per cent of energy consumption. Table 2.19 shows India's average annual compound growth rates (AAGR) of consumption of petroleum products and their specifications.

Over the years, the domestic production of crude oil has not kept pace with demand. Self-reliance on crude oil has dropped dramatically in recent years with the spurt in refining capacity and presently it stands at a mere 30 per cent. The parameters of energy security in India can be readily set out. India is already importing over 75 per cent of its crude oil needs. Even if India raises its domestic output by half—from nearly 35 million tonnes per annum at present to, say, 50 million tonnes—over the next two decades, owing to the high growth rates of import, dependence will only rise to 85 per cent and beyond. As for natural gas, which is increasingly substituting for crude oil in many applications, India is short by 50 per cent of current

Table 2.19

AAGR of Consumption of Petroleum Products

(Per Cent)

	1974-1979	*1979-1980*	*1980-1985*	*1985-1990*	*1992-1997*	*1997-2002*	*2002-2007*
Products	*V Plan*	*Annual*	*VI Plan*	*VII Plan*	*VIII Plan*	*IX Plan*	*X Plan*
LPG	8.7	0.5	18.4	18.9	10.0	12.6	8.2
MS	-0.1	-0.6	6.9	10.9	6.8	7.2	7.3
Naphtha	10.4	-4.1	5.3	1.4	6.4	20.1	-3.5
Others	-1.7	-8.7	1.2	14.2	7.2	38.7	–
Light Distillates	5.6	-2.7	7.2	8.3	7.5	15.3	–
ATF	8.2	-0.9	3.2	5.8	6.7	0.9	3.2
SKO	3.7	-2.0	9.0	6.7	3.9	0.5	0.0
HSD	9.8	13.5	6.9	8.6	9.1	0.9	5.6
LDO	-1.0	4.1	-1.1	4.4	-3.5	5.4	0.0
Others	0.0	12.3	0.2	3.0	8.8	5.2	–
Middle Distillates	6.7	7.6	6.6	7.7	7.4	1.0	–
Lubes	-2.3	4.0	3.2	6.9	1.7	2.3	4.7
FO/LSHS	2.4	6.2	2.3	2.1	4.6	2.4	2.6
Bitumen	-2.4	13.4	-2.6	12.6	5.9	2.6	3.0
Others	1.6	16.6	5.5	8.5	4.9	27.6	–
Heavy Ends	1.5	7.3	2.0	4.0	4.6	4.4	–
Total Consumption	4.8	5.8	5.4	6.9	6.8	4.9	3.7

Note: (i) LPG is liquefied petroleum gas, MS is motor spirit, ATF is aviation turbine fuel, SKO is superior kerosene oil, HSD is high speed diesel, LDO is light diesel oil, FO is fuels oil, LSHS is low sulphur heavy stock; (ii) Growth rates are based on consumption including private parties imports; (iii) – means not available.

Source: Petroleum Planning and Analysis Cell (PPAC), Government of India, 2007.

requirements. Even a doubling of current levels of domestic gas output by 2025 will leave India with the same level of relative deficit—50 per cent or, perhaps, even more. The widening gap between domestic production and demand is depicted in Figure 2.12.

Figure 2.12

India's Oil Product Consumption and Domestic Production Widening Gap between Demand and Domestic Supply

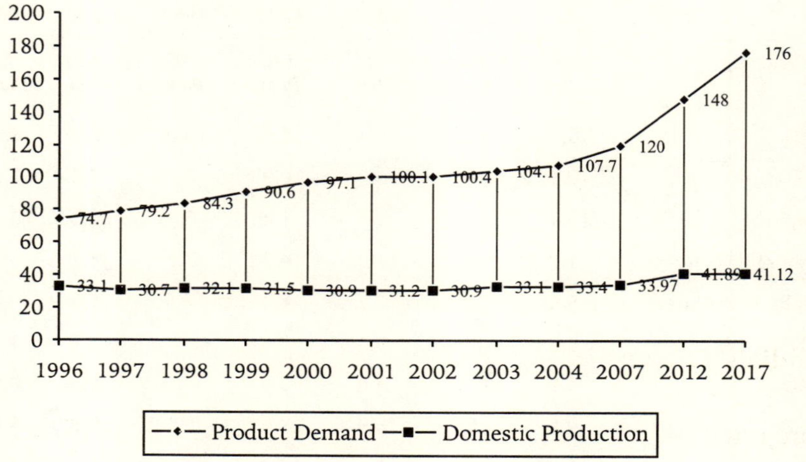

Source: MoPNG, *Basic Statistics on Indian Petroleum and Natural Gas*, GoI, Various issues and *India Hydrocarbon Vision 2025*.

India's dependence on crude oil and natural gas is increasing day by day, compared to domestic production and reserve accretion. India imports about 70 per cent of oil for domestic consumption while only 30 per cent is produced domestically. The import of natural gas will increase substantially in the future, as it is being used in large volumes in electricity generation and other productive processes in the country. The share of oil and petroleum products in total imports has risen to 34 per cent in 2004-05 compared to 25 per cent in 1999-2000 and 15 per cent in 1998-99. This has happened due to the high oil prices in 2004 and early 2005. While India's share of global oil production of crude oil in 2001 was less than 1 per cent, its share in world consumption was 2.15 per cent. Imports of crude oil exceeded domestic production for the first time during 1992-93. It is to be noted that with the positive downstream fundamentals and expansion of capacity, India has also become able to export products recently especially, HSD and MS products. Table 2.20 shows the trends of India's net oil and products imports, both in quantity and value terms.

Table 2.20

India's Net Imports of Crude Oil and Products,

(Quantity in MMT and Value in million $)

Year	Net Imports	
	Quantity	Value
1997-98	55.08	7719
1998-99	62.85	6327
1999-00	73.66	12314
2000-01	74.99	15369
2001-02	75.63	12415
2002-03	78.92	15330
2003-04	83.68	16703
2004-05	87.16	22953

Source: Prepared from *Basic Statistics on Indian Petroleum Sector*, MoPNG, GoI, Various Issues.

India's Future Energy Trends

The total primary commercial energy supply in India has been projected to grow at an annual average rate of 3.2 per cent over the period 2002-2025.[20] These growth rates would mean a doubling of energy requirements to reach 709 mtoe from the current level of 325 mtoe by the year 2030.[21] Fossil fuels are likely to dominate India's energy mix. The share of various fuels in India's energy mix is shown in table 2.21. Though the share of coal is expected to decline from 55 per cent to 50 per cent by the year 2025, it will still remain the largest energy source in India's energy matrix. The share of natural gas and nuclear are also expected to constitute 20 per cent and 3 per cent of the energy mix respectively by the same period.

Table 2.21

Share of Future Energy Supply in India

(Per Cent)

Year	Coal	Oil & Gas	Hydro	Nuclear
1997-98	55	42	2	1
2001-02	50	47	2	1
2006-07	50	47	2	1
2010-11	53	44	2	1
2024-25	50	45	2	3

Source: Up to 2011 from *Technical Note on Energy*, Planning Commission, GoI, 1998-99. Beyond this period the figures have been extrapolated.

20. Energy Information Administration, US Department of Energy, 2003.
21. International Energy Agency, 2002.

As per the available projections, India's demand for oil is expected to grow at a compound rate of 4.2 per cent per annum over the period 2002-2025 to reach about 274 MT assuming a refinery loss of 8 per cent; the refinery throughput would be 295 MT in 2025. The current indigenous production falls far short of this projected demand and India would be importing about 88 per cent of the total consumption by 2006-07.

The *India Hydrocarbon Vision 2025* identifies natural gas as the fuel for the future. On the demand side, power and fertiliser sectors are expected to be the biggest consumers of gas. Figure 2.13 depicts the demand and domestic production of gas outlook in India. Thus, the growing demand for gas along with oil has made it imperative to an overwhelming dependence on imports in the future.

Figure 2.13

India's Demand and Domestic Production of Natural Gas, BCM

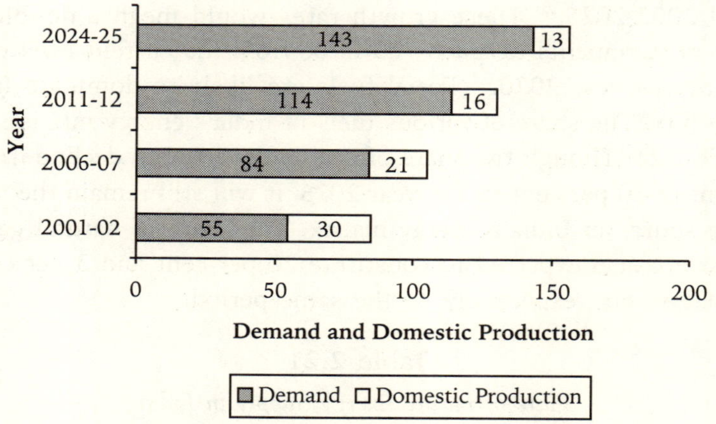

Source: Prepared from *India Hydrocarbon Vision 2025*.

It is also expected that India will continue its present trend[22] in the consumption of oil and natural gas in the near future. Thus, the most important outcome regarding the Indian oil and gas trends is that India will continue heavily on imports, as neither its domestic reserve/ production, nor, the regional reserve/production (Asian) can really be adequate to meet the ever burgeoning demand for oil and gas.

22. The trends of India's oil and consumption will be discussed fully in Chapter 3.

Thus, oil and gas demand in reflection to the rapid economic growth in India and other Asian countries is poised to experience sizeable growth rates in the foreseeable future. Because increase in economic activity and income brought about by economic growth can expand energy requirements in various ways, as discussed above. India with a large population and impressive growth rate will require huge energy inputs to fuel and augment the growth engine. However, both India and its neighbours have limited domestic and regional oil and gas supplies to meet this rising demand. This is because of the factors such as limited resource base, high costs of new energy infrastructure investments, energy transportation bottlenecks and growing concern about environmental problems. These imbalances in the oil-gas demand-supply in India and the whole of Asia will bring out heavier dependence on imported energy from outside the Asian region. Figure 2.14 shows the oil import outlook of the region.

Figure 2.14

Oil Import Outlook in Asia, mb/d

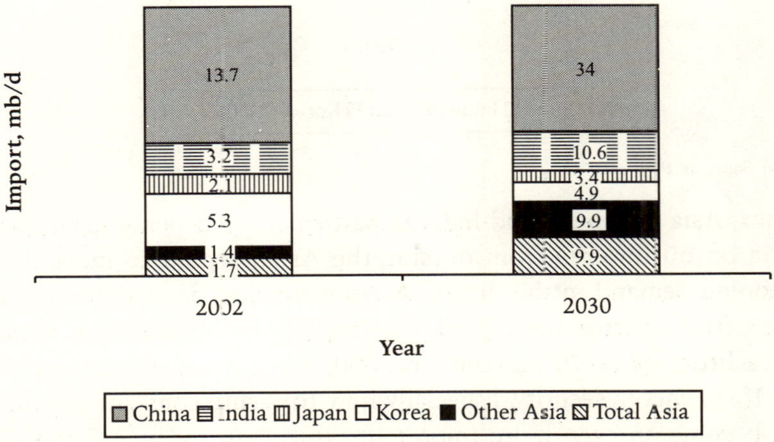

Source: Institute of Energy Economics (IEE) (2003). *Oil Market Report*. Japan, April.

Moreover, it is significant to note that the share of countries in the total imports of the region is likely to undergo a radical change. Japan importing 38.7 per cent of the total Asian imports in 2002 is likely to be having an import share of only 14.4 per cent in 2030, Korea too shows a decline in import share from 15.35 per cent to 10 per cent for the same period, but China shows a rise of 12.4 per cent to 20.1 per cent, followed by India from 10.2 per cent to 15.6 per cent (Figure 2.15).

Figure 2.15

Share of Main Asian Countries in Total Asian Oil Imports

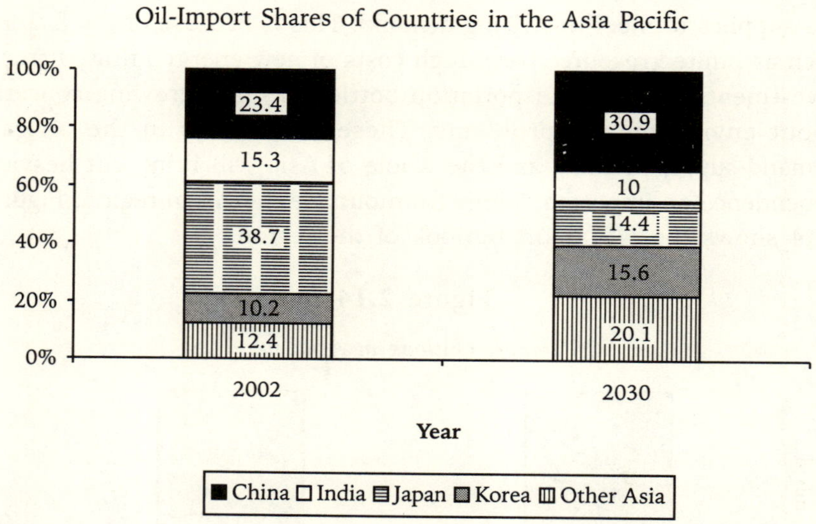

Source: Same as Figure 2.14.

Thus, Asia in general and India in particular are depending and will depend on oil imports from outside the Asian region to meet their burgeoning demand in the future. Asian countries' dependence on oil imports from outside the region, particularly the Middle East, which stood a little above 70 per cent in 2000, can outrun 90 per cent by 2030. If so, energy security, especially how to secure constant supplies, could become an even more important issue than today.[23] Given the fact that the Gulf being the only immediate and the only oil exporting region will be the target of India and other burgeoning Asian markets, which have also implications for the oil and gas exporters in the Gulf region. In the preceding section it will be analysed why these oil and

23. Fujime, Kazuya (2003). *Asia Need to Construct a Framework of Energy Cooperation and Joint Research*. Japan: IEE. March.

gas fundamentals of Asia in general and India in particular is important for the GCC oil and gas exporters.

Fluctuation in Gulf Cooperation Council Oil Exporters' Global Clout

The most important aspect of the present global oil and gas regime is the fluctuating clout of the OPEC in general and the Gulf[24] in particular. The phenomenon of fluctuation in OPEC's/Gulf's international clout can be aptly described by looking at the phenomenon from the demand side and the supply side, as well as a quick historical review[25] and in the light of domestic economic constraints.

Supply Side Factors

First from the supply side, it can be noted that, after the 1970s new oil was discovered in several parts of the world. In addition, non-OPEC countries helped push global supply level to the point where prices started to drop. For instance, oil production in Mexico, China, Egypt, Malaysia, Britain, Norway, India and other countries all helped increase in global supply. Today even more oil is expected to be pumped from wells in the Caspian Sea and other locations around the world including Eastern Siberia, the Gulf of Mexico, Canada's tar sands deposits, and Venezuela's Orinco Belt.[26] Second, by the 1990s, most OPEC members were pumping out more oil than they were supposed to, thus increasing world supply. This occurred in part because of the world's oil-rich countries were struggling economically.

The economies of the GCC members of the OPEC countries relied—and continue to rely—almost exclusively on oil; for many, oil accounts for 75 per cent of their national incomes. In the case of Kuwait, over 90 per cent of its revenues were coming from oil. Even Saudi Arabia, the leading oil supplier and producer in the world and

24. Since the major oil-exporting members of the Gulf Cooperation Council (Saudi Arabia, Kuwait, and UAE, Qatar) are also the members of OPEC, the analysis for OPEC also reflects the situation in these countries.

25. This aspect has been descriptively discussed in Chapter 1.

26. Fisher, Robert W. (1997). "The Future of Energy", *The Futurist*, September/October. pp.43-46.

the political leader of OPEC, faced debt problems and economic recession. In 1997, for instance, Saudi Arabia earned about $45 billion from oil exports. In 1998 it earned only about $30 billion. This led to a budget deficit of nearly $13 billion.[27] As a result of the economic difficulties in the major oil producing countries, each individual OPEC member had an inclination to sell more oil in the market. This resulted in more supply and hence a drop in the price of oil as per the market dynamics. This is exactly what has been happening in the 1980s and particularly in the 1990s. This action is referred to as the 'free rider problem'[28] which refer to the phenomenon that an OPEC member state cheating on the cartel's agreement to keep world supplies low and prices high or by passing the 'quota principle' and pumping more oil through covert bilateral negotiation with importing countries to earn the much needed revenue to maintain the political as well as economic *status quo*.

Demand Side Factors

The demand side factors responsible for GCC/OPEC members' declining international clout are: world recession, the Iran-Iraq War and the Asian financial crisis of the late 1990s, increased fuel (oil) substitution, augmented energy conservation programmes, and disagreements among OPEC members. The worldwide recession that followed the two oil shocks of the 1970s dampened the global oil demand, which was further exacerbated by the Asian financial crisis of 1997, as Asia was the second largest oil-consuming region in the world next to North America. Secondly, since the 1970s the massive inter-fuel substitution in the industrialised countries in particular, in which oil is being substituted by natural gas, coal and nuclear power has subscribed to dampen the world oil demand. This has become possible due to the sophisticated technology in these countries, which had increased the energy efficiency indicator of these economies. For example, as per one estimate,[29] between 1973 and 1982, Western

27. "The Suffering Gulf", *The Economist*, October 24, 1998, p.41.
28. 'Free Rider Problem' is a form of cheating, like an individual riding a bus for free, associated with countries benefiting from membership in an international organisation without having to bear any of the political, military, or economic costs. See Duncan, W. Raymond, *et al.* (2002), *World Politics in the 21st Century*. New York: Longman. p.524.
29. Joan E. Sepro and Jeffry A. Hart (1997). *The Politics of International Relations*, 5th edition. New York: St. Martin's Press. p.290.

countries became 31.1 per cent more efficient in their energy use. This also throws light on the Western countries energy conservation programmes that have in fact been witnessed in these countries declining reliance on oil as a source of energy. This can be substantiated from the trends of OPEC oil export shares in major consuming areas of the world as shown in Figure 2.16.

Figure 2.16

OPEC Crude Oil Export Market Share by Region (%)

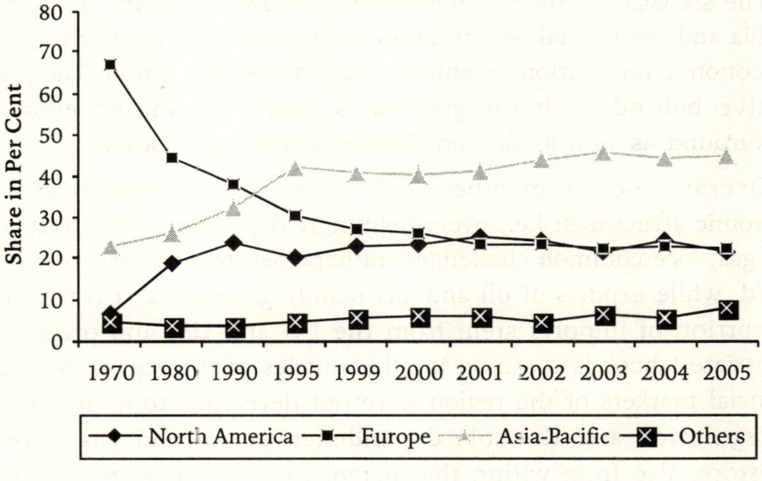

Source: Prepared from OPEC *Annual Statistical Bulletin 2005*.

As evident from the Figure, the OPEC oil export share in Europe has declined considerably over the years from 66.8 per cent in 1970 to 22.4 per cent in the year 2005. Its share in the North American market reached its peak in the year 2001 and is consistently decreasing afterwards except the year 2004 during the same period. However, OPEC's oil export share in the Asia Pacific region has increased considerably from 22.9 per cent in 1970 to 45 per cent in the year 2005. In a way this signifies the significance of the Asia-Pacific region for the OPEC in general and Gulf oil exporters in particular, and the conviction that other oil importing regions, such as North America and Europe are increasingly dependent on imports within their regions respectively. Moreover, in such a case, emerging major importers in the Asia Pacific region like China and India, are crucial for the OPEC and Gulf oil exporters.

Lastly, the internal strife, which is the culmination of differences among members within the OPEC, has also contributed in this regard. Since the OPEC heydays of the 1970s, the members have never completely controlled global oil prices due to their differences over output targets.

Broad Characteristics of GCC Economies

The six GCC member states, Bahrain, Kuwait, Oman, Qatar, Saudi Arabia and the United Arab Emirates, envisage completing the process of economic integration by entering into a customs union. The pivotal motive behind such integration is based on shared economic background as well as on common language and history.

Overall, the six member GCC states are similar in terms of economic structures; i.e., overwhelmingly dependent on export of oil and gas, face common challenges, rather open towards the rest of the world, while exports of oil and gas mainly go to Asia, a considerable proportion of imports stem from the EU and US, and presence of expatriate labour is common in all countries of the region. Moreover, financial markets of the region have not developed to a large extent, as regulation and the sole dependence on oil and gas have led investors, also from within the region, to prefer investment outside the region. The common challenge of the states of the GCC has been to diversify their economic base from oil and gas in order to address the structural deficiencies and emerging challenges of the bulging population. The GCC economies as a block represent a market of 35 million people and an aggregate GDP of about US $465 billion (2004 figures). The oil and gas sector contributes more than one-third of GDP in the GCC. Other contributing sectors, albeit much smaller, are construction, tourism and banking. Due to the peculiar arid climate, agriculture is of negligible importance. The trends in nominal GDP and export values are closely related to global oil prices.

However, despite these broad similarities, there are also considerable differences. Oil and gas endowments differ greatly among countries, and reserves will soon be exhausted in some countries and in the distant future in others. Pressure on the labour market is less acutely felt in some countries, and diversification efforts have not been equally successful everywhere. There are, however, important differences among the GCC countries. Per capita income ranges from less than $8,000 in Oman to $28,400 in Qatar. The structures of GCC economies and the composition of their exports are also changing. The weight of the manufacturing sector has been growing very rapidly in Saudi Arabia, as has *entrepôt* trade and related activities in the United Arab Emirates, while the banking and insurance sector is by far the single most important sector in Bahrain. In Qatar, natural gas is well on the road to bypassing oil as the key sector in the economy, and in Oman the growth strategy centred on developing its natural gas resources and tourism has just begun to bear fruit. Reflecting these trends, non-oil growth has varied across the GCC area. Domestic inflation—albeit low—has differed across countries, leading to diverging paths for real effective exchange rates. Differences also remain in bank regulatory practices, particularly regarding entry restrictions, liquidity requirements, and loan classification and provisioning. Notwithstanding progress toward economic diversification, growth of the non-oil sector has remained weak relative to the growth of the domestic labour force in most of the GCC countries. Table 2.22 shows the latest major macroeconomic indicators of the GCC economy.

Overview of Economic Developments and Policies

Since the substantial increase in international oil prices during the 1970s, economic developments and policies in the GCC countries can be broadly divided into four periods: (i) the oil boom period (1981-1985), when historically high—albeit declining—oil prices increased export receipts, allowing the GCC countries to record large external current account surpluses and to build up foreign reserves; (ii) the oil bust (1985 to 1990)—with the continued erosion of oil prices, economic conditions weakened further and large internal and external financial imbalances emerged; (iii) the economic adjustment process being disrupted by the regional crisis (the Iraqi invasion of Kuwait); and (iv) the declining oil prices and global economic slowdown in the aftermath of the crisis.

Table 2.22

GCC Macroeconomic Indicators 2006

Economic Indicators 2005	*Bahrain*	*Kuwait*	*Oman*	*Qatar*	*Saudi Arabia*	*UAE*	*GCC*
Constant GDP Growth (%)	6.9	8.5	3.8	5.5	6.5	8.0	6.5
Constant GDP (US $ bn)	10.71	50.98	22.63	30.07	265.19	107.71	487.29
Population (mn)	0.7	2.9	2.5	0.8	24.6	4.1	36.4
Population Growth (%)	2.6	7.5	2.0	7.5	2.3	7.0	4.8
Per capita GDP (US $)	16, 195	17, 560	10, 501	38, 316	11,493	26, 271	20056
Consumer Price Inflation (%)	3.7	1.8	1.9	3.0	1.0	6.0	2.9
Fiscal Balance as % of GDP	7.9	36.5	11.1	23.0	17.5	24.6	20.1
Exports (US $ bn)	9.89	41.19	17.20	22.62	190.97	108.73	390.64
Imports (US $ bn)	8.66	12.48	10.48	5.43	54.36	46.77	138.18
Trade Balance (US $ bn)	1.23	28.71	6.72	17.23	136.62	44.0	252.48
Current Account Balance (% of GDP)	5.8	43.3	7.0	45.6	28.3	22.0	25.33
Government Debt (% of GDP)	31.7	13.1	11.0	30.5	46.5	8.4	23.53
Oil and Gas Indicators, 2004							
Oil Production (mn bbls)	13	914	231	290	3, 432	893	5, 774
Oil Reserves (mn bbls)	125	104, 000	5, 606	15, 207	266,810	97, 800	489, 448
Gas Production (bcf)	346	343	622	1384	2260	1617	6, 572
Gas Reserves (tcf)	3.25	56.02	29.28	910.52	241.84	214.40	1455.3
Oil & Gas as % of Gov. Revenue	72.6	91.4	66.2	55.3	84.1	77.7	74.6
Oil & Gas as % of Total Revenue	73.8	82.8	81.3	83.7	86.8	35.8	69.1
Oil & Gas as % of GDP	23.3	47.6	43.8	62.2	45.3	32.5	42.4

Source: Gulf Research Centre (2006). *Economic Report*. September.

The policy objectives of improving the social and physical infrastructure, diversifying the economic base, and containing inflationary pressures were addressed through a two-pronged strategy. First, with a view to insulating their economies from foreign inflation, the GCC authorities abandoned the link between their currencies and a depreciating SDR, and established a *de facto* peg with the US dollar, which led to a significant real effective appreciation of all GCC currencies. Second, expenditures on development projects increased, and some countries actively pursued policies to promote basic industries based on their vast hydrocarbon resources.

The sizeable budget surpluses started to diminish from 1982 as expenditures continued to increase in some countries while revenues declined due to the steep slide in oil prices. While some countries had large budgetary deficits in 1984-1995, the region as a whole recorded an annual average deficit of only 1 per cent of GDP and an external current account surplus equivalent to 7 per cent of GDP during 1981-1985. Foreign reserves positions were very comfortable and inflation decelerated to an average rate of less than 1 per cent per annum, but real output contracted.

In response, the authorities implemented adjustment policies involving primarily cuts in expenditure, particularly capital outlays which declined from an average of 21 per cent of GDP during 1981-1985 to 13 per cent of GDP during 1986-1989. Adjustment was further facilitated by the significant real effective depreciation of GCC currencies.

Despite the expenditure cuts, and given the severity of the decline in oil revenue, the aggregate budget deficit increased to 4 per cent of GDP during 1986-1989, while the external current account position shifted to a deficit of 1 per cent of GDP during the same period. External borrowing by some GCC countries limited the drawdown in foreign reserves.

Notwithstanding the sharp jump in oil prices in the initial phases of the conflict and the higher oil production in some countries, crisis-related expenditures and transfers created significant pressures on the budgets and external current account positions of the GCC countries.

Those countries directly involved in the conflict suffered the worst: the budget deficit in Kuwait exceeded an estimated 100 per cent of GDP in 1990-91; that of Saudi Arabia increased to 17 per cent of GDP in 1991; and the combined external account deficits of the two countries amounted to US $54 billion in 1991 alone. Excluding Kuwait, the aggregate external current account deficit of the GCC countries increased to 7 per cent of GDP, and their combined official foreign reserves declined further.

Economic growth in the GCC moderated to an average of 2 per cent per annum in 1992-1994, real per capita GDP declined, and the lingering expenditures and transfers related to the conflict prevented significant reductions in the internal and external imbalances. For the region as whole, the average budget deficit in 1992-1994 (10 per cent of GDP) was higher than that of the pre-crisis period (4 per cent of GDP), despite the much lower levels of capital expenditure. Similarly, at 6 per cent of GDP, the aggregate external current account deficit was higher than the average during the 1986-1989 period (1 per cent of GDP) and foreign reserves positions eroded further. By 1994, although the stock of external debt stabilised at about 12 per cent of GDP, debt service payments had increased sharply.

From 1995 most GCC countries intensified their adjustment efforts in response, *inter alia*, to an unfavourable oil market outlook. In particular, Kuwait, Oman, and Saudi Arabia introduced medium-term plans incorporating balanced budgets by the year 2000, as well as measures to promote private sector growth and human resource development. In other countries, similar policies are under consideration or are being formulated.

Recent Performance

The GCC region is currently experiencing an economic boom that is mainly stimulated by high international oil prices and strong global demand for both oil and non-oil goods and services. The rise in oil revenues and buoyant stock and real estate markets have led to greater wealth in the Gulf Cooperation Council (GCC), thereby lifting private consumption and boosting investment. In fact, the economic boom in the GCC has positive spillover effects on the economies of the West

Asian region, which has resulted in increasing workers' remittances, exports and tourist receipts.

According to the latest estimates, average real growth in the GCC countries was 6.9 per cent in 2005.[30] In 2006, GDP growth in the GCC region is forecast to decelerate by approximately a percentage point, at 5.8 per cent. The average annual price of oil from the Organization of Petroleum Exporting Countries (OPEC), which surged from $28.1 per barrel in 2003 to $50.65 in 2005, is expected to remain high in 2006 and in the range of $50-$60 per barrel. With the anticipated average daily oil production in the GCC countries set to exceed the level of 16.1 million barrels in 2005, oil revenues are likely to increase during 2006, albeit at a decelerating rate, thereby providing less relative stimulus to GDP growth than in 2004 and 2005. However, owing to the significant increases in oil revenues of the past two years, the countries of the GCC have recorded large current account and budget surpluses. In 2006, public spending is expected to increase substantially as national budgets partially reflect the recent surge in oil prices with expanding expenditure.

As the oil revenues of the region increase, countries of the GCC will be more confident to spend larger portions of these revenues rather than save them. Consequently, a strong fiscal stimulus is expected to spur economic activity in the GCC economies during 2006. In addition, efforts by Governments in the GCC to diversify economies and to foster private sector development have resulted in a positive, albeit speculative, investment climate. Moreover, a reduction of investment regulations is enhancing competitiveness in these economies.

On the monetary side, given that all the national currencies of the GCC are pegged to the United States dollar, the cycle of interest rate increases is likely to continue during the first half of 2006, trailing policy decisions of the United States Federal Reserve.

Overall, it is expected that real GDP growth in 2006 in Bahrain, Saudi Arabia and the United Arab Emirates will be similar to growth in 2005. Owing to its relatively diversified economy, real GDP growth

30. ESCWA. *Survey of Economic and Social Developments, 2005-06.*

in Bahrain is forecast at 6.3 per cent for 2006, compared to 6.2 per cent in 2005. Over the same period, real GDP growth is expected to decrease from 6.8 per cent to 6.0 per cent in Saudi Arabia and, more substantially, from 8.0 per cent to 6.0 per cent in the United Arab Emirates. In Oman and Qatar, significant accelerations of real GDP growth in 2006 are forecast. In Oman, real GDP growth in 2006 is forecast at 5.5 per cent, compared to an estimated 4.2 per cent for 2005; and in Qatar, real GDP is expected to expand to 8.0 per cent in 2006, compared to 7.6 per cent in 2005 owing to the high rate of public investment in that country. In Kuwait, GDP growth is expected to decline substantially from 6.5 per cent in 2005 to 4.1 per cent in 2006 as oil revenue growth tapers off and export possibilities to Iraq stabilise. Table 2.23 shows the latest trends of growth of real GDP in the GCC region.

Table 2.23

GCC's Real GDP Growth Rate 1980-2005

(Per Cent)

Country	*1980*	*1985*	*1990*	*1995*	*2000*	*2001*	*2002*	*2003*	*2004*	*2005*
Bahrain	7.5	-0.9	7.3	3.9	5.3	4.5	5.1	5.7	5.5	5.3
Kuwait	-20.4	-4.3	-26.2	1.4	1.9	0.7	-0.5	9.7	7.2	3.2
Oman	6.1	14.5	8.4	4.8	5.5	7.5	1.7	1.4	2.5	3.6
Qatar	-1.0	-13.0	-14.6	5.5	9.1	4.5	7.3	8.5	9.9	5.1
Saudi Arabia	7.9	-4.1	10.6	0.5	4.9	0.5	0.1	7.2	5.3	4.1
UAE	-1.8	-2.5	16.6	7.0	12.3	3.5	1.9	7.0	5.7	4.5

Source: IMF (2006). *World Economic Outlook*.

The overflow of investments in the region's equity and real estate markets contributed to boom conditions that prevailed for a while in these sectors and that subsequently sparked fears of major market corrections. In fact, there were serious financial market fluctuations in most countries of the GCC in the first few months of 2006, which resulted in a financial crash in March. Specifically, by 27th March 2006, stock market indices in Dubai and Abu Dhabi, in the United Arab Emirates, and in Qatar dropped by some 40 per cent, 16 per cent and 20 per cent, respectively, from highs of 1,101.63 in Dubai, 5,279.96 in

Abu Dhabi and 11,291.71 in Qatar. Similarly, the market index in Saudi Arabia, which had witnessed gains of more than 21 per cent during the first two months of 2006, began a steep decline at the beginning of March and resulted in a drop of approximately 24 per cent from its highest level by 27 March 2006. Equity market activities experienced less dramatic declining trends in Bahrain and Oman, where indices dropped by 11.49 per cent and 3.6 per cent, respectively, relative to their highest levels.

Thus, over the past three decades the member countries of the Cooperation Council of the Arab States of the Gulf (GCC)—Bahrain, Kuwait, Oman, Qatar, Saudi Arabia, and the United Arab Emirates—have witnessed an unprecedented economic and social transformation. Oil proceeds have been used to modernise infrastructure, create employment, and improve social indicators, while the countries have been able to accumulate official reserves, maintain relatively low external debt, and remain important donors to poor countries. Life expectancy in the GCC area increased by almost 10 years to 74 years during 1980–2000, and literacy rates increased by 20 percentage points to about 80 per cent over the same period. Average per capita income in the GCC countries was estimated at about $12,000 in 2002, with their combined nominal GDP reaching close to $340 billion (more than half the GDP of all Middle Eastern countries. With very low inflation, overall real economic growth has averaged 4 per cent a year during the past three decades, while the importance of non-oil economic activities has grown steadily, reflecting GCC countries' efforts at economic diversification. Moreover, central bank international reserves alone in some GCC countries are equivalent to about 10 months of imports. This progress has been achieved with an open exchange and trade system and liberal capital flows, as well as open borders for foreign labour. The GCC area has become an important centre for regional economic growth.

Despite generally favourable economic conditions in the region measured in terms of macroeconomic stability, robust oil prices and high GDP growth rates, market corrections are expected to persist for a while, thereby impacting propensities to invest and consume in the private and household sectors. Volatility is expected to remain high in the months ahead. Moreover, while the recent initiatives have significantly strengthened the adjustment process that began in the mid-1980s, the nature and extent of emerging challenges are also different in at least two important areas; (i) The fiscal deficits have become more structural in nature; and (ii) The GCC countries are undergoing major demographic changes characterised by a rapidly growing and young population, with important implications for the labour market.

In earlier periods, fiscal retrenchment was carried out through cuts in development expenditure without seriously affecting growth prospects. In the meantime, the maintenance costs have increased, and there is a need to replenish the ageing capital stock. In addition, the investment income, which in some GCC countries comprised a large share of government revenue, has declined while debt servicing has increased. Expenditure on social sectors has increased in line with a growing population, and outlays on defence and security have remained high. Pressures on expenditure also come from a large and growing government wage bill.

Traditionally, the government sector has absorbed a large number of new entrants to the labour force, reflecting the policy of guaranteed employment, higher wages, and the social status and other benefits associated with government employment. Fiscal constraints limit this possibility at a time of an increasing number of entrants into the labour market. The policy challenge in the period ahead therefore is to meet the dual objectives of maintaining high levels of employment while reducing the role of the public sector in favour of the private sector.

Against such a background and given the trends as reflected in the global oil industry, it may be pointed out that GCC countries' economic resilience and forward momentum crucially hinges on the oil market trends and fundamentals that point to the strategic importance of major consuming countries like India in the Asia Pacific region.

Moreover, with the structural changes of the global oil and gas regime, it is interesting to look at the role of oil producing governments, especially the GCC states and the effects of these changes on their economies. The relationship between the oil and gas sector and the national economy in most of the developing oil producing countries, especially in the GCC has changed in a fundamental way over the past two decades. The oil and gas sector is no longer an exogenous sector immune from the broader economic and financial realities and pressures. More than ever before, the economic constraints have become binding at all levels. Perhaps the most significant consequence for the global oil and gas regime is the fact that the hydrocarbon sector in the GCC countries was pushed into 'the politics of the budget',[31] to carry on social charity in order to restrain the emerging public consciousness.

Very few GCC countries still have the financial resources that they had a few years ago. Not only have their real oil revenues come down drastically in the past 10 years or so, but also most GCC states have exhausted the vast financial surpluses accumulated during the golden days of the 1970s and early 1980s. Instead these countries have accumulated huge foreign debt on account of successive deficit budgets and surmounting public expenditure. This evinced from the fact that, the net assets[32] of OPEC member states crashed from just under $160 billion in 1980 to almost negative $60 billion in 1995. However, the depletion of assets and successive accumulation of huge foreign debt, in and of itself, is not the problem. The real problem facing these economies and these governments is the fact that the windfall revenues from oil exports was never disposed off rationally. This is vindictive of the fact that none of the oil exporting GCC states has managed to develop a productive non-oil sector that can grow and create wealth independent of government spending and subsidies. This is a peculiar phenomenon of a depleting-resource-based economy. Thus, at a time of declining global market share and dire need of huge investments in the oil and gas sector in order to meet the challenges of the global environment of emerging potential markets (Asia in general and India and China in particular) and the sustained penetration of new players (non-OPEC oil and gas producing countries, Russia, etc.) in the global oil regime, the political pressures

---

31. Vahan, Zanoyan (1999). "A Relevant Framework for Understanding the Global Crude Oil Market", in ECSSR, (ed.), *Gulf Energy and the World: Challenges and Threats.* UAE, Abu Dhabi: ECSSR. Chap. 2. p.38.

32. Net assets refer to total foreign assets less total foreign debt. The trends are sourced from, *IMF Financial Statistics.* January 1997.

on the governments to spend on either current or military items has, more often than not, deprived the oil and gas sectors of the strategic necessary investment funds. This is why the budgets of national oil companies, which in the GCC economies do not represent important political constituencies, were the first to be cut.

Incidentally, just when the demands on declining revenue base started to take their toll on the governments' freedom of flexibility in formulating domestic policy, their capacity to influence the world oil market is virtually being eroded. The mounting domestic economic pressures implies that most governments could not afford the short-term revenue consequences of an exercise/campaign to raise their market share; nor could they afford to neglect a host of regional and global political repercussions while considering short-term oil price targets.

Most GCC countries that depend on the West for security are generally constrained not only by the political imperative to spend on Western military and civilian imports, but also by the necessity to take western economic interests into consideration while formulating oil policy. The former reduces their freedom to cut spending; the latter reduces their chances of raising oil revenues. Moreover, the domestic constraints are intimately related to the fact that most oil exporting GCC countries have failed to come to terms with the new post-oil boom socioeconomic realities in their respective countries. This tendency or popular psyche of 'carefree attitude' has been strengthened by chronic deficit spending by the GCC governments and in fact created the illusion that the free period of the 1970s and early 1980s could be indefinitely prolonged. In addition the cost-cutting measures if adopted with iron intent cannot become successful because of the inherent fundamental structural and institutional bottlenecks.

The external policy options for the GCC countries have changed radically in recent years. Perhaps the most damning aspect of that change for oil exporting GCC countries is the extremely stubborn and widespread 'supply complacency' that has overwhelmed the oil consuming world for almost a decade. The fact that three members of OPEC are under US trade embargo (i.e., Iraq, Libya and Iran) is indicative of the degree of supply complacency. The resilience of the supply complacency becomes more remarkable when one considers the fact that it has survived major political and military upheavals, including two major wars in the Gulf, along with substantial reductions in excess production capacity in the world in the past few years. Part of the reason for the supply complacency stems from the fact that the OECD countries in the aegis of IEA have accumulated substantial strategic petroleum reserves after the first oil shock, which in fact provided a level of comfort for the industrialised world and the global regime. Another part is the emergence and consolidation of paper markets[33] and hedging practices in the present regime, which have somehow instilled transparency and stability in the global oil and gas market. Another part is the rapid increase in production capacity in countries outside of the Gulf. The most important feature is that the capacity addition in the non-OPEC countries have been undertaken by international companies, while the operations in this regard in the GCC countries have been undertaken by the national oil companies with stringent budgets and government constraints.

Thus, the GCC countries are facing daunting challenges to sustain themselves. The challenges facing the GCC countries are well analysed by some analysts.[34] Over the past 20 years, real economic growth in the GCC had not exceeded 2.5 per cent annually, or half the average annual growth rate recorded in other developing countries. The per capita income in the GCC countries had declined over the past 20 years, whereas in other developing countries it had increased by some 60 per cent. The GCC countries are confronting five major challenges to sustain themselves such as follows; population growth and labour productivity due to high birth rate, growth in budgets and public debt, dominance of public sector, restricting the development of a vibrant private sector, failure to tap enough foreign investment due to the unattractiveness of the domestic rigid institutions. The independent analysis of each of the above factors will reflect the extent of GCC countries' vulnerability in augmenting economic growth.

33. In fact, the volume of trade in the paper markets and hedging practices is 10 times higher than the overall physical oil trade in recent years.

34. For details see *MEES*, Vol. 45(18), 6 May 2002, p.B4, and Oweiss Ibrahim M. (2000). *The Arab Gulf Economies: Challenges and Prospects.* UAE: ECSSR.

Challenges Facing the GCC Countries

Population Growth and Labour Productivity

Rapid population growth rate in comparison to labour productivity in the GCC countries is the most important problem. The growth rate in population—nationals and non-nationals—is one of the highest in the world, having averaged 5 per cent between 1970 and 1995. The GCC countries are witnessing high birth rates coupled with low but declining death rates, as health conditions and sanitation improve over time. A summary of population statistics is given in Table 2.24. This rapid growth has in turn led to a surge in demand for jobs, with the labour market now roughly accounting for one-third of the population, of which foreigners account for roughly for two-thirds. The number of new entrants to the labour market—local and foreign—increases annually by an average of 3.7 per cent. The national labour force is estimated to increase by 6 per cent as a result of increased fertility rates and consequently some 7 million nationals are expected to enter the labour market during the current decade. In each of these six countries, the dependency on oil prices as the main source of government revenues make it difficult to devise long-term economic policies, given oil price fluctuations and ever changing trends. Assuming stable government revenues against a high population growth rate, the per capita income will shrink and the standard of living will worsen over time.

Table 2.24

Population Statistics for GCC Countries

	Bahrain	*Kuwait*	*Oman*	*Qatar*	*Saudi Arabia*	*UAE*
Population, 2005 (million)	0.7	2.7	2.6	0.8	24.6	4.5
Projected Population, 2020 (million)	0.9	3.7	3.3	1.0	32.9	5.8
Annual Growth Rate (2000-05)	2.1%	3.8%	0.9%	5.1%	2.5%	4.7%
Population in age group 0-14 of total	26.3%	23.7%	33.8%	21.8%	34.5%	19.9%
Population in age group 15-24 of total	16.1%	16.0%	21.5%	13.9%	18.5%	16.3%
Population in age group 15-59 of total	69.3%	73.1%	62.0%	75.5%	61.3%	78.3%
Population in age group 60+ of total	4.5%	3.1%	4.3%	2.7%	4.2%	1.8%
Median age	28.8	29.2	22.5	31.3	23.3	29.4

Source: Calculated from United Nations Population Division. *World Population Prospects, 2007.*

The population of the six GCC countries is expected to increase by 55 per cent in a 15-year interval. In the absence of evidence that oil prices will increase by the same ratio, the per capita income is bound to decline and budget deficits will increase. While examining the rate of population growth against sources of economic growth it has been found that labour productivity contributed only 9-11 per cent of their overall economic growth rate. This is in sharp contrast to industrialised nations where the contribution of labour to growth is in the neighbourhood of 75 per cent. Given that the source of growth in these economies is natural resources, the growth accounting against such rapid population growth and lower labour productivity indicates that the per capita income will decrease. Another worrying trend is that in UAE, Qatar and Kuwait the foreign labour force accounts for 80 per cent of the total population.

Heavy Budgets and Surmounting Public Debt

With the exception of Kuwait and Qatar, the internal and external debt of the GCC countries has reached critical levels. The deterioration in the financial position of these countries has been caused by fluctuations in the oil market, especially in the late 1980s and early 1990s when oil prices reached low teens and declining market share of these oil-exporting countries due to the penetration of other oil producers to the international oil market. Another factor is the increasing level of current expenditure in these countries.[35]

Public Sector Dominance

As per the latest statistics (2000), the public sector dominates the GCC economies, ranging from 35 per cent in UAE, to 54 per cent in Saudi Arabia and 61 per cent in Oman. The growth of public sector in these economies can be attributed to the fact that the governments in these countries accumulated massive wealth from oil revenue at a time when the private sector was virtually absent. This prompted the state to take initiatives and provide all the basic public services. At the same time the states in this region penetrated in the industrial sectors

35. Barnett, Steven and Rolando Ossowski (2002). "Operational Aspects of Fiscal Policy in Oil-Producing Countries," *IMF Working Paper* 02/177. Washington: International Monetary Fund.

by investing in petrochemicals, banks and the iron and steel industries among others.

Failure to Tap the Flow of FDI and the Restrictions on Foreign Investment

Foreign direct investment in the GCC countries is relatively low because of a host of negative factors, notably the small size of the market, the lack of investment opportunities and the availability of liquidity locally. There are also other problems such as obstacles to foreign investment in trading services and the acquisition of real estate and inequality in tax treatment and the provision of services and subsidies. Moreover, fluctuations in economic activity act as a deterrent to foreign capital because government expenditure is a function of oil revenue.

Another disquieting trend is the failure of the GCC states to attract foreign investment in the present global regime of liberalisation and globalisation. This is not only peculiar to the GCC countries alone, but also to the whole Middle East region.[36]

Economics of Oil and Gas

Another major challenge to the GCC economies is to find a means by which they can cope with an ever-changing pattern of oil market fundamentals, which are determined by a complicated set of market variables in recent years. As discussed earlier in this chapter, the GCC countries are sensitive to demand disruptions dampening their revenue sources. Therefore, they are in constant search for a viable and stable market for their oil and gas exports. This is also consonant with the interdependent policies adopted by OPEC in the late 1980s to secure stable outlets for their exports. Given the emergence of the Asian region in general and India in particular, and the greater trading affinity of the Gulf region with these emerging regions, it is now up to the GCC policy makers to devise and implement suitable policies to reap long-term benefits.

36. See MEES, "Arab Countries Fail to Capture Proportionate Share of FDI", *MEES*, Vol. 45(11), 18 March 2002, p.B3, and also see, Sadek, Ali T. and Ali A. Bolbol (2001). "Capital Flows, FDI, and Technology Spillovers: Evidence from Arab Countries", *World Development Journal*, Vol. 29(12): 2111-23.

Therefore, it can be contended that the GCC countries have wasted the opportunities offered by the generous flow of gigantic volumes of oil revenues in conspicuous expenditures, instead of using the funds for diversification of their narrow economic base. As rightly pointed out,

> The spectacular opportunity given to the Arab States in the Gulf 'to tackle their massive development requirements and build Arab unity on the basis of fruitful economic cooperation' has been dissipated in wasteful expenditures domestically and internationally.[37]

Thus, the GCC countries face important policy challenges and opportunities in view of an uncertain oil market outlook and the evolving trends in the regional and international economy. These are compounded by domestic developments, particularly the growing number of nationals entering the labour markets. Indeed, the GCC countries are at a crossroads. One path, built on insufficient policy response to less favourable external conditions, carries the risk of low rates of economic growth, rising unemployment, and growing financial imbalances and indebtedness. The second, stressing economic adjustment supported by structural reforms, promises financial stability, growing employment opportunities, and sustained economic growth.

Thus as evident from the above discussion, the global oil and gas regime has undergone radical changes and transformations over the years. The market fundamentals have altered the global game in the favour of none. Both the producers and consumers are now overwhelmingly dependent on market solutions for their survival in the global oil and gas regime. The demand as well as the supply side of the regime has altered. The Asian countries have taken centre stage in the demand side of the global regime due to their surmounting consumption of imported energy ignited by their economic growth rate. In the Asian region, after China, India with its gigantic population is poised to be the largest energy consumer in the world. Given the fact that GCC countries are the traditional sources of India's energy provider this will open new opportunities for the GCC energy

37. El-Beblawi, Hazem (1983). "The Oil Decade: An Appraisal in Perspective", *The IBK Papers*, Series No.10. Kuwait: The Industrial Bank of Kuwait K.S.C. p.43.

exporters to tap the booming energy situation in India as well as the whole of Asia. India's heavy reliance on imported energy especially from the Gulf region is looking inevitable in the near future. On the other hand, from the global supply perspective, the GCC countries have lost their early leverage (1970s and early 1980s) to the outside players who have emerged in the regime due to the institutional, strategic, economic factors and due to the inherent instabilities in the world market. Nevertheless, these countries (GCC countries) are likely to play a crucial role in the future, as most of the world's reserves lie in these countries and the cost of production is the lowest in this part of the world, if they consolidate themselves to the new realities of the times.

In this backdrop the emergence of India and the whole of Asia as a strategic force in the global energy consumption front, it is time for the GCC countries to take the appropriate policies and reap the benefits to ensure their survival in the new environment and to earn much needed leverage in the global regime. And this seems evitable as one analyst has talked of the emergence of a 'global demand heartland' comprised of China, India and rest of Asia and a 'resource periphery' around the region from Central Asia, Persian Gulf to Indonesia and South China.[38]

---

38. Singh, Jasjit. "Geopolitics of Energy and its Security", in Jasjit Singh (ed.), *Oil and Gas in India's Security.* New Delhi: Knowledge World and Institute for Defence Studies and Analysis (IDSA) p.13.

3

India and GCC Countries

An Emerging Pattern of Energy Interdependence

The analysis in the previous chapter reveals that the present global oil and gas regime is radically different from that of the past years. While on the one hand, the major players of the regime of the yesteryears—the GCC countries are in the process of losing streak due to the penetration of other players; on the other hand, the industrialised West is being replaced by the newly industrialising countries of the East—the Asian economies in general and India in particular, in the world energy consumption map. Despite continuous decline in export market share (especially western market) there are clear indications of GCC countries retaining their position in the regime in view of the growing dependence of Asia.

This chapter attempts a 'SWOT (strengths, weaknesses, opportunities and threats) Analysis' of the oil and gas fundamentals in India and the GCC countries. This will reveal how an increasing pattern of interdependence based on current energy market fundamentals is emerging in the present global regime. The first section deals with the Indian oil and gas sector from the days of its evolution till the present phase of deregulation and restructuring. The second section focuses on the various emergent issues in the GCC oil and gas sector and their relevance to the stability and sustainability of the GCC countries in the present regime. The last section attempts to delineate the emerging pattern of interdependence between India and the GCC countries.

SECTION I

Indian Oil and Gas Sector: A Brief Historical Account

The Indian petroleum industry is one of the oldest in the world, with oil being struck at Makum near Margherita in Assam in 1867,[1] nine years after Col. Drake's sensational discovery in Titusville. Indian oil exercise started at a time when exciting technological innovations in the post-Industrial Revolution period marked heavy and persistent World (especially the Western) dependence on a key resource like petroleum. H.B. Medicott of the Geological Survey of India first started oil exploration in India in 1865 in the Makum area. The most astounding Indian oil history was made on 26th March 1867 by Striking oil at 118 ft. It was India's first oil well and Asia's first mechanically drilled well. Then came the discovery of oil at 178 ft., on 16th October 1889 in Digboi, which marked the birth of the Indian petroleum industry in November 1890. A small oil refinery was set up in Margherita in 1893 to process Digboi crude. However, the Assam Oil Company commissioned India's first oil refinery at Digboi in December 1901. Production from Digboi was initially 20,000 tonnes in 1934. Another area in upper Assam named Surma Valley, was opened up for exploration in Badarpur prospect in 1915. A small oil deposit was discovered, which was later abandoned in 1933 after a total production of about 3,20,000 tonnes.

The Formative Stage

In terms of evolution, the period 1947-1960 and more precisely the decade of the 1950s could be designated as the formative stage of the growth of the Indian oil sector. Independent India adopted a centrally planned socialistic economic system with mixed economy articulations reflected in some areas of industrialisation. The greatest Indian oilman, the late Keshava Deva Malviya—the father of the modern Indian Oil industry, very wilfully and committedly took up the responsibility of

1. The efforts and findings worth mentioning in this respect are of Lt. R. Wilcox in Supkhong (1825), C.A. Bruce in upstream Makum (1828), W. Griffith in Kamrup Putar (1837), Lt. W. Bigge in Namrup (1837), Capt. Francis Jenkins in Borhat and Makum (1835), Capt. H. Vetch in Makum (1842), and a few unnamed explorers. The Indian exercises in this field have been well documented by S.N. Visvanath in his book (1990). *A Hundred Years of Oil: A Narrative Account of the Search for Oil in India.* New Delhi: Vikas Publishing House.

transcending the Nehruvian vision into realities of a national oil industry. His efforts led to the discovery of two oil fields in Nahorkatiya in June 1953 and a relatively smaller one in Moran in November 1956, which added considerable strength to the Indian energy economy. To give boost to the exploration activities an Oil and Natural Gas division was created within the Geological Survey of India in December 1955, which was upgraded to Oil and Natural Gas Commission (ONGC) on 14th August 1956. ONGC started exploration in the Sibsagar district in Upper Assam and in the central part of Gujarat in the Cambay basin in 1956-57. The efforts soon resulted in the form of two giant discoveries of oil fields in Lunej and the biggest onshore oil field at Ankleswar. In the downstream sector the second oil refinery owned by the Standard Vaccum Oil Company was commissioned in 1954. The third refinery in Mumbai owned by Burma-Shell Refineries Ltd. and the fourth refinery in Visakhapatnam owned by the Caltex Oil Refinery (India) came on stream in 1955 and 1957 respectively. The Indian Refinery Limited was formed in 1958 and for marketing the petro-products, the Indian Oil Company came into being in 1959. On the other side, Oil India Private Limited got incorporated on 18th February 1959 as a Rupee Company with two-third shares held by the AOC-BOC combine and one-third by the Government of India (GoI). This arrangement was further modified; equal shareholding of this company between the GoI and Burma Oil Co. (BOC) was effected from 27th July 1961.

The Developing Stage

This stage covers two decades the 1960s and 1970s, when the efforts, growth and success of the Indian petroleum industry in its upstream and downstream sectors were of significant proportions. Oil exploration was spread out to almost all the first and second grade petroliferous Indian basins. Success of discovering a good number of mega, macro, medium, moderate, mini and also micro size oil-gas fields, both in onshore and offshore areas, irrevocably confirmed the presence of oil and gas beyond Assam. The decade of the 1960s is therefore designated as the "saga of elephantine serendipities, exemplary sacrifices and determined struggle for discovering, developing and utilising the petroleum resources of the country."[2] Of the total oil-gas find achieved in this decade, the discoveries, mentioned in Table 3.1 are technically and economically most significant.

Table 3.1

Important Oil-Gas Discoveries of 1960s and 1970s in India

Discovery (Oil/Gas)	*Basin*	*Date of Discovery*		*Field Size*
		Month	*Year*	
Cambey (Lunej)	Cambay	November	1958	Mini
Ankleswar	Cambay	May	1960	Mega
Rudrasagar	Upper Assam	December	1960	Medium
Kalol	Cambay	June	1961	Macro
Lakwa-Lakhmani	Upper Assam	December	1962	Mega
North Kati	Cambay	April	1967	Medium
Geleki	Upper Assam	April	1968	Macro
Sonthal	Upper Assam	October	1971	Medium
Bombay High (Oil & Gas)	Bombay Offshore	February	1974	Giant
Panna (Oil)	-do-	March	1976	Macro
South Bassein (Gas)	-do-	April	1976	Mega
Heera	-do-	October	1977	Mega
South Tapti	-do-	February	1978	Medium

Source : Bose, B.K. (1999). *Oil Asia*, January-March, p.7.

In the refinery sector, the first public sector refinery at Guwahati (1961), World's first crude conditioning plant at Nahorkatiya (1963), Cochin Refinery (1966) and Madras Refinery (1969) came on stream in the 1960s. A few pipelines were also commissioned. They were the Nahorkatiya-Guwahati pipeline, the first long distance product pipeline in India from Guwahati Refinery to Siliguri (1964), 16" dia pipeline from Ankleswar to Koyali Refinery (1965). In the organisational front, Indian Refineries Ltd. and India Oil Company merged to form the Indian Oil Corporation Ltd. (IOC) on 1st September 1964.

The period of the 1970s may be termed as the decade of exploration excellence. In this period the exploration concepts, efforts and also the expectations got progressively refined. Offshore exploration was started and India's oil giant Bombay High and the gas-mega Bassein level was

2. Bose, B.K. (1999). *Oil Asia*, January-March, p.5.

discovered much to the rejoice of the nation. Bombay High was brought to commercial production in 1975 and gas supply from the field for power generation and fertiliser manufacturing started in 1978. But the biggest disappointment of the developing stage was the lack of exploration success in the Bengal basin, Ganga Valley, Mahanadi basin, Kutch-Saurashtra and the Andamans. The American companies, named Carlsberg-Namotas and Reading & Bates respectively, in the mid-1970s took offshore acreages in the Bengal basin and Kutch, but failed to make any headway in exploration.

During this period, indigenous oil production increased significantly. At the time of Indian independence in 1947, oil production was a meagre 5,047 b/d, while in 1970 it became 1,42,000 b/d, an amazing increase of more than 28 times. The level of self-sufficiency of the Indian economy in oil, however was then only around 35 per cent. In the refinery side, the fuel sector of Haldia Refinery came on stream in 1975. Next year, the Burmah Shell Refineries was fully taken over and renamed Bharat Refineries Ltd., while Esso refinery on Government take-over was renamed as Hindustan Petroleum Corporation Ltd.

The Maturing Stage

This stage resulted in a rapid increase in exploration activities and also inventories of non-economic and marginal fields. Despite a few impressive discoveries, almost 85 per cent of the discoveries of the 1980s were of micro size. The situation characterises the matured stage of exploration efforts in an area. Field production and development increased manifold in this stage. In fact, Indian domestic oil production reached the then highest ever peak of oil production around 6,92,000 b/d in 1989-90. Also, Indian self-sufficiency in oil touched an all time high of 68 per cent. The Krishna-Godavari and Cauvery basins both onshore and offshore came up on the Indian and global map with substantial discoveries (Table 3.2). Some of the discoveries in Bombay offshore and the Gandhar oil-gas field in Cambay had been the most rewarding assets of this period.

Table 3.2

Important Oil-Gas Discoveries of 1980s

Discovery (Oil/Gas)	*Basin*	*Date of Discovery*		*Field Size*
		Month	*Year*	
Mukta (Oil & Gas)	Bombay Offshore	August	1981	Medium
Gandhar (Oil-Gas)	Cambay	March	1984	Mega
Narimanam (Oil)	Cauvery Onshore	July	1985	Moderate
Pasrlapudi (Gas)	Krishna-Godavari (K-G) Onshore	January	1987	Medium
Neelam (Oil & Gas)	Bombay Offshore	January	1987	Mega
Ravva (Oil & Gas)	K-G Offshore	July	1987	Macro
Mandapeta (Gas)	K-G Onshore	September	1988	Medium
PY-3 (Oil)	Cauvery Offshore	September	1988	Mini

Source : *Oil Asia Journal*, January-March. 1999. Table 3. p.8.

The other important development during this stage was the government's take-over of Oil India Ltd., which became a fully 100 per cent public sector company in 1981. During this period, the supply of natural gas also got intensified. Gas from Bombay High started getting up to HBJ (Hazira-Bijaipur-Jagdishpur) pipeline from 1987-88. One LPG plant at Uran (near Mumbai) was commissioned by ONGC in 1985-86. This period witnessed the emergence of two jewels of the oil-gas sector, such as the Indian Oil Corporation (IOC) and Oil and Natural Gas Commission (ONGC).

This decade however marked the induction of foreign players into the Indian oil regime, though slowly. It was realised that foreign technologies, expertise and above all capital would be essential to deal with the future challenges and commitments of the Indian oil economy. The first step towards this end was the opening up of Indian exploration acreage to competitive global bidding. The first strategic initiative was taken in 1979-80 of offering 32 exploration blocks (17 offshore and 15 onshore) covering 8 basins for global bidding.[3] In fact, the first strategic alliance in the Indian oil sector started in the year 1953-54 when the Indo-Stanvac Petroleum Project (ISPP) was organised for oil exploration in West Bengal offshore and Kutch

3. Ministry of Petroleum and Natural Gas (1990). *Annual Report*. New Delhi: Government of India.

offshore and they were assigned to Carlsberg-Namotas and Reading & Bates respectively in 1975. However, the options of phased liberalisation of the Indian oil-gas sector started getting nationally debated and seriously considered since the end 1980s.

Global Regime in India

Before discussing the stage of the Indian oil-gas sector in the 1990s, it would be interesting to focus on the implications of the global regime on the Indian oil economy. It is to be noted that, when India achieved political independence in 1947, oil, more than any sector, was the weakest link in its economic structure. The powerful foreign oil monopolies, especially the British, with the full backing of the colonial administration, had seen to it that India remained backward and totally dependent on them in this vital front. They did not show interest in developing crude production or refining in India.[4] The imperialist interest in oil was to supply the Indian market, on terms advantageous to them, from rich oil fields of the Middle East and Latin America, which the international monopolies operated. The activities of global oil cartels in India were confined to establishing sales network rather than making investments on building an integrated oil industry. Though the American monopolies, as part of their worldwide competitive requirements, sometimes evinced interest in oil exploration in India, particularly during the first two decades of the 20th century, the British due to its colonial political power restricted their moves.[5]

However, after World War I, with the balance of power shifting in favour of the Americans, the Americans penetrated the Indian oil and gas sector. This period witnessed cut-throat competition between the British and the American monopolies in India, which was later resolved by an agreement for the carving up of the Indian market in 1927. This was at about the same time as the top seven international oil companies entered into elaborate cartel arrangements for the world

4. Mehta, Balraj (1974). *India and the World Oil Crisis*, Part II. New Delhi: Sterling Publishers Private Ltd. p.31.

5. When in 1902, the Standard Oil of the US sought permission to prospect for oil in India, it was curtly refused on the specific ground that, "it is not desired by the Government of India to introduce any American oil companies, or their subsidiary companies, into India," see Mehta, Ibid.

market as a whole. The British became more accommodative to share the Indian market with the Americans, though the major share of about 70 per cent rested with them, till the 1950s. It is to be noted that the Americans lost interest in exploration in India and whatever desultory exploration was undertaken, was more to hide than to search for oil.

However after Independence, when policy makers became restive about the vulnerable position in this vital sector the multinationals advanced the false theory that there was no oil in India.[6] The foreign companies propagated this myth even after oil had been struck in the first few years of exploration in the public sector with Soviet assistance. The most decisive factor in this period has been the success of the efforts to develop the industry in the public sector during the late 1950s. Nevertheless, the foreign oil monopolies had always hedged their efforts of collaborations with many unacceptable conditions and terms and there had been no progress in this direction. Thus, there was virtually no oil industry in India at the time of independence. There was a small refinery in India and six marketing companies, all with their head offices outside India. Three of the marketing companies were subsidiaries of the international oil majors—the Burmah Shell, the Stanvac, later turned into Esso and the Caltex. The three together controlled 90 per cent of the sales of petroleum products to the Indian market. The Digboi refinery with less than half a million tonnes capacity, also wholly owned by a subsidiary of the Burma Oil Co—a British concern which holds 50 per cent partnership in Burma-Shell, covered only a small part of the consumption.

The growing demand for petroleum products had to be met by increasing imports through the companies, on which they made enormous profits. This openly colonial pattern in the Indian oil-gas sector continued till the early 1950s. Though the Government in its 1948 Industrial Policy took some bold steps to revamp the sector from the colonial pattern, it failed due to the transition phase in the aftermath of the Second World War. Meanwhile, the oil monopolies strategised new ways of consolidation in the Indian oil economy. The new plans took stage with the commissioning of three new coastal

---

6. Mehta *op. cit.*, No. 4.

refineries between 1954 and 1957, since after World War II, the oil monopolies had intended to locate the refineries in consumption centres rather than in the centres of crude oil production due to political, strategic and economic reasons. This also forestalled the implementation of Government of India (GoI)'s 1948 Industrial Policy Resolutions. The oil monopolies not only succeeded in consolidating their hold over the Indian market, but also they won away special refinery arrangements from the GoI, which was arbitrary and irrational. It is to be noted that the GoI played into the hands of the oil monopolies at the formative stage of the Indian oil economy. This was exacerbated by the then prevailing situation in the global regime in which there was scepticism regarding cut off of future oil supplies to India, due to the nationalisation of the British oil cartel in Iran and successive American and British threats.

The whole *raison d'être* of the companies putting their refineries on the Indian coasts was simply to tie up the rapidly expanding Indian market with their own sources of crude supply, which automatically tied the Indian oil sector with their global operations. It was designed to strengthen and consolidate their hold on the Indian market rather than develop the Indian oil industry. When in order to mitigate foreign exchange stringency, the Soviet Union offered to supply crude to India on rupee payment basis for refining, the companies bluntly refused to process it in their refineries and got away with it, by invoking the refining agreements. It was also equally significant that the product pattern of the refineries established in India did not cater to more crucial Indian demand patterns such as kerosene, aviation jet fuel and lubricants which were of economic and strategic importance for the country. Thus, the entire pattern of the companies' operations and organisation in India was developed to achieve the objective of establishing a small link in the chain of their world operations.

Moreover, the operations of smaller independent companies were insignificant in comparison to the majors. Between 1928 and 1933, for instance, some independent distribution companies were floated in India but they had to face a fierce cut-throat competition and underselling by the giants and as a result, they collapsed or remained out of business. Even after Independence, such attempts got foiled. An Indo-Iranian oil company was set up during the Anglo-Iranian oil conflict in the early 1950s. It even concluded a contract with the National Iranian Oil Company (NIOC) to buy oil products for sale in India. But the power of the monopolies was so great that the company was liquidated before it could start business.

However, the monopoly of the cartels got challenged with the setting up of the 100 per cent public sector owned Indian Oil Company in 1959 with supply assured to it by the Soviet Union. The process of development of a national oil industry was slow. Even in 1964-65, the IOC sales were still only 17.2 lakh kilolitres, against 52.12 lakh kilolitres sales of the Burmah Shell Company in 1963, Esso's 31.22 lakh kilolitres in 1962 and Caltex's 19.70 lakh kilolitres in 1963.[7] Only due to the compulsions of foreign exchange stringency and the multinationals' persistent intransigence, the government at last decided in 1965 to cut off the import of products through the cartels and confined their sale operations to the products of their own refineries in India. The IOC then jump-started its sale operations in one year to double its turnover.

Thus, in the system of majors' operation in India, there was necessarily no place for exploration and production of crude, the primary source of their super-normal-profit. India was placed very low in the order of priority for exploratory efforts in the global operations of the international oil majors. Even in such cases where prospects for exploration were established to be good, the companies sought special rights and concessions, reimbursement of expenditure in event of failure and control over disposal of crude. Only the BOC agreed to participate in crude exploration and production in the Assam area, at especially favourable terms, because it already held profitable investments in the Digboi refinery and wanted to expand further. The result was the formation of the Oil India Ltd., in which the BOC first secured 70 per cent share and subsequently agreed to a 50:50 partnership with the government, and a guarantee of 9 to 13 per cent profit to the BOC. During the first year of its working when the profits were not good, the return to the company was ensured through government subsidies to the tune of Rs. 60 and more per tonne of crude production.

By the mid-50s, it became clear to the government that there is no

7. Visvanath *op. cit.*, No. 1.

alternative to building a national oil industry in the public sector. In this regard, the Oil and Natural Gas Commission (ONGC) was set up in 1956 and was converted into a statutory body in 1959. After the first success in oil exploration by the ONGC, the government started to plunge into the refining sector and subsequently in early 1965, the public sector refining company and the IOC were merged to form the Indian Oil Corporation (IOC). This setup in the public sector oil had to rival the power of the monopolies. The existence and growth of the public sector in oil for 10 years between 1956 and 1965 was a source of great strength to the economic and security capability of the country.

The decision to develop a national oil industry in the public sector had naturally met with hostilities from the international companies. This hostility expressed itself in various economic as well as political forms over a prolonged period of tussle for the public sector oil to establish itself. The setting up of public sector refineries especially met with stronger resistance since it threatened the interests of the companies immediately. In this regard, the attitude and position of world bodies like the World Bank is noteworthy:

> The World Bank in its two reports submitted in 1956 and 1958 went out of its way to specifically oppose the public sector oil programme in India. In the 1956 report it remarked, 'It would be a mistake to insist on such a measure of government participation in the exploitation and development of oil resources as to discourage foreign oil ventures.' Again in its report in 1958 it reported: 'The (India) government's insistence that refineries must be in the public sector and its reluctance to grant new exploratory concessions to oil companies inhibited the participation of foreign capital.' The Federation of Indian Chamber of Commerce and Industry (FICCI) also echoed the same line and demanded that foreign capital should be allowed in the oil sector.[8]

Meanwhile, favourable conditions had begun to operate in the global regime. While in the initial phases, Soviet and Romanian assistance alone could be counted upon to develop the national oil industry new developments in the world oil industry were also taking

8. Mehta *op. cit.*, No. 4, p.49.

place at about the same time to reduce somewhat the monopoly grip of the cartels in this vital sector. The sweep of national liberation movements in the countries of Asia and Africa had important repercussions for the global oil regime. It gave birth to the drive of nationalisation of oil industries in the oil-producing countries, earlier owned by the multinationals. Most of these countries were able to release wholly the oil concessions from the cartels' control and establish national oil companies. This provided a new basis for international collaboration between India and countries in the West Asian region. The countries in West Asia were eager to penetrate into the potentially vast oil market in India. Also, India had developed technical expertise to some degree in various fields which West Asia could use viably and economically. The first instance of this cooperation was a deal with the Iranians which included the setting up of a refinery at Madras and participation of India in oil exploration in the Iranian offshore areas. Similar prospects afterwards came up in relation to other oil producing countries, the most important being the deal with Iraq.

Another major development having bearing on the development of the national oil industry in India was the growth of national oil companies in the consuming countries of Europe such as France and Italy as well as the emergence of independent oil companies in the West as a whole, including the US. In their search of business opportunities as a measure of self-defence, these national oil companies and the independents were willing to accept terms of collaborations. This resulted in the refinery construction at Cochin with the American company Philips accepting a minority holding. In the field of exploration also, India attracted foreign expertise and capital from independent sources such as from the ENI of Italy and the French government.[9] The cartel remained completely out of any such venture. These developments made it possible for India to confront the international oil companies in India from a position of comparative strength and self-confidence. The result was the companies' retreat in the form of offer to terminate the special refinery agreements as a sop to the national sentiment and to operate under ordinary industrial

9. Mehta Ibid.

licenses. However, the offer was conditional in that the government had to allow the tie up of the companies' refineries with their own sources of crude supply. This implies that the companies wanted to maintain their international monopoly in India. Thus, the 1960s witnessed a significant decline in the operations of international oil cartels in India.

The energy sector in India was completely nationalised by the mid-1970s, and the government started using the sector as a vehicle to provide subsidies to its population as well as to provide employment. While on the one hand these sectors were straddled with employee numbers far beyond those required and the accompanying labour problems, on the other hand there was never a position in these public sector enterprises to generate any substantial internal resources to augment the budgetary support provided to them by the government. Additionally, the subsidised energy provision resulted in scant regard being paid to energy efficiency by the consumer. This resulted in a situation where demand growth outstripped supply growth, thereby leading to sub-optimal investment choices.

The Transforming Stage

One of the significant aspects of the public sector development of the oil-gas sector in India is the grant of substantial budgetary support, which resulted in the present maturing stage of the industry. The 1990s witnessed a phase of transformation in the oil and gas sector in India as well as other sectors of the Indian economy. The oil-gas sector witnessed a transition from a state of complete protection to the phase of open competition. For several decades, India pursued protectionist 'import substitution' trade policies, which impaired the flow of foreign capital into the country. Dictated by a balance of crisis, mainly due to sky-rocketing world oil prices in the event of the Gulf War (1990-91), India began to open up to foreign investment and trade. Given the fact that petroleum product consumption has increased substantially over the years and there is every likelihood of these trends continuing, an assessment of the current and future scenario in the Indian hydrocarbon sector became important. As a result, factors basic to promotion, progress and prosperity of the oil-gas business in India have been altering since the early 1990s. This is commensurate with the general economic reforms and restructuring going on in the Indian economy since the early 1990s.

Economic reforms in India have followed an approach. In the process, though these reforms have been undertaken slowly, it has been argued that the process has avoided many cataclysmic effects that have accompanied reforms in several other countries. The tackling of the reforms at the macro level got succeeded by 'mesoeconomic reforms', i.e., reforms in the more critical sectors of the economy. There are certain reasons for prioritising reforms in the hydrocarbon sector, such as:[10]

- The horrible experiences of the oil shocks of 1973-74, 1979-80 and the period during and after the Gulf War of 1990-91 made the policy makers devise policies and prepare the Indian economy to absorb the shocks and uncertainties of any future oil market upheavals.
- Given the growth in demand for petroleum products, the excessive dependence on oil imports needs to be curbed either through indigenous production or from equity oil that India may be able to establish in other oil producing and exporting countries. Even though export earnings in general have been buoyant in the 1990s, the cost of increased outflow of foreign exchange required to import petroleum products could become high and hence need to be guarded against.
- The oil and gas industry worldwide went through a period of reform which had important lessons for India that became the guiding principles for restructuring and reorganising the sector. While the decade of the 1970s was a period of growth and emergence of national entities, the 1990s represented a period of reforms in the national oil companies and organisations in the industry. In fact, the oil-gas industry today represents the cutting edge of economic reforms in many countries. The experiences thus served well for reform in the oil and gas sector in India.

Thus, a process of transition of the Indian oil-gas sector has started since the mid-90s from its protective into a competitive future. The

10. For details see Government of India (GoI) (1996). *Restructuring Group Report.* New Delhi.

oil-gas sector is also gearing up to suitably transform into a competitively responsive industry. The causes and contents of the forces driving the need of transformation are arising from the ground realities of the various sub-sectors of the oil-gas sector such as the upstream, mid-stream and downstream sectors. A detailed analysis of the sectors will reveal the basic realities/fundamentals of the oil-gas sector in India.

Upstream Sector

Resources and Reserves

Total hydrocarbon resources, inclusive of deep waters, are estimated at around 28 billion tonnes oil and oil-equivalent of gas (O+OEG). As on 01.04.2006, initial in-place oil and oil-equivalent gas of 8.46 billion

Table 3.3

Basin-wise Hydrocarbon Resources of India

(MMT)

Basin	*Offshore*	*Onland*	*Total*
Mumbai (MUM)	9,190	—	9,190
Assam-Arakan Fold Belt (AAFB)	—	1,860	1,860
Cambay (CBY)	—	2,050	2,050
Upper Assam (UA)	—	3,180	3,180
Krishna-Godavari (K-G)	555	575	1,130
Cauvery (CY)	270	430	700
Rajasthan (RAJ)	—	380	380
Kutch (KUT)	550	210	760
Andaman-Nicobar (AN)	180	—	180
Kerala-Konkan (K-K)	660	—	660
Saurashtra Offshore (SAU)	280	—	280
Ganga Valley (GV)	—	230	230
Bengal (BEN)	30	160	190
Himalayan Foreland (HF)	—	150	150
Mahanadi (MN)	100	45	145
Deep Water (DW)*	7000	—	7000
Grand Total	**18,815**	**9,270**	**28,085**

Note : *–HC resources in deep water off East Coast likely to increase further by about 4,000 MMT as per interpretation results of reconnaissance surveys carried out by DGH.

Source : Directorate General of Hydrocarbons (DGH).

tonnes and ultimate reserves of 3.25 billion tonnes have been established. The resources estimated by DGH for its 'internal use', for the country, are 32 billion tonnes (O+OEG). Table 3.3 shows basin-wise hydrocarbon resources of India.

Seismic Surveys

During the year 2005-06, 2-D seismic data acquisition comprised 7,265.17 LKM onland and 12,780.48 LKM offshore data. In respect of 3-D seismic data, 4,415.64 sq. km onland and 39,344.10 sq. km offshore data were acquired. A total of 16 2D seismic parties and 27 3D seismic parties were deployed in onland areas. Eight (8) seismic vessels were engaged to carry out 2D and 3D seismic surveys in offshore areas.

Drilling

Of the total of 418 wells drilled, 198 were exploratory and 220 development wells. A total of 11,09,480 metres were drilled, including 561,620 metres of exploratory and 547,860 metres of development drilled.

Production

Total oil production during the year was over 32.18 MMT and that of gas 32.20 BCM. The contribution of Pvt./Joint Venture companies was about 18 per cent of the total Oil & OEG production.

Privatisation Efforts by Pvt./JV Companies in E&P Sector

Directorate General of Hydrocarbons (DGH) has decided to publish every quarter, performance of E&P Companies operating in India under the New Exploration Licensing Policy (NELP) and Pre-NELP regime. Details regarding performance of various E&P companies are given in Table 3.4.

Recent Significant Discoveries

National Oil Companies

In the last 6 years (2000-2006), the NOC's *viz.*, ONGC and OIL made 38 significant hydrocarbon discoveries of which 13 are in offshore and 25 in onland. Out of 13 offshore discoveries, 8 were made

Table 3.4

Performance of Various E&P Companies in India

Name of the Company	No. of Blocks Awarded			Total Blocks	Total Acreages (Sq.km)	No. of Wells Expl. Committed	No. of Wells Drilled (Exp+App +Dev)	No. of Discoveries	Success Ratio (Per cemt)	Investment Made (US $MM) (Upto March 2005)	No. of Wells Drilled in 2004-05 (Exp+App +Dev)	No. of Discoveries (2004-05)	Success Ratio (Per cent) (2004-05)
ONGC	13	14	20	47	430335	78	13	Nil	Zero	415.58	9	Nil	Zero
RIL	3	16	13	32	288976	47	32	18	56	566.79	15	7	47
CEIL	2	2	1	5	21949	17	147	21	33	645.6	54	8	37
OIL	6	Nil	Nil	6	25220	3	Nil	Nil	NA	2.95	Nil	Nil	NA
HOEC	2	1	Nil	3	4074	1	3	1	66	2.46	2	1	66
GSPCL	4	1	Nil	5	4760	36	30	4	40	21.04	7	2	29
JOGPL	3	Nil	Nil	3	2360	13	Nil	Nil	NA	Nil	Nil	Nil	NA
GAZPROM	Nil	1	Nil	1	7818	2	Nil	Nil	NA	6.59	Nil	Nil	NA
CANORO	1	Nil	Nil	1	1444	1	Nil	Nil	NA	1.91	Nil	Nil	NA
HARDY	Nil	1	Nil	1	859	2	1	Nil	Zero	10.14	Nil	Nil	Zero
ESSAR	2	Nil	Nil	2	430	9	5	1	20	6.31	1	1	34
PHOENIX	2	Nil	Nil	2	9486	9	3	Nil	Zero	6.79	3	Nil	Zero

in Kutch and Mumbai Basins, Western Offshore, and 5 in KG basin, Eastern Offshore. All these offshore discoveries were by ONGC. In 2005-06, discoveries made by ONGC are B-9-1 (Gas) within Daman Fm. in Saurashtra-Dahanu and RV-1 (Gas) within Panna Fm. in Western Offshore and GS-15-E-1 (Gas) within Ravva Fm. in (KG) Eastern Offshore.

Out of the 25 Onland discoveries, 13 discoveries were made by OIL in the Upper Assam Shelf and 12 discoveries were made by ONGC in Rajasthan, Cambay, Cauvery, K-G and in the Assam Arakan Basins. In 2005-06, discoveries made by OIL were Moran-109 (Gas) in Oligocene Barail Sand, Bazaloni-1 (Oil & Gas) in Oligocene Barail Sand, Moran-107 (Oil & Gas) in Lakadong+Therria Sand of Eocene age, Baghjan-2 (Oil & Gas) and Barekuri-4 (Oil & Gas) in Langpar Sand of Late Cretaceous age. The discoveries made by ONGC were Turputallu (gas) in K-G and Mekeypore (Oil) in the Upper Assam Shelf.

Private/JV Companies

In the last 6 years, under the PSC regime Pvt./JV companies have made 59 significant hydrocarbon discoveries (as on September, 06), both in the NELP and Pre-NELP blocks. These discoveries were made in five major areas: Krishna-Godavari offshore, Mahanadi–NEC offshore, Gulf of Cambay, onland Rajasthan and Cambay Basins.

M/s RIL made a series of oil & gas discoveries in their deep water block KG-DWN-98/3 through the drilling and testing of Dhirubhai wells 18, 19, 22, 23 and 26. In the block KG-OSN-2001/2 Reliance has discoveries oil & gas in Dhirubhai-24 and 25. Recently in the block KG-OSN-2001/1 M/s RIL has discovered Oil & Gas in Dhirubhai #28. Recently gas discoveries namely Dhirubhai–20, 21 in Upper Miocene Pay Sand made by M/s Reliance India Ltd (RIL) in shallow offshore block NEC-OSN-97/2 located in the Mahanadi-NEC basin have upgraded the category of the basin from Cat.-III to Cat.-II. When these discoveries are put on production along with earlier discoveries, the category of the basin will be further upgraded to Cat.-I and will become the 8th basin with established commercial production.

In deepwater block KG-DWN-98/2. M/s. ONGC made three important discoveries: DWN-A-1 (Gas), U-1 (Gas) & W-1 (Gas).

Figure 3.1

New Significant Discoveries

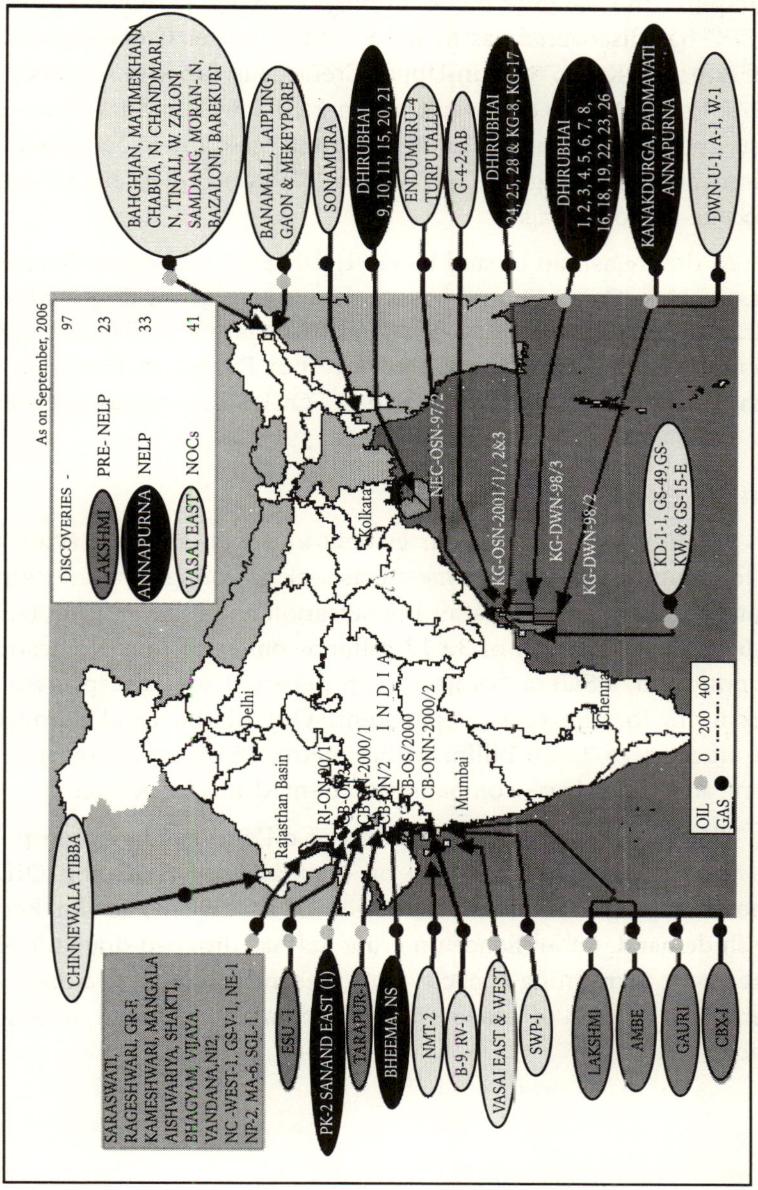

Source: Director General of Hydrocarbon (DGH), E&P Reports, 2005-06.

Recently in block CB-ONN-2000/1, M/s. GSPC has discovered oil & gas in Sanand East (1) Olpad. It also discovered oil in Kalol in well Tarapur-1 in CB-ON/2 block. In offshore block KG-OSN-2001/3, M/s. GSPC has discovered gas in KG-8 well in Lower Cretaceous Sand and oil & gas in KG-17 well in Upper Cretaceous Sand. In CB-ON/3 block, M/s. Essar Oil has discovered oil in ESU-1 well and its commerciality was approved in August, 2006. In Panna-Mukta field M/s. BGEPIL has discovered oil and gas in SW Panna (SWP-1) in Bassein Limestone of Eocene-Oligocene age.

In the Rajasthan onland block RJ-ON-90/1 in Barmer-Sanchor sub-basin, M/s. Cairn Energy has made a string of oil & gas discoveries *viz.*, NI-2, NC-west-1 & GS-V-1 in Fathegarh Fm. These discoveries along with previous discoveries have put Rajasthan firmly on the oil map of India. In RJ-ON/6 block M/s. FOCUS Energy has discovered gas in SGL-1 well (see Table 3.5).

Oil-Gas Production

The dominance of PSUs is evident in the oil and gas sector, though a few numbers of both domestic as well as foreign private companies have entered the sector after liberalisation and restructuring (see Table 3.6). In 2005-06, out of 32.18 million tonnes of total domestic crude production, PSUs account for 86 per cent and the private sector accounts for the rest 14 per cent. Out of the total domestic gas production of 32.20 billion cubic metre, PSUs accounted for 77 per cent and the private companies accounted for 23 per cent.

The exploration and production of oil and gas has been primarily in the hands of two national oil companies: ONGC and OIL. Over the years, the domestic production of crude oil has not kept pace with demand. Self-reliance on crude oil has dropped dramatically with the spurt in refining capacity and presently stands at a mere 30 per cent. The trends of crude oil production and demand are shown in Table 3.7.

Table 3.5

Discoveries made by Pvt/JVs in NELP and Pre-NELP Blocks and Fields

Sl. No.	Year	Block/Field	Bidding Round	Operator	Name of Discovery	Oil/Gas	Date of Discovery	Present Status
1.	1999-2000	Ravva	Field	Cairn	Ravva Sattelite	Gas	May 1999	On production since Nov 1999
2.		RJ-ON-90/1	Pre NELP	Cairn	Guda	Oil	Aug-99	Under Evaluation by operator
3.	2000-01	CB-OS/2	Pre NELP	Cairn	Lakshmi	Gas/Oil	May, 2000 /April '02	Producing since Nov. 2003.
4.					Ambe	OiVGas	November, 2000	Declared commercial on 5.04.06.
5.					Gauri	Oil/Gas	Dec, 2000	Production since April 2004.
6.					Parvati	Oil	January 2001	Relinquished
7.	2001-2002	RJ-ON-90/1	Pre NELP	Caim	Saraswati	Oil	Nov.'2001	Development plan approved on 27.05.06
8.		KG-DWN-	NELP I	Cairn	Annapuma	Gas	June, 2001	Discovered by Caim.
9.		98/2			Kanak Durga	Oil/Gas	August, 2001	Now Block is with
10.					Padmavati	Oil/Gas	October, 2001	ONGC.
11.	2002-2003	RJ-ON-90/1	Pre NELP	Cairn	Rageshwari	Oil	February 2003	Development plan approved on 27.05.06
12.		KG-DWN-98/3	NELP I	RIL	Dhirubhai-1	Gas	October, 2002	Dhirubhai-1,2&3 declared as commercial.
13.					Dhirubhai-2	Gas	October, 2002	Development plan for Dhirubhai 1&3 approved.

contd. ...

...contd. ...

Sl. No.	Year	Block/Field	Bidding Round	Operator	Name of Discovery	Oil/Gas	Date of Discovery	Present Status
14.					Dhirubhai-3	Gas	October, 2002	
15.					Dhirubhai-4	Gas	January, 2003	Commerciality under review
16.		CB-ONN-2000/2	NELP II	NIKO	Bhima-1	Gas	Nov,02	On Prod from Oct, 04
17.					NS	Gas	Jan, 03	On Prod from May, 04
18.	2003-2004	RJ-ON-90/1	Pre NELP		Kameshwari	Oil	October'03	Under Evaluation by operator
19.					Mangla	Oil	January'04	Development plan
20.					Greater Rageshwari (GR-F)	Gas	Jan'04	approved on 27.05.06
21.				Cairn	NA (Aishwarya)	Oil	March'04	
22.		CB-OS-2	Pre NELP	Caim	CBX Structure	Gas	Feb 04	Development plan approved on 28.02.06
23.		RavvaRavva	Field	Cairn	Dhirubhai-5	Gas	July, 2003	Under Evaluation by operator
24.			Field	Cairn	Dhimbhai-6	Gas	July, 2003	Commerciality under review
25.	2004-2005	RJ-ON-90/1	Pre NELP	Caim	NC (Shakti)	Oil	April'04	Commerciality under review.
26.					NV (Bhagyam)	Oil	August, 04	
27.					NR-1	Oil	Sept, 04	Under Evaluation by operator
28.					NR-2	Oil	September 2004	Under Evaluation by operator
29.		KG-DWN-98/3	**NELP I**	**RIL**	Dhirubhai-7	Gas	May, 2004	Commerciality under review.

contd. ...

...contd. ...

Sl. No.	Year	Block/Field	Bidding Round	Operator	Name of Discovery	Oil/Gas	Date of Discovery	Present Status
30.					Dhirubhai-8	Gas	May, 2004	
31.					Dhirubhai-16	Gas	August, 2004	
32.		NEC-OSN-97/2			Dhirubhai-9	Gas	June'04	Commerciality approved on 02.05.2006.
33.					Dhirubhai-10	Gas	June'04	Commerciality approved on 02.05.2006.
34.					Dhirubhai-11	Gas	June'04	
35.					Dhirubhai-15	Gas	August, 2004	
36.		CB-ONN-2000/1	NELP II	GSPC	PK#2	Oil	August, 2004	Under Evaluation by operator
37.	2005-2006	RJ-ON-90/1	Pre NELP	Caim	NI#2	Oil	June 2005	Under Evaluation by operator
38.					GS-V-1	Gas	November 2005	Under Evaluation by operator
39.					NC-West-1	Oil	November 2005	Under Evaluation by operator
40.		CB-ON-2		GSPC	Tarapur-1	Oil	July, 05	Commerciality ap proved on 4.08.06
41.		CB-ON-3		Essar Oil Limited	ESU-1	Oil	July, 05	Under Evaluation by operator
42.		KG-DWN-98/3	NELPI	RIL	Dhirubhai-18	Gas	April 2005	Under Evaluation by operator
43.					Dhirubhai-19	Gas	April 2005	Commerciality under review.

contd. ...

...contd. ...

Sl. No.	Year	Block/Field	Bidding Round	Operator	Name of Discovery	Oil/Gas	Date of Discovery	Present Status
44.					Dhirubhai-22	Gas	August 2005	
45.					Dhirubhai-23	Gas	October 2005	
46.		NEC-OSN-97/2	NELPI	RIL	Dhirubhai-20	Gas	April 2005	Commerciality approved on 02.05.2006
47.					Dhirubhai-21	Gas	April 2005	Under Evaluation by operator
48.		KG-OSN-2001/3	NELP III	GSPC	KG-8	Gas	June 2005	Under Evaluation by operator
49.		KG-OSN-2001/2		RIL	Dhirubhai-24	Oil/Gas	December 05	Under Evaluation by operator
50.				ONGC	Dhirubhai-25	Oil/Gas	December 05	Under Evaluation by operator
51.		KG-DWN-98/2	NELPI	Cairn	DWN-U-1	Gas	January 06	Under Evaluation by operator
52.					DWN-A-1	Gas	January 06	Under Evaluation by operator
53.	2006-2007	KG-DWN-S 98/2	NELPI	ONGC	DWN-W-1	Gas	April 06	Under Evaluation by operator
54.		Panna-Mukta	Field	BGEPIL	SWP-1	Oil/Gas	May, 06	Under Evaluation by operator
55.		RJ-ON-90/6	NELP II	FOCUS	SGL#1	Gas	May, 06	Under Evaluation by operator
56.		KG-OSN-2001/3	NELP II	GSPC	KG-17	Oil/Gas	June 06	Under Evaluation by operator

contd. ...

...contd. ...

Sl. No.	*Year*	*Block/Field*	*Bidding Round*	*Operator*	*Name of Discovery*	*Oil/Gas*	*Date of Discovery*	*Present Status*
57.		KG-DWN-98/3	NELPI	**RIL**	Dhirubhai-26	Oil	June 06	Under Evaluation by operator
58.		CB-ON/2	Pre NELP	GSPC	Tarapur-G	Gas	July,06	Under Evaluation by operator
59.		CB-ONN-2000/1	NELP II	GSPC	Sanand East (1)	Oil & Gas	July,06	Under Evaluation by operator
60.		KG-OSN-2001/1	NELP **III**	**RIL**	Dhirubhai-28	Gas	Sept, 06	Under Evaluation by operator
61.		MN-OSN-2000/2	NELP II	ONGC	MDW-2A	Gas	Dec,06	Under Evaluation by operator
62.		KG-DWN-98/2	NELPI		DWN-UD-1	Gas	Dec,06	Under Evaluation by operator
63.		CY-OS/2	Pre NELP	HARDY	FANA-1	Gas	January, 07	Under Evaluation by operator
64.		KG-DWN-98/3	NELP-1	**RIL**	Dhirubhai -31	Gas	Mar-07	Under Evaluation by operator
65.		NEC-OSN-97/2	NELP-1	**RIL**	Dhirubhai -32	Gas	Mar-07	Under Evaluation by operator

Table 3.6

Oil & Gas Industry Structure in India, 2004-05

Company	*Share (in Per cent)*
E&P: Total Domestic Production-33 MMT	
ONGC	78
Oil India Ltd	9
Pvt./JV: Reliance, Cairn, HOEC, Premier, GSPC, etc	13
Refining Capacity- 127.36 MTPA	
IOCL (IBP, CPCL, BRPL)	42
HPCL	10
BPCL (KRL, NRL)	14
Reliance	26
Others (Essar, Shell, ONGC-MRPL, OVAL)	8
Distribution: Total Retail Outlets- 27056	
IOCL	50
HPCL	24
BPCL	24
RIL	1
EOI	1

Source : MoPNG, 2004-05.

Downstream Sector

Refining

As of April, 2006 there are a total of 18 refineries in the country comprising 17 in the Public Sector, and one in the private sector. To meet the growing demand of petroleum products, the refining capacity in the country has been gradually increased over the years by setting up of new refineries in the country as well as by expanding the refining capacity of the existing refineries. The total refining capacity in the country as on 1.4.2006 stands at 132.46 MMTPA. Table 3.8 details company-wise locations, installed capacities and throughputs of all the refineries.

The public sector share in the total refinery capacity stood at 75.08 per cent. The rest is in the private sector: the 9.69 MTPA Hindustan Petroleum Corporation Ltd (HPCL)/AV Birla Group JV at Mangalore,

Table 3.7

Trend of Crude Oil Production and Demand in India 1990-91–2005-2006

(MT)

Year	Production		Domestic Total	Net Import	Total Demand	Import as Per cent of Demand
	Onshore	Offshore				
1990-91	11.83	21.19	33.02	20.70	53.72	38.53
1991-92	11.38	18.96	30.34	24.00	54.34	44.17
1992-93	11.20	15.75	26.95	29.25	56.20	52.05
1993-94	11.65	15.38	27.03	30.82	57.85	53.28
1994-95	12.01	20.23	32.24	27.35	59.59	45.90
1995-96	11.85	23.32	35.17*	27.34	62.51	44.73
1996-97	11.37	21.53	32.90*	33.91	66.36	50.76
1997-98	11.44	22.37	33.86*	34.50	68.36	50.47
1998-99	11.50	21.20	32.70*	39.80	72.50	54.90
1999-00	11.20	21.30	32.50*	53.50	86.00	62.21
2000-01	11.71	20.72	32.43*	74.09	103.44	71.62
2001-02	11.81	20.22	32.03*	78.70	107.27	72.77
2002-03	11.39	21.65	33.04*	81.98	112.55	72.83
2003-04	11.45	21.91	33.37*	90.43	121.80	74.24
2004-05	11.59	22.39	33.98*	95.86	127.40	75.24
2005-06**	11.43	20.76	32.19*	99.40	130.14	76.37

Note: * includes oil production through Pvt./JV Companies; ** Provisional.

Source: Ministry of Petroleum and Natural Gas (MoPNG) (various years). *Basic Statistics on Indian Petroleum and Natural Gas*. GoI.

Karnataka, and the 33 MMTPA refinery of Reliance Petroleum Ltd at Jamnagar, Gujarat. Following the recommendation of the Nitish Sengupta Committee on the merger of stand-alone refineries with integrated refining-marketing companies, the government sold its stake in the Kochi Refineries Ltd (KRL) and the Numaligarh Refinery Ltd (NRL} to BPCL and that in the BRPL (Bonaigaon Refineries and Petro-chemicals Ltd) and the CPCL (Chennai Petroleum Corporation Ltd) to the IOC. After the restructuring, the IOC accounts for the major share of the country's refining capacity with a total capacity of 41.3 MMTPA. Map 3b shows the location of all the existing and proposed refineries with relevant details.

Table 3.8

Installed Capacity and Refinery Throughput

(million tons per annum, MMTPA)

Refinery/Location	*Installed Capacity*	*Refinery Crude Throughput*						
	As of 1st April'06	*1990-91*	*2000-01*	*2001-02*	*2002-03*	*2003-04*	*2004-05*	*2005-06*
Public Sector	99.4	51.7	77.4	77.6	82.0	89.4	93.1	96.9
IOC, Guwahati	1.0	0.7	0.7	0.6	0.4	0.8	1.0	0.8
IOC, Barauni	6.0	2.4	3.1	2.8	2.9	4.3	5.0	5.5
IOC, Koyali	13.7	9.3	12.0	11.6	12.4	12.7	11.6	11.5
IOC, Haldia	6.0	2.8	3.8	4.0	4.5	4.5	5.4	5.5
IOC, Mathura	8.0	7.8	7.1	8.0	8.2	8.2	6.3	7.9
IOC, Digboi	0.6	0.5	0.6	0.6	0.5	0.6	0.6	0.6
IOC, Panipat	6.0	0	5.7	5.8	6.1	6.3	6.3	6.5
Total IOC	41.3	23.7	33.2	33.7	35.2	37.6	36.6	38.5
BPCL. Mumbai	12.0	6.9	8.6	8.7	8.7	8.7	9.1	10.2
HPCL, Mumbai	5.5	5.7	5.5	5.6	6.0	6.1	6.1	6.2
HPCL, Visakhapatnam	7.5	3.4	6.4	6.7	6.8	7.5	8.1	7.9
Total HPCL	13.0	9.2	11.9	12.3	12.9	13.6	14.2	14.2
KRL, Kochi	7.5	5.0	7.5	6.7	7.5	7.8	7.9	6.9
CPCL, Manali	9.5	5.6	6.0	6.1	6.1	6.3	8.1	9.6
CPCL, Marimanam	1.0	0	0.5	0.5	0.6	0.6	0.7	0.6
Total CPCL	10.5	5.6	6.6	6.6	6.8	7.0	8.9	10.3
BRPL, Bongaigaon	2.3	1.1	1.4	1.4	1.4	2.1	2.3	2.3
NRL, Numaligarh	3.0	0	1.4	2.3	1.8	2.2	2.0	2.1
ONGC, Tatipaka	0.08	0	0	0.01	0.09	0.09	0.09	0.09
MRPL, Mangalore	9.7	0	6.4	5.4	7.2	10.0	11.8	12.0
Private Sector	33.0	0	26.0	29.6	30.5	32.3	34.3	33.1
RPL, Jamnagar	33.0	0	26.0	29.6	30.5	32.3	34.3	33.1
Total	132.4	51.7	103.4	107.2	112.5	121.8	127.4	130.1

Note: CPCL and BRPL are subsidiaries of IOC; KRL and NRL are subsidiaries of BPCL; and MRPL is a subsidiary of ONGC.

Source: MoPNG, 2007.

Consumption

The demand for petroleum products is linked with the energy requirements of the country, which is a function of the level of economic activity as measured by the GDP. Presently, India is undergoing major economic and industrial reforms for integrating its economy with the global economy. In the liberalised scenario, the

Table 3.9

Sale of Petroleum Products in India, 1997-98 to 2005-06 ('000 Tonne)

Products	1997-98	1998-99	1999-00	2000-01	2001-02	2002-03	2003-04	2004-05	2005-06*
LPG	4803	5352	6421	7016	7728	8351	9305	10245	10304
Mogas	5182	5507	5909	6613	7011	7570	7897	8251	8648
Naphtha	6590	8891	10801	11673	11728	11929	11868	13993	12262
NGL	768	330	91	6	27	32	0	0	0
Others	523	451	1309	4006	3124	3873	5265	2712	2283
Light Distillates	17866	20531	24531	29314	29618	31755	34335	35201	33497
SKO	11065	12243	11898	11307	10432	10405	10230	9395	9359
ATF	2108	2112	2197	2249	2256	2269	2484	2813	3299
HSD	36071	37217	39295	37958	36546	36644	37074	39650	40152
LDO	1235	1278	1512	1399	1592	2063	1619	1477	885
Others	424	480	532	554	613	684	616	572	505
Middle Distillates	50903	53330	55434	53467	51439	52065	52023	53907	54200
FO	7168	7973	7690	7664	8451	8027	8312	9136	8842
LSHS/HHS	4323	4537	4763	4989	4531	4711	4633	4404	3890
Lubes	1081	1097	1243	1115	1137	1250	1427	1348	2104
Bitumen	2178	2412	2879	2774	2584	2986	3373	3339	3515
Petroleum Coke	227	393	328	448	1798	2563	2877	3129	4432
Paraffin	28	36	53	43	45	41	41	80	232
other waxes	45	76	89	62	51	13	20	0	96
Others	471	177	76	198	778	715	710	1090	1112
Heavy Ends	15521	16701	17121	17293	19375	20306	21393	22526	24223
Total	84290	90562	97086	100074	100432	104126	107751	111634	111920
Refinery Fuel	3514	3700	5544	6900	7273	7650	8240	8537	9125
Grand Total	87804	94262	102630	106974	107705	111776	115991	120171	121045

Note: * Provisional. 1994-95 onwards total and product-wise consumption includes private sales also.

Source: MoPNG, 2007.

hydrocarbon sector has been identified as one of the main areas of focus. Major policy changes are planned for the vital sector to make the oil industry globally competitive. With the reforms package formulated and expected high growth in all economic sectors, the demand for petroleum products is expected to show a compound growth of about 7 per cent. In absolute terms, the demand for petroleum products by the year 2006-07 is expected to increase from the present level of 80 million tonnes to 155 million tonnes per annum.

The demand for petroleum products registered an increase of 47 per cent during the period 2000-01 to 2005-06 (Table 3.9). In 2005-06, HSD accounted for the highest share in total petroleum product sales in the country followed by LPG sales and naphtha sales (see Figure 3.2).

Figure 3.2

Product-wise Share in Total Sale of Petroleum Products, 2005-06

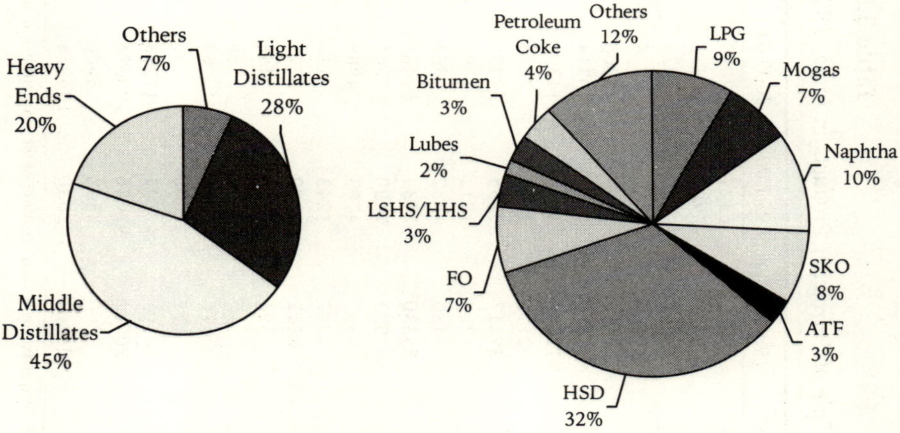

Source: Prepared from MoPNG, 2007.

Based on the 2005-2006 data, the share of the public sector in total petroleum product sales was 85.9 per cent, up from 84.8 per cent in the previous year. Further, over the period from 1997-98 to 2003-04, the annual average growth rate of private sector has been 23.3 per cent as compared to 2.2 per cent for the public sector. This has resulted in a jump of private sector share from 5.3 per cent in 1997-98 to 15.2 per cent in 2004-05. Major products in the portfolio of private players in the market are naphtha and raw petroleum coke which make up 48 per cent of the total private sector sales. The total production of petroleum products has been 119.7 MT in 2005-06, up from 118.6 MT in the previous year. India for the seventh year in a row emerged as a net exporter of petroleum products. For 2005-06, India had a net export of 9.9 MT of petroleum products.

Natural Gas

The start of gas utilisation in India can be traced back to the period after the commissioning of the Hazira-Bijaipur-Jagdishpur (HBJ) gas pipeline in 1986, which linked the gas producing areas in the western part of India to the consuming states in the north-western part of India. Since then the government of India has appointed a number of committees to assess the optimum use of gas. Initially, gas in India was allocated for fertiliser production. Over the years, however the utilisation of gas has taken place for other purposes such as generation of electricity, etc. the structure of gas consumption has also changed. Current gas consumption for power generation equals that for fertiliser production, with each sector accounting for about 40 per cent of the total gas consumption in India.

Although the gas industry has witnessed a rapid development since, gas usage accounted for only 8.4 per cent of the total primary energy consumption in the country in 2006. The demand for natural gas in India has been growing rapidly. Gas sales in the country increased at an annual rate of 9.5 per cent during the period 1990-91–2005-2006. Gas has been primarily used as fuel in power generation and as feedstock in fertiliser production. Gas production in 2005-06 was 32.2 billion cubic metres. The three main producing basins in the country—the Western offshore region, the Cambay basin in Gujarat, and the Upper Assam region—are in the mature phase of exploration. As per the projections of the Sub-group on Utilisation of Natural Gas constituted under the *Hydrocarbon Vision 2025*, domestic gas availability is expected to decline to about 16 BCM by the year 2011-12. On the other hand, the demand for natural gas in the country has been growing rapidly. Netting of LPG production and gas for ONGC's own use, gas sales aggregated 23.8 billion cubic metres. Table 3.10 shows the detailed area-wise and sector-wise gas consumption pattern in India for the period 1999-2000.

Moreover, with gas production in the country set to increase by 50 per cent when Reliance' gas comes to the market, the gas marketing scenario is all set to change. If Reliance is unable to sell its entire production in the east coast at a lucrative price, this may find its way into the west coast of the country where it will compete with domestic as well as imported LNG. Map 6 shows the prominent LNG terminals, proposed gas import pipelines and National gas grid.

Demand and Supply of Natural Gas

Natural gas offtake at 31,025 MCM (million cubic metres) in 2005-2006 was higher as compared to 30,775 MCM in 2004-2005. Seventy-one (71) per cent of total natural gas used was for energy purposes, while the rest was used as feedstock in fertiliser and petrochemical industries (Table 3.11).

Table 3.10

Area-wise and Sector-wise Gas Consumption in India, 1999-2000

(MMSCMD)

Region/State	*Fertiliser*	*Power*	*Sponge Iron*	*Others*	*Total*
Western Offshore:					
Uran	4.8	3.6	1.5	0.8	10.7
Hazira	2.8	—	1.7	0.9	5.4
HBJ	13.4	11.0	—	2.8	27.2
Sub-Total	21.0	14.6	3.2	4.5	43.3
Western Onshore	1.2	4.1	—	1.4	6.7
Krishna	1.8	2.5	—	0.1	4.4
Godavari Basin	—	—	—	—	—
Rajasthan	—	0.4	—	—	0.4
Cauvery Basin	—	0.0	—	0.2	0.2
North East	—	1.4	—	0.1	1.5
Total	**24.0**	**23.0**	**3.2**	**6.3**	**56.5**

Source : Gas Authority of India Ltd (GAIL).

As shown in Table 3.11, the use of Industrial fuel showed the highest percentage growth over last year (6 per cent), followed by captive use (2.1 per cent). Under the directives given by the Supreme Court of India, there has been an increase in the use of CNG (compressed natural gas) as a fuel for the transport sector. IGL (Indraprastha Gas Ltd.) in Delhi and MGL (Mahanagar Gas Ltd.) in Mumbai are engaged in developing city gas distribution projects for the supply of CNG and PNG (piped natural gas) in these cities. IGL is catering to the needs of over 90,000 vehicles of different categories through 121 CNG stations, at present. Delhi has the world's largest fleet of around 13,400 CNG buses, which includes around 4,500 mini buses. MGL has also set up 75 CNG stations that cater to more than 1,00,000 vehicles, which are mainly three-wheelers and taxis.

The current gas demand is constrained by supply. To bridge this gap, public and private sector companies are pursuing several gas import options. Many LNG terminals have been planned along the east and west coasts of the country, while several pipelines are also in the planning stage.

Table 3.11

Sectoral Consumption of Natural Gas (MCM)

Consumption	*1990-91*	*2000-01*	*2001-02*	*2002-03*	*2003-04*	*2004-05*	*2005-06*
Energy Purposes	6375	17199	18234	19767	20940	21328	22052
Power Generation	3634	8801	9214	10510	11478	12099	11878
Industrial Fuel	827	2870	2979	2939	3099	3569	3780
Tea Plantation	89	151	147	119	142	142	151
Domestic Fuel	50	335	485	654	93	343	75
Captive usage/ LPG shrinkage	1775	5004	5339	5409	4865	4944	5048
Others	0	38	70	136	12163	231	1120
Non-Energy use	6391	10661	9803	10197	9966	9447	8973
Fertiliser Industry	5612	8480	7957	7955	7889	8173	7762
Petrochemicals	409	779	909	1027	1128	1236	1175
CNG	0	0	0	0	1	0	0
Others	370	1402	937	1223	948	38	38
Total	12766	27860	28037	29964	30906	30775	31025
			Percentage to Total Consumption				
Energy Purposes	49.9	61.7	65.0	66.0	67.8	69.3	71.1
Non-Energy Purposes	50.1	38.3	35.0	34.0	32.2	30.7	28.9

Note: Excludes gas supplied to IGL, MGL, Bhagyanagar Gs, TNGCL, BMC & CGCL and sponge iron use.

Source: MoPNG (2006-07). *Basic Statistics*.

Demand Projections

Oil Demand

Generally, demand projections are made in the short- as well as long-term period, so that appropriate policies can be devised and implemented in time of need. The short-and long-term outlooks for oil demand are essentially supply driven, considering the trends in the domestic as well as world scenarios. And, the trends in the present scenario are extrapolated to reach possible scenarios in the near or distant future.

The demand for oil compared with an other primary source, i.e., coal in India is expected to grow vigorously in the coming decades resulting from economic growth, population changes, increases in disposable incomes of households, and changes in the capital intensity of the Indian economy and as environmental factors and the cost of rehabilitation of land in coal-mining areas add significantly to the cost of coal mining. In addition, given the fact that coal reserves are predominantly located in the eastern and south-eastern part of the country, transportation costs, particularly where new transport capacity additions are involved, would make the price of coal at consumption points in other parts of the country much higher than current levels.

As per one short-term estimate,[11] the oil demand of 75 MMTS in 1995-96 is expected to reach 115 MMTS by the year 2001 and to 155 MMTS by the year 2006. This estimate is based on a 6 per cent GDP growth rate during the 1990s. Another estimate[12] projects the crude oil demand of 91 MMTS in 1999-2000 to reach 364 MMTS by the year 2024-25. The details of the estimate are given in Table 3.12.

One set of forecasts made by the TEESE[13] (TERI Energy Economy Simulation and Evaluation) model shows an increase in demand for oil products from 119 MTS in 2001 to 157 MTS in 2011. However, TERI has made another set of forecasts up to the period 2047. The demand for oil in the base case scenario in the forecast, has been extrapolated

11. See *Oil Asia*. January-March 1999. p.16.

12. MoPNG (2000). *Hydrocarbon Vision 2025*.

13. As cited in MoPNG (1997). *Restructuring Group Report 1996*. p.5.

from the present trends and practices, adds up to 667 MTS by 2047.[14] In this sectoral projection for oil has also been made, which shows that the transport sector continues to drive the demand for oil in the country. In addition, oil demand for non-energy uses, e.g. feedstock, industrial consumables (greases, waxes, lubricants, etc.), and bituminous carpeting, and by industries is also high. Table 3.13 shows the estimates.

Table 3.12

Projections of Supply/Demand—Petroleum Products 1999-2000–2024-2025

(MMTS)

Year	*Demand (without meeting gas deficit)*	*Demand (with meeting gas demand)*	*Estimated Refining Capacity*	*Estimated Crude Requirement*
1999-2000	91	103	69	69
2001-2002	111	138	129	122
2006-2007	143	179*	167	173
2011-2012	195	195**	184	190
2024-2025	363	368	358	364

Notes : * Assuming 15 MMTSPA of LNG import by 2007.
** Assuming that by 2012, adequate gas is available through imports and domestic sources.

Source : MoPNG (2000). *Hydrocarbon Vision 2025.*

Table 3.13

Sectoral Oil Demand (MTS) Projections: The Base Case Scenario

Year	*Industries*	*Non-Energy*	*Transport*	*Agriculture*	*Commercial*	*Domestic*	*Power*	*Total*
1997	12	13	39	1	2	14	3	84
2019	40	38	101	2	14	25	14	234
2047	126	119	292	4	50	35	41	667
1997-2047 (%)*	4.7	4.6	4.1	3.1	6.3	1.9	5.7	4.2

Note : * Compound Annual Growth Rate.

Source : TERI (2001). *TERI Directions, Innovations, and Strategies for Harnessing Action (DISHA).* p.280.

14. TERI (2001). *TERI Directions, Innovations, and Strategies for Harnessing Action (DISHA).*

Supply Projections

Domestic crude production is expected to fall short of the targets. Though the Planning Commission has set a target of 180 MTS during the Ninth Five-year Plan period, it is estimated that actual production will be much lower, at about 162 MTS, according to the mid-term review of the Plan. Crude production in 2000-01 aggregated 32.7 MTS as against a refining throughput of 90.8 MTS. With an increase in domestic refining capacity, crude imports have increased considerably with imports in 2001-02 expected to be about 77 MTS.

Thus as the trends show large imports of crude are inevitable, which is also strengthened from the fact that improved domestic refining activity will prompt more imports of crude to feed the refineries which will increase value-added in the economy. The long-term import requirement of India has been well summarised by TERI DISHA, as shown in Table 3.14. Map 4 shows the existing and proposed crude pipelines in India.

Table 3.14

Projected Demand and Supply of Crude Oil:
The Base Case Scenario

(MT)

Year	*Demand*	*Refinery Throughput*	*Domestic Production*	*Imports*
1997	83	69	34	35
2019	234	246	80	166
2047	667	702	80	622

Note : Indicative refining throughput (assuming refinery fuel and loss at 5 per cent and no product imports) is compared to domestic crude production to estimate import requirements.

Source : TERI (2001). *TERI Directions, Innovations, and Strategies for Harnessing Action (DISHA)*. p.280. New Delhi.

As evident, India is poised to depend on oil supplies from overseas to meet its surging demand in the future. As per the IEA, India's external oil dependency will increase from the present level of around 65 per cent (2002) to 77 per cent by the year 2010 and to 86 per cent by the year 2020 (Figure 3.3).

Figure 3.3

India—External Oil Dependency Outlook

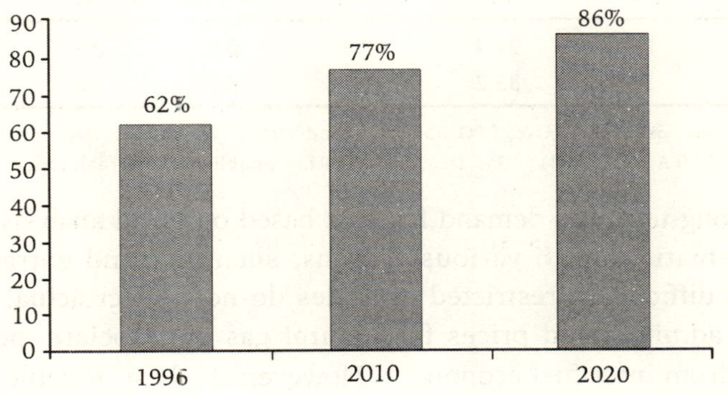

Source : IEA, March 2000.

Natural Gas Demand Projections

The short-term outlook for gas demand is essentially supply driven, with project expansions being linked to gas imports. LNG imports on the west coast are expected to materialise by 2005. Additional gas from LNG terminals would cater to: (i) current deficits of existing gas consumers, i.e., the difference between gas allocated to them and actually supplies received; and (ii) new gas based projects. In case of the power sector, current shortfalls add up to 10.3 MMSCMD. In addition, new gas based power projects would require about 20.6 MMSCMD of gas. Total additional short-term gas requirements are expected to be about 30.9 MMSCMD. With regard to gas demand for fertiliser production, the Planning Commission has estimated a demand-supply gap for urea of 3 MMTS by 2004.[15] For other sectors, new capacities/projects have not been considered and the short-term outlook essentially reflects the difference between current allocation to various sectors and sales. Table 3.15 shows the short-term gas demand outlook.[16]

15. Planning Commission (1998). *Ninth Five Year Plan Documents*. GoI.

16. TERI/FACTS (2003). "Gas Demand". TERI, Unpublished Internal Paper.

Table 3.15

Short-term Gas Demand Outlook

(MMSCMD)

Year	*Power*	*Fertiliser*	*Industry*	*Transport*	*Domestic*	*Total**
1999	25.0	24.4	9.1	0.1	0.1	59.4
2005	55.9	33.2	11.9	0.5	1.3	102.7

Note : * Gas for Captive Use, LPG Shrinkage and Other Non-Energy Uses.
Source : TERI/FACTS (2003). "Gas Demand". TERI, Unpublished Internal Paper.

The long-term gas demand forecast based on trend analysis in India is problematic due to various reasons, such as trend extrapolation becomes difficult as restricted gas sales do not reflect actual demand and the administered prices for natural gas disassociate 'perceived' demand from inter-fuel economics. However, the best possible scenario for forecasting gas demand is that which is based on criteria such as population growth and more importantly the economic growth rate, which is called GDP indexed demand growth (GIDG).[17] Table 3.16 summarises the available forecast studies on gas demand in India, apart from the well-used TERI technique.

Supply Projection

A sub-group on the Development and Utilisation of Natural Gas under the *Hydrocarbon Vision 2025* offers different scenarios of the likely production of domestic gas by 2024-25. The analysis is based on the estimates provided under the 'given scenario' based on production profile of existing fields. The trends have been interpolated to assess the gas production in 2019 and extrapolated to estimate the same in 2047, as shown in Table 3.17.

As shown in the table, domestic gas production is expected to be marginal by 2047. These are very conservative estimates based on the rate at which existing fields are being depleted and assume that no new discoveries are made. However, in the absence of any reliable estimates or targets for the future (unlike oil in the *Hydrocarbon Vision*), these figures have been adopted. This implies that projected import requirements will change as and when new gas fields are discovered and exploited.

17. The GIDG parameter is the innovation of TERI.

Table 3.16

Various Gas Demand Projections

(MMSCMD)

Scenario I: Gas Master Plan					*Scenario II: Hydrocarbon Vision 2025*				
Year	*Power*	*Fertiliser*	*Others*	*Total*	*Year*	*Power*	*Fertiliser*	*Others*	*Total*
2001	40	38	12	89	2001	40	54	23	117
2006	73	38	12	122	2006	67	66	33	166
2011	112	38	12	161	2011	90	83	43	216
					2024	153	105	64	322

Scenario III: TERI/FACTS Study

Year	*Power*	*Fertiliser*	*Industry*	*Transport*	*Domestic*	*Total**
1999	25.0	24.4	9.1	0.1	0.7	59.4
2005**	55.9	33.2	11.9	0.5	1.3	102.7
2010	69.3	40.3	15.6	0.7	1.7	127.6
2015	78.8	46.3	21.9	1.0	2.7	150.8
CAGR	7.4%	4.1%	5.7%	15.4%	8.9%	6.0%

Notes : * Short-term Estimate (Supply Driven).
** Gas for Captive Use, LPG Shrinkage and Other Non-Energy Uses.

Source : TERI/FACTS Study. 2003.

Table 3.17

Projected Domestic Gas Production (BCM)

Year	*Production*
2001	25.6
2006	21.2
2011	16.4
2019	14.3
2024	13.1
2047	0.4

Source : *Hydrocarbon Vision 2025.*

The Deregulated Indian Oil and Gas Sector

Though the above analysis reflects the deregulation process in the Indian oil and gas sector, yet an in-depth analysis will reveal the emerging opportunities and challenges in the sector. The section below starts with a brief historical background of deregulation in the Indian oil and gas sector and focuses on various aspects and issues in the deregulated oil and gas regime in India.

Brief Historical Background of Deregulation

The period after the 1970s saw nationalisation of the oil industry, which resulted in the public sector dominance of the oil industry through buying up of private entities. In all public sector undertakings (PSUs), the government of India holds a stake of 51 per cent or more of the paid-up share capital. However, with the restructuring of the Indian economy in the 1990s the process of deregulation started in all sectors and also in the oil and gas sector with a view to transforming it into a vibrant and globally competitive industry. In this regard by April 2002, the sector became fully deregulated.

In the early 1950s, pricing was based on a system of 'valued stock account' (VSA). Under this system, the basic selling prices of major petroleum products were determined as the sum of free on board (fob) Ras Tanura price, ocean freight, insurance, ocean loss, import duty, interest and other charges as well as 10 per cent remuneration. However, the government decided to abandon this system of pricing as it was based on assumed costs rather than actual costs. Consequently, an Oil Price Enquiry Committee was set up in 1960, under the chairmanship of Mr. K.R. Damle.[18] The committee recommended that ceiling selling prices for bulk refined products should follow the 'import parity principle'.[19] Moreover, by the 1970s, it was felt that the refining capacity of the country was adequate to meet the needs and thus the dependence on imports of petroleum products was less. It was also felt that the West Asian product prices, which were the basis for determining the import parity prices, did not necessarily reflect the actual cost pattern and operations of Indian refiners. Thus the government introduced the 'Administered Pricing Mechanism (APM)'[20] in 1977, which was later modified by the Oil Cost Review Committee

18. See Mehta *op. cit.*, No. 4, pp.93-100.

19. For detail understanding of the principle of 'import parity', refer Horsnell *op. cit.*; and also see, International Trade Centre (1995). *International Procurement of Crude Oil and Petroleum Products.* Guide No. 24. UNCTAD/WTO (Import Management).

20. The APM essentially constituted a cost-plus pricing regime wherein costs were reimbursed as per standards laid out with respect to throughputs, yield pattern, fuel and loss, operating cost, capital employed, etc. companies were allowed a 12 per cent post-tax return on their net-worth and reimbursed their borrowing costs. For a clear understanding of the mechanism of APM and OPA and its different components, see Rao, Saudamini (2001). "The Indian Oil and Gas Sector Bracing for Deregulation", *Oil Asia Journal.* Mumbai. January-April-June. pp.25-54.

in 1984. The Oil Co-ordination Committee was set up in 1975 to manage Oil Pool Accounts and to coordinate supply and other matters in the oil and gas sector.

The APM was aimed at ensuring continuous availability of petroleum products to consumers at fairly stable prices and crude to the refiners, while ensuring the socioeconomic objectives of the government. However, in April 2002 the government dismantled the APM formula to initiate market determination of prices of petroleum products on import parity basis to get rid of subsidies—the major source of budget deficit.

Initiatives Prior to Deregulation

As mentioned in the earlier section of this chapter, exploration bidding rounds to attract private investment started in 1979, but were unsuccessful. Private participation in the refining sector in the form of joint ventures with the public sector was announced in 1986. The marketing of lubricant-based stocks was allowed in 1992. The government had allowed parallel marketing of LPG and SKO in 1993, under which the import of these products were decanalised and private parties were allowed to market them at market determined prices.

Rationale for Deregulation

There are various factors that have contributed significantly in initiating and carrying forward the deregulation process. Some of the factors have already been mentioned in this chapter. The other main factors can be analysed as follows:

- The main reason for the deregulation of the sector were the serious loopholes in the APM mechanism and its unintended effects, which were economically unsustainable. Oil pricing has been used as a tool for achievement of the objectives of the government of the day, divorced from the basic economic realities. The prices of politically sensitive products do not reflect the economic cost of the producer. Subsidies and cross-subsidies have resulted in wide distortion in consumer prices and the consumption pattern of petroleum products which resulted in dieselation of the economy and consequent automobile fleet of the country. In case of highly subsidised products, the low pricing much below its economic value has led to inefficient, wasteful use resulting in sub-optimal inter-fuel substitution. Political compulsions often dictate price administration and pricing system is thus inflexible to changes in global prices. In a country, where more than 50 per cent of the demand is met through imports of crude as well as products, such inflexibility can prove to be hazardous for the economy. The pool deficit became a source of serious concern. The APM provided little incentive for improving efficiency or productivity as returns were guaranteed on the capital employed. Competition was stifled with marketing companies acting as mere distribution companies.

- Over the last two decades, the import of petroleum products soared ten-fold from over 2.2 MTS in 1975 to nearly 18 MTS in 1995. Given the high level of imports in the Indian economy, the APM, which insulated the oil economy from the global market, had lost its utility. Further, it was estimated that during the 9th Plan period, an investment of about Rs. 1,24,000 crores would be required to create the necessary infrastructure to meet the surging demand, it was recognised that such a scale of investment was not possible to be initiated by the public sector. Participation of the private sector was therefore imperative, as before the APM was not attractive to the private investors.

So in 1995, the Ministry of Petroleum and Natural Gas (MoPNG) set up the Oil Industry Restructuring Group ('R' Group) to come up with a time bound programme for reforms in the petroleum sector. The Group prepared a blueprint for phased reform of the petroleum sector. As a follow up of the 'R' Group recommendation, the government had appointed an Expert Technical Group (ETG), an inter-ministerial committee, which was required to examine the various scenarios reflecting the impact of different levels of duty structure on various sectors. The ETG recommended a time bound programme of reforms to move towards a market-driven pricing mechanism for petroleum products in the country.

In addition, the refining sector was de-licensed in 1998. Further, while naphtha exports were de-canalised with effect from June 1998, furnace oil imports were de-canalised under the provision of the export-import policy in July 1998. Freight under-recoveries on HSD to the extent of 20 per cent were passed on in selling prices in January 1999. However, it may be noted that HSD prices are not being fixed at import parity, despite the government notification on the subject. Subsidies on HSD have, thus, inflated the deficit in the oil pool account. Administered HSD prices constitute a major distortion of the reform agenda.[21]

In a significant move towards deregulation, the GoI in 2001 announced decontrol of ATF prices and the disinvestment in IBP with bidders being required to commit themselves to an investment of Rs. 2,000 crores in exploration and marketing, refining, pipelines or terminals.

Features of Deregulation

Main features of deregulation as per the Gazette Notification[22] are as follows:

- Crude price payable by refineries will be on import parity.
- Retention price concept will be abolished for existing and new refineries.
- The tariff on crude and petroleum products will be rationalised in phases by 2001-02.
- Refineries will be free to decide their product prices except for LPG, MS, SKO, ATF and HSD. The refinery gate price for these five products till 2001-02 will be fixed by the Oil Coordination Committee (OCC) at adjusted import parity for existing refineries. The government in the beginning of every year will announce the adjustment factor.

Impacts on Different Aspects of the Oil-Gas Sector

As a result of deregulation the oil industry in India is witnessing penetration of private players and there is also indication of intense

---

21. TERI (2001). "Roadmap to Deregulation of the Indian Petroleum Industry", in *Reforms in Energy Sector*. New Delhi.

22. Acharya, K.K. *et al.* (1993). "Challenges in Deregulated Scenario", in *Hydro-Carbon Technology*. Centre for High Technology. August. p.1.

competition in the future as and when the reform process became fully operational. This can be substantiated from the developments in the sector. When the Indian lubricants market was decontrolled in 1993 to parallel marketing, there were 20 new entrants who captured about 12 per cent of the market share in just five years, eating into the market share of established players like the IOC and Bharat Petroleum Corporation Limited (BPCL). The market also witnessed a spate of joint ventures as the Indo Mobil between Mobil and IOC to blend, package, distribute and market the Mobil brand lubricants throughout India. Similar restructuring of the industry may be expected with the decontrol of transportation fuels—while the increase in number of new players may not be as high as in the case of lubes, primarily on account of conditional marketing rights, the degree of competition in this sector would be more severe. In fact, some of the private companies are now marketing super quality transport fuels for two-wheelers in the metro cities of the country.

Another impact of the deregulation can be noticed in the sourcing of crude oil. Till 2001, all PSU refineries had to source crude through the IOC, which was the sole canalising agent. Only the joint sector and private refineries had freedom in crude sourcing and importing. On March 14, 2001, the government extended this freedom to all PSU refineries. The move was welcomed by the industry as imports could now be tailored to suit the exact requirements of a particular refinery.

External Policy Initiatives

With regard to the external policy initiatives, two things can be considered. One is the attempt to diversify the source of oil imports either through holding oil equity in areas outside the Gulf or through joint ventures. Second are the policy initiatives for the import of LNG. In case of the first, except some achievement in the form of joint sector development in the Sudan and Russia's Sakhalin Project, nothing substantial has been achieved so far. This implies that India's dependence on its traditional supplier—the GCC countries—is most likely to continue for long.

Considering the burgeoning gap between the demand and supply of natural gas, the government has started promoting utilisation of natural gas. For this, in 1996, Petronet LNG was formed to facilitate imports of LNG. Four public sector hydrocarbon majors—IOC, BPCL, ONGC and GAIL promote this company. The LNG projects have been proposed by companies like Shell at Hazira, CMC Energy/Unocal/Grasim at Ennore, IOC/Petronas at Kakinada, Tata/Totalfina/GAIL at Mumbai and British Gas at Pipavav.

As the above analysis shows there are tremendous business opportunities in the deregulated Indian oil and gas regime. The prospective business opportunities in the form of volume of investment required in each sector can be summarised as follows (also see Annexure 3.6):

- *Exploration*: Investment perspectives for petroleum exploration till 2010 might be of the order of about US $4-6 billion. This amount covers the G&G (Geology and Geophysics) and exploratory drilling activities for oil and gas. Investment for other alternative energy exploration (Coal-Bed Methane, Gas-Hydrates, etc.) in this period could be around US $200 million.
- *Oil-Gas Production*: Rehabilitation and redevelopment of some of the major oil-gas producing fields has become one of the principal investment agenda, which need substantial investments. It is estimated that the production side of the upstream sector might require an investment of about 1 billion during the next 10-12 years. Therefore, the Indian owners of these fields are often looking for suitable partners who can participate in recharging, rehabilitation, and redevelopment of the fields on mutually acceptable terms.
- *Refining*: Investment opportunities in the Indian refining sector during the next 8-10 years aggregate to about US $20-25 billion, in order to achieve capacity addition of about 110 MMTS.
- *Natural Gas*: The quantitative mega images of the emerging investment opportunities in the business of natural gas in India for the next 15 years are as follows:

- Proposed sub-sea pipeline from Oman to India for importation of LNG from Oman: US $5 billion.

- Setting up of LNG terminals of 2.5 MMTSPA-10MMTSPA: US $1.1 billion.
- Southern Gas Grid: US $2.4 billion.
- Domestic Transportation Network of 2000 km: US $3.0 billion.
- Downstream (GAS) Business: US $10 billion.
- Importation of gas from Iran and/or other neighbouring countries and other related activities: US$ 5 billion.
- City distribution projects and technological development in principal sectors of the gas business in India: US $3.5 billion.
- Total: US $30 billion.

Source: *Oil Asia Journal*. January-March 1999. p.16.

The latest development[23] in the policy front by the Government of India also signifies major emerging opportunities in the oil and gas sector. The government in January 2004 lifted almost all curbs on foreign direct investment in the petroleum sector. Foreign investors will now be able to bring in 100 per cent FDI in refineries, marketing, explorations and pipelines—both natural gas and LNG. While removing existing FDI caps in these sectors, the government has also allowed investments via the automatic route instead of the existing Foreign Investment Promotion Board (FIPB) route. This investor-friendly move will encourage investments and do away with procedural delays.

The sectors where 100 per cent FDI has been allowed via the automatic route include refineries, marketing, investments in small and medium sized exploration blocks and petroleum product pipelines. However, these foreign investments are subject to sectoral conditions and guidelines. For instance, in the case of retail marketing where the existing cap of 74 per cent has been done away with, 100 per cent FDI has been allowed subject to the existing sectoral policy and regulatory framework. The policy requires companies to invest Rs. 2,000 crores in the petroleum sector either in refining, exploration or infrastructure (relating to the petroleum sector) to qualify for marketing licence. The licence is to be issued by the regulator in the oil and gas sector. This

23. "Full FDI Flow for Oil Exploration, Refining & Sales", *Times News Network*. Friday, 16, 2004 01:20:33 AM. Online at *http://www.indiatimes.com*

move is expected to attract foreign investments given the market size of the country and the growth potential of the industry.

In case of refining, where the government has allowed 100 per cent foreign equity investments via the automatic route, as against the existing policy of going through the FIPB route, it has been specified that this policy will not include PSU refineries where the cap of 26 per cent remains, but only be applicable for private sector refineries. However, given the existing refining capacity in the country which is in surplus to the demand in the country, it will be sometime before foreign investments come into this sector. In the case of pipelines, while the existing cap of 51 per cent has been removed, 100 per cent FDI via the automatic route has been allowed only in the petro-product segment. As far as natural gas and LNG pipelines are concerned, investments will have to be approved by the FIPB.

The new policy also removes the present FDI limit in oil exploration of 60 per cent in unincorporated joint ventures and 51 per cent in incorporated joint ventures. The government has allowed 100 per cent FDI via the automatic route in both small and medium sized fields subject to the policy on private participation in exploration of oil and the discovered fields of national oil companies.

Thus as the above discussion shows, India is vastly growing to be one of the largest energy markets of the world. It is a developing economy transiting from state regulated centrally planned economic discipline to the options, imperatives and practicalities of a competitive market economy. Therefore, it can be said that the Indian oil-gas sector is in the process of transformation from its normative present to a combative future. As mentioned by one analyst,

> The sector is confronted with reserve replacement, stagnant oil production, surmounting oil-gas demand, depleting and/or dysfunctioning reservoirs of some of the major oil fields, vastly expanding oil demand of the national economy, technological deficiencies, impacting the development of a deregulated oil-gas regime, and massive need of capital. All these problems and hazards are radically altering the risks, rewards and rationalising the future of business in the Indian oil-gas sector. On the other side, it is throwing up new possibilities and attractive opportunities for those countries/organisations/companies who are not threatened with the

impermanence of corporate prosperity in a constantly changing business world.[24]

Prognosis of segment-wise investment potential for the next 10-12 years (Table 3.18), of both upstream and downstream sectors of the Indian petroleum industry, opens up new opportunities for the oil and gas exporting GCC countries, given that, the GCC countries are the traditional energy suppliers to India and presently the GCC countries as a whole account for 65 per cent of India's energy imports.

Table 3.18

The Oil Demand of Investment in Indian Oil-Gas Sector till 2010

(US $ Billion)

Segments	*Investment Requirements*
1. Oil-gas and Coal Bed Methane Exploration	4-6
2. Oil-Gas Field Development, Rehabilitation and Production	15-20
3. Natural Gas and LNG, Storage, Importation, Transportation, Distribution and Marketing	20-30
4. Oil Refining	20-25
5. Product Pipelines	7-10
6. Tankage, Storage and Port Facilities	5-7
7. LPG Import, Distribution and Marketing	20-25
8. Oil Products Distribution and Marketing	
Total	**91-123**

Source : *Oil Asia Journal*, January-March 1999, and p.44.

SECTION II

GCC Oil and Gas Sector

GCC countries play a crucial role in the world energy scenario. The strategic importance of the GCC countries in the global oil regime over the years is attributed to the availability of prolific reserves and the low cost of production of oil. However, this position has been challenged in recent years by rising penetration of outside OPEC players into the global oil-gas regime, major restructuring and cost cutting by international oil firms, technological breakthroughs, conservation programmes, environmental legislation, and taxation

24. Bose *op. cit.*, No. 2.

adopted by industrial countries. Besides these events have been accompanied by two major developments: first, the declining influence of Gulf oil *vis-à-vis* OPEC in a new world oil market and second, major changes in the politics and economics of the Gulf oil producing countries that have increased the dependence on oil revenues, while at the same time arresting the growth of the national oil industry, rendering it unprepared to meet the ever-changing global developments.

Gulf Oil as a Unique Oil Supply Phenomenon

Since the early 1950s, outside the United States and the Former Soviet Union (FSU), Gulf oil has been the source of about 45 per cent of total world supply. Its enormous contribution to global oil supply has, even so, been overshadowed by the region's share of proven reserves. This has ranged from a low of about 61 per cent in 1981 to a high of 78 per cent in 1960, suggesting that the prolific nature of oil occurrence in the Gulf has never been matched by an equivalent dependence on its production, in spite of the extremely low cost of oil discovery and development in the region.[25] As mentioned by one analyst,

> The continuing indication for the past 40 years of a flat-or nearly flat-long run supply price curve for the Middle East oil up to potential level of production which, if they had been achieved, could have served most of the world's demand outside the FSU and the United States.[26]

It is also to be noted that the role of Gulf oil was critical to the industry's ability to meet the burgeoning demand during the 25 year period of a near 8 per cent per annum rate of increase in the use of oil from the early 1950s. Table 3.19 shows aspects of the changes in the international oil industry *vis-à-vis* Gulf oil.

As shown in Table 3.19, in 1965, total world production of oil was 1566.33 MT, of which about 27 per cent was produced in the Middle East and 17 per cent was produced by the GCC countries. But GCC's share was 60 per cent of the oil produced in the Middle East region. By

---

25. See Adelman, M.A. (1993). *Economics of Petroleum Supply*. Cambridge, MA: MIT Press.

26. Odell, Peter R. (1997). "The Global Oil Industry: The Location of Production-Middle East Domination or Regionalisation", *Regional Studies*, Vol. 31(3): 311-22.

Table 3.19

Global, Middle East and GCC Oil Production, 1965-2005

(Million Tonnes)

	1965	*1970*	*1975*	*1980*	*1985*	*1990*	*1995*	*2000*	*2005*
World Oil Production	1566.335	2355.23	2734.405	3087.94	2792.12	3170.59	3280.92	3613.8	3894.98
Middle East Oil Production	418.2	691.745	979.85	934.15	516.94	851.875	978.94	1138.625	1208.08
ME as Per cent of World Total	26.7	29.4	35.8	30.3	18.5	26.9	29.8	31.5	31.0
GCC_5	254.82	414.71	586.04	718.37	326.45	552.43	718.78	771.02	872.57
GCC_5 Per cent of World Total	16.27	17.61	21.43	23.26	11.69	17.42	21.91	21.34	22.40
GCC_5 as Per cent ME Total	60.93	59.95	59.81	76.90	63.15	64.85	73.42	67.72	72.23

Note : GCC_5 means Kuwait, Oman, Qatar, Saudi Arabia and the UAE.

Source : *BP Statistical Review of World Energy, 2006.*

1980 world output was almost two times higher (3087.94 MT) of which the Middle East produced almost 30 per cent. In 2005, the Middle East's share in world oil production was 31 per cent. However, the Middle East's share in world oil exports which was 54.17 per cent in 1980 declined to 38. 14 per cent in 1985 and in 2005 it was 40 per cent (Table 3.20).

Table 3.20

Middle East's Share in World Oil Exports

(Thousand Barrels Daily)

	1980	*1985*	*1990*	*1995*	*2000*	*2005*
Middle East	17510	9340	14212	16651	18944	19820.69
Total World	32324	24488	31441	36410	42402	49905.99
ME as Per cent of World Exports	54.17	38.14	45.20	45.73	44.68	39.72

Source : BP, 2006.

The beginning of the 1970s witnessed the geographical concentration of oil supply in the Middle East. Additionally, the companies had moved in to exploit oil in certain new countries of the region—especially in the new low-cost Middle East producers such as UAE, Qatar and Oman—as per the contracts granted to them by respective governments. Company/government negotiations over their relationships in the Middle East, as well as in North Africa, in the early 1970s had in essence confirmed the perceived mutually advantageous relationships, albeit in the context of higher excise taxes imposed by governments on concessionary companies. Such changes in favour of the host governments were, however, matched, or even more than matched, by similar tax changes elsewhere so that the companies producing oil in the Middle East maintained their cost advantages. Thus, they continued to expect further growth in demand for oil from their Middle East concessions.[27] Thus, at that time, it was highly likely that the companies would continue to exploit the Middle East's oil resources to a degree, which would further enhance the region's

27. For instance, ARAMCO, the single concessionary company in Saudi Arabia, foresaw its output rising from 400 to 1000 Mts. per year over the rest of the century, as cited in Adelman *op. cit.*

share in global oil production for the indefinite future, providing only that the oil exporting countries did not change fundamentally the way in which the production and development processes were organised.

Adverse Supply Trends in the Gulf

The post-1975 period witnessed radical change in the pattern of the Middle East oil supply, as in the aftermath of the first oil crisis (1973-74), the countries concerned decided to terminate the concession-type arrangement and constitute national ownership over the resources and national control over the levels of production.[28] Within a few years, total or controlling ownership of both production and reserves in the entire main and small oil producing countries of the region had reverted to the nation-states and their state oil companies. The previous concessionary companies retained some influence through management agreements with the state corporations and in some cases secured preferential rights to the supply of agreed minimum/maximum volumes of oil. However, these arrangements were short-lived so that by the end of the 1970s all-important major decisions on Middle East oil production and supply were the monopoly of national entities. Importing countries' fears for the security of oil from each individual country in the region now became greatly enhanced. There was, moreover, concern for the security of Middle East supplies overall in the context of the main producers' membership of OPEC and its decision to operate as a cartel, with its quota for each member. This development eliminated the flexibility of supply, which the companies had previously enjoyed by virtue of their ability to play one nation off against another. These supply uncertainties were further intensified by the concomitant decline in the west's political influence in the region. This emerged partly because for possible expansionist policies into the region by the Soviet Union; partly because of a heightened concern for the installation of radical regimes in individual countries; and partly because of the rise of inter-state rivalries within the region for both political and religious reasons.[29]

28. Odell, P.R. (1986). *Oil and World Power*. 8th Edition. Harmondsworth: Penguin.

29. Soviet incursion into Afghanistan in 1979; the overthrow of the Shah of Iran in the same year and the declaration of war by Iraq on Iran in 1981 illustrated the validity of the concerns. See, Peterson *op. cit*.

The consequential 'away from Middle East oil' policies by many countries (in the more general context of away from oil policies because of its high price and the widely held perception of oil as a scarce commodity) expressed the unacceptability of too much oil from the Middle East. Moreover, the high price of oil after 1974 (five times up on 1970 prices) and the even higher price by 1980, coupled with the production/export limitations imposed by producers themselves, helped them to make Middle East oil unaffordable or even unobtainable. Given that OPEC had determined to price its oil up to the cost of alternative energy supplies, hitherto low-cost oil supplies from the Middle East became available only at prices which included very high excise taxes imposed by the governments of the oil producing countries. These taxes eliminated the economic advantage of buying Middle East oil. Additionally, political concerns over security of its supply made sure that it would not be bought if any alternatives were available. Middle East oil was, moreover, on average, more distant from markets than all alternative sources, so that the geography of international trade in oil would inevitably respond to the transport-costs related, unfavourable location of the region's oil.[30] Thus, the Middle East's share of world oil production peaked in 1975—the year following the first oil price shock—at 35.7 per cent. It then fell year by year to 1985 when it reached a low of only 18.5 per cent, with a volume of production which was only a little more than half that of 1975. Also the exports from the Middle East was at its peak in 1975, when they accounted for 61 per cent of all internationally traded oil; by 1985, the volume of exports had more than halved and their share of world trade was only 35 per cent. The dramatic changes in the international oil regime, thus, had undermined the hitherto dominant position of Middle East oil in the world oil market. Likewise the nationalisation of oil companies' assets brought the long ongoing expansion of Middle East proven oil reserves of the region from fewer than 20 billion tonnes (bt) in 1956 to 55 billion tonnes by 1974, to an end. By 1980, the proven reserves of the region had fallen to fewer than 50 bt and they did not recover to their 1975 level till 1987. The changed Gulf industry was unable to sustain the reserve accretion process, in spite of the huge economic

30. Weiner, R.J. (1991). "Is the World Oil Market 'One Great Pool'", *The Energy Journal*, Vol. 12(3): 95-108.

rent that the low cost producers of the region earned against the very high unit price of oil over this period.[31] Against a full cost of production of no more than $1 per barrel for the most expensive barrel required, the unit price (measured in dollars of 1973) rose from about $3 per barrel in 1973 to a high over $20 in 1981 and still as much as $13 in early 1986, immediately prior to the price collapse later that year.

Post-1986 Developments in the Regime and Its Impact on the Gulf

Thus, as discussed above, the changes in the international oil regime from the mid-1970s undermined the previously economically dominant and highly competitive low-cost oil potential of the Gulf. In fact, it was the recognition of the severe implications of these changes for the producers which eventually led to Saudi Arabia's decision in 1986 (later joined by Kuwait and UAE) to sell its oil for whatever price it would fetch in the market.[32] As a result the average price of international traded oil fell from $27.10 per barrel in January 1986 to a low of $8.96/b in July that year. This price collapse was followed thereafter by a modest recovery, as OPEC succeeded in restraining production of its members. Since then, except for some months in 1990-91 during the Gulf War, the international oil price stabilised at about 60 per cent of its level in 1985, measured in current dollars. In real terms, however, it is now priced at only about 45 per cent of its 1985 value. Though the price fall has been steep over the years, it has, nevertheless, been moderated by two factors; first, by the supply interruptions caused by the Iran-Iraq War from 1980 to 1988 and by the events of the Gulf War in 1990-91 and since then the absence of Iraqi oil in the market; and second by the OPEC agreed and generally observed limitations on production by its members.

In spite of these constraints, Middle East oil made a comeback to the international market. This is in part because of the re-expansion of global oil demand in the context of lower oil prices: from 1985 to 1995 world output grew from 2,800 to 3,250 MT. In part, however, it

31. Adelman *op. cit.*, No. 25.

32. Hartshorn *op. cit.*

arises from the specific ability of the Middle East to take advantage of the location of the growth in oil consumption in the Far East where alternative sources are less readily available than in the Atlantic basin. This also in a way explains the importance of the region to the prospects of the major oil exporters in the Middle East. Thus as shown in Table 3.18, over the 15 year period to 2000, Middle East production has grown by 85 per cent and its share of world oil production from 18.5 per cent in 1985 to 30 per cent in 1995 and to near about 32 per cent in 2000. Likewise, its share of world trade grew from 35 per cent in 1985 to near about 45 per cent in 1995 and by 2000 it was near about 41 per cent. On the basis of these data and in the context of an expected continuing expansion of oil demand, especially the Asian factor in general and India in particular, many analysts are predicting the near future predomination of Gulf oil in the international oil market.

In the event, however, the Middle East producers especially the GCC oil producers lost the market share they were realising earlier. The market share of the Gulf decreased from 49 per cent in 1979 to 36 in 1996.[33] From the early 1990s until 1998, oil market perceptions were characterised by:[34]

- The ability of the OPEC to maintain a fair degree of cohesion amongst its members that helped to stabilise oil prices at artificially high levels and for a long period. The embargo on Iraqi oil was instrumental in maintaining OPEC's supply regulatory system, because it allowed many OPEC countries, especially Saudi Arabia and Venezuela, to increase their market share substantially without damaging price stability. OPEC's capacity to sustain oil prices at higher levels encouraged investment in new oil, despite the economic and political risks arising from investing in that part of the world.
- The oil technology revolution led to a spectacular reduction in the cost of finding and developing high-cost oil, so that even when the OPEC price declined from US $28/b in 1985 to US

---

33. Porter, Edward D. (1999). *Non-OPEC Supply and World Petroleum Markets: Past Forecasts, Recent Experience and Future Prospects*. Washington DC: American Petroleum Institute.
34. Chalabi, Fadhil J. (2000). "Gulf Oil *vs*. The Oil of the Caspian Sea", in ECSSR (ed.), *Caspian Energy Resources: Implications for the Arab Gulf*. Chapter 3. UAE: ECSSR. p.156.

$17-18/b thereafter, the economics of investments in the area were still favourable. Investing company profits were enough to include them into further investment towards expanding their operation in this high cost area.

- Between 1994 and 1997, non-FSU world demand for oil grew at robust rates with annual incremental demand exceeding 1.4 mb/d, a substantial proportion of which (41 per cent) originated in the Asia-Pacific, whose economies were growing at fabulously high rates.
- Until the mid-1990s, most OPEC countries were persistent in the policy of closing their national industries to foreign investors, a factor that pushed the latter to find alternative investment opportunities.

All these favourable factors and market perceptions justified economically the rush to the areas outside OPEC, especially outside the Gulf, notwithstanding the high cost of developing the new oil and transporting it through difficult, costly and politically hazardous routes. The oil companies' penetration into outside the Middle East was in line with the wave of huge investments in frontier areas, where costs are very high and risks are not negligible. This happened as a result of OPEC's past policies, which, with their self-defeating and uneconomic approach to oil, encouraged investment in those areas, to its own detriment. The result was that the OPEC itself, especially the GCC producers, paid a heavy price in terms of losing their market share in favour of the newcomers. The various factors responsible for such down fall of OPEC can be summarised as follows:

- OPEC's past price-shock policies (which took the price of oil from US $3 per barrel in mid-1973 to US $34-36 per barrel in 1981) secured a very high margin of profits for investments in 'new' high-cost oil, which surpassed all the incumbent economic risks. For the whole of the 1970s and for part of the 1980s, OPEC policy makers naively thought that no matter how high the price they imposed on their oil, the market demand for their oil would increase. Unfortunately for them, the excessive high prices led to, among other things, investments in upstream oil outside their territories in new production capacities, irrespective of cost differences.

- More important, is that in its policy of keeping oil prices at artificially high levels, OPEC adopted the production quota system, which secured, for the new high-cost oil producers, marketing precedence over the OPEC, especially the Gulf. The system is based on the concept of 'swing producer' (residual supplier) which means that OPEC limits its production (the ceiling, which is the sum of all members' quotas) to the difference between world demand, on the one hand, and the oil supplies from outside OPEC including the FSU's net export, on the other hand. Buyers lift non-OPEC oil first and then turn to OPEC oil to fill the gap of their requirements. By doing so, OPEC, and especially the GCC producers, became suppliers of the last resort with a shrinking market share.
- Until the very late 1980s, OPEC followed the system of fixed prices of crude oil under which the members are not allowed to sell their crude but leave the refined product to be priced according to market forces. This meant firstly, crude oil sellers from outside the organisation were free to sell according to the market price, thus enjoying a competitive advantage over OPEC and crude oil-sellers; secondly, crude oil sellers within the OPEC, like Saudi Arabia, were placed under pressure to reduce their production in order to safeguard the price—a system from which other OPEC members with more sale of refined products like Venezuela benefited. While OPEC generally had to reduce its production and lose its market share in order to keep prices at an artificially high levels, thus carrying the burden of price protection from which non-OPEC producers benefit, Saudi Arabia and certain other member countries became the swing producers within the OPEC itself, carrying an even greater burden to protect prices, and hence losing greater market share than other members. The beneficiaries of these policies were the new, high-cost oil producers at the cost of the Gulf producers.
- To put themselves at a greater disadvantage, OPEC policies of full state ownership (except in the case of the UAE, which retained 60 per cent concessions of the former Iraq Petroleum Company Group for the national oil company, leaving the remaining 40 per cent for the latter) benefited the high-cost producers mainly at

> the expense of the Gulf. Full state ownership of the oil industry in the Gulf led to a massive shift of capital away from the Gulf towards upstream investment in new, high-cost oil. Following wholesale nationalisation of the oil industry in OPEC (either through legislation, as in the case of Iraq, or by agreement with the oil companies as in the case of Saudi Arabia and Kuwait), international oil companies started looking for new investment opportunities outside OPEC. It is estimated, for example, that during the period 1980-1995 over US $350 billions were invested in the upstream sector of the oil industry in new areas. This contributed to a great expansion of new oil development, at the expense of OPEC.

North Sea oil is the classic example of how OPEC policies were instrumental in shifting investments from low-cost, oil abundant areas in the Middle East to limited, high-cost areas. The recoverable reserves in the North Sea now stand at around 17 billion barrels, similar to that of the Caspian basin (1.5 per cent of the world total). North Sea epitomises spectacular production and the enhancement and recovery of reserves from a limited resource base through huge investments and technological breakthroughs. In 1973, the North Sea's recoverable reserves were estimated at 14.5 billion barrels, against 16.9 billion barrels in 1999. In the meantime, production grew from 0 to almost 6.3 mb/d in 1999 and the cumulative throughput 1973-1997 amounted to 28.7 billion barrels. In other words, additions of new reserves in the North Sea since 1973 were more than three times the size of reserves that had been estimated then.

Following these developments which favoured investments in high-cost areas outside the Gulf, sweeping changes have taken place in the geography of oil and in the respective market shares. A new phenomenon presents itself, whereby oil from a limited, rather uneconomical resource base and high-cost oil from other frontier areas has been replacing oil from OPEC and especially the prolific, low-cost oil of the Gulf. World oil production outside OPEC, the US and the FSU (new oil) increased from 10.5 mb/d in 1977 to 26.6 mb/d in 1998, or an annual increase of about 850,000 b/d. North Sea production alone increased during that period from about 1 mb/d to 6.5 mb/d. Accordingly, 'new' oil's share in meeting non-FSU world consumption increased from 20 per cent to 40 per cent during the same period. This spectacular expansion of new high-cost oil was at the expense of Gulf oil. In 1998, the combined production of the 5 major Gulf producers was about 1.8 mb/d lower than that of 1977, at a time when non-FSU world consumption increased by 17 mb/d. This means that the Gulf' oil share in meeting world consumption fell from 42 per cent in 1977 to 29 per cent in 1997.[35] Although OPEC, as a whole, was losing market share in favour of the new oil, it was Gulf oil that lost market most heavily from this change, caused by OPEC price policies. The share of non-Gulf OPEC members in world consumption fell by only 1.7 per cent during these 20 years compared with the Gulf's loss of 13 percentage points.

Impact of the Changes on GCC Countries' Oil Revenues

Oil revenue constitutes the lifeblood of the GCC economies. However, the transformations and changes witnessed in the global oil regime over the years have adversely affected the flow of oil revenue to the GCC countries. This has happened due to the fact that the revenue stream is highly sensitive to uncertain and changing factors such as price elasticities for oil demand, non-OPEC supplies and world economic growth.[36]

During the heydays of OPEC, particularly during 1979 and 1981, the Gulf as well as OPEC was able to attain price and revenue records and came pretty close to reaching the 1977 records for market share and production. In 1979, OPEC oil revenue reached an all time high of about $276 billion, only to be followed by yet another record in 1981 when the average price of Arabian light crude climbed up to $34/b. many things have happened since OPEC's golden years, but the peaks attained at that time remain elusive till date. While OPEC's production has recovered considerably from its nadir of about 15.5 mb/d in 1985 to the current level of about 26.5 mb/d in 1999, international oil prices and OPEC revenue remain only a fraction of what they were in the 1979-1981 period. Only a decade ago, when prices were hovering around $28/

---

35. "Oil Market Intelligence (OMI)", *Petroleum Intelligence Weekly* (PIW). London. December 1998.
36. Gately, Dermot (1984). "A Ten Year Retrospective: OPEC and the World Oil Market", *Journal of Economic Literature*, Vol. 22(2): 11-14, and also, Gately, Dermot (1995). "Strategies for OPEC's Pricing and Output Decisions", *The Energy Journal*, Vol. 16(3): 1-33.

b, the market perceptions were that if OPEC allowed the price to drop temporarily to the low teens, non-OPEC producers would be decimated in a matter of a couple of years. Consequently OPEC would re-emerge with the market power. But as evident from the developments, nothing could have been more incorrect than these predictions.

During the 1990s (up to 1998), the real price of oil in US dollars stood at around less than 30 per cent of the 1981 level, yet non-OPEC production outside the US and the FSU continued to increase. North Sea production has continued to rise. Table 3.21 shows the major increase in the non-OPEC productions up to the year 2002.

Table 3.21

Major Increases in Non-OPEC Productions, 2007

('000 b/d, including Ngls)

Country	*1990*	*1995*	*2000*	*2001*	*2002*	*2003*	*2004*	*2005*	*2006*
Argentina	517	758	819	830	818	806	754	725	716
Azerbaijan	254	185	282	301	311	313	315	452	654
Brazil	650	718	1268	1337	1499	1555	1542	1715	1809
Canada	1965	2402	2721	2677	2858	3004	3085	3041	3147
China	2774	2989	3252	3306	3346	3401	3481	3627	3684
Colombia	446	591	711	627	601	564	551	554	558
Denmark	121	186	363	348	371	368	390	377	342
Ecuador	292	395	409	416	401	427	535	541	545
India	732	804	780	780	801	798	816	784	807
Italy	90	101	88	79	106	107	105	117	111
Kazakhstan	551	434	744	836	1018	1111	1297	1356	1426
Mexico	2977	3065	3450	3560	3585	3789	3824	3760	3683
Norway	1716	2903	3346	3418	3333	3264	3188	2969	2778
Romania	169	145	131	130	127	123	119	114	105
Russian Federation	10405	6288	6536	7056	7698	8544	9287	9552	9769
Turkmenistan	120	84	144	162	182	202	193	192	163
United Kingdom	1918	2749	2667	2476	2463	2257	2028	1809	1636
USA	8914	8322	7733	7669	7626	7400	7228	6895	6871
Uzbekistan	69	172	177	171	171	166	152	126	125

Source: BP Statistical Review of World Energy, 2007.

The trend of oil revenue of the OPEC can be ascertained from the latest statistics. OPEC's 2001 net oil export revenue are estimated to have fallen by 21 per cent from the 2000 levels to around $191.3 billion and for 2002 they are forecast at $177.7 billion, or 27 per cent below the 2000 levels (Table 3.22). With the established declines, OPEC net oil revenues in real terms will return to the levels of the early-to-mid-1990s, but will remain far below the levels from 1974 through 1985, prior to the oil price collapse of 1985-86. This boom-bust cycle of oil revenues in the OPEC countries in general and in the overwhelming oil revenue dependent GCC countries in particular, is making budgetary planning difficult and also complicating efforts in many cases to deal with balance of payment deficits, accumulated debt, budgetary deficit, and rapid population growth. In real terms (constant 2000 dollars), OPEC revenues peaked in 1980 at $598 billion and registered the worst year in constant dollar terms since the early 1970s in 1998, when revenues fell to only $113 billion in constant 2000 dollars, slightly below the previous low revenue year of 1986 ($117 billion) following the oil price collapse late 1985-early 1986. OPEC revenues for 2001 are estimated at about $186-billion (constant $2000), which is less than one-third of 1980 revenues, but around 64 per cent higher than 1998 revenues. For the 1990s as a whole (1991-2000), OPEC oil export revenues (in constant 2000 dollars) were

Table 3.22

OPEC Oil Export Revenue

(Billion Dollars)

Country/Year	*1972*	*1980*	*1986*	*1998**	*2002F*
Algeria	5.5	27.5	7.2	3.9	10.7
Indonesia	3.7	31.8	7.7	2.8	2.8
Iran	17.1	28.0	9.1	8.1	19.1
Iraq	6.0	57.8	10.6	4.9	12.1
Libya	12.2	47.6	7.4	4.6	10.1
Venezuela	12.7	38.9	11.1	8.9	18.1
Nigeria	8.7	51.0	10.2	7.4	16.4
Qatar	1.8	11.4	2.3	2.4	5.9
Saudi Arabia	19.3	223.2	31.2	23.6	48.6
UAE	4.3	40.3	10.5	7.5	16.2
Total	**102.8**	**597.5**	**117.2**	**80.6**	**170.2**

Notes : All figures are estimates. * The 1998 figures are in constant 1990 levels and all others are in constant 2000 levels. F means forecast for 2002.

Source : Energy Information Administration (EIA), Department of Energy (DOE), USA.

$1,600 billion, compared to $2,400 billion in the 1980s and $3,300 billion in the 1970s. Thus, total OPEC oil export revenues in real terms during the 1990s were less than half of revenues in the 1970s.

Moreover individual OPEC members' shares of total oil export revenues have fluctuated over the past three decades, but several trends are apparent. First, Saudi Arabia has consistently earned more oil export revenues than any other single member of OPEC, with the Saudi share ranging from below 16 per cent in 1971 to a high of 46 per cent in 1981 and 29 per cent in 2001. Second, Iran's revenue share fell after the 1978-1979 Iranian Revolution (followed soon thereafter by the Iran-Iraq War for much of the 1980s), and has not recovered since. Presently, Iran accounts for about 11 per cent of total OPEC oil export revenues, down from 17-19 per cent in the 1970s. Third, Iraq's oil export revenue share has fluctuated sharply from a high of around 14 per cent in the late 1980s, to basically 0 per cent for several years following its August 1990 invasion of Kuwait. After the UN oil-for-food deal, which permits Iraqi oil exports and the share of Iraq in total OPEC oil revenue became around 7-8 per cent. Thus, OPEC per capita oil export revenues (in inflation adjusted terms) are far below the peaks reached in the late 1970s-1980s. For OPEC as a whole, per capita oil export revenues are expected at $327 for 2002, down 10 per cent from the $365 per person figure for 2001, and less than one-fifth of the $1,816 per capita revenues achieved in 1980. This has significant implications for OPEC oil price preferences and policies, especially combined with the fact that OPEC countries' populations are growing rapidly (mainly in Gulf OPEC countries), and that many Gulf OPEC countries, despite their seeming oil wealth, are heavily indebted. This is partly as a result of low prices for most of the period from the mid-1980s through the late 1990s. Table 3.23 shows the oil revenue dependence of OPEC countries and non-OPEC countries estimated by the IMF for the year 2001.

Thus, as discussed above, there now remains, to a high degree, a situation, which reflects the implementation of energy policies adopted by the OPEC members and especially the GCC countries which have encouraged oil production outside the Middle East. Moreover, the policies adopted by the main consuming nations have made the transition swiftly from the Middle East countries and in fact these policies conveniently fall into place within the context of three regional political-economic entities built around the main geographical groupings of the OECD countries, *viz.*, North America, Western Europe and Japan/Australia.[37]

However, in the recent years, after 2000, there has been a spurt in OPEC oil exports and a consequent increase in current account balances due to the high oil prices. The historically high oil prices of

Table 3.23

IMF Estimate of Oil Revenue Dependence for Selected Major Exporters, 2001

Country	*Government Hydrocarbon Revenue*		*Crude + Product Exports (1998)*	
	Per cent of Total Revenue	*Per cent of GDP*	*Per cent of World Exports*	*mb/d*
Bahrain	64	18	0	0.2
Kuwait*	68	45	4	2
Saudi Arabia	79	29	14	7.9
Qatar	78	26	1	0.7
UAE	60	23	4	2.4
Oman	85	40	2	0.9
Nigeria	82	38	4	1.9
Angola	90	51	1	0.7
Yemen	76	33	1	0.3
Venezuela	58	17	5	2.9
Mexico	31	7	3	1.8
Russia**	30	5	7	3.7
Norway	29	13	6	3.2
Syria	28	9	1	0.3
Algeria	77	30	2	1.2
Iran***	67	22	5	2.7
Libya	67	29	2	1.3
Ecuador	36	11	1	0.3
Azerbaijan	37	8	0	0.2
Cameroon	30	6	0	0.1
Gabon	67	23	1	0.3
Equatorial Guinea	88	25	0	0.1

Notes : * Fiscal Year 1999-2000; ** Fiscal Year 2000-01 and
*** Government Oil revenue estimate imprecise due to classification issues.

Source: *Middle East Economic Survey (MEES)* (2002). Vol. 45(4). February. p.A15.

37. Tahmassebi, Cyrus H. (1995). "The Changing Structure of World Oil Markets and OPEC's Financial Needs". *OPEC Bulletin*. March.

the last five years as a result of increasing demand from the Asian region, especially China, India and from the US, declining spare production capacity, fall in non-OPEC production and the geopolitical environment has resulted in an economic boom in oil exporting countries. This can be substantiated from the latest estimates of petroleum export values and current account balances of these countries (Tables 3.24 and 3.25).

Table 3.24

OPEC Members' Value of Petroleum Exports

(US $ Billion)

Country/Year	*1970*	*1980*	*1990*	*2000*	*2001*	*2002*	*2003*	*2004*	*2005*
Algeria	-0.13	0.25	1.42	8.93	7.03	4.85	7.03	10.17	17.62
Indonesia	-0.31	3.01	-3.24	7.99	6.90	7.82	8.16	2.88	3.00
IR Iran	-0.51	-2.44	0.33	12.48	5.99	3.59	0.82	3.99	13.27
Iraq	0.11	14.71	3.80	4.09	1.79	-0.81	-0.94	-12.22	-6.51
Kuwait	1.21	15.30	3.89	14.67	8.33	4.25	9.42	18.88	32.63
Libya	0.65	8.21	2.20	7.74	3.42	0.12	3.64	3.71	10.73
Nigeria	-0.37	5.18	2.47	7.02	2.17	0.58	8.15	10.30	25.57
Qatar	0.15	2.65	0.31	4.58	4.16	3.82	5.75	7.55	7.06
Saudi Arabia	0.07	42.76	-4.15	14.32	9.35	11.87	28.05	51.93	87.13
UAE	0.13	10.07	5.23	12.16	9.60	3.41	7.55	12.94	18.54
Venezuela	-0.10	4.73	8.28	12.11	2.06	7.42	11.45	14.58	23.36
OPEC	0.90	104.43	20.53	106.07	60.78	46.66	89.07	124.70	234.39

Source : OPEC (2005). *Annual Statistical Bulletin.*

Issues in the GCC Countries' Oil and Gas Sector

The GCC accounts for 49 per cent of the world's proven oil reserves[38] and almost 15 per cent of proven gas reserves. Oil is the lifeblood of GCC economies. Revenue from oil exports accounts for the largest shares of each country's export earnings and government revenues also see figure. Government expenditure represents a significant proportion of GDP. Taken together, the oil and government sectors account for a large part of each country's GDP, with oil exports

38. Calculated from the *BP Amoco Statistical Review of World Energy*, 2001.

Table 3.25

OPEC Members' Current Account Balance

($ Billion)

Country/Year	*1970*	*1980*	*1990*	*2000*	*2001*	*2002*	*2003*	*2004*	*2005*
Algeria	0.68	12.97	9.59	14.20	11.74	12.37	16.48	23.05	32.88
Indonesia	0.45	15.60	7.40	7.74	6.90	6.54	7.12	7.62	9.25
IR Iran	2.36	11.69	16.83	25.44	21.42	12.22	26.12	34.29	48.29
Iraq	0.79	26.10	9.59	19.77	15.69	12.59	7.52	17.75	23.40
Kuwait	1.58	18.94	6.39	18.19	14.98	14.06	19.01	26.68	42.58
Libya	2.38	21.91	10.72	12.23	10.88	9.47	13.57	18.65	28.32
Nigeria	0.72	24.93	13.27	20.04	17.19	17.08	22.18	33.31	46.77
Qatar	0.23	5.37	3.27	7.83	6.96	6.89	8.81	11.69	18.63
Saudi Arabia	2.42	101.42	40.13	70.87	59.79	63.82	82.27	110.90	164.71
UAE	0.52	19.39	14.85	26.15	22.41	21.77	25.15	38.10	49.70
Venezuela	2.37	17.56	13.91	27.87	21.75	21.53	22.03	31.92	48.06
OPEC	14.49	275.87	145.94	250.34	209.70	198.34	250.32	353.95	512.60

Source : OPEC, *Annual Statistical Bulletin*, 2005.

as the driving force in each economy. The significant fact is that a large proportion of the revenue of state oil companies is transferred to governments. For example, between 1970 and 1990 the share of Saudi oil export revenue transferred to the government from the oil companies varied from a low of 53 per cent in 1970 to a high of 96 per cent in 1982.[39] In 1990, the share was about 78 per cent. Since investments in oil and gas infrastructure have historically come from cash flow, changing the share transferred to the government have affected investments in the oil and gas sectors in these countries. Lower international crude oil prices since 1985, coupled with government financial requirements have resulted in inadequate investments in the oil and gas sector over the years.

As mentioned in Chapter 2 (section on GCC), the GCC countries are at the threshold of real challenges and stumbling blocks to

39. Oil export revenue is not the total income of the national oil companies, since money is also earned from domestic sales. It is also not known how much domestic sales of crude oil and refined products amount to in Saudi Arabia, but limited data suggest that domestic revenue is not included in the above data. See, IEA/OECD (1995). *Middle East Oil and Gas*. Paris: IEA.

augment their economic growth rate. The oil and gas sector, the mainstay of these countries is not in a position to derive leverage from the global regime, due to the lack of foresight of the policy makers in devising domestic as well as external policies. As noted earlier in this section the major drawback of such policies adopted in the GCC countries in this regard has been the overwhelming presence of the public sector in the oil and gas sector. While the low oil revenues due to almost stagnant international oil prices in the 1990s (except for a high in a few years) have restricted the flexibility in managing budgets of national oil companies, the almost insularity of the oil and gas sectors from private foreign investments in these countries have proved fatal. The result is that, while on the one hand the global market share of the GCC oil exporting countries is on the wane; on the other hand they are not in a position to devise suitable policies to reverse their hold on the global regime, experienced during the 1970s and early 1980s.

Another disquieting factor is surmounting domestic energy consumption in these countries, including that of oil and oil products, ignited by population growth and economic advancement (Table 3.26 and 3.27).

Table 3.26

Total GCC Countries' Energy Consumption 1995-2000

('000 boe/d)

Country	*1970*	*1995*	*1996*	*1997*	*1998*	*1999*	*2000*	*Average 1970-2000*
Bahrain	10.3	151	153	162	173	178	185	149.4
Kuwait	119.0	240	249	278	285	295	303	226.3
Oman	1.0	76	80	84	88	93	98	77.5
Qatar	18.8	141	145	159	161	167	173	142.8
Saudi Arabia	58.3	1,469	1,691	1,702	1,725	1,750	1,790	1,533.0
UAE	2.3	498	499	510	517	534	549	460.2

Source : *MEES*, Vol. 45(32), August 2002, p.A10.

Table 3.26 presents the GCC countries' estimates of consumption of oil products for the period 2001-2015.

Table 3.27

GCC Countries' Estimates of Consumption of Oil Products for the Period 2001-2015

Country	*2001*	*2005*	*2010*	*2015*	*Average Growth Rate, 2001-15 (in Per cent)*
Bahrain	7.4	7.6	8.0	8.6	-1.4
Kuwait	53.5	55.5	58.4	61.8	1.2
Oman	15.6	18.4	23.3	30.7	4.8
Qatar	8.0	8.9	10.5	12.6	3.3
Saudi Arabia	247.8	255.3	266.3	279.6	0.5
UAE	100.9	104.0	108.0	112.4	0.8

Source : *MEES*, Vol. 45(32), August 2002, p.A10

Energy Policies of GCC Countries and Implications

The heavy dependence on oil revenues concurrent with the low global oil prices compelled the GCC countries to adopt pragmatic energy policies, through changing their mix of energy exports either by adding new products or by changing the balance of existing products (crude oil, refined products, natural gas/LNG and petrochemicals), in order to raise revenue. All the GCC countries except Bahrain export crude oil, refined products and petrochemicals; only the UAE exports natural gas in the form of LNG. In general, the GCC countries tried to maximise revenue from liquid hydrocarbons by exporting lighter crude oil and more NGLs[40] and refined products. For instance, Saudi Arabia substituted production of lighter crude for heavier crude in 1994. Since lighter crude has a higher value per barrel, the effect is to increase revenue per barrel and total revenue, most of which accrues to the government. Therefore, production of NGLs increased about 53 per cent to 1.8 mb/d in 2000. This followed a mass expansion of refineries in the GCC countries. Qatar and Saudi Arabia expanded their refinery capacity and Kuwait and the UAE followed suit. Moreover, the governments are now attempting to earn additional income by participating in ventures outside their borders. For example, Kuwait has become a partner to several companies that

40. NGLs (natural gas liquifieds) are not classified as crude oil; they have higher unit value than heavy or medium crude and they are not counted in Gulf OPEC quota commitments. So these exports not only earn more revenue per barrel, but also they bring in additional revenue, as these are not replacing crude oil.

develop oil production and pipelines in the North Sea and the United States. Saudi Arabia and Qatar are owners or joint venture partners in foreign refineries.[41]

In the 1990s, government financial constraints made the national oil companies to rely on debt to finance energy-related projects. Governments or state run companies resorted to borrowing internationally and domestically. Historically, the GCC countries guaranteed loans for energy projects where projects were not financed from cash flow, but financial pressures are changing this approach. State oil and gas companies are now expected to obtain their own finance for projects. The effect will be to substantially decrease governments' financial burden. For instance, in 1992, Saudi Aramco and its tanker subsidiary, Vela, borrowed about US $2.5 billion on the international market. The Qatari government is developing major gas projects with 'non-resource' finance (that is, with debt service tied to future project earnings, not to government guarantees). This is necessary because the cost of the two large LNG projects, Qatargas and Rasgas, is so high—more than twice the Qatari GDP. Non-resource finance lets the government continue its regular business while developing large-scale projects. This Qatari experiment has become a hallmark in the GCC to be emulated by other members in the future.[42]

Further, in an attempt to cut government deficits the national oil companies initiated cost-cutting measures. Cost reduction measures took various forms from increasing the efficiency of existing company to reducing the unit cost of production to decreasing the share of government participation in oil and gas projects. In Saudi Arabia, the former domestic oil marketing company, SAMAREC was merged in 1993 into Saudi Aramco, with one goal being to improve the overall operating efficiency of the state oil industry. Saudi Aramco then started competitive bidding of various projects. Kuwait adopted horizontal drilling techniques to increase oil well productivity, thereby reducing

---

41. This is substantiated from the participation of GCC countries such as Qatar, Oman, Kuwait, and Saudi Arabia in various projects in India.

42. For a more complete discussion of this topic see, "The Investment Requirements for the Development of the Arab Oil and Gas Sector and Related Downstream Activities until the End of the Decade", Arab Petroleum Investment Corporation, presented at the *Fifth Arab Energy Conference*, Cairo, 7-10, May 1994, as cited in *MEES*, Vol. 45(12), 27th May 1994.

the cost per barrel produced. Kuwait Petroleum Corporation worked with foreign oil companies as a source of new technology and a means of completing projects at lower costs. In the UAE and Qatar the state oil companies also adopted similar policies.

Another feature of GCC oil policies is that despite not much success, the trend of foreign participation in the domestic oil-gas operation in the GCC countries is continuing because the financially burdened governments are allowing this. For example, in Abu Dhabi, where foreign oil companies were never asked to relinquish all their operations when other Gulf countries were nationalising, ADNOC now has its own Cray supercomputer and has developed in-house reservoir modelling capability. In 1994, Qatar signed two production sharing agreements, with the US oil companies Pennzoil and Occidental, to bring capital, expertise and new technology to Qatar. For several years the government of Qatar attempted to get Shell to extend its production sharing agreements, but was unable to do so because the terms it was offering were not that attractive to Shell. In the new agreement, the government improved the contract as per which Occidental will invest US $700 million over 25 years. Kuwait announced its production sharing agreements in 1996. After the Gulf War, Kuwait signed BP and Chevron to technical service contracts to evaluate its oil reserves. The main reason behind this exercise was to infuse technological expertise and management expertise of multinational oil companies. Saudi Arabia has recently opened up its upstream sector to foreign companies.

In short, production sharing, or a variety of agreements have been the usual procedure in most of the GCC countries to enhance foreign participation. The only exception has been Saudi Arabia. Because the Saudi state oil company—Saudi Aramco—has the financial strength to carry operations in new oil-gas projects on its own. There are enormous investment opportunities in the GCC oil and gas sector.

Kuwait has experienced a difficult end of the decade, but it is well placed to recover, holding roughly 9 per cent of the world's total oil reserves. The country has a population of around 2 million people and is one of only a few oil-producing countries that have significant excess oil production capacity. Its government has for years applied some of its oil revenue to subsidising services for the citizens. However, world pressure on oil prices and a stated government desire to privatise state-owned business to reduce the government's spending on subsidies indicates a willingness to consider foreign investment or participation in previously highly controlled and financed national businesses. In 1999, Kuwait made a major policy change regarding involvement of foreign oil companies in the upstream operations. Kuwait plans to increase its oil production capacity to more than 3 mb/d by the year 2006 from its current level of 2.4 mb/d.[43] In pursuit of this objective, Kuwait has sought foreign investment in the northern fields. Regarding downstream operations there are proposals for setting up refineries with the aim of expanding its overseas operations to Asia and Europe.

Revenues from oil account for 40 per cent of Oman's GDP and 75 per cent of government revenue. However, compared with other oil-dependent GCC countries, Oman has limited oil resources. In fact, at current production levels, Oman is expected to exhaust its oil reserves by the year 2020. To offset the decline in oil reserves, the country has embarked on a plan to diversify its sources of revenue and has become more receptive to foreign investments. The country's oil resources are controlled by Petroleum Development Oman Ltd., in which the Oman government has a 60 per cent share and another 40 per cent is held by foreign oil companies, including Shell and TotalFina. The government plans to increase current production capacity from 9,000 b/dto 1 mb/d by 2004. To achieve this goal, the assistance and investment of foreign oil companies is being actively sought in exploring for and developing new fields. Several bidding rounds have been undertaken and concession agreements have in recent years been signed with foreign oil companies. Oman is also pursuing an economic growth strategy of exploring gas development. Much of the investment in this sector has been sought from private parties. Official projections expect gas projects to contribute about 15 per cent of GDP by 2004.[44] The LNG plant located near Sur built with a cost of $2.5 billion, promises a bright future.

43. *Oil and Gas Journal* (OGJ), January 13, 2000.

44. Stevenson, Michael J. and Paul Suddaby (2000). "Middle East Petroleum Sector Offering More Foreign Investment Opportunities", *Oil & Gas Journal*, February 14, Special Issue, pp.34-40.

Qatar has the third largest gas reserves in the world and is poised to be the major exporter of LNG in the world. Qatar exports about 600,000 b/d of oil. In an attempt to increase revenues, Qatar is investing huge amounts in the petrochemical industries, as it will earn more per barrel of oil equivalent produced by exporting value-added products. Such investments also create jobs and reduce the increasing dependence on the government. During the 1990s, Qatar was at the forefront of attracting foreign investments and funding into the region. The country has been successful in raising over $10 billion and has partnered with multinationals such as ExxonMobil Corp., TotalFina, ARCO, Occidental Petroleum Corp., and Philips Petroleum Co. notwithstanding existing foreign investment in Qatar, much of which has focused on developing the North Dome gas reserves, the decision to open the Doha Securities market to GCC citizens has become the signal regarding the government's commitment towards greater participation with countries in the era of liberalisation. The general environment in the country is receptive to foreign investment, and indications are that this will continue to be so under the guidance of the current Emir. The scope of foreign investment is likely to be less in comparison to the recently completed projects such as Qatargas and Rasgas grassroots LNG projects. The larger upcoming development projects will probably focus on petrochemical projects such as Q-Chem, Qatar Vinyl Co., and expansion of Qafaco-4 and a toluene di-isocyanate project. One of the major proposed projects that is creating a great deal of interest among investors and financiers is the Dolphin Gas project backed by the UAE Offsets Group (UOG), which involves the offtake of 3 bcfd from North Dome. In March 1999, the UGO and QGPC signed a Statement of Principles for the Dolphin Project. In March 2000, the UOG signed an agreement with Enron and TotalFinaElf to build the necessary infrastructure and pipelines.[45] The initial phase involves a transport pipeline to distribute 0.08 bcm daily of natural gas. This phase will require an investment of about $4 billion. A further $4-6 billion will be spent on downstream developments over a period of 6-7 years. In short, this project is one of the largest energy-related developments in the world.[46]

---

45. Jones, Mathew (2000). "Enron and Elf in the Mid-East Venture" *Financial Times*. 2nd March. On the web, *www.ft.com*.

46. Rhodes, Anne (2000). "UAE Offsets Moves Westward", *OGJ*, Vol. 98(36): 31. September 04.

Saudi Arabia holds one quarter of the world's proven oil reserves and has the world's fifth largest gas reserves. Through the exploitation and marketing of oil, the country has established strong ties with the US and other western countries. In 1998, Saudi Arabia supplied 16 per cent of US crude oil imports. The country's oil and gas sector dominates its economy. However, there are increasing signs that the government is seeking to diversify its income streams and is in the process of enhancing the process of privatisation. Because of the huge need for continued capital investment and the requirement to use current technology, the government considered new avenues in terms of developing its hydrocarbon assets. For example, in September 1998, Crown Prince Abdullah invited proposals for investments in the energy sector from foreign oil companies. This resulted in the oil majors submitting proposals for consideration. A ministerial committee has studied the proposals and submitted its report in July 1999. In January 2000, an 11-member Council for Petroleum & Minerals Affairs was established to determine all matters regarding investment in the Saudi upstream and downstream sectors.[47] Notwithstanding, the formation of the Council, foreign direct investment in the upstream sector has been banned because presently, Saudi Arabia has an excess production capacity of 3 mb/d. As per industry sources, Saudi Arabia is looking for foreign investment in the downstream sector that would help in developing and producing additional gas volumes. In this regard, the Saudi government started negotiations with multinationals such as BP Amoco, TotalFinaElf, Royal Dutch Shell, Eni, and ExxonMobil. It is expected that these foreign firms will bring in billion of dollars of investment.[48]

Several characteristics can be identified in Saudi gas initiative.[49] First, there is a pressing need to provide a sufficient volume of gas at commercial prices to support the development of competitive industries. Secondly, the proposed projects will be wholly financed by the companies, without the kingdom shouldering any financial responsibility. Thirdly, each area of investment will carry both

47. *MEES*, 17 June 2000, p.A3.

48. Middle East Economic Digest (2000). "Deadline Looms for IOCs Gas Proposals", *Middle East Economic Digest* (MEED), Vol. 44(22): 8. June 02.

49. Bahgat, Gawdat (2001). "The Geopolitics of Natural Gas", *OPEC Review*. September, p.278.

upstream and downstream obligations. Fourthly, the international companies' bids will be assessed on their financial positions, technical ability and the extent to which they will provide job opportunities and training for indigenous Saudis. And fifthly, this initiative is a part of a wider effort by the Saudi government to diversify and reform its economic system.

The UAE is a key player in the world oil and gas market, holding 10 per cent of the world's oil reserves and being one of the top five countries having gas reserves of about 205 tcf. The UAE has reserves sufficient for more than 150 years at current levels of oil production of about 2.5 mb/d. The UAE is one of the most diversified economies in the GCC. Nevertheless, with oil and derivative products accounting for about 78 per cent of the UAE's total exports, the oil price crash in 1998-99 put considerable pressure on the economy. During the 1970s and 1980s, the focus on investment was primarily oil related. In recent years, however, OPEC production quotas and increased domestic consumption of electricity have provided the incentives for the UAE to develop its gas reserves. As part of this development process, the UAE has embarked on major projects costing up to $10 billion to upgrade its onshore and offshore gas extraction and distribution systems, and to transfer the Taweelah commercial district into a gas-based industrial zone. Unlike countries such as Saudi Arabia and Kuwait, the UAE while maintaining control over its natural resources, has engaged in a number of joint ventures in developing its fields, such as with Conoco Inc., BP Amoco, TotalFinaElf and ExxonMobil.

Dolphin, one of the largest energy-related projects in the world, was launched in March 1999, to offtake gas from Qatar's northern fields and for construction of a pipeline connecting Qatar with UAE and Oman. This project also envisages the construction of gas and liquid processing facilities with other downstream activities relating to the development of new and existing industrial clusters in the UAE, Qatar and elsewhere in the GCC region. To add value, the Emirates of Abu Dhabi and Dubai have separately sponsored projects to increase their downstream capacities. Downstream developments include Borogue, a joint venture of Borealis and Abu Dhabi National Oil Co. (ADNOC) which let a contract valued at more than $600 million to a joint alliance of Germany's Linde AG and Bechtel for construction of an ethylene plant at the Ruwais petrochemical complex. Other new developments in the downstream projects include Emirates National Oil Co.'s $300 million condensate refinery at Jebel Ali and an independently owned naphtha-processing plant being constructed by ISO Octane. Also, during 1999-2000, a restructuring of various elements of ADNOC's activities in order to enhance efficiency saw the creation of two new companies, the formation agreements of which provide for the possibility of private sector investors at a future date. As a consequence of efforts to increase environmental awareness in the country, investment opportunities are also arising for business proposals such as the US-Oman joint venture, OnSite Arabia, which is setting up two hydrocarbon recovery facilities in the UAE.

These developments in the GCC countries share similar characteristics. First, the somehow insulated oil and gas sector of these economies are now opening up to foreign investments in the upstream as well as in the downstream sector in order to enhance production and recovery to sustain themselves in the world oil market by penetrating into the emerging economies. Secondly, the interest in gas exploration and development in the Gulf region is a new phenomenon. Only in the last decade or so has the gas industry attracted well-deserved attention and the necessary resources in the GCC states. The gas resources in the early 2000s are still largely underutilised and underdeveloped. Nonetheless, both production and consumption are soaring. Thirdly, the governments in these countries are continuing to negotiate with the IOCs for greater cooperation in the oil-gas sector in the future. The degree of opening up to foreign investment varies from country to country in the GCC, but all of them are, increasingly, showing signs of reforming their energy sector.

As per estimates, total investment required for oil, gas, refining and petrochemical sectors in the Arab countries during the period 2002-2006 stood at around $84 billion, of which $21 billion will go for increasing oil production capacity (25 per cent of the total), $36 billion for the gas sector (43 per cent), $7 billion for refining (8 per cent) and $20 billion for petrochemicals (24 per cent), Table 3.28 and 3.29.

Table 3.28

Projected Financial Requirements for Maintenance and Expansion of GCC Oil Sector, 2002-06

($ Billion)

Country	Cost of Maintenance of Available Capacity	Cost of Expanding Capacity	Total Cost
Bahrain	0.1	—	0.1
Kuwait	2.3	0.9	3.2
Oman	1.5	0.2	1.7
Qatar	1.0	0.1	1.1
Saudi Arabia	9.3	5.2	14.5
UAE	2.8	2.1	4.9
Total	**17.0**	**8.5**	**25.5**

Source : *MEES*, Vol. 45(21), 27th May 2002, p.A5.

Table 3.29

Projected Investments in GCC Gas, Refining and Petrochemical Projects, 2002-06

($ Million)

Country	Natural Gas	Refining	Petrochemicals	Total
Bahrain	—	600	—	600
Kuwait	—	126	3,500	3,626
Oman	980	870	2,060	3,910
Qatar	9,390	400	2,800	12,590
Saudi Arabia	5,000	1,500	5,085	11,585
UAE	3,400	900	—	4,300
Total	**18,770**	**4,396**	**13,445**	**36,611**

Source : Same as Table 3.25.

Thus as shown above, governments in the GCC countries, while in the past have resorted to wrong policies, now in the amidst of change and realities, are putting in place various appropriate measures to sustain themselves in the global oil and gas regime. In this regard, given the fact that they still rely on oil revenue, the emerging markets in Asia and particularly India is of strategic importance to these countries. From the perspective of the global oil demand trends in the future, centering on the demand growth in the buoyant Asian economies in general and huge Indian economy, in particular, the future of the GCC countries and OPEC can be ascertained.

Forecast to 2010

Non-OPEC production has expanded by 1 to 1.5 per cent per annum on an average since 1988. This has been accomplished during a period when prices were either stable or declining, with the brief exception of increases during the Gulf War. A combination of technological advances and discoveries of new basins in South America in deep water and elsewhere contributed to this gain. Should this trend continue, non-OPEC production could reach 54 mb/d by the year 2005 and 58 mb/d by 2010, roughly 64-68 per cent of anticipated global demand of between 80 to 85 mb/d in 2005 and 61-69 per cent of forecast global oil demand between 84 mb/d to 94 mb/d by 2010, assuming continuation of average historical price trends.[50] Such a forecast would imply that OPEC would need to hold back significant volumes of anticipated productive capacity for 2010 to balance supply with demand in 2005 and 2010 and promote moderate oil prices in the high teens. Given expected OPEC capacity gains for countries such as Venezuela, Iraq, Iran and Libya, among others, OPEC might need to shut-in between 8 mb/d to 15 mb/d by 2005-2010 just to keep prices above current levels. By contrast, OPEC shut in 2 to 3 mb/d of productive capacity in 1998.[51] Ironically, as noted earlier, GCC countries such as Kuwait, Oman, and the UAE are pursuing foreign private investment to raise output capacity, despite expectations of lower oil prices. Saudi Arabia continues to guard its market share relative to other producers and refuses to return to the role of 'swing producer' to defend prices.

Thus, one rationale of market share-oriented strategy in the Gulf is that lower oil prices will discourage development of competing high-cost reserves such as those found in the Caspian basin. This market strategy makes sense but may not be able to wrest back as much market share as the GCC producers would like. In the very short term,

50. See Jaffe, Amy Myers (2000). "Price vs. Market Share for the Arab Gulf Oil Producers: Do Caspian Oil Reserves Tilt the Balance", in ECSSR (ed.), *Caspian Energy Resources: Implications for the Arab Gulf.* Chapter 7. UAE: ECSSR. p.146.

51. IEA (1999). *Monthly Oil Market Report.* January.

low oil prices will neither force many oil field closures, nor cancellations of major investments. Environmental and other considerations can also render it more costly to shut-in high-cost oil production wells than to operate at a loss for considerable periods of time. High-cost oil producers burdened with short-term expenses will likely wait to react to falling prices until it is clear that the price decline will be substantial and sustained. Some producers are hedged in forward, futures and derivatives markets and therefore will be immune to oil price swings for a period of time. This fact has shorn up US lower 48-state production (US oil production excluding Alaska and Hawaii) despite the sharp drop in oil prices in 1998. In the first 11 months of 1998, US production declined by only 60,000 b/d to 6.3 mb/d from the levels of a year ago.[52]

Eventually, nonetheless, there is some evidence that in the longer run, lower oil prices will stimulate increased consumer demand for oil. On a worldwide basis, many analysts believe global price elasticity of demand is unitary or less, meaning that the revenues of the world's oil producers would not be enhanced through consumption additions alone as price fall. But, to the extent that the GCC producers attract some of the limited foreign exploration investment dollars for their own fields, thereby diverting significant investment from oil fields outside their domain, the Gulf market share could be enhanced further. Moreover, if lower oil prices can stimulate economic expansion of the economies of oil consuming countries, oil producers—in particular, those large producers of the Gulf—can benefit. The possibility that additional energy taxes could be imposed in consuming countries, especially in the industrialised countries could hinder the GCC producers' ability to garner enough sustainable additional market share for themselves at a lower oil price level to boost revenues overall.

However, the Energy Information Administration (EIA) has predicted a bright outlook for the Gulf producers.[53] The IEA forecast based on latest estimates expects the global oil demand to register 2 per cent growth rate per annum and the world consumption to increase from its present level of 75 mb/d to more than 115 mb/d by 2020. Oil

52. Ibid.

53. EIA (2001). *International Energy Outlook*. Washington DC: US Department of Energy.

demand grows faster in developing countries, slower in developed countries. This is based on an estimated gradual increase in oil prices to US $23 per barrel in 2020 (1996 dollar). Transportation is assumed to be the major sector driving demand growth. In the reference case, IEA predicts that the increase in world oil supply of about 40 mb/d by 2020 will come from OPEC countries, particularly from the low-cost Gulf producers. It has been assumed on the basis that the low-cost Gulf producers will make the necessary financial investments to expand capacity. Other assumptions include that the non-OPEC supply from proven reserves including the North Sea where production is estimated to peak at 7.6 mb/d in 2003 and then begin to decline gradually and oil production in the FSU increases to 9.5 mb/d by 2005 and exceeds 13.1 mb/d by 2020, of which just under 5.7 mb/d is exported mostly from the Caspian basin. This is based on the argument that "in potential major oil and gas exporting countries such as these, production will probably depend more on finance and export opportunities than on the full success of internal economic reforms. However, the latter can speed up the process considerably by attracting additional domestic and foreign funds and promoting the timely installation of infrastructure necessary for oil and gas development. While the higher GDP growth generated by intensified reforms will entail more domestic energy use, the incremental amounts of consumption are assumed to be substantial than the additional energy exports made possible through increased production."[54]

As mentioned earlier, the steady increase in non-OPEC supply since 1988 has surpassed all expectations. But out of some 1,010 billion barrels of estimated proven reserves, only 230 billion barrels (23 per cent) lie in non-OPEC countries and a significant proportion of that is in high-cost areas. Yet, the potentialities cannot be taken lightly with the changes in technology and operational efficiency recently in the global oil regime. There are numerous opportunities for the GCC countries in the present global oil regime. Considering the Asian factor in the global energy consumption where the booming Asian countries in general and India in particular are poised to experience sizeable oil consumption growth rate in the near future, the GCC countries being

54. IEA (1998). *Caspian Oil and Gas.* Paris: IEA/OECD.

close to these economies will strive hard to penetrate into these economies.

Another aspect of the transformation with regard to the supply side of the global oil and gas regime in the perspective of the GCC countries witnessed in recent years is the overwhelming dependence of Gulf oil in Asia. The Asian region in general and countries such as India and China—the main growth centres of world oil and gas consumption—have been the market for the Gulf oil exports.

Thus as the above discussion shows that after the sharp decline in oil prices in 1997-98, the GCC states reevaluated their longstanding economic weaknesses, in particular the generous system of social benefits they provide to their citizens. However, the strong expectations in these countries of continued benefits led the Gulf countries to look to other ways to reform their economies. Rather cut benefits, impose or raise taxes, or dramatically reduce their defense budgets, some of the GCC countries have chosen to try to reduce economic vulnerability by attracting international capital to their economies, into the energy sectors in particular. Thus, there are opportunities and challenges for the GCC countries to sustain in the regime.

SECTION III

Interdependence: Concept and Framework

The concept 'Interdependence' is often used in different conflicting ways. To put it, the term can be used both ideologically as well as analytically. As a political verb, interdependence is conjugated, "I depend; you depend; they rule." As an analytical word, interdependence refers to, "situations in which actors or events in different parts of a system affect each other." Simply put, interdependence means "mutual dependence." Such a situation is neither good nor bad in itself, and there can be more or less of it. In other words, interdependence is not merely an exchange relationship rather it is the capacity where the two parts/parties are faced with a situation of 'no substitution' or high cost of substitution.

The dimensions of interdependence can be explained through four different distinctions: its sources, benefits, relative costs and symmetry. Interdependence can originate in physical (i.e., in nature) or social (economic, political, or perpetual) phenomena. The distinctions make clear the degree of choice in situations of mutual dependence.

Generally speaking, economic interdependence[55] is similar to military dependence in that it is the substance of traditional international politics and has a high degree of social, especially perpetual, origin. Economic interdependence involves policy choices about values and costs. For example, in the early 1970s there was concern that the world's population was outstripping global food supply. Many countries were buying American grain, which in turn, drove up the price of food in American supermarkets. A loaf of bread cost more in the US because the Indian monsoon failed and because the Soviet Union had mishandled its harvest.[56] Social choices as well as physical shortages affect economic interdependence in the long run. Therefore, it has been argued that it is always worth considering the long-term perspective when making short-term choices.

The benefits of interdependence are sometimes expressed as 'zero sum' and 'non-zero sum'. In a zero sum situation, one's loss is another's gain and vice versa. In a positive sum situation, both gain; in a negative sum situation, both lose. Dividing a pie is zero sum, baking a larger pie is positive sum, and dropping it on the floor is negative sum.[57] Both zero sum and non-zero sum aspects are present in mutual interdependence. Some liberal economists tend to analyse interdependence in terms of joint gain, that is, positive sum situations in which everyone benefits and everyone is better off. This type of view though ignores the political aspects of interdependence, yet it is true that both sides can gain from interaction. This approach has been adopted in the analysis of interdependence between India and the GCC countries in the present study.

The costs of interdependence can involve short-run sensitivity or long-run vulnerability. Sensitivity refers to the amount and rapidity of the effects of dependence; that is, how quickly does change in one

---

55. For details see Jones, R.J.B. (1987). *Globalisation and Interdependence in the International Economy*. London: Pinter.

56. Nye Jr, Joseph S. (1999). *Understanding International Politics: An Introduction to Theory and History*. New York: Longman. p.179.

57. Ibid.

part of the system bring about change in another part? For example, in 1987, the New York stock market crashed suddenly because of foreigners' anxieties about US interest rates and what might happen to the prices of bonds and stocks. It all happened very quickly; the market was very sensitive to the withdrawal of foreign funds. More recently, in 1998, weakness in emerging Asian markets had a contagious effect that undercut geographically distant emerging markets in Russia and Brazil. A high level of sensitivity, however, is not the same as a high level of vulnerability. Vulnerability refers to the relative costs of changing the structure of a system of interdependence. It is the cost of escaping from the system or changing the rules of the game. The less vulnerable of the two parties is not necessarily the less sensitive but rather the one that would incur lower losses from altering the situation. For instance, during the 1973 oil crisis, the US depended on imported energy for only about 16 per cent of its total energy uses. On the other hand, in 1973, Japan depended about 95 per cent on imported energy. The US was sensitive to the Arab oil embargo in so far as prices shot up in 1973, but it was not as vulnerable as Japan was. In 1998, the US was sensitive but not vulnerable to the Asian crisis. The financial crisis cut half a per cent off the US growth rate, but with a booming economy the US could afford it. Indonesia, on the other hand, was both sensitive and vulnerable to changes in global trade and investment patterns. Thus, vulnerability involves degree.[58]

India and GCC Countries: Interdependence in the Global Oil Regime

Before discussing the pattern of interdependence between India and GCC countries in the present global oil and gas regime, it is to be noted that there are certain similarities between the oil-gas fundamentals of both India and the GCC countries, which has resulted in interdependence. Consider:

- The oil and gas sectors in India and in the GCC countries have travelled full circle—from multinational domination to nationalisation and again to privatisation, though the extent of

58. This aspect of interdependence will be discussed in the next chapter.

privatisation is limited to some extent in case of the GCC countries.

- The oil-gas fundamentals have put both in the focal point of the global oil-gas regime—India on the consumption front and the GCC countries on the supply front.
- Both are in search of market solutions to solve the intricacies of energy sector problems. While India being aware of the pernicious effects of supply disruption is trying to secure stable sources of supply, GCC countries are striving hard to secure stable outlets for their energy exports.
- Presently, the GCC countries as a whole account for near about 65 per cent of India's oil imports.[59] There is every likelihood of this trend to continue in the future due to the ground realities of the Indian oil-gas fundamentals. The attempts for diversification of import sources have not resulted in substantial results either due to economic or geopolitical bottlenecks.

The evolving energy sector interdependence between India and the GCC countries is itself part of the changing pattern of the global energy regime, in which India is on the way to becoming the GCC countries' most important customer; and the GCC countries are the only source of energy for India. As discussed in the Chapter, the pattern of interdependence between India and the GCC countries is consolidated on the basis of the oil-gas fundamentals.

India-GCC energy interdependence propelled primarily because of India's heavy dependence on cheap Gulf oil imports given that most of the oil resources of Southeast Asia, Africa and North America and the Caspian basin are traditionally by and large committed to the North, Gulf oil resources were the ultimate source for India. Moreover, with the changing of fortune of the GCC countries in the global regime due to the penetration of a number of players, thereby making dents in the market share of OPEC in general and the GCC oil exporting countries in particular; the emerging markets like India and the rest of Asia are the only hope of revival of the GCC countries' fortunes, as these are and will continue to be the major oil-gas consuming and

59. This figure has been calculated from CMIE (Centre for Monitoring the Indian Economy), (2001). "Foreign Trade and Balance of Payments". Mumbai: CMIE. July. p.217.

importing countries. The various initiatives taken both by India and GCC countries in this regard points to the growth of the pattern of interdependence.

Interaction between India and GCC Countries in the Interdependence Framework

The energy sector interdependence is an important component of India's illustrious relations with GCC countries, premised basically on three factors:

- India's economic interaction with the Gulf region dated back to centuries old.
- India's dependence on the region for its energy requirements.
- Heavy presence of Indian migrant workforce in these countries.

As mentioned earlier in the section 'Global oil regime in India', the first instance of energy interdependence between India and the GCC can be traced back to the then period of Indian oil history, when a deal with the Iranians was finalised which included the setting up of a refinery at Madras and participation of India in oil exploration in the Iranian offshore areas. Similar prospects afterwards came up in relation to other oil producing countries, the most important being the deal with Iraq.

Reliance on Crude Oil Imports from the Gulf

In the recent past, India's oil demand has been growing rapidly as a result of its vibrant economic growth. This growth averaged 5.6 per cent per year from 57.90 million tonnes in 1990 to 114.07 million tonnes in 2005. On the other hand, crude oil production remained virtually unchanged, moving only from 34.80 million tonnes to 36.20 million tonnes over the same period. As a result, the oil supply-demand gap widened, and this in turn led to a sharp growth in imports. A breakdown of imports (crude oil, petroleum products) reveals conspicuous increases in crude oil imports since the mid-1990s.[60] At the same time, progress has been made in increasing

60. In the mid-1990s, refining capacity failed to keep up with the growing oil demand, and petroleum product imports, particularly diesel, increased considerably. As a result, the share of crude oil imports in total oil imports had plunged to about 60 per cent by FY 1995.

India's refining capacity. Partly as a result of Reliance, a private company, having put its newly built giant refinery (capacity 27 million tonnes) on stream in July 1999, India's crude oil imports in 2003-04 reached some 65 million tonnes and occupied a high 77.5 per cent of total oil imports.

Among the constituents of India's crude oil imports in recent years, an increasing share of African crude oil, particularly from Nigeria, has been noted. This is attributable to various factors. Firstly, in view of the greater preponderance of white oils in India's oil demand mix and upgraded specifications (lower sulfur contents) of petroleum products, the Indian refining sector is basically in need of low-sulfur crude oil. Among others, although African crude oil prices are primarily linked to North Sea Brent, the market's supply-demand relations have often made African crude less expensive, so that crude oil imports from Africa make good sense economically. Nonetheless, although it is true that African crude oil imports have been growing rapidly, Middle East crude at present still constitutes the mainstream of India's crude oil imports. The background to this includes the following factors:

- The short distance between the Gulf and India means that economic advantages exist in points such as transportation cost.
- The Gulf has sufficient supply potential to cover India's import requirements.
- India and the Gulf have long standing economic/trade relations and have virtually formed a single 'market zone'. For these reasons, most of India's incremental crude oil requirements are likely to be met by imports from the Gulf.

On the basis of these projections, India has considered a number of projects to build new refineries in joint ventures with the Gulf oil-producing countries. Such projects are expected to be beneficial to both sides: introduction of capital from Gulf oil producers will enable India to mitigate its financial burdens incurred in refinery construction, while stable crude oil supplies can be secured at the same time. The oil-producing countries for their part will be able to secure a stable outlet for their crude oil and gain a foothold in India's vast market place. In reality, however, most of such refinery projects have been cancelled, or have ended in pullouts by the Gulf oil-producing countries. This outcome is the result of various factors. First, new refinery construction involves total investments on an enormous scale. Second, owing partly to the Asian economic crisis, refining margins remain sluggish in Asia, casting doubt on the economic viability of massive investments in the refining sector. Among others, India's moves to deregulate and free its oil downstream sector remain uncertain. In addition, it is significant that India, the host country of investments, failed to offer any especially favourable treatments/incentives to the joint venture projects with the Gulf oil-producing countries in return for securing oil imports.[61] In fact, the decision whether or not to support a specific project appears to have been decided on the basis of the respective economics in each case.

Basically, both the Gulf oil-producing countries and the majors seem to be highly interested in the Indian market, in which expansion and liberalisation are likely to be realised before long. The Gulf oil-producing countries, with their massive crude oil production capacities and interest in acquiring security/expansion of outlets, are expected to continue searching for approaches to India's downstream oil sector while keeping a watchful eye on market trends.[62]

Natural Gas Import Plans

Natural gas currently accounts for about eight per cent of India's total primary energy consumption and occupies the position of the third energy source after coal and oil. Natural gas is principally used in power generation and fertiliser production. When combined, the two consuming sectors alone account for about 80 per cent of the country's total natural gas consumption.[63] With these two sectors occupying centre stage, India's natural gas consumption grew sharply by 7.5 per cent/year from 12.70 MTOE (12.5 billion cubic metres) in 1990 to 21.40 MTOE (23.7 bcm) in 1999. During the period, natural

61. As already mentioned, for India to receive oil supplies from the Middle East is sometimes viewed by Indians as being entirely natural. This derives from the concept that, as India is a 'natural market' for Middle Eastern crude, its security should involve no extra cost.

62. Among recent moves, Kuwait (KPC) is reported considering equity participation in Reliance Refinery and Mangalore Refinery.

63. As of 1998, the natural gas consumption mix consists of fertiliser production 39.4 per cent, power production 38.7 per cent, and other industrial uses 13.4 per cent.

gas production has grown favourably along with consumption,[64] and the entire domestic demand has been met by domestic output. However, it is believed in some quarters that India's 'potential demand' for natural gas is greater than its actual consumption, which has been regulated by supply restraints involved in domestic production.[65] The potential demand—i.e., the possibility of expanding consumption— is believed to originate from the two above-mentioned sectors of power generation and fertiliser production. India's basic electricity demand is on the rise in reflection of its economic development, and there is a constant demand for generating fuels. As will be discussed later, while the principal generating fuel is coal, from the viewpoints of environmental conservation in urban areas and accessibility to fuel coal (distance and transport cost from mines), in certain locations natural gas-fired power generation often proves superior. Furthermore, in agriculture-based India, expansion of the fertiliser supply is among the top priorities in the country's efforts to increase output and self-sufficiency in foods. This means there is a massive demand for fertiliser feedstock. Accordingly, it is considered that once the supply of natural gas becomes sufficiently available at affordable cost, potential demand will be realised by the same margin as incremental supply, thus leading to a expansion of actual consumption.

The first option in boosting the natural gas supply is to increase the domestic natural gas output. At present, India is giving clear-cut priority to this option of enhancing domestic gas production, and is implementing the (previously mentioned) NELP to that end. However, as hopes should not be pinned only on sharp domestic output increases, natural gas imports are under consideration as the second option for increasing supply. Natural gas imports are roughly divided into pipelined imports and LNG imports, and India appears basically to prefer the former. This is because, although distance from the supply source has to be taken into account, pipelined gas supply is considered to be economically advantageous if the other conditions remain constant. At present, there are two pipeline gas supply

64. India's natural gas production grew sharply from 11.80 MTOE in 1990 to 22.40 MTOE in 1999.

65. This view was often expressed by people we interviewed at Indian government organisations, etc.

projects to India. One is an export project from Bangladesh, and the other from Iran. However, owing to factors such as deviating policies and conflicts with the transit country (Pakistan),[66] neither of these projects stands much chance of realisation for the time being. LNG projects have therefore been highlighted in recent years as being more feasible.

A succession of LNG import projects are being considered in major coastal and near-coastal cities from the point of view of favourable transport cost. Particularly on the West Coast, large numbers of projects are being examined or are under way, assuming imports of LNG from the Middle East. By the end of the year 2002, there were reportedly more than 15 LNG projects targeting the Indian market. Regarding contents and actual states, however, many of these are still at the study stage. The few that are actually in progress include the Dabhol project, Petronet LNG project, Pipavav project and Trombay project. The most advanced of these is the Dabhol project, which was being carried out under Enron's leadership. This project, studies for which were started in the early 1990s, is designed to construct an LNG import terminal, build and operate a power plant, and supply natural gas to gas distribution business in Maharashtra Province.[67] Fuelled by naphtha in its first phase, the power plant was commissioned as early as May 1999. The second phase of the power plant includes capacity expansion and fuel switching to LNG. Construction works, etc. at first made good progress toward the second-phase commission slated for November 2001.[68] But however, the project got a severe jolt in the aftermath of the Enron financial scam and consequent liquidation of the firm in late 2003. Table 3.30 depicts the major LNG projects of India and the GCC countries.

---

66. As Bangladesh gives top priority to domestic supply, a government permit for the export project is at present unlikely to be granted. The Iranian project also faces many difficulties at home and abroad as the pipeline runs through Pakistan, whose relations with India are tense due to the Kashmir dispute, etc.
67. LNG receiving capacity is designed at 5.00 million tonnes. Of this, 2.20 million tonnes will be used by the power plant built under this project.
68. With LNG supply scheduled to start in the fourth quarter of 2001, sales-purchase agreements (SPA) were concluded with Oman LNG (20 years, 1.60 million tonnes) and Adagas (20 years, 480,000 tonnes). Also, a letter of intent was signed with MLNG Tiga, from which India would buy 2.60 million tonnes of LNG for 20 years to be used for industrial use.

Table 3.30

Major LNG Projects of India with Qatar and Other GCC Countries

Consortium	*Location*	*LNG Required*	*Period*	*Supplier*	*Status*
Petronet LNG	Dahej (Gujarat)	5 MT	25 yrs	RasGas	SPA concluded
Petronet LNG	Kochi	2.5 MT	25 yrs	RasGas	SPA concluded
DBEC	Ennore	2.5 MT	20 yrs	RasGas	Heads of Agreement
Reliance	Jamnagar (Gujarat)	2.5-3.0MT	20-25 yrs	Qatargas	Talks in progress
Gujarat Pipavav LNG	Pipavav (Gujarat)	2.5 MT	20 yrs	Qatargas	Talks in progress
INGC (Tata-Total)	Trombay (Mumbai)	3.0 MT	–	–	Preliminary talks
India Gas Co.	Manappad (T.N.)	1.5-2.5 MT	25-30 yrs	–	Preliminary talks
Enron	Dabhol (Mah.)	2.1 MT	20 yrs	ADGAS/ Oman LNG	SPA concluded

Source : *http://www.indianembassy.gov.qa/iqhyd.html*

Majors and Producing Countries Strengthening Commitments to Greater Investment Opportunities

Trends and developments in India such as soaring energy demands, policies of introducing foreign capital to facilitate domestic energy development, deregulation and liberalisation of energy markets, and reorganisation of energy industries, are providing the international energy industry with big investment opportunities. During the turbulent days of sluggish crude oil prices until early 1999 followed by skyrocketing crude oil prices, the international oil/energy industry has undergone a series of reorganisation/restructuring moves. Amid the resultant turmoil, major players on the market have been under pressure to introduce streamlining/efficiency-improvement measures, while it has become a matter of vital importance to secure promising investment targets for the sake of growth and better earnings in the future. Accordingly, the leading market players—notably the majors and Gulf producing countries (state-run oil companies)—currently appear to have China and India in their sights as priority investment targets.

In fact, the majors and Gulf oil producers have made increasingly aggressive commitments to the Indian market in recent years, and various developments have been noted. In their approaches to India, the majors are also focusing on gas (LNG) businesses and oil downstream operations. Regarding the former, particularly because LNG supply from the Middle East is expected to become the nucleus, the majors are struggling to secure outlets and increase sales of specific LNG projects in which they have become involved. Furthermore, in an effort to secure LNG marketing, moves are also being made toward participation in downstream operations (LNG terminal construction, gas marketing).[69] Regarding the latter, while carefully watching moves to abolish the APM and liberalise the market as discussed in Chapter 2, the majors are seeking chances to enter downstream oil operations. By trying to establish their brand image through expansion of already freed lubricant marketing, among others, the majors are steadily preparing the ground for a rosy future. The Gulf oil producers, for their part, intend first to secure and increase sales of crude oil, their most important commodity, in both China and India. One reason for this is their expectation of an enlarging 'pie': they feel that oil demand and imports by these countries are likely to keep growing in the long run. They also have other reasons that justify their approach, including the facts that:

- the European/American markets, important outlets so far, are now exposed to intensifying competition from the former Soviet republics, Africa, Latin America, etc. and do not allow easy market expansion; and
- Asia-bound crude oil can be sold for higher prices than that destined for Europe/America.[70]

On the Indian market, joint-venture refinery projects have since 1990 been under consideration between Gulf national oil companies and their Indian counterparts. These have included Saudi Aramco and

69. For example, TotalFinaElf is joining in the Trombay project and RD Shell in the Hazira project. Also, in March 2001, RD Shell announced it had decided on $3-billion investments in gas projects (construction of pipeline and gas-fired power plant) in India.
70. The so-called "Asia Premium". There was a premium of about $1-1.5/bbl on average in 1990-1999.

HPCL, Kuwait's KPC and IOC, Oman's OOC and BPCL, OOC and Essar Oil, OOC and HPCL, and the UAE's ANDOC and IOC. Although these JV projects have made little progress for reasons already cited, the producing countries' interest in the Indian market has basically remained high. More recently, as demonstrated by KPC's plans for equity participation in existing refineries as well as entries by establishing partnerships with majors, tentative new approaches have been noted.[71] Incidentally, Iran's approach to planned pipeline gas exports now under negotiation is somewhat exceptional among attempts to tap into the Indian gas market, in that most such initiatives at present consist of efforts to increase LNG sales in partnership with majors.

The GCC countries and India have engaged themselves in various upstream and downstream projects over the years. As per one report, the GCC counties have planned to invest $6 billlion to build refining capacity in India.[72] This was illustrated by the agreements signed between India and Oman in June 1993. The three agreements signed between India and Oman included construction of a gas pipeline with estimated investment of $5 billion covering 900 miles by Oman linking two countries and setting up of two refinery projects in India: Bina Refinery and Deogarh refinery projects. These refineries are expected to refine Omani crude and it is a joint venture of the Oman Oil Co. and two Indian firms, Hindustan Petroleum Corporation and Bharat Oil Co. A memorandum of understanding has also been signed between India and Oman for the construction of a gas based fertiliser plant for the production of ammonia and urea in Oman. The Kuwait Petroleum Corporation has also agreed to participate in an Indian Oil Corporation venture with 26 per cent equity in the joint venture refinery to be set up by the IOC in Daitari, Orissa.[73] Kuwait is also interested in other refinery projects

71. Good examples are KPC's plans for equity participation in Reliance Refinery, etc. and an alliance between Saudi Aramco and RD Shell in downstream operations in Asia region-wide, including India.

72. Pant, Girijesh (1999). "The Changing Gulf Market and India: Trends and Prospects", in A.K. Pasha (ed.), *Perspectives on India and Gulf States*. New Delhi: Détente Publishers. pp.112-126.

73. *MEED* (1995). "KPC to Set up Indian Oil Refinery", *MEED*, January 27, p.21.

in India. Qatar with its gas reserves is also interested in setting up joint ventures in the Indian oil-gas sector. Qatar has signed an agreement with Enron to develop massive new LNG facilities to penetrate the booming Indian market. Besides crude oil supplies and the refining sector, there are tremendous potentialities in the petrochemical sector to be incorporated in the interdependence. In fact, the GCC countries have become a source of investment in India, mainly in the refineries sector. The total investment of about US $694.44 million has been committed by the Oman Oil Co., KPC and Saudi Aramco.[74] However, the Oman Oil Co. dropped its plan in 1997 and the Saudi Aramco went ahead in the refinery project in Phulo Khari in Punjab to expand the capacity of their joint venture from 6 MT to 9 MT at a cost of US $2.5 billion. The most noteworthy Indian investments in the Gulf region are the two fertiliser joint ventures in Oman, UAE.[75] The recent Qatari proposal for the setting up a petrochemical plant in Kerala is also worth mentioning.[76] To put it briefly, there are interactions between India and the GCC countries in the framework of interdependence and given the location of both in the present regime, the framework of interdependence will consolidate into a very vibrant and solid form in the coming future.

The framework of interdependence between India and the GCC countries in the coming years will be based on the following aspects of the oil and gas sectors in both countries:

- Given the fact that Indian consumption of oil, products, and natural gas will register impressive growth rates, and the inadequate domestic availability of these, India will continue to rely on the GCC countries. Moreover, the recent capacity expansion in Indian refineries will call for increased crude imports from the GCC countries.
- The GCC countries as an emerging market to penetrate into the Asian products markets can use the improved refinery sector in India.

---

74. *MEED* (1996). 16 February, p.14.

75. Roy Choudhury, Rahul (1995). *Sea Power and Indian Security*, London: Brassey's Inc., p.89.

76. See *Oil Asia Journal*, June-September, 2001.

- India can make use of the advanced technologies of the GCC countries for domestic exploration through joint ventures. India can also get some concessions for exploration and development in the GCC countries.
- There are tremendous opportunities in the natural gas front due to the future viable interdependence between India and GCC countries.

Interdependence in the Liberalised Economic Regimes in India and the GCC Countries: Emerging Opportunities

Another important aspect of interdependence is the vast opportunities emerging in the liberalised economic regime in India and the GCC countries. The GCC countries are implementing policy reforms to accelerate non-oil growth and create employment opportunities for a rapidly increasing labour force in a sustained fashion, while reducing vulnerability to oil price shocks. They are aware of the need to adjust to the challenges from regional integration and the globalising world economy.

Following the sharp drop in oil prices in 1998–99 and the associated financial pressures, the authorities in the GCC have reinforced their structural reform programmes[77] (Box 3.1). Since the programmes are driven by specific pressures in each country, they are at different stages of implementation. In all GCC countries, progress has been made over the past few years toward fiscal consolidation, lessening the budgets' vulnerability to terms of trade shocks from oil price volatility. Some countries have made progress in separating public expenditure decisions from short-term developments in oil revenues, including (as in Kuwait and Oman) through formal oil savings and stabilisation funds. Attempts to raise non-oil revenues have met with mixed results; they are expected to be more successful in the medium term. Moreover, containment of public expenditure has proven to be harder than expected: reducing public sector employment and curtailing the scope and budgetary impact of

77. Fasano, Ugo (2001a). "With Limited Oil Resources, Oman Faces Challenges of Economic Diversification, Structural Reforms," *IMF Survey*, July 30, pp.254-57.

subsides have been difficult and the generous welfare systems have remained largely unchanged.

The restructuring and privatisation of utilities and related services have been placed at the top of the agenda in many GCC countries. Oman, Qatar, and the United Arab Emirates are presently relying on the private sector and foreign direct investment to fund and manage infrastructure projects in the energy and water sectors, while Saudi Arabia has moved aggressively to privatise telecommunications. The state enterprise reform and privatisation can be sustained by a more sequenced approach, including establishing a process-monitoring system, further reducing regulation, offering common treatment of investors, implementing time-specific programmes to improve the efficiency of state enterprises, and gradually increasing energy and water tariffs to recover costs.[78]

New incentives have been recently adopted in all GCC countries to attract foreign direct investment. These include the establishment of regulatory, institutional, and legal frameworks to govern foreign capital inflows under a generally liberal exchange and trade system. In fact, 100 per cent foreign ownership of companies has been allowed in most non-hydrocarbon sectors. Corporate income tax on foreign corporations has been reduced substantially, administrative steps for investment approval streamlined, and foreign investors' access to local stock markets improved.

More significantly, the banking systems of all GCC countries have remained resilient to the volatility in oil prices, as high capitalisation and strengthened prudential oversight, together with cautious monetary policies, have helped preserve the quality of banks' assets. Steps have also been taken to deepen the financial system through the promotion of capital and equity markets in a number of GCC countries.

---

78. Barnett, Steven, and Rolando Ossowski (2002). "Operational Aspects of Fiscal Policy in Oil-Producing Countries", *IMF Working Paper* 02/177. Washington International Monetary Fund.

Box 3.1

GCC Countries: Recent Key Structural Reforms

Financial Sector

Bahrain	Issued the first Islamic government bills to complement the working of the Islamic financial institutions; took steps toward improving prudential regulations for Islamic banking; ratified anti-money laundering legislation in 2001; and enforced the Bahrain Stock Exchange rules and regulations.
Kuwait	Adopted a foreign investment law allowing foreigners to own and trade shares of joint-stock companies listed on the Kuwait Stock Exchange, subject to specific limits.
Oman	Expanded repossession facilities to the inter-bank market; implemented a capital market law to restructure the Muscat Securities Market into three separate bodies dealing with regulations, trading and exchange, and depository registration; and adopted a new banking law in 2000. The central bank has reactivated the issuance of certificates of deposits to manage liquidity, and implemented measures to reduce the risk of over-lending to individuals, corporations, and their related parties. Oman has taken steps toward full compliance with the Financial Action Task Force (FATF) recommendations on money laundering and combating the financing of terrorism. The central bank is also strengthening risk-management assessment.
Qatar	Removed interest ceilings on local currency deposits in February 2001; strengthened bank supervision, resulting in tightening of non-performing loan criteria; and introduced a new scheme to enhance liquidity management. Under this scheme, commercial banks can deposit their excess liquidity with, or borrow from, the central bank at rates determined by the central bank, which are fixed on a daily basis.
Saudi Arabia	Allowed foreigners to trade on the stock market through open-ended mutual funds and approved a new capital markets law to deepen the financial markets and

Contd...

...contd...

	strengthen the stock market. Enforced recommendations in line with Financial Action Task Force (FATF) guidelines relating to the prevention of money laundering.
United Arab Emirates	Established formal stock markets in 2000, and regulatory body for capital markets; enacted a new Securities Law to address volatility and malpractices that plagued security markets in 1997 and 1998, and adopted comprehensive anti-money laundering legislation along with combating the financing of terrorism in January 2002. The central bank is implementing a comprehensive pilot risk-management module for banks.
	Foreign Direct Investment
Bahrain	Eased rules on non-GCC firms to own buildings and lease land; established a one-stop shop to facilitate licensing procedures; and permitted foreign ownership to increase from 49 to 100 per cent of businesses in all but a few strategic sectors (e.g., oil and aluminum).
Kuwait	Passed a law allowing foreigners to own 100 per cent of Kuwaiti companies and reduced corporate taxes from 55 per cent to 25 per cent. Established Foreign Investment Capital Office to process foreign direct investment applications.
Oman	Allowed 100 per cent foreign ownership of companies in most sectors; reduced income tax disparity between Omani and foreign companies by raising the single rate for the former from 7.5 per cent to 12 per cent and lowering the rates for the latter from 15–50 per cent to 5–30 per cent; redefined 'foreign' company as one with more than 70 per cent foreign ownership instead of currently 49 per cent; and allowed foreign, non-GCC, firms to own buildings and lease land. Opening up the service sector to full foreign ownership in line with WTO agreements, starting in 2003 with the information technology sector.
Qatar	Allowed 100 per cent foreign ownership in agriculture, industry, health, education, and tourism sectors, and streamlined investment approval procedures. Reduced

...contd...

	maximum corporate tax from 35 per cent to 30 per cent.
Saudi Arabia	Enacted a new Investment Law and established the associated investment authority Saudi Arabian General Investment Authority (SAGIA) to facilitate foreign direct investment processing, including the establishment of a one-stop shop. Allowed for 100 per cent foreign ownership of business in most sectors, including gas, power generation, water desalination, and petrochemicals. Cut the highest corporate income tax on foreign investment from 45 per cent to 30 per cent. Permitted non-Saudis to own real estate for their business or residence, except in the two holy cities.
United Arab Emirates	Launched several new free trade zones intended to establish the emirate as a global centre for trade in gold bullion, research and development of technology, and financial activities. Relaxed restrictions for foreign investment in specific real estate projects.
	State Enterprise Reform and Privatisation
Bahrain	Privatised the Public Slaughter House and the capital's waste collection and incineration. Other privatisations are under way, including the public transport company (bus) and tourism facilities. The telecommunications and postal services sectors are being liberalised.
Kuwait	The privatisation law, approved by the Finance Committee of the National Assembly, established a comprehensive framework for large-scale privatisation, identified areas and modes of privatisation, and set up a pricing mechanism and safeguards against job losses. The government plans to offer for sale to the private sector most of the 62 public sector entities still under its control.
Oman	The power sector is at the forefront of privatisation efforts, with three power plants now under construction by foreign investors under a build-own-operate basis. Existing government power plants are being restructured for their future privatisation. Oman has also recently privatised the management of airport services. Other

Contd...

...contd...

	services to be privatised in the near future include water distribution, waste water network, postal services, and tele-communications. The government also plans to gradually sell its participation in the few remaining non-oil public companies listed in the local stock market.
Qatar	Partially privatised the Telecommunications Company at the end of 1998. Corporatised the electricity and water sectors and sold most of the government's power generation plants to Qatar Electricity and Water Company, which is majority-owned by the local private sector. Construction is under way of the first independent power and water plant, which is majority-owned by a foreign developer. Sold 60 per cent of the government's stake in a recently created company—spun off from Qatar Petroleum—to take over the local distribution of gasoline.
Saudi Arabia	Announced in June 2002 a new privatisation strategy under which autonomisation of management would be followed by deregulation (corporatisation) and ultimately private ownership. Twenty sectors are presently identified for privatisation, including telecommunications, electricity, industrial parks, postal services, water, railroad, education, and air transportation. Saudi Arabia has recently privatised 30 per cent of the Saudi Telecommunications Company. Eight regional electricity companies have been merged into the Saudi Electricity Company, and a regulatory authority was established to set tariff rates and regulate market access to new entrants.
United Arab Emirates	Embraced utility privatisation, embarking on new power projects through joint ventures with foreign investors, and selling some existing assets.
	Labour Market Reform
Bahrain	Recently developed a new National Employment Strategy that includes providing fiscal subsidies for training nationals in the private sector and financial aid for the unemployed. Introduced measures to improve general education standards, and vocational and technical training

Contd...

...contd...

	programmes, and increased employment quota of Bahrainis in small- and medium-sized companies while abolishing the 'free visa' system to the expatriate labour force.
Kuwait	Established Manpower and Government Restructuring Programme (MGRP) in July 2001 to implement the labour law, provide unemployment benefits to unemployed Kuwaiti nationals, and provide training and facilitate employment of Kuwaiti nationals in the private sector. Approved, in September 2002, quotas for the proportion of Kuwaitis that private companies must employ; companies that fail to meet this target would be subject to a fine and sanctions such as exclusion from bidding for government contracts.
Oman	Introduced measures to improve vocational and technical training programmes, and set a uniform minimum wage for Omanis at RO 100 (plus RO 20 as transportation allowance) instead of the previous two-tiered (skilled/unskilled) minimum wage. The authorities are also modernising the educational system at all levels. A new ministry of manpower was created in 2002 and a new labour law adopted in May 2003.
Qatar	Formally ended the policy of automatic employment for Qatari graduates. Now assists job seekers by maintaining information on job openings and by counselling and training. Established a department in the ministry of civil service with responsibility for this function.
Saudi Arabia	Created the Human Resources Development Fund (HRDF)—with financial participation of the private sector—to provide training of the Saudi labour force in skills required by the private sector, and development of a database for matching and placement of Saudi workers in the private sector.
United Arab Emirates	Established the National Human Resource Development and Employment Authority to help improve skills of UAE nationals looking for jobs; and established a national labour market database to facilitate nationals' job searches.

Source: Fasano *et al*. (2003).

Implications of Adjustment in the GCC Countries for India

Given the traditional links with India, economic diversification and fiscal retrenchment in the GCC countries would be expected to influence the economic performance of the rest of the region through a number of channels: the flow of workers' remittances, financial aid, merchandise trade, as well as the flow of investment to the region.

Employment opportunities in the GCC countries for foreign labour are likely to become more limited in the short run. The contraction of the oil sector would initially dampen non-oil activities, and large-scale infrastructure development has reached saturation in several countries. Moreover, there is a recent trend in the GCC countries to substitute Asian workers for workers from the region. In addition, most of the GCC countries have initiated long-term programmes of nationalisation of their labour force through employment policies.

These factors suggest that with reduced reliance on foreign labour, the larger share of adjustment would possibly fall on workers from the region. In addition to the direct balance of payments impact, there would also be effects on investment and growth associated with the loss of remittances, as these flows have traditionally financed small-scale private investments (mostly in construction) in the recipient countries.

Over the past two decades, the GCC countries have been an important source of financial support for India, both directly through grants and soft loans, and indirectly through contributions to other socioeconomic projects in India. During the 1974-1994 period, concessional financial assistance from the GCC countries to other developing countries totalled about US $90 billion, representing three per cent of donors' GDP. Budgetary constraints have made it difficult to maintain high levels of official financial assistance. Further expenditure restraints would be expected to result in relatively limited aid flows to India.

Looking forward, the expansion of domestic economic base and export diversification in the GCC countries would be expected to lead, over time, to higher exports from the GCC countries to India, particularly in areas where the GCC countries have a clear comparative advantage (e.g., secondary and tertiary petrochemical products) and consequent higher imports from India in other fields where India has expertise such as electrical goods, software, automobile parts, textiles, etc.

Finally, in the present liberalisation era, the prospects of macroeconomic stability, supported by simplification of investment procedures and the lowering of the barriers to entry of foreign capital in India would offer opportunities for increased investment by the GCC countries. Moreover, the prospects of peace in the Gulf region, combined with sound economic and financial policies, would improve investment incentives and create opportunities for joint projects that have not been fully exploited because of socio-political risks. Although most GCC countries would be expected to pursue economic diversification based on domestic investment, their comfortable overall capital position would still allow large investments in the region. There are only a few other capital surplus economies in the region that could benefit from the opening of equity markets and privatisation programmes in the GCC countries. Hence, India has numerous opportunities to penetrate the booming GCC countries in the future.

Another important aspect of the interdependence between India and GCC countries in the present regime can be identified as the synergy between energy (oil and gas) and knowledge, which in fact describes the respective deficits of both. India being a leader in the global knowledge industry of the present era will play a major role in the GCC countries' attempts at building a knowledge society. In recent years, there are renewed efforts by both India and GCC countries to devise strategies to fill up the deficits of both in the framework of interdependence.

Thus, India and GCC countries are becoming prominent in the present global oil and gas regime. The GCC countries though have lost their supremacy due to different policies as well as developments in the past regimes, yet they are in the process of consolidating themselves to place them in the regime again. They are carrying out policies to penetrate in the emerging potential markets such as India in the framework of interdependence to secure their position. India on the other hand being geographically close to the GCC countries and additionally having historical links with the region is in the process of establishing secure source of energy supplies from the GCC countries in the framework of greater interaction. Moreover besides the hydrocarbon interdependence there are other avenues of sustaining the interdependence framework especially the newer arenas precipitated by the liberalised economic regime such as the knowledge sector amongst other.

4

Interdependence and Mutual Vulnerability

Issues in Energy Security

The oil and gas fundamentals of India and the the GCC countries will result in greater interdependence in the present global regime. The sectoral interdependence may have costs as well as benefits, owing to the cyclical fluctuations in economic and oil and gas market fundamentals. The costs of interdependence involve sensitivity and vulnerability. While sensitivity refers to the amount and rapidity of the effects of dependence; that is how quickly does change occur in one part of the system bring about change in another part? Vulnerability refers to the costs of changing the structure of the system of interdependence. Vulnerability involves degree.

Energy dependence and especially energy import dependence on Gulf sources and energy security has been a debatable issue for quite a long time. On the one hand, it has been argued that there is no direct link between energy import dependence and energy security,[1] on the other hand, arguments run that increased dependence on imported energy, especially oil and gas from the Middle East, is a threat to energy security,[2] have provided a driving force for energy policies and strategies in the past. This chapter explains the interdependence framework with its implications for energy security of both the oil and gas importing countries (India), and the oil and gas exporting countries of the GCC.

---

1. See Lichtblau, John H. (1994). *Oil Import and National Security: Is there still a Connection*. New York: Petroleum Research Foundation and also Koyama, Ken (1998). "Oil Supply Security in Asian Economies: Growing Oil Imports and their Response Measure", *Energy in Japan*. Japan: Institute of Energy Economics (IEE). January.
2. Yergin, Daniel (1991). *The Prize: The Epic Quest for Oil, Money and Power*. New York: Simon & Schuster. pp.582-632.

The Concept of Energy Security

Security in common parlance refers to the abilities, capacities and preparedness to confront the challenges, uncertainties and effects of an inevitable crisis. Therefore, energy security can be defined as the capabilities to mitigate the vicissitudes of uncertainties in the event of a crisis in terms of energy supply as well as demand disruptions during a period of time. The term 'energy security' covers a wide range of issues and many different resources. Energy security refers to the degree of vulnerability accruing from dependence on particular form of energy, say oil or gas or electricity. Therefore, 'energy security' in this study refers to the degree of dependence on oil and gas as sources of energy.

Moreover, energy security is defined in terms of the physical availability of supplies to satisfy demand at a given price. The security problem therefore involves a quantity risk and a price risk. It also has a long-term and short-term component: a long-term trend of rising prices for energy imports have a different implication for an economy rather than sudden price hikes or prices volatility. The difficulty in addressing energy security is defining the nature of the problem in these terms and attempting to evaluate the costs of failing to meet security objectives.[3]

Thus, energy security is a function of energy dependence, since energy dependence determines the degree and extent of energy security. Energy dependence can also be defined as the dynamic problem of short- and long-run market power. The potential monopoly of an oil or gas cartel depends on its world market share and the elasticities of demand and supply for the energy (oil or gas), while the sensitivity and vulnerability of energy importing countries depends most directly on the quantity of imported oil/gas and their respective cost share in the GDP of the importing countries.

The concept of energy security has thus two dimensions such as demand as well as supply. In other words, there is a different perception of energy security for energy producing and exporting countries and energy consuming and importing countries. For most

3. IEA/OECD (2001). *Towards a Sustainable Energy Future.* Paris. p.76.

industrialised countries, energy security remains synonymous with ensuring access to foreign oil supplies at reasonable prices. For oil-gas producing and exporting countries, energy security means the physical protection and transport of oil-gas to markets at reasonable prices. Both consumers and suppliers must therefore concern themselves with events that could jeopardise oil-gas's physical security, its delivery to market and price.[4] Thus, the dynamics of energy security can be analysed from two aspects such as demand disruptions affecting the energy producers and exporters and from the supply disruption aspects affecting the energy consumers and importers.

In addition, the economics of energy security also implies energy security differently for developed industrial consuming countries and developing consuming countries. It has been argued that,[5] for the main economies (which are developed industrialised and trading countries), relative costs and risks of energy security are critical in the sense that they are sensitive to supply disruptions. This has attracted attention recently due to the movement towards liberalisation of the energy sector in these economies. Though liberalisation of energy sector in many developed countries reflects a choice of competition as the best means of procuring and delivering final energy like other goods and services at the lowest possible cost, yet, the consumers in these countries can be affected during the transition period in case of supply disruption. On the other hand, for most developing countries, security of supply means security of expanding supply in line with their economic growth. Liberalisation to achieve lower costs may compound the difficulties which under-funded state monopolies (or private utilities squeezed by price controls) face when investing to expand (as the case in India). And for developing countries dependent on oil exports (as the GCC countries) there are additional challenges. Their economic growth will not be sustainable unless the revenues gained from exports are sufficiently combined with the human, social and economic capital of their countries to diversify future economic growth. Energy exports themselves may create barriers to that

4. Kemp, Geoffrey (1998-99). "The Persian Gulf Remains the Strategic Price", *Survival*, Vol. 40(4): 132-49, Winter. Washington DC: International Institute for Strategic Studies.
5. Mitchell, J.V. (2002). *Renewing Energy Security*. London: The Royal Institute of International Affairs, Sustainable Development Programme. July.

development and diversification. Export rents flowing into a narrow structure of elites may increase social divisions, perpetuate authoritarian regimes, and fund civil or regional military conflicts, which will impair global energy security.

The recent manifestation of the concept of energy security has been expressed on the basis of apprehensions of terrorist attacks on vital installations of oil and gas infrastructure or supply routes. Therefore in the aftermath of 9/11 terrorist attacks, concerns expressed about energy security from the perspective of supply interruptions by questioning the relevance of benign dependence. As *The Economist* observed,

> The previous arguments assume that Middle Eastern oil producers will know what is good for them. But if a Taliban-like regime were ever to gain control of the Saudi oilfields, could it be relied on to maximise profits in a sensibly self-interested fashion? It might decide to blow up the wells, in pursuit of driving out poverty and punishing the West for its corruption. An indefinite cessation of production from what is now Saudi Arabia is not something the West could take in its stride, with or without flexible markets. And going to war for the oil might not be straight forward, especially if one postulates nuclear arms in the possession of such a state.[6]

Such apprehensions and policy measures are vindictive of the fact that America raised its war on terror on Iraq to dethrone the regime on the plea of possession of WMDs, but there are questions regarding the real motive behind such exercise. Analysts are in fact pointing towards the so-called 'oil factor' behind the impulsive American exercise in Iraq. The increasing long-term dependence of the US economy on imported supplies of oil has been well documented:

> The National Energy Policy Development, under the leadership of Vice President Dick Cheney, reported in May 2001 that US oil production would fall by 12 per cent over the next two decades. With US oil consumption expected to rise by one-third over the same period, this means that US dependence on imported oil, which has risen from one-third in 1985 to more than half today, will climb to two-thirds. According to the Cheney report, Persian Gulf producers

6. "Energy and Geopolitics: Addicted to Oil", *The Economist*, December 13, 2001. On the site, *http://webs.wichita.edu/physics/labs/111/articles/Energy%20and%20geopolitics.doc*

alone will supply up to two-thirds of world oil exports in 2020. This means that control of the region will become even more important in the future than it has been in the past. The significance of Iraq under these conditions has been remarked on many times. It has the world's second largest oil reserves, 115 billion barrels, and a figure that may rise to as much as 220-250 billion barrels when potential reserves are fully explored.[7]

Notwithstanding the terrorist threat or war for oil assertions behind the energy security debate nowadays, there are real apprehensions from this perspective for the consuming countries, especially like India. As per press reports,

India's most significant oil field at the Bombay High is under threat from terrorist attacks. The Navy reckons the Bombay High oil rigs could be targets of "9/11-type attacks" or its sea-borne variants. Bombay High produces about 11 million tonnes of the 30 million tonnes domestic oil production that's absolutely vital for the Indian economy. Well-established terrorist groups have enough maritime resources to cause damage and disruption to the off-shore infrastructure.[8]

Brief History

Concern about the security of petroleum supplies has been a key element of strategic planning since the First World War. The United Kingdom was the first major power to suffer from vulnerabilities of oil supply disruption during wartime. This has been well summarised as:

First Lord of the Admiralty Winston Churchill's decision just before World War I to shift from coal to oil to fuel the Royal Navy's warships was based on sound military logic, but it forced Britain to acquire bases and sources of oil capable of supporting an oil-filled fleet. Unlike the US, the UK did not possess a domestic supply. At the outbreak of war, Britain set out to control new oil resources in Iraq. The UK's failure to amass sufficient domestic oil reserves did not greatly affect the conduct of military operations until February 1917, when Germany resumed its campaign of unrestricted submarine warfare. The effectiveness of the U-boats nearly

---

7. Beams, Nick (2003). *Oil and the Coming War against Iraq*. On the site, *http://www.wsws.org/articles/2003/*
8. *The Statesman*, February, 28, 2004.

immobilised the Royal Navy for lack of oil, leaving an indelible impression on British military planners.[9]

Moreover, access to oil reserves also played an important role in Axis and Allied Strategy during the Second World War. The Axis Powers (Germany, Italy and Japan) were desperately short of fuel supplies, and both Germany and Japan were greatly influenced by the need to secure petroleum resources. The Nazi-Soviet Pact of 1939 contained several secret clauses concerning oil and the Middle East that in fact influenced early war strategies.[10]

During the 1950s, the control of oil and of its distribution woke up the concerns about energy security in the precipitation of two crises such as: first, the Iranian nationalisation of the jointly owned Anglo-Iranian Oil Company in 1951; and second, the nationalisation of the Suez Canal by Egypt in 1956, in retaliation for the decision by the US, supported by Britain, to cancel a World Bank loan to Egypt to build a dam on the river Nile. The UK and France went to war with Egypt in part to ensure control over oil supplies from the Gulf to Europe via the Canal.

Following the 1973 Arab-Israeli War and the subsequent Arab oil embargo, the issue of energy security again assumed strategic dimensions for three reasons. First, the emergence of OPEC as a powerful counterweight to the industrialised countries campaign of a fundamental redistribution of international power, with the oil-exporting countries becoming, in effect, the world's bankers. Second, the crisis coincided with the growth of the Soviet Union's military power projection capabilities and apprehensions that Moscow and its supporters would resort to oil supply cuts from the Middle East and Africa in future crisises. In fact, this prompted the Western military strategies to protect oil supplies, especially from the Persian Gulf and to defend sea lines of communication across the world's oceans. A third factor was the rise of environmental movement and the emergence of an influential doomsday literature that predicted 'limits

9. Kemp *op. cit.*, No. 4, p.133.

10. Ibid.

to growth,[11] and advocated abandoning the ethos of capitalist expansion reflected in the success of the OECD. However, the gloomy situations as predicted by the doomsday advocates did not happen and the Western countries concentrated on development of energy sources outside the Gulf through economic incentives, establishing strategic petroleum stockpiles and production sharing agreements and investing on new technologies to improve efficiency and adaptation.

The West's resilience in the face of energy disruption was tested again in the mid-1980s when, during the Iran-Iraq conflict, Baghdad embarked on a 'tanker war' to curtail Iran's oil exports. Teheran responded by attacking Arab tankers. However, the oil market was saturated due to slackening demand from the industrialised West, economic recession and abundant new sources of supply. A more serious threat to global order emerged in August 1990, when Iraq suddenly invaded Kuwait and moved his forces to the Saudi border which had ripples flown across the world economy due to triggered high prices of oil.

In the mid-1990s, new forecasts were made of another energy crisis around the end of the century, driven in part by the booming Asian economies and the growing energy needs of large populated and modernising economies such as China and India.[12] While the fundamental problem of meeting Asia's energy demands still remains a challenge, in late 1997 another energy-security problem emerged, this time precipitated by Asia's financial crisis. The crisis coincided with a warm winter, resulting in a sharp drop in demand for petroleum and a significant fall in its benchmark price. It soon became clear that the decline in oil prices was itself a factor undermining the economic stability of key oil exporting countries, especially the GCC countries. Another significant effect of the downturn in oil prices has been the slow capital investment in new oil development, including in the promising areas of the Caspian basin.

---

11. Thirty years ago, a group of academic theorists called the Club of Rome put forth the "limits to growth" theory, predicting disaster for humankind unless we abandoned natural resource-depleting economic and technological progress, for details see, Gerlagh, Reyer, and Michiel A. Leyzer. *Limits to Growth Theory.* On the site, *http://130.37.129.100/english/o_o/instituten/IVM/org.*

12. "Power to the People: A Survey of Energy", *The Economist*, 18th June 1994. p.14.

Thus it can be argued that, energy security in today's world is the concern of both oil/gas producers/suppliers and the oil/gas consumers/importers. Both are sensitive and vulnerable in the wake of any possible either supply or demand disruptions.

The late 2002 and the early part of 2003 witnessed another round of discussion regarding energy security in the event of possible American war against terror in Iraq to get rid of the regime in Iraq of weapons of mass destruction. Though there was no concrete focus regarding the outcome of this campaign, yet everywhere, at least in the oil consuming and importing countries, like India, there was heated discussion going on. However, the aftermath of the campaign witnessed no such apprehensions regarding energy security as the oil exporting countries of the OPEC assured the world that there were sufficient oil in the market and oil can never be used as a political weapon. It can be argued that these assurances by the oil exporting countries are in fact the recognition of the pernicious long-term effect of previous oil crises on their domestic economic conditions as demand for OPEC oil declined, adversely affecting their fiscal position. However, though the price of oil increased substantially, yet market fundamentals along with geopolitical imperatives create concerns about supply security. The latest concern has been the nuclear face off involving Iran and US, the peak oil demand and apprehensions of price spiral of more than $100 per barrel in the medium term.

In today's world, concerns about energy security focus less on the possibility of a global confrontation between major powers, and more upon the possibility of oil prices.[13] Oil is a fungible commodity, universal commodity that commands a worldwide benchmark price. If supplies from one region, such as the Gulf, are disrupted, prices will rise in the short-term until the market adjusts itself. From an economic viewpoint it does not matter that North America and Western Europe import only 20 per cent and 29 per cent respectively from the Gulf, whereas Asia imports 74 per cent.[14] All three regions will be equally affected if oil supplies from the Gulf or from any other region are disrupted, or their transportation endangered.

13. Kemp *op. cit.*, No. 4, p.136.

14. Energy Information Administration (IEA) (2000). *International Energy Outlook*. Washington DC: US Department of Energy. p.36.

Fluctuations in oil prices can have serious consequences for consumers and producers. For the industrial countries, in the short-term, a rapid price increase is a concern because, in the short-term, the demand for petroleum products in industrial countries is relatively inelastic: for a given increase in price, there will not be a proportional decrease in demand because it is difficult to find substitutes for petroleum products. The high oil prices affect everybody, since the cost of energy is closely linked to the general price level. In the long-term, significant rises in oil prices will invariably lead to lower demand and fall in prices. The industrial countries have efficient mechanisms for adjusting over time to high oil prices through conservation, innovation and taxation. Furthermore, the oil-sharing programme set up by the International Energy Agency in 1974 are still effective and the US and others still maintain a strategic petroleum reserve which they could draw upon to lower the market price of oil. But, for many countries such as the developing countries, steep rise in oil prices can be disastrous. The short-term spike in oil prices in 1990-91 pushed India to the brink of bankruptcy and forced massive reforms in the country. Many emerging economies are today in similar position; the impact of sudden oil-price spikes on the economies of emerging economies therefore have serious repercussions.

Similarly, a significant fall in oil prices generates immediate economic benefits for importing countries, but poses serious problems for the oil producing and exporting countries. The low oil prices in 1997-98 bear testimony to the vulnerable position of the oil/gas exporting GCC countries, as oil revenues constitute the major proportion of these governments' revenue and international prices are linked to their budget preparation. In addition, demand disruptions due to economic crisis in the importing countries also affect directly the exporting countries. This has been witnessed during the Asian financial crisis, dampening the oil/gas imports of the countries in Asia and thereby affecting the oil/gas exporters, as Asia has become the major oil/gas-consuming region in the world. The only reprieve of low oil prices for the exporting countries is that it induces consumption and thereby the market share of major producers such as the GCC countries increases and moreover, the investments in the search for new oil in high-cost regions get delayed. But the direct effect of low oil prices directly affects the revenues and therefore budgets, of the GCC countries, causing serious political problems. Falling oil revenues also restrict the options of new investments in the oil and gas sector in the GCC countries. As a consequence, pressure is growing on the GCC member countries to modify their restrictive and nationalist oil policies, which can be vindicated from the recent policies of allowing foreign investments in oil/gas sectors in some of the countries.

Thus, ironically, both producers and consumers are becoming more financially interdependent just when economic hardships of the major oil/gas producing countries, especially in the GCC countries may cause domestic instability, which can affect energy security concerns.

Supply and Demand Disruptions

As mentioned earlier, supply disruptions can be defined as the physical scarcity of supplies to meet demand at a given price. And demand disruptions refer to the lack of demand to adjust to the available supply. These terms thus refer to the quantity component of energy security.

Oil supply disruptions have occurred rather frequently (Table 4.1)—over the past half-century, there have been at least 14 significant disruptions involving a loss of 0.5 mb/d or more crude oil. Most of these disruptions were related to either military or political upheavals, especially in the Middle East. Since 1973, four major crises—the 1973 Arab-Israeli War, the 1978-79 Iranian Revolution, the 1980 Iran-Iraq War and the 1990-91 Gulf War—resulted in initial shortfall of between 3.0 and 3.5 mb/d. It is to be noted that, virtually all past disruptions have been short, typically no more than six to nine months. Moreover, the politically motivated supply disruption can be broadly grouped into two categories such as: first, random shocks, caused by internal unrest in OPEC countries such as the Iranian Revolution in 1978-79, the Nigerian Civil War of 1967-1970 or wars involving OPEC states like the Iraq-Iran War and the Gulf War of 1990-91; and second, strategic shocks involving wilful exercise of market power by the oil cartel such as by the Middle East oil producers (Arab oil embargoes) in 1957, 1967 and 1973-74.

Table 4.1

World Oil Supply Disruptions

Dates	*Supply Disruption*	*Magnitude of Supply Disruption (mb/d)*	*World Oil Consumption (mb/d)*	*Per cent of Consumption*
Mar. 1951-Oct.1954	Iranian Fields Nationalised	0.7	13.2	5.3
Nov.1956-Mar.1957	Suez War	2.0	17.5	11.4
Dec.1966-Mar.1967	Syrian Transit Fee Dispute	0.7	34.3	2.0
Jun.1967-Aug.1967	Six Day War	2.0	40.0	5.0
Jul.1967-Oct.1968	Nigerian Civil War	0.5	40.1	0.3
May 1970-Jan.1971	Libyan Price Controversy	1.3	48.0	2.7
Apr.1971-Aug.1971	Algerian-French Nationalisation Struggle	0.6	50.2	1.2
Mar.1973-May1973	Lebanese Political Conflict	0.5	58.2	0.9
Oct.1973-Mar.1974	October Arab-Israeli War	4.3	58.2	7.4
May 1977	Damage at Saudi Oil field	0.7	62.1	1.1
Nov.1978-Apr.1979	Iranian Revolution	5.6	65.1	8.6
Oct.1980-Jan.1981	Outbreak of Iran-Iraq war	4.1	60.4	6.8
Mar.1989-Apr.1989	Exxon Valdez Accident	<0.5	51.6	<1.0
Apr.1989-Jun.1989	UK Cormorant Platform	0.5	51.6	1.0
Aug.1990-Jan.1991	Iraqi Invasion of Kuwait	4.3	66.3	6.5

Note: Initial Production loss only, in some cases, this was quickly made up by production increases elsewhere.

Source: IEA/OECD (2001). *Towards a Sustainable Energy Future.* Chapter 4. Table 7. Paris. p.79.

Demand disruptions actually occurred in the global oil regime during the period of nationalisation of Iranian attempts, when the industrialised countries put an embargo on Iranian oil supplies from being marketed. And recently the embargo on oil by the US on Iraq,

Libya and Iran can also be considered demand disruptions, as the oil supplies of these countries are not in the market. These disruptions can be attributed to the asymmetry of interdependence whereby the balance of power is in favour of powerful consuming nations due to the structural intricacies (that means the consumers can do away with the supplies from these countries as supplies are substantial in relation to demand) of the global oil regime. Moreover, the market forces domination in the present regime saw demand disruption due to domestic economic crisis in the consuming countries such as in Asia in 1998, affecting the world demand and thereby the oil revenue dependent Gulf countries.

The Energy Security Debate

The scarcity of energy sources such as oil in the global energy scenario sparked off the debate about energy security. Consistent with economic doctrine, a group of energy experts argue that a commodity in scarce supply becomes more expensive. This encourages conservation and discovery of new sources of energy and new supply sources and technological breakthroughs making energy efficiency production process. These factors make it highly unlikely that the world can run out of a key resource like petroleum. While others argue that in the short term, unexpected supply disruption and price instability can be extremely damaging and have negative effects on inflation, growth rate, productivity, and balance of payments position of the importing economies. Therefore, suitable policies should be devised and strategically adopted to counteract the energy crisis.

However, questions arose as to the possibilities that the world would someday run out of petroleum and therefore everybody should be cautious. In order to vindicate such types of queries, it is necessary to delve into the economics of natural resources and the controversies that the literature in this field has engendered.[15] Economists in the Malthusian mould always forecast ultimate doom because of resource scarcity in relation to the world population growth and thereby assert prime importance to energy security. But by any standard, until the

15. Marcus, A.A. (1992). *Controversial Issues in Energy Policy*, Vol. 2. New York: Sage Publications Inc. p.25.

mid-1900s, resources were plentiful in the US and other industrialised countries. Concern for energy security to sustain economic growth therefore made little sense. Even with a growing population, economists believed that technological advances would assure adequate supplies of energy. As time progressed, low-grade resources simply would take place of the high-grade resources. Technological changes and advances that would ease the transition would accompany the replacement of one type of resources by another. Such cycles in resource use were common, which could be seen in the historical experience of minerals such as iron ore.[16] But the oil embargo of 1973 rekindled the controversy about whether the process would actually work as economists have predicted before. The dominant view was that any supply problem, should it exist, was distant. Vast potential new supplies of high-grade oil and natural gas were still available. Yet, the worldwide energy crisis of 1973 woke up the concerns of supply disruptions owing to short-term price fluctuations. After the multinational oil corporations (e.g., Exxon, Mobil, Shell, etc.) lost ownership of crude oil production to the oil producing states, the producing states controlled production levels and prices. They restricted the role of the multinationals to transportation and downstream refining. These actions brought on worldwide energy crises: the near quadrupling of oil prices that followed the Arab-Israel War (from $3.50/barrel in 1973 to $13.50/barrel in 1974) and near tripling of oil prices that followed the Iran-Iraq War (from $13.50/ barrel in 1979 to $34.50/barrel in 1980).[17] These abrupt price shocks created havoc in the world economy and the energy security debate gathered momentum.

The development of energy security issues in the international oil and gas market can be analysed in two ways: first, from the aspect of the implications of the structural changes of the global oil and gas regime to the oil-gas supply issues and secondly, from the aspect from the recent phases of the regime. These issues can be summarised as Box 4.1.

---

16. For details regarding the energy transition, see Smith, V.K. (1981). *Scarcity and Growth Reconsidered.* Baltimore, MD: John Hopkins University Press.

17. The detail causes and consequences and events, which led to the above crises, have been illustrated in chapter 1 of this study.

Box 4.1

Development of Oil/Gas Supply and Demand Security Issues in the Global Oil and Gas Regime

Structural Changes of the Global Oil Regime and its Implication to the Oil Supply and Demand Issues

- Sluggish oil demand in the industrialised countries and in the main oil-consuming OECD countries, promotion of alternative energy development and massive energy conservation.
- Rise of non-OPEC production, shifting investments from OPEC in general and GCC countries in particular, technological innovations and increasing production in high-cost areas.
- Development of futures/spot trading markets, shift of oil pricing mechanism to market-related type.
- Oil-producing countries' recognition of interdependence with oil consuming and importing countries (the learning effect from the era of the high oil prices up to the early 1980s).
- Establishment of emergency preparedness in the industrialised West (formation of IEA in 1974 and stockpiling build-ups).
- Stagnated oil prices and prevailing outlook for low oil prices in the 1990s and consequent lower revenues for the oil exporting countries, market search by the oil producing countries for increasing revenues.
- The Asian Currency Crisis and lower oil demand affecting the major oil producing countries in the GCC and investments in the new areas and in the GCC capacity expansion attempts.

Recent Issues on Oil Supply Security

- US-Iran Nuclear face off.
- Peak oil doctrine: Shrinking world surplus crude production capacity and its concentration in a few politically unstable Gulf countries.
- Regional (Asia) energy shortages have become acute. Signs of rising dependence on the Gulf where 65 per cent of reserves of oil and 16 per cent of gas reserves lie.
- Domestic instability in major oil producing countries (economic difficulties in the Gulf countries and problems in the non-OPEC region such as Caspian basin oil being marketed).

Contd...

...*Contd*...

- Liberalisation and privatisation in the energy sectors in the developed and developing countries. Private oil companies' policy to keep their stocks at minimum level, its effects on the deregulated energy markets such as in India.
- Steady rises expected for oil and gas demand in the long-run future, particularly in India and its impact on the various sectors of the Indian economy.
- The outlook of India's heavy dependence on the Gulf for energy supplies and the risks.
- Possible economic breakdown in India affecting its oil/gas imports and its impact on the GCC oil/gas exporting countries.

As a result of surging non-OPEC output since the late 1970s and slowdown in world oil demand spurred by the energy conservation and alternative energy development policies of the industrialised countries (which account for more than 50 per cent of world oil demand), the OPEC's share in the global oil production capacity dropped significantly from 53 per cent in 1973 to less than 30 per cent in 1985. Though OPEC's share recovered after the late 1980s due to the combined effects of robust oil demand in developing countries and slowdown in non-OPEC production due to lower oil prices; yet it remained at around 40 per cent in the 1990s. Moreover with the emergence of new high-cost oil producers in the market, the degree of concentration of crude oil supply market dropped. The concentration of crude oil supply market, measured by the 'Herfindahl Index',[18] indicates that, from a peak of 1,158 recorded in 1981, the degree of concentration of crude oil supply market dropped to a low of 628 in 1999. This signifies the loose grip of the global oil regime from the OPEC.

With the changes in oil supply and demand and market structure as discussed in chapter I and II, as the background, oil pricing mechanism in the global oil market has transformed into market related type over the years. Particularly, both future oil prices and spot market prices, having significantly developed since the 1980s, came to

18. Herfindahl Index is the sum of the squared market share of each supplier.

serve as the indicator of global oil price, thereby evolving transparency in global oil pricing mechanism.[19] One analyst has aptly summarised the implication of the market domination on the OPEC:[20]

> The major development that has curbed OPEC's role as the arbiter of prices is the advent of news and telecommunication systems—the thousands of instant market-monitoring, computerised devices that tell bankers, oil traders and commodity market speculators what the price of oil is at any moment. They also relay news that affects those prices. That development has encouraged wild growth in the trading of oil futures, placing hundreds of new investors in the oil markets whose role is limited to trading 'paper barrels' for the sake of bettering on oil's price. Such trading on the New York Mercantile Exchange alone reached 40 million barrels a day in 1987. By comparison, world oil consumption that year was 49 mb/d. This means the speculators' ability to influence oil prices approaches the power of OPEC and non-OPEC producers combined ....OPEC, however, is a consistent, and sore, loser in this game. When prices drift too low, it is obliged to promise meetings or curbs on output that prop up its image as the protector of oil prices, a role it can no longer veritably perform. The organisation has not helped itself by its constant failure to meet the goals of the ceilings on production that it sets. OPEC members consistently either produce above their quotas or discount their oil to stimulate their sales, or both.

As discussed in the previous chapters, many OPEC nations, especially those in the Gulf (the GCC countries) are facing difficult social, economic and political challenges, because they are overwhelmingly dependent on oil revenues. This situation of the GCC countries further worsened in the beginning of the year 1997, which marked the 'reversal oil price shocks', affecting the oil export revenues, balance of payments, budgets and overall economic conditions of these countries. Low oil prices since late 1997 till late 1999 have been caused by several main factors, including OPEC's December 1, 1997, agreement to raise the organisation's production quota by 10 per cent, a warmer than normal winter in the Northern

---

19. For details see, Horsnell, Paul and Robert Mabro (1993). *Oil Markets and Prices: The Brent Market and the Formation of World Oil Prices.* Chapter II. Oxford: Oxford University Press.

20. "OPEC: Cartel Facing the Fact that some Producers are Beyond its Reach", *International Herald Tribune*, April 9, 1988, as cited in Nye Jr., Joseph S. (1999). *Understanding International Conflicts: An Introduction to Theory and History*. 3rd edition. Chapter 7. New York: Longman. p.192.

Hemisphere, increasing Iraqi oil exports, and reduced demand stemming from the severe economic crisis in East Asia.

Collapsing oil prices till late 1998 actually threw GCC countries' budgets into chaos, as they scrambled to cut expenditure, raise revenue and minimise budgetary deficits. These situations in the GCC countries have been discussed in chapter III. Thus, the GCC countries and other OPEC members, having enjoyed high oil prices up to the early 1980s, came to realise the effects of their 'process of self-destruction', which resulted in penetration of high cost non-OPEC producers in the world oil-gas regime, stagnation in world oil demand and decline in demand for OPEC oil. The declining demand for OPEC oil coupled with duping international oil prices since the oil price slump in 1986, made GCC countries' oil revenue stringent and consequently damaged their economic stability. The situation of the Gulf countries has been well summarised by one analyst as,

> Things have changed in the kingdom (Saudi Arabia), and in the Gulf as a whole. The welfare states built in the 1970s, with seemingly limitless resources for very small populations, are now strained by high population growth rates and flat oil prices. Indigenous middle classes created by state education and employment policies except remunerative employment and increasingly seek an outlet for their hope of political participation.[21]

The oil exporting GCC countries are therefore in the threshold of a major threat, not only due to their substantial loss of market share, but also due to their further inability to meet their overall revenue needs. This situation thus precipitated a policy dilemma before the GCC governments: while a continuation of recent trends in market share could be disastrous in the long run, any attempt to recapture the lost market share through 'controlled-production management mechanism', carries with it enormous short-term financial risks. Because of this 'learning effect', oil producers in the OPEC, especially the GCC countries therefore, began respecting interdependent relations with consuming nations, as well as they became keen to secure stable outlet for their energy exports in the emerging markets.

21. Gause, Gregory F. (1997). "The Gulf Conundrum: Economic Change, Population Growth, and Political Stability in the GCC States", *The Washington Quarterly*, Vol. 20(1): 145-65 Winter.

Recognising the first oil crisis as the turning point, industrialised countries have advanced such establishments of emergency preparedness for oil supply disruption as oil stockpiles and this is why it can be argued that the IEA was formed in 1974 as an international framework to tackle oil supply disruptions. In a sense, the IEA could play an important role in stabilising the world oil/gas market. In fact, it helped to calm down the international oil market through its coordinated actions during the Gulf Crisis in 1990-91. In fact, the IEA has used the strategic reserves very effectively recently in 2001 to control oil price spikes.[22]

Thus, until the 1980s, oil was often regarded as a strategic commodity, used as a weapon to manipulate productions, costs and prices owing to the whims or political intentions of oil producing states' or the OPEC's cartel behaviour, but with the changes described above oil has become a 'market leading commodity', of which supply-demand and prices are dictated by free forces of the market mechanism. Since the early 1970s when energy security was debated seriously, considerable changes in oil and gas markets have altered the picture. Suppliers have increased, as have proven reserves and stocks, and prices have become flexible and transparent, dictated by market forces rather than by cartel arrangements. Moreover, global as well as regional conflicts are lessening and trade is flourishing and becoming freer. It is to be noted that suppliers have not imposed any oil/gas sanctions since the early 1980s, nor have there been any real shortages anywhere in the world. Instead, the major consuming country (US) has imposed trade sanctions on some of the producing countries such as Iran, Iraq and Libya. Though, this has not resulted in supply disruption, yet it has created demand disruptions in the world market, not only affecting the producing countries in question, but also, in a way the world market, because had there not been any sanctions, then the supplies from these countries would have resulted in more world supplies and consequent low prices—some relief from the energy security point of view for the high energy consuming and importing countries like, India. In other words, all this points to the present abundance of oil/gas supplies.

---

22. The US released 30 million barrels from its strategic reserves to bring down prices, which were hovering over more than $35/barrel. This controlled prices temporarily.

Moreover, in today's market environment energy security is a shared issue for consumers/importers as well as producers/exporters. As much as importing countries are anxious to ensure security by having sustainable sources, exporting countries are anxious to export to ensure sustainable income.[23] History reveals that oil supply disruptions have negative effects on oil exporting countries. As consumers in importing economies shift away from oil, the lower demand causes severe economic damage to the exporters. In addition, many oil exporting countries, especially Gulf countries have recently obtained stakes in downstream operations in importing countries. This can be vindicated from the involvement of some Gulf countries in OECD countries, thereby contributing to the energy security of the OECD countries, as supply disruption could mean a loss of opportunities for both oil exporters and importers.[24] In this sense, concern about oil supply security due to oil producers' political intention and price manipulation by producers has been viewed as less relevant. Thus, in those circumstances, the issue of oil supply security, which used to be given priority by the market participants, has become somehow less relevant nowadays. In addition, the oil exporting countries of the GCC have become intensely vulnerable in the process of transition of the global regime over the years.

Yet, the recent developments in the global oil and gas regime have shown emerging moves noteworthy for considering the issue of oil supply security, as summarised in the box above. Moreover, analysts have challenged the contention that market forces domination of the regime really dampens the possibility of future supply disruption, as market forces will automatically match demand with supply. The critics argue that despite market forces and the structural changes in the regime, geopolitics is and still has an important bearing on the energy security phenomena.[25]

23. Mitchell, J.V. (1997). *Will Western Europe Face an Energy Shortage?*. Strasbourg Energy Council of Europe.

24. United Nations (2001). *World Energy Assessment and the Challenge of Sustainability*. Chapter 4. p.118.

25. See for details, Mitchell, John *et. al* (1996). *The New Geopolitics of Energy*. London: Royal Institute of International Affairs and also see, United Nations (2001). *World Energy Assessment and the Challenge of Sustainability.*

Security of Crude Oil Supply

Over the past two decades many changes in the oil market have improved the overall security of the global energy market. The world economy has become less dependent on oil, as most consuming regions have diversified their energy sources. Oil constituted almost 46 per cent of world commercial energy sources in 1973, compared with 40 per cent now (year 2002). There is also diversification of supply. In the early 1970s, the OPEC accounted for more than half of the world's oil; today it provides only 42 per cent. The world now has 80 oil-producing countries. The oil markets have now become more like traditional commodity market, with futures markets, transparent and able to respond quickly to changing circumstances. Big strides have been made in energy efficiency, gradually reducing the dependence of economic growth on increased oil consumption (particularly in developed countries). Advances in technology have led to discoveries, and significantly improved the recovery rate, increasing oil resource base to an estimated 2,3000 trillion barrels. World trade has flourished in recent years. In 1998, it was three times that in 1980 and now (2002) accounts for 44 per cent of global GDP, compared with 39 per cent in 1980.[26] Both energy exporters and importers benefit from trade. Most exporters, especially the GCC countries are low-income countries that badly need oil income for development.

Even with the increase in the number of oil producing countries, the fact remains that almost two-thirds of the world's oil reserves are in the Middle East, mostly in the Gulf[27] region. Although these countries now (2002) account for only 36 per cent of global crude oil supplies, they are expected to double their share to 52 per cent in 2010.[28] The Gulf countries have not been historically known for political stability and security. There is also likelihood of the world depending more on oil from the Middle East, especially from the Gulf region. Moreover, the global surplus crude oil production capacity,

26. These figures are adapted from International Monetary Fund (IMF) (2002). *Direction of Trade Statistics*.
27. The Gulf region here includes the Islamic Republic of Iran, Iraq, Saudi Arabia, Kuwait, Qatar, and UAE.
28. United Nations (2001). *World Energy Assessment and the Challenge of Sustainability*. Chapter 4. p.120.

which helped to stabilise the market at the time of oil supply disruption in the past, has sharply dropped from 10.10 mb/d in 1996 (excluding Iraq) to nearly 3.00 mb/d in 1997 and to 6.7 mb/d in 1999. Most OPEC countries, especially those in the Gulf have spare productive capacity due to the current oil market conditions precipitated by weak demand and high incremental non-OPEC oil production. Among the Gulf producers, Saudi Arabia due to its large reserves maintains the largest spare production capacity, estimated at between 2-2.5 mb/d and the total OPEC spare capacity is around 5.3 mb/d. This is expected to go even further over the foreseeable future.[29] To add to the matter, the current surplus capacity concentrates only in a few GCC countries, i.e., Saudi Arabia, Kuwait and UAE. Table 4.2 shows world's greatest oil and gas reserves.

Table 4.2

Greatest Oil and Natural Gas Reserves by Country, 2006

Country	*Oil Reserves Thousand Million Barrels*	*Country*	*Gas Reserves Trillion Cubic Metres*
Saudi Arabia	264.2	Russian Federation	47.82
Iran	137.5	Iran	26.74
Iraq	115.0	Qatar	25.78
Kuwait	101.5	Saudi Arabia	6.90
United Arab Emirates	97.8	United Arab Emirates	6.04
Venezuela	79.7	USA	5.45
Russian Federation	74.4	Nigeria	5.23
Libya	39.1	Algeria	4.58
Nigeria	35.9	Venezuela	4.32
USA	29.3	Iraq	3.17

Source: BP, 2006.

Table 4.3 shows the breakup of idle capacities of OPEC countries in the first half of the year 2001.

29. *MEES*, 17 September 2001.

Table 4.3

Idle Capacities of OPEC Countries in the First Half of 2001

(mb/d)

Member Countries	*Idle Capacity*	*Average Production*
Algeria	0.07	0.83
Indonesia	0.01	1.24
Iran	0.08	3.82
Iraq	0.66	2.14
Kuwait	0.31	2.09
Libya	0.10	1.40
Nigeria	0.08	2.12
Qatar	0.04	0.70
Saudi Arabia	2.32	8.18
UAE	0.30	2.18
Venezuela	0.13	2.91
OPEC	4.13	27.60

Source: Prepared from various issues (18 June, 16 July, and 30 July 2001) of *MEES*.

In the current low oil demand, high oil price scenario, demand for OPEC and Gulf oil is rising at a snail's pace. However, even in this low growth world and with steadily increasing non-OPEC production, the call on OPEC through the end of the 2003 is estimated around 25.5 mb/d.[30] About 17 mb/d and including another 19 mb/d from North Africa representing 67 per cent of current OPEC production or 22 per cent of global oil production comes from the Middle East.[31] There is no way the world could adjust to a scenario without the Middle East oil for any length of time short of facing a calamity. Moreover, many global oil supply assessments conclude that incremental non-OPEC production will slow, if not decline, later in this decade even at currently prevailing prices. All scenarios point at a sharply rising demand for Gulf oil in the next decade (2010-2020). As per the projections of both the IEA and EIA, significant growth in demand for Gulf oil is expected even in this decade. Though their timing and extent of dependence on Middle East oil differs, all analysts agree that the importance of the region in meeting future global oil demand will steadily rise. The EIA's *International Outlook 2002* estimates global demand on the Gulf in 2010 as high as 28 mb/d in its reference scenario, with the share of Saudi Arabia

30. Petroleum Economics Ltd., London; *MEES*, 45:37, September 2002, p. D3.
31. Ibid.

estimated in excess of 12 mb/d. In either case, Saudi Arabia remains the number one world oil exporter (Table 4.4).

Table 4.4

World Oil Production by Region and Country, Reference Case, 1990-2025

(mb/d)

Region/Country	*History (Estimates)*		*Projections*				
	1990	*2001*	*2005*	*2010*	*2015*	*2020*	*2025*
OPEC							
Persian Gulf	16.2	20.6	21.7	24.8	29.2	34.6	40.5
Other OPEC	8.3	9.8	9.9	11.3	12.2	13.6	15.1
Total OPEC	24.5	30.4	31.6	36.1	41.4	48.2	55.6
Non-OPEC							
Industrialised							
United States	9.7	9.0	9.0	9.2	9.0	9.4	9.4
Canada	2.0	2.8	3.1	3.4	3.6	3.8	4.1
Mexico	3.0	3.6	3.8	4.2	4.5	4.6	4.8
Western Europe	4.6	6.9	6.6	6.5	6.0	5.6	5.1
Other	0.8	0.9	0.9	1.0	1.0	0.9	0.9
Total Industrialised	20.1	23.2	23.4	24.3	24.1	24.3	24.3
Eurasia							
China	2.8	3.3	3.5	3.6	3.5	3.5	3.4
Former Soviet Union	11.4	8.8	9.7	11.6	13.3	14.4	15.9
Eastern Europe	0.3	0.2	0.3	0.3	0.3	0.4	0.4
Total Eurasia	14.5	12.3	13.5	15.5	17.1	18.3	19.7
Other Non-OPEC							
Central and South America	2.4	3.8	4.3	4.7	5.7	6.2	6.7
Pacific Rim	1.7	2.5	2.5	2.6	2.8	2.7	2.6
Other	3.5	4.8	5.4	6.1	7.3	8.1	9.4
Total Other Non-OPEC	7.6	11.1	12.2	13.4	15.8	17.0	18.7
Total Non-OPEC	42.2	46.6	49.1	53.2	57.0	59.6	62.7
Total World	66.7	77.0	80.7	89.3	98.4	107.8	118.3
Persian Gulf Production as a Percentage of World Consumption	24.6	26.7	26.8	27.7	29.6	32.0	34.1

Note: Production includes crude oil (including lease condensates), natural gas liquids, other hydrogen hydrocarbons for refinery feedstock, refinery gains, alcohol, and liquids produced from coal and other sources. Totals may not equal sum of components due to independent rounding.

Sources: *History*: Energy Information Administration (EIA), Energy Markets and Contingency Information Division. *Projections*: EIA, System for the Analysis of Global Energy Markets (2003); and US Department of the Interior, US Geological Survey, *World Petroleum Assessment 2000*. Reston, VA. July 2000.

Table 4.5 shows Saudi Arabia's oil production, OPEC oil production and Saudi share in OPEC production from 1980 to 2001.

Table 4.5

Saudi Oil Production and its Share of Total of OPEC

('000b/d, 1980-2005)

Year	*Saudi Production*	*OPEC Production*	*Saudi % of OPEC*
1980	9,990	27,445	36.40
1981	9,985	23,380	42.70
1982	6,695	19,930	33.59
1983	5,225	18,425	28.35
1984	4,760	18,470	25.77
1985	3,565	17,215	20.70
1986	5,150	19,555	26.33
1987	4,600	19,345	23.77
1988	5,720	21,605	26.47
1989	5,635	23,215	24.27
1990	7,105	25,135	28.26
1991	8,820	24,692	35.72
1992	9,098	26,074	34.89
1993	8,962	26,875	33.34
1994	8,873	27,204	32.61
1995	8,890	27,466	32.36
1996	9,036	28,252	31.98
1997	9,213	29,553	31.17
1998	9,219	30,821	29.91
1999	8,549	29,368	29.10
2000	9,115	30,901	29.49
2001	8,768	30,181	29.05
2002	8,680	28,240	30.73
2003	8410.3	26884.6	31.28
2004	8897.0	29549.2	30.10
2005	9353.3	30673.3	30.49

Source: Prepared from *BP Statistical Review of World Energy*, various issues.

Moreover, as the single largest reserve holder, Saudi Arabia has a unique oil policy that is designed to maximise the benefit of holding so much of the world's oil supply. Saudi Arabia's goal is to assure that oil's role in the international economy is maintained as long as possible. It has been argued that Saudi policy has always denounced efforts by industrialised countries to wean themselves away from oil dependence, whether through tax policy or regulation.[32] In fact, Saudi strategy focuses on three different political arenas, reflecting the oil strategy. The first involves ties between the kingdom and other OPEC countries. The second concerns the kingdom's relationship with other non-OPEC producers such as Mexico, Norway, and Russia. Finally there is Saudi Arabia's links with the major oil importing regions—most importantly North America, but also Europe and Asia. Given the size of the Saudi oil sector, the kingdom has a unique and critical role in setting world oil prices. Since its overridding objectives are maximising revenues generated from oil exports and extending the life of its petroleum reserves, Riyadh aims to keep prices as high as long as possible. But the price cannot be so high that it stifles demand or encourages other competitive sources of supply. Nor can it be so low that the kingdom cannot achieve minimum revenue targets. The critical balancing act of Saudi policy therefore is to maintain the price within a reasonable band. Stopping oil prices from falling below the minimum level requires cooperation from other OPEC and occasionally from non-OPEC countries. Preventing prices from rising too high requires keeping enough spare production capacity to use in an emergency situation. The kingdom can afford to maintain this spare capacity because of the abundance of oil reserves and the comparatively low cost of developing and maintaining reserves. In today's soft market, in which Saudi Arabia produces around 7.4 mb/d, the kingdom has close to 3 mb/d of spare capacity. Its spare capacity is usually ample enough to entirely displace the production of another large oil-exporting country if supply is disrupted or a producer tries to reduce output to increase prices. This spare capacity is greater than the total oil exports of all other oil-exporting countries—except Russia. In addition, even in the low demand, high non-OPEC production growth scenario, the Middle East still accounts for 65-70 per cent of OPEC production and more than 20 per cent of global oil production. Saudi Arabia would account for 25-30 per cent of OPEC production and 8-11 per cent of global production. Under

---

32. Morse, Edward L., and James Richard (2002). "The Battle for Energy Dominance", *Foreign Affairs*, March-April, pp.16-31.

any scenario (even the most conservative demand outlook), Saudi Arabia would need to produce between 7 mb/d and 9 mb/d to meet global oil demand, even taking into account prospects for a slighter adjustment of OPEC quotas. Saudi Arabia would remain the single largest oil exporter in the world and the only country with sufficient spare capacity to continue to play its role as one of the pillars of global oil supply security. No other producer will be able to challenge the position of Saudi Arabia as the largest oil exporter and prime provider of oil supply security in this decade.[33] This spare capacity has helped the kingdom to maintain cordial relations with major oil consuming/ importing countries such as the US in the past. Therefore, Saudi Arabia is the most important element in energy security. Saudi Arabia supplies, more than 9 mb/d (2002) which is expected to rise to 13-15mb/d in 2010 to meet growing oil demand and offset resource depletion in non-OPEC countries. In fact, as one analyst has outlined that, "global oil security rests on the twin pillars of the strategic stocks of the IEA member states and Saudi Arabia's spare capacity."[34] Though Saudi Arabia has the potential and the reserves to meet projected demand but the expansion will call for massive investment. And given the social, economic, and political condition in Saudi Arabia, the implementation of suitable policies is the need of the hour to ensure energy security of the world. And the necessary investment should easily flow into the country to ease the task. It has been, therefore, argued that, disruption of Gulf oil supplies is a major threat to energy security, which would lead to global recession.[35] Thus, short-term supply disruption due to regional conflict cannot be ruled out.

However, over the years the means to overcome such disruptions have developed in the global regime. The best illustration of this is the minimal effect of the Iraqi invasion of Kuwait in 1991 on the world oil market. Although 4 mb/d oil dropped from the market, Saudi Arabia increased its production and restored stability to the oil market and

33. Franssen, Herman (2002). "Arab-US Energy Needs in Perspective", *MEES*, Vol. 45(37), 16th September, pp.D1-D7.

34. Ibid.

35. David, S.R. (1999). "Saving America from the Coming Civil Wars", *Foreign Affairs*, Vol. 78(1): 103-16.

prices within a week. Instruments for stabilising the oil market are improving year after year—strategic stocks held by oil companies and major oil consuming countries, development and liberalisation of oil markets, and regional and global energy agreements. For instance, the enormous expenditure on the 1990-91 Gulf War, totalling several hundred billion dollars, was meant to ensure energy security for major oil importing countries. The six GCC states, which control nearly 45 per cent of the world's recoverable oil reserves contributed more than $60 billion to the US led allied offensive to eject Iraqi forces from Kuwait in 1991.[36] This also signifies the vulnerability of GCC countries in the wake of any possible supply disruption due to regional conflicts.

Another factor in determining energy security is the quantity of stocks—the cushioning against supply disruption. Oil stocks are usually held by oil companies for operational purposes, and by countries and state utilities to provide a cushion against unexpected surges in demand and possible disruptions in imports. Oil companies usually hold stocks that account for 55-65 days of consumption. IEA members are required to hold emergency oil stocks equivalent to at least 90 days of import. But in case of developing countries it is not easy to hold oil stocks. Because of the cost, their stocks are relatively smaller than those of the IEA countries, which amount to only 25-55 days of consumption that is also typical of oil companies in these countries. In 1997, world oil stocks were about 5,500 million barrels, equal to 70-80 days of average global consumption. Though this implies that there are enough stocks, yet this is only for a short period. This can be substantiated from the experience of past years. Oil stocks/stockpiles in the US/Europe dwindled in 1998, which reflects the western oil companies' policies of maintaining stocks minimum in their effort to slim management to survive in the phase of liberalisation. In addition various governments (in France, US) have used the stock either selling in the market to secure fiscal discipline[37] or to meet statutory standards for their regional trade union.[38] The

36. AFP (Agence France-Presse) (1998). "Gulf States can not Afford to Finance another War", *Jordan Times*, 16th February, p.10.

37. In March 1996, the US government decided to sell part of the strategic petroleum reserves to secure fiscal revenues and the SPR sold in 1996 reached a total of 23 million barrels.

38. In July the German government decided a partial (of about 14 million barrels) sale of national reserves to meet the EU standards for the monetary union.

reduction in the level of stockpiles, the shock absorber for supply disruption, indicates that the world emergency preparedness was impaired. Thus, energy security depends on the policies of industrialised countries in this regard. Moreover, with the continued growth of non-OECD oil consumption, centering on the Asian growth factor, it can be argued that stocks will function less effectively. Their size relative to the global oil market is small; since most developing countries do not maintain emergency oil stocks (may not be able to afford them). On this trend it can be said that, vulnerability to sudden and substantial oil supply disruption is enormous.

Another aspect of energy security is the liberalisation of energy markets in importing countries. Liberalisation and deregulation, coupled with the development of oil futures and forward markets, mean an easier and more secure flow of oil from exporting to importing countries. Most oil producing countries are now inviting foreign oil companies to participate in oil development, which significantly enhances security of the global oil market. Although, security in terms of flows of oil and gas to importing countries is improving, the security of supply to consumers faces new challenges. Liberalisation, the withdrawal of government responsibility for supply, and competition among private suppliers are creating challenges in securing reliable supply to individual consumers. In this regard, it is worth analysing the concept of 'energy security externality',[39] which has implications for consumers in a deregulated scenario of energy sector. A security cost that energy consumers can take into account in their private decisions is not an externality. For instance, companies who buy a particular fuel may in various ways buy insurance against supply interruptions; however, since they bear this cost themselves it is not an externality. External costs are those that accrue to others in the economy. In the case of energy security externality, the costs for emergency measures, diversification and other instruments to manage the risk of supply disruptions would be borne by the importers and

39. An 'energy security externality', associated with the use of a given fuel, is "the cost of an interruption in its supply that is not borne by purchasers of the fuel," for details see, IEA/OECD (2001). "Safeguarding Energy Supply Security", in *Towards a Sustainable Energy.* Paris: IEA/OECD. pp.75-98.

eventually the consumers of the fuel that causes the externality. Though attempts have been made to estimate the economic costs of a supply disruption or sudden price spikes, it is not possible to distinguish between the internal and external costs in a comprehensive way. However, one study carried out by the US Department of Energy (US DOE), an annual external cost for the period 1990-2020 lies in the range of US $0.44-1.27 per barrel of oil consumed. The estimate is reduced to US $0.17-0.49/bbl if the strategic petroleum reserve is taken into account. As per these estimates, the oil security externality for the United States amounts to some 1-3 per cent of current US crude oil spot prices.[40]

Another development in the dynamics of energy security is the face off and diplomatic wrangling between the USA and Iran over the latter's proposed nuclear development and its implications for the security of the global oil regime. Given the fact that the Middle East region has been historically unstable, any possible military strike on Iran will put the whole region into turmoil, which will have serious short- and long-term implications for the world and especially energy security. This issue is crucial in the present market environment of overheating demand, low spare production capacity, peak oil and projected higher oil prices and OPEC's latest production cut decision.

Besides these issues, another most important issue regarding oil security is the transit route. Since bulk of the oil and gas reserves are in the Persian Gulf region, Strait of Hormuz is counted as the potential choking point. As per one estimate,

> Over 14 mb/d of oil flows through this strait to Japan, United States, Western Europe and other countries. It is the world's most important oil chokepoint. At its narrowest, it consists of 2-mile wide channels for inbound and outbound tanker within the Omani side of the Strait, and a 2-mile wide buffer zone...The US Department of Energy reference case indicates that exports through the Strait must more than double by 2020, reaching 42 mb/d. This implies that up to three times more tankers will transit the Strait in 2020 than transit it today. Closure of the Strait of Hormuz would require use of longer alternate transportation routes at increased costs and these routes

40. Ibid.

cannot meet anything approaching current export levels. The routes include the 4.8 mb/d capacity Petroline, the 2.2 mb/d IPSA- I & II lines and the Abqaiq-Yanbu natural gas liquids line across Saudi Arabia to the Red Sea. [41]

The sensitivity of the issue needs to be appreciated in view of the emerging markets in the Asia Pacific region with China and India as the leading destinations. It has been argued that, "sharp increased tanker traffic in particular the number of ships passing through, raises the question of providing security for the increased volume of trade and securing the requisite number of ships not to mention the prospects of oil spills and ship accidents."[42]

Security of Natural Gas Supply

Natural Gas is slowly gaining importance in the world energy scene. Between 1987 and 1997 gas consumption increased from 1,756 giga cubic metres to 2,197, at an annual growth rate of 2.27 per cent, compared with 1.47 per cent for total primary commercial energy consumption. Over the period until 2020 natural gas demand is expected to still faster-at an annual rate of 2.6 per cent, compared with 1.9 per cent for oil. And natural gas supply, since it is starting from a much lower base, than oil supply, is not expected to peak until well beyond 2020.[43] International traded natural gas accounted for 19 per cent of gas consumption in 1998, compared with 44 per cent for oil. So just as for oil, though to a lesser extent, there is mismatch between the location of gas supply and its consumption. Security of gas supply, therefore, is critical. But the physical characteristics of natural gas make the supply security more critical. Unlike crude oil, natural gas requires expensive pipelines or LNG infrastructure. These delivery systems of natural gas are inflexible, since, pipelines cannot be moved or built overnight, and LNG, although somehow portable, still requires an expensive receiving terminal. Moreover, gas is difficult

---

41. Cordesman, Anthony H. (1999). *Are Energy Wars Still Possible?*. Washington DC: Center for Strategic and International Studies. February 11.

42. Pant, Girijesh (2002), "India's Energy Security: The Gulf Factor", *GSP Occasional Paper Series*, GSP 2002/2. New Delhi: GSP, CWAAS, SIS, JNU. p.8.

43. IEA (1998). *World Energy Outlook 1998*. Paris: IEA/OECD.

to store in significant quantities. The energy content per unit of volume is much lower for gas than for oil.

At the simplest level, gas supply security can mean operational reliability—in other words that gas flows to the consumer when it is required. Security of supply also involves reducing strategic risk, mainly the risk of a major disruption to supplies caused either by political factors or by major technical failure. Strategic risk is growing in parallel with the growing share of natural gas in meeting countries' primary energy requirements. The long-term risk is to ensure that consuming countries can secure future and additional supplies as their existing supplies are depleted. This represents a challenge as the bulk of the world's gas reserves are in the areas that are far from current markets and also often have a high level of country risk. With the increase in internationally traded gas, as expected in coming decades, political risks to gas supplies and security of inter-regional grids have come to the forefront of energy security discussion.

Another important fact in considering the security of gas supplies is the implications of liberalisation of gas markets for security. Traditionally, the international gas trade has been conducted on the basis of long-term 'take-or-pay contracts',[44] which is completely different from a commodity market, where supply and demand balance at whatever is the market-clearing price. The traditional system is also frequently involved either monopsony or oligopoly buyers such as the European and Japanese utilities. However, it has been argued that such a system was the only way to match supply with demand, ensure orderly development of the market, and allow all parties to recoup their investments. In fact, from importing countries' viewpoint, it has evidently worked: the record on gas supplies security in Europe and Japan.

But recently in the phase of liberalisation, where third party access

44. Under 'take-or-pay' contract system, designed to manage risk, the buyer agrees to take a certain volume over a period of time and to pay for that volume regardless of whether it is actually used. In effect the buyer takes all the volume risk (the risk as to how much gas the end-use market will actually consume). The seller agrees to sell a certain quantity at a price indexed to such factors such as the price of competing fuels, the price of electricity and producer inflation. The sellers therefore take the risk that this price will cover its cost of production and provide a return on its investment. For details see, Chambers, Ann (1999). *Natural Gas and Electric Power in Non-technical Language.* Tulsa, Oklahoma: Penwell Pub. Co.

is being given, so that any producer has the ability to transport its product to the end market, and any customer can buy gas from any producer/wholesaler, the security aspect is being talked of. Though this system has worked succeeded in ensuring gas supply security in the US, yet it cannot be emulated in other markets. Long-term take-or-pay contracts do not completely eliminate political or commercial risks. If a country is unable or unwilling to export its gas reserves for whatsoever reason, who has legal title to them is irrelevant. However, it has been argued that such contracts can do and have done in the past is to give the parties a degree of confidence in the viability of a project and help securing financing. The separation of transport from supply, liberalisation, over the long term will encourage producers able to supply the market at the lowest cost to meet consumers' demand. This has become successful in the United States, where pricing of gas supply and associated services are transparent and explicit, and making market participants searching for the most cost-effective ways of ensuring gas supply. However, the result of such a policy depends upon the structure of industries and players and regulative structures in countries' concerned.

Another most important aspect while considering the issue of gas supply security in recent years has been the impression that major gas producers' possible cartelisation and its impact on world gas supply security, in the lines of the illustrious OPEC to increase revenue or for other motives. Against the backdrop of liberalisation and the changing structure of the gas industry—which has developed security sensitiveness among consuming and importing countries—the recent initiative of the major gas producers and exporters, at Algiers in February 2002, to establish a Forum of the Gas Exporting Countries (FGEC), to protect their mutual interest, has attracted a great deal of attention and prompted concerns that they may move to assume an OPEC-like role in managing the world gas market. This attempt by the major gas producers and exporters is jeopardising the effort to promote competitive energy markets in consuming and importing countries.[45]

Despite their differences in terms of their reserves, production and

45. Aissaoui, Ali (2002). "Gas-Exporting Countries: Towards Cartelisation", *MEES*, Vol. 45(32): D1-D3, 12th August.

exports, the 15 gas producing and exporting countries (Table 4.6) which have so far shown interests in some form of consultation, are now seen to have the potential to wield more power than OPEC. Indeed, they contribute 63 per cent of the global gas trade, as compared to 47 per cent for OPEC oil, and control 84 per cent of LNG exports.

Table 4.6

Adherents to the Forum of Gas Exporting Countries: Reserves, Production and Exports (2001, bcm).

Country	*Proved Reserves*	*Net Production****	*Exports*	
			Pipeline	*LNG*
Algeria	4,250	78.2	32.2	25.5
Bolivia*	680	4.1	2.5	
Brunei	390	11.4		9.0
Egypt*	1,000	21.0		
Indonesia	2,620	62.9	1.0	31.8
Iran	23,000	60.6	0.1	
Libya*	1,310	5.4		0.8
Malaysia	2,120	47.4	1.5	20.9
Nigeria	3,510	13.4		7.8
Norway**	1,250	57.5	50.5	
Oman	830	13.4		7.4
Qatar	14,440	32.5		16.5
Russia	47,570	542.4	126.9	
Turkmenistan**	2,860	47.9	4.2	
Venezuela*	4,180	28.9		
Total 15 (bcm)	110,240	1,027.0	218.9	119.7
World's Share (Per cent)	71	42	53	84

Notes: *** net production excludes gas flared or re-injected. * Countries which joined the FGEC at its second meeting in Algiers. ** Countries which participated in the Teheran meeting but dropped out of Algiers.

Source: *MEES*, 12th August 2002, Table 1, p.D2.

Analysts have so far dismissed the potential of an OPEC-like cartel 'cartelisation' of gas exporting countries on the grounds that, in contrast to oil, there is no world gas market. According to these analyses,[46] gas markets are essentially regional as a result of high

46. See MacDougall, Michael, and Peter T. Linder (1992). "Long Term Outlook for World Gas Trade: 1990-2015", *Calgary*. Canada: Canadian Research Institute and also see, Gray, Dale (1995). "Reforming the Energy Sector in Transition Economies: Selected Experience and Lessons", *World Bank Discussion Papers* No. 246. Washington DC.

transportation costs and physical inflexibility. In addition, the structural and regulatory features of the gas industry in each region have resulted in different market values for gas and, as a consequence, different levels of prices even though gas prices have directly or indirectly been linked to those of oil. This therefore explains, even when acting within the institutional framework of OPEC, gas exporters have been unable to coordinate their pricing policies. However, the establishment of FGEC is a clear indication that gas-exporting countries have resorted to act independently of OPEC, which have serious implications for energy security.

Income (Demand and Supply) Security[47] of GCC Oil/Gas Exporters

As pointed out earlier, the GCC countries have become vulnerable to possible demand as well as supply disruptions. These countries depend on oil/gas revenue not for income only, but for their overall economic development. Their dependence on oil/gas export revenue is not restricted to them only; the benefits spread to other countries in the form of trade and investments and also to their region as wage remittances and financial assistance to other regions. In the GCC countries, oil export revenue accounts for almost two-thirds of government revenue. The dramatic drop in oil prices in 1998 and early 1999 led not only to budgetary problems in these countries, but also to unemployment and significant drop in income level. Such economic problems were not only restricted to the oil exporters, but were also experienced by their neighbouring countries, which depend on revenues from exports of goods and services to these countries and on remittances from workers in these countries. For energy-exporting countries, export security is becoming as important as energy import security is to resource-scarce countries. All this is therefore enhancing the prospects for global energy security, in a sense.

Dependence on energy exports has an additional implication for the GCC countries. These countries are worried about the possible long-

47. Income security here can be defined as the secure revenue sources for oil/gas exporting countries.

term impact on export demand of policies to mitigate environmental impacts, promote energy efficiency; and increase use of renewable energy sources. Although exaggerated in the short-term, the potential impact could pose long-term problems for countries, adversely affecting their economic and social development. Having met the needs of global energy needs over the past years, oil-exporting countries are asking for compensation if mitigation actions start to bite. This request is being reviewed in international organisations and negotiations. It may be many years before exporting countries' income is affected. Meantime, it is expected that with international assistance and compensation, they will be able to diversify their income sources and reduce their dependence on oil/gas exports.

In addition to the above factors, all forecast studies suggest global oil demand will maintain a modest growth rate of near about 2 per cent per year, as compared to 0.3 per cent per year during the 1980s. This strong growth in oil demand is solely attributable to developing Asian economies in general and India and China in particular; which are poised to register higher demand growth rates in the coming years in reflection to their strong economic growth rate and the fact that these countries are starting oil/gas consumption from a lower base. This factor is expected to be the main driving force for the world oil/gas demand growth.

Thus in the backdrop of recent developments in the global oil and gas regime, it can be aptly argued that as the oil/gas demand continues to grow centering on the Asian factor, the world is expected to become more and more dependent on oil supplies from politically volatile region—the Gulf—and that with the oil stockpiles becoming lean, vulnerability to oil/gas supply disruption is gaining momentum as a strategic global issue once again.

Energy Security of Developing Asian Countries

The most notable point in considering issues of energy security since the end of the Cold War is the fact that, along with the rapid rise in population and impressive economic growth of developing countries, the demand for energy by these countries is continuing to follow a sharply rising trend. In recent years, the Asian countries, in general, and China and India, in particular, have taken the centre stage in world economic growth and maintained high growth rates in the climate of recession in most of the industrialised West. Though, these countries' per capita energy consumption is still very low compared to that of the developed countries, yet these countries are experiencing increases in the consumption of every form of energy. An issue of growing importance, therefore, is that for Asian countries and India, to sustain economic growth rate, long-term energy supply sources will have to be found, since regional reserves and production are insufficient to match either current demand or future demand.

Under such a scenario, because local crude oil/gas production/reserves are inadequate to meet demand, energy imports in the Asian region increased substantially. Asia's total net oil imports grew from a total of 6.60 mb/d in 1990 to 11.7 mb/d in 1997 and due to the East Asian currency crisis, it steadied around 11.0 mb/d in 1998. From now on, given outlooks for their primary energy supply-demand and crude oil production, net oil imports of the Asian region is projected to rise to 16.7 mb/d in 2005. Meanwhile by 2005, Asia will have five economies, aside from Japan growing into big oil importers with their net oil imports exceeding a 1 mb/d each. The five economies include the Republic of Korea with 2.6 mb/d, China with 2.0 mb/d, India with 1.8 mb/d, Thailand with 1.2 mb/d and Taiwan with 1.02 mb/d. Another fact is that even now, Asia registers by far higher dependence on oil/gas imports from the Middle East and particularly from the Gulf region (77 per cent), more than the US and Europe.[48] And many projections indicate that Asia's dependence on the Gulf will keep rising in the short-term and long-term. Thus, Asia is particularly vulnerable to any future supply disruption, unlike the sensitive Western countries. Moreover, except the Republic of Korea, no Asian country has any provision of energy stockpiles, only maintenance stocks held by either government utilities or private companies. As mentioned in earlier sections of this chapter, the liberalisation process going on in the energy sectors of these economies add to the concerns of supply security. Further, in Asia, there is no organisational framework to confront the vulnerabilities of energy supply disruptions, unlike the IEA for OECD countries.

---

48. Details regarding this can be accessed on line at, *http://www.eia.doe.gov.*

It can be mentioned that in the background of high energy imports by the Asian countries in the near future and their thrust for oil and gas supplies from overseas, a competitive environment in the Asian region itself is in the making, which will have multidimensional regional as well as global implications. Moreover, the intensity of competition among the Asian players is seen as an emerging dimension to contemporary energy security concerns. It is argued that,

> With the end of the Cold War, economic competition may replace ideology as the focus of international conflict. Oil will remain the critical strategic and economic commodity. Most importantly, developing oil shortages in Asia could lead to a stress on a global scale and if not handled well the situation could lead to a new global war.[49]

Another analyst has given a more alarming prognosis of the Asian competition. According to him,

> As oil commerce in increasingly global and transparent markets has come to be shaped more by transport costs than political relationships, a largely bifurcated global market has arisen: oil flows from the Middle East gravitating to Asia; oil supplies from the Western Hemisphere (Mexico, Venezuela, Colombia and Canada) to a large degree displacing Gulf oil in the US markets.[50]

Gulf and Asia: Energy Interdependence and Vulnerability

All energy experts are unanimous on the view that Asia, not Europe and the OECD is the global hotspot for energy demand growth caused mainly by the relatively high tax effect on the consumption in other energy consuming parts of the world and the fuel-switch which is sweeping in that part of the world. While oil demand in Europe reduced by 0.8 per cent and 0.5 per cent in 1999 and 2000 respectively, consumption in the Asian region grew by 3.6 per cent in 1999 and over 5 per cent in 2000. According to the latest statistics, most of Asia's growth in oil demand is accounted by four economies of the region, i.e., Japan, China, South Korea and India, which

---

49. "Oil, Technology and War in the Next Decade", Crustal Fluids GP/PE/GES 200, *Spring Quarter*, 1995/1996, *http://srb.stanford.edu/nur/classes/otw.html*.

50. Manning, Robert A. (2000). "The Asian Energy Predicament", *Survival*, Vol. 42(3). Spring. The International Institute for Strategic Studies.

together import 60 per cent of their total oil consumption. The IEA expects this figure to increase to 90 per cent by the year 2020. More importantly, virtually all these imports will originate from the Gulf region, as only the OPEC producers are strategically located to these markets. Hence any supply disruption or abrupt price hikes will severely affect these economies and ultimately the Gulf countries, as this region is the latest hope for the Gulf's re-establishment in the global oil regime.

This interdependence between Asia and the Gulf countries is a major factor in the global energy security conundrum. The main concern for the Asian countries is the instabilities in the Gulf region and its pernicious effects on ensuring energy security. Moreover, this interdependence between Asia and the Gulf countries has developed concerns among Western policy makers, as they think; the greater interdependence will hamper their long-term political, strategic calculations, which may swing in favour of these emerging countries. As one has put it,

> With a pacific region importing 20-24 mb/d from the region in 2020, the benign commercial relations between the two regions are likely to see a qualitative change including the possibility of an 'Islamic-Confucian Civilisation Alliance'-one of the West's worst nightmares.[51]

The implications of energy interdependence between the Asian countries and the Gulf countries has been aptly analysed through three different scenarios—the near term (to 2010) and tangible; the long term and intangible and potential nightmare scenarios:[52]

> The first scenario underlines the growing interdependence in terms of mutual need to trade and invest in the energy sector. According to one estimate, by 2010, if Asia is importing 17 mb/d from the Middle East at $24 a barrel, the result would be capital transfers to the Middle East to the worth of $124 billion annually. Even in today's global financial markets, where nearly $2 trillion a day floats through cyberspace, that is serious money. Such revenues could, in part, be recycled into downstream investment in dynamic Asian economies. Expanding capital flows to the Middle East would also go some

51. Ibid.

52. Pant *op. cit.*, No. 42, p.10.

distance towards ameliorating a growing list of problems in major oil exporting countries such as Saudi Arabia, Kuwait, Iran and Iraq. Riyadh for example has seen a significant decline in living standards over the past 15 years, has a large demographic bulge of young adults to absorb into its economy, and has accumulated foreign debt of $130 billion.

In the second scenario it is visualised that 'such capital flows could also accelerate efforts to obtain a new cycle of modern weapons including WMDs'. If at least the rough lines of anticipated economic and financial consequences of the Middle East-Asian energy interdependence for the global economy are discernible, the political and security implications enter the realm of the intangible and speculative. In the 1930s, it was energy security that led Japan to occupy Indonesia (then the Dutch East Indies) and take control of its oil fields. Indeed the US oil embargo was an important factor leading Tokyo to attack Pearl Harbor, bringing the US into the Second World War. Some analysts see in China, a rising power with a new found energy dependence, the potential for twenty-first century repetition of these experiences. The problem for Asian stability, growing with each barrel of Chinese oil imports, is now clear-asserts Kent Calder in an influential book on energy and security in Asia. It is the danger that China's attempts to safeguard its oil supply lanes and defend its historical sovereignty in adjacent seas poses threats for other nations, especially Japan. China claims 80 per cent of the South China Sea as territorial water, 70 per cent of Japan's oil supplies pass that way. Thus logic runs, as Chinese imports steadily rise, defending the fragile sea-lanes to the far off Persian Gulf becomes a new security imperative for the PLA Navy.

In the third scenario, such speculation begins to move from the merely intangible into the category of nightmare scenarios, in which China deploys destroyers and aircraft carriers to interdict tanker traffic in a confrontation over the disputed Spartly Island in the South China Sea, goes to war with Japan over the virtually inhabited Senkaku Island, or, worse still, allies with Iraq or Iran in a future Gulf War. It is easy to conjure up such scare stories. The number of oil tankers navigating the waters of the Indian Ocean, through the straits of Malacca and the South China Sea for ports in Pusan, Yokohama and Shanghai, in the two decades ahead is likely to increase three-fold. But whether this prospect poses a security threat depends to a considerable degree on whether China elects to view energy security geo-strategically or geo-economically.

However, discounting the possibility of tensions among the Asian consumers, one analyst sees such ensuing competition among the Asian players will act as a founding stone towards the establishment of a framework of co-prosperity. As pointed out,

> The new pattern of supply and transport has created a reasonable rather than destructive rivalry among Asian countries. There is no stampede to sign contracts at any price or to offer unreasonable terms. In today's transparent oil market, prices are based on futures markets or other formulas. Indeed no major producer in the Middle East sets its own prices today. The Asian rivalry is based on an economic mandate to form strong economic and energy bonds with the Middle East and to create linkages that ensure the smooth flow of oil and gas. This is a two way street. Key Middle East suppliers recognise that Asia is their best market and try to ensure credibility and consumer satisfaction. The Asians seek to negotiate the best deals, but do not wish to depend solely on one economy or region. All this has mitigated the fears regarding Asia's energy security problems. The issue of the reserve base is no longer a critical energy security concern because there are enough identified resources in the Middle East.[53]

The latest concern among major Asian importers has been the increasing penetration of China into the energy sectors of the Gulf region and successful joint development and investment proposals in the framework of crisscross deals, i.e., recently concluded pact between China and Saudi Arabia is a case in point. This has raised eyebrows in the global policy discourse and in the regional scenario also.

Energy Security in India

A modest growth rate and sustenance of that growth rate in an economy has become essential in recent times due to the process of globalisation sweeping across continents. The maintenance of a modest growth path considerably depends on the availability of substantial energy sources, as energy is used as strategic input in every economic activity. India, an emerging vibrant economy, presently

---

53. Fesharaki, Fereidun (1999). "Energy and the Asian Security Nexus", *Journal of International Affairs*, Vol. 35(1), Fall. New York: Colombia University.

achieving a modest annual growth rate of 6 to 7 per cent in average need substantial energy supplies to sustain the growth rate in the foreseeable future. In such a scenario, energy security debate is being debated in the country every now and then. The gigantic volumes of oil/gas consumption, scarce domestic reserves and stagnant productions, and consequent voluminous energy imports have made energy security in India imminent and pertinent. In such regional and global scenario, as discussed in earlier chapters, India is poised to be a significant factor in regional (Asia) and global energy scenario in the coming years. Table 4.7 shows worlds' top 10 oil importers and India is in the 7th place (also see figure 4.1).

Table 4.7

World Oil Consumption, Production and Imports

(Million Tonnes)

	Consumption	*Production*	*Net Imports*
USA	944.6	310.2	**634.4**
China	327.3	180.8	**146.5**
Japan	244.2	0.1	**244.1**
Russian Federation	130.0	470.0	-340.0
Germany	121.5	0.1	**121.4**
India	115.7	36.2	**79.5**
South Korea	105.5	0.1	**105.4**
Canada	100.1	145.2	-45.1
France	93.1	0.1	**93.0**
Mexico	87.8	187.1	-99.3

Notes: 1. Production includes crude oil, lease condensate, natural gas liquids, other hydrocarbons and alcohol, and refinery gain.

2. Net imports are calculated by subtracting estimated production from consumption.

Source: BP (2006). *BP Statistical Review of World Energy 2006*.

As pointed out earlier India is taking strides in world energy demand, consumption, and imports. There are also clear projections regarding India's potential growth in the future. Thus, energy security is of vital concern to India's global standing and sustenance in the future.

Figure 4.1

Top Net Oil Imports, 2006

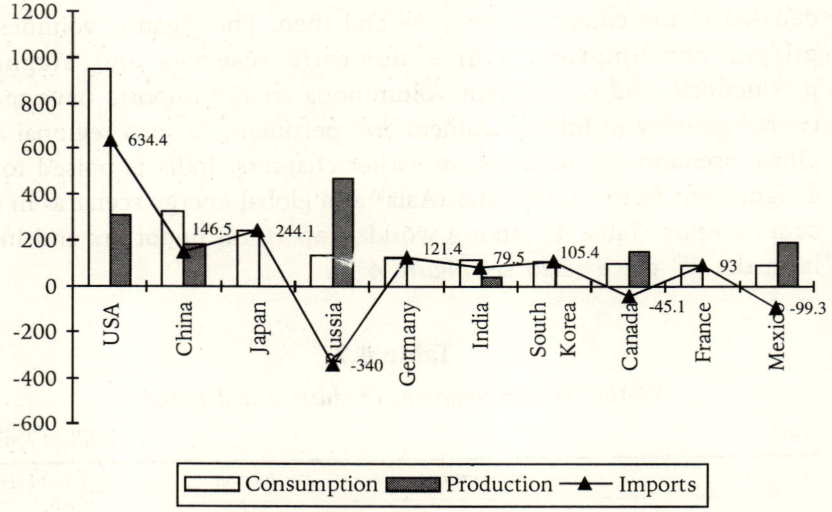

Source: Prepared from BP Statistical Review of World Energy 2006.

Vulnerability of India's Energy Security

In India, commercial fuels constitute about 68 per cent of the total energy consumed. Crude oil is the second largest commercial fuel (accounting for 27 per cent), after coal (61 per cent), and followed by natural gas (9 per cent). Oil and now natural gas are critical inputs to every sector of the Indian economy. India is emerging as a leading consumer of petroleum products with consumption rising at 6.4 per cent annually. India's dependence on crude oil and now natural gas is increasing day by day, compared to domestic production and reserve accretion. India imports about 70 per cent of oil for domestic consumption while only 30 per cent is produced domestically (Table 4.8). Though till now, the imports of natural gas has not taken place, yet, as discussed in earlier chapters, the import of natural gas will increase substantially in the future, as it is being used in large volumes in electricity generation and other productive processes in the country. The share of oil and petroleum products in total imports has risen to 31 per cent in 2000-01 compared to 25 per cent in 1999-2000 and 15 per cent in 1998-99. This has happened due to the high oil prices in 2000 and early 2001. While India's share of global oil production of crude oil in 1998 was less than 1 per cent, its share in world consumption was 2.15 per cent. Imports of crude oil exceeded domestic production for the first time during 1992-93.

Table 4.8

India's Imports and Exports of Crude Oil and Products

(Thousand Tonnes)

Year	*Total Imports Crude Oil*	*Petroleum Oil and Lubricants (POL)*	*Total Exports POL*
1990-91	20699	8660	2648
1994-95	27349	13951	3254
1995-96	27342	20335	3435
1996-97	33906	20265	3162
1997-98	34493	22970	2381
1998-99	39808	23772	720
1999-2000	57805	16608	746
2000-01	74097	9267	8365
2001-02	78706	7009	10085
2002-03	81989	7228	10289
2003-04	90434	8001	14620
2004-05	95864	8828	18211
2005-06*	99409	11677	21505

Note : * Provisional.

Source : Prepared from *Basic Statistics on Indian Petroleum Sector* (various issues). MoPNG. GoI.

The most important aspect is the fact that, GCC countries account for more than 65 per cent of India's oil imports. India is the one most dependent country on the Gulf region. Table 4.9 shows India' source of oil imports. Table 4.10 shows GCC countries' share in India's total imports.

Table 4.9

Sources of India's Import of Crude Petroleum and Products

(US $ Million)

Country	*1995-96*	*1996-97*	*1997-98*	*1998-99*	*1999-2000*
Bahrain	807.11	778.19	500.83	361.81	260.97
Kuwait	1872.38	2276.44	2109.66	1334.55	1740.11
Qatar	0.87	16.77	7.84	7.80	119.33
Oman	3.88	0.08	0.07	0.02	47.10
Saudi Arabia	1539.76	2140.93	1769.73	1191.81	2420.99
UAE	1050.52	1328.73	978.69	909.90	1798.57
Iran	433.69	677.14	429.32	256.25	1028.21
Iraq	–	24.82	185.60	150.90	199.76
Egypt	49.91	57.86	168.68	161.99	411.78
Yemen	17.15	12.20	10.04	1.78	251.73
USA	58.16	93.42	36.39	42.37	55.19
France	77.52	97.95	48.56	8.83	17.89
Germany	9.33	5.15	4.94	8.04	10.00
Italy	165.50	80.13	45.44	13.51	9.55
Spain	12.98	14.26	7.13	0.81	8.95
Greece	41.35	8.82	9.70	0.14	7.42
Netherlands	24.66	81.78	10.48	7.42	6.60
South Africa	1.33	0.34	4.35	10.31	7.36
Nigeria	716.29	1478.68	1033.57	1108.91	2871.69
Singapore	268.46	243.35	227.06	410.35	425.26
Japan	11.00	13.10	14.89	15.19	11.79
South Korea	15.07	5.08	65.06	36.27	181.37
Thailand	–	–	9.45	16.30	9.55
Malaysia	104.89	157.98	170.25	256.87	529.49
Indonesia	33.54	114.80	112.64	37.12	110.52
China	9.98	8.33	34.62	27.58	12.19
Pakistan	–	–	0.14	3.05	8.29
UK	33.52	32.90	43.37	8.59	15.84
Mexico	–	–	–	–	42.72

Source: CMIE (2001). *Foreign Trade and Balance of Payments*, July, Mumbai, p.217.

Table 4.10

GCC Countries' Share in India's Total Imports of Crude Oil and Products

(Per cent)

Country	*1995-96*	*1996-97**	*1997-98**	*1998-99**	*1999-2000**
Bahrain	10.71	7.75	6.13	5.66	2.07
Kuwait	24.84	22.66	25.81	20.86	13.78
Oman	0.05	–	–	–	0.37
Qatar	0.01	0.17	0.10	0.12	0.95
Saudi Arabia	20.43	21.31	21.65	18.63	19.17
UAE	13.94	13.23	11.97	14.22	14.24
Total GCC	70	65.12	65.66	59.49	50.58

Note: * Implies figures for Oman are not available.

Source: Prepared from, CMIE (2001). *Foreign Trade and Balance of Payments*. Mumbai. July, p.217.

Moreover, India is far more dependent than the US or Europe on the import of crude oil from Middle East. In 2004, about 70 per cent of India's total imports were from the Middle East region (see Figure 4.2).

Figure 4.2

Share of Regions in India's Crude Oil Imports

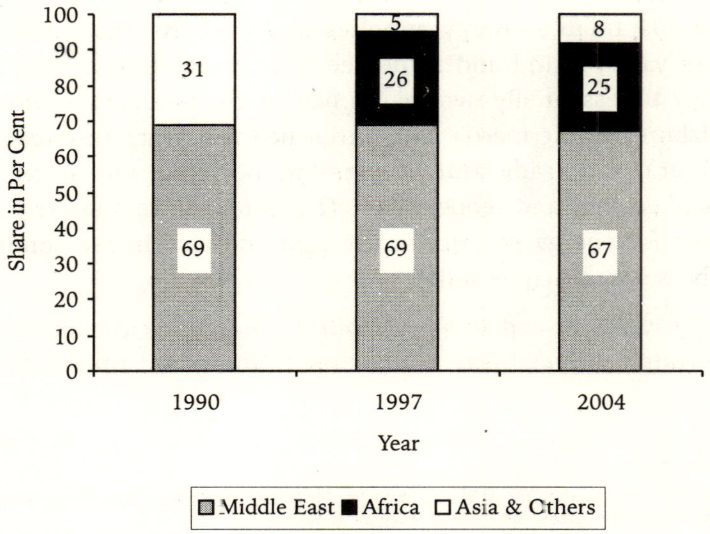

Source: Calculated from Planning Commission Data. GoI. 2005.

Thus it is the soaring of oil consumption, the low level of domestic production and productivity and the lack of development of alternatives that have given rise to vulnerabilities in energy security. For example, productivity of oil consumption or the energy intensity levels have been very week, as reflected by the figures: oil consumption per $1000 of GDP has risen by 13 per cent in India during over the period 1981-1991, while the same has decreased by 45-60 per cent in developed countries.

The past experiences of world oil shocks reveal the vulnerability of India more vividly. During the first oil shock of 1973-74, India's import bill rose by over 50 per cent in the first year. During the Gulf War of 1990-91, the net value of oil imports rose by 50 per cent and that of petroleum products by 72 per cent to Rs. 11,000 crores. The abrupt rise in oil prices has pernicious effects on the Indian economy. It has been estimated that every one dollar increase in oil prices drags down the GDP growth rates by 0.04 per cent and increases the inflation level by one percentage point.[54]

The study by FICCI-IDSA has descriptively analysed the vulnerability and impact of an oil shock on the various sectors of the Indian economy. The findings are summarised in the Box 4.2.

There are several key obstacles in realising India's quest for stable, secure and sustainable energy supplies at relatively stable prices. While these vary in kind and in degree from one energy source to another, they are essentially two-fold in nature: the internal, problems of political/bureaucratic inertia and entrenched resistance to outward looking liberalised trade and investment policies; and built-in constraints of geology and geopolitics.[55] The various factors underlying India's quest for energy security in the past and also in the coming years can be summarised as follows:

- *Lack of expertise and technical ability, financial constraints and inadequate policy decisions*: India's oil refining and oil recovery

---

54. FICCI-IDSA (2001). "India's Energy Security and Managing Oil Shock", *FICCI-IDSA*. New Delhi. November.

55. Manning, Robert A. (2000). *The Asian Energy Factor: Myths and Dilemmas of Energy, Security, and the Pacific Future*. New York: Council on Foreign Relations.

Box 4.2

Effects of Oil Shock on Indian Economy

Sectors

Transportation, Industry, Agriculture, Power, Tours and Travel, Equity Market

Impacts

- Transportation is by far the largest oil-consuming sector accounting 62 per cent of total oil consumption. Crude oil is crucial for this sector-be it road, sea or air transport. The impact of an oil shock would be transmitted through this sector. For example, heavy metals and first moving consumer goods, which depend on this sector, would be directly hit. A further sectoral impact would be a fall in demand for industrial products consuming fuels such as motor vehicles and oil engines.
- Naphtha as a feedstock in fertiliser industries accounts for 75 per cent. An oil shock would have a deep impact this sector, which will ultimately affect the agricultural sector and this may call for subsidies, which have adverse fiscal implications.
- The travel and tourism industry is hardly hit in the post-terrorist strike on Iraq. This shows that possible supply disruption now will result in recession in this sector.
- Equity markets are indirectly affected by oil price shocks. In equity markets an increase in oil prices generally lead to an initial weakening in the earnings of firms producing energy intensive output and their market valuations. This occurs both through higher production costs, which would be particularly severe in the traditional manufacturing and transportation companies, as well as through the slowdown in demand.
- Big price movements due to oil price hikes such as that of 1998 are disastrous because they curtail investment plan and also affect human capital and corporate performance.
- Consumer confidence could also plunge. For example, during the 190-91 Gulf War, the conference board's index of consumer confidence fell 74 points from August, the month of invasion to January 1991, the end of the war.
- High oil prices will affect the general price level, employment and thereby overall growth of the economy.

capabilities and overall energy technology is inadequate to meet the challenges of recent changes in the global energy sector. Though some public and private sector entities like ONGC Videsh Ltd. and Reliance Pvt. Ltd. have recently entered into technological alliances with foreign partners, a lot is to be done to overcome these hurdles.

- The meagre equity levels and financial strength of Indian oil and gas companies has affected the international presence. High interest rates in India relative to other countries have acted as a liability for the Indian oil and gas companies to compete for equity oil abroad. Moreover generating loans in the international market for oil and gas sector operations has not been successful due to India's lower position in world financial markets' country ranking. In addition, neither Indian banks nor the Indian government have provisions of special incentives in the form of soft loans for equity oil projects.
- Overall, the policy-making loopholes have affected adversely the quest for energy security. India doesn't have a coordinated energy policy till date.
- *Geopolitical Hurdles*: Regardless of the efficacy of India's reforms, India's hopes of diversifying supply as a means of enhancing energy security have been—and will continue to be—constrained by its political geography for the foreseeable future. India's geopolitical realities in regard to oil and gas resources are in many respects, the reverse of many other Asian actors. For example, Japan has spent tens of billions of dollars over the past three decades searching for oil fields in the Middle East or pursuing oil and gas schemes with Russia in an effort to diversify supplies. More recently, as we have seen, China has also purchased oilfields from Sudan to Central Asia and entertained the idea of constructing massive pipelines that have little economic rational in the hope of diversifying supplies in the name of geopolitics and energy security.
- *But for India, the Opposite is True*: energy projects that have a compelling economic logic are stifled by the geopolitical realities of South and Southwest Asia. Positioned on the Arabian

Peninsula, only 835 miles separate India's westernmost bulge from Oman on the tip of the peninsula, a major supplier of oil and gas. Turkmenistan's enormous gas reserves are also within range of commercially viable pipelines to India. Only its land border with Pakistan physically separates India from Iran. And of course, northeast India shares a long border with gas-rich Bangladesh, whose independent national existence was obtained with Indian support in 1971. India has sought oil and gas relationships with all these actors with the exception of Oman, where technical/economic problems have sidelined plans for an Oman-Bombay pipeline.

- Some prime examples of this dilemma involve Turkmenistan gas, Iranian oil and gas, and Bangladeshi gas. In the case of Turkmenistan gas, a Unocal-led consortium had laid the legal financial groundwork for building a 1,400 km pipeline from Turkmenistan through Afghanistan to Multan, Pakistan, with an additional 600 km connecting link to New Delhi. By the end of 1995 agreements were reached between Turkmenistan, Pakistan, and the Unocal group to build the pipeline, which could send some 1.6 billion cubic feet of gas a day into Pakistan and some portion to India. Construction was due to begin by the end of 1998, with initial deliveries to Pakistan in 2001. Yet in November 1998, continued instability and conflict in Taliban-led Afghanistan led Unocal to cancel the project. Another eventual obstacle may have been the pathology of Indo-Pakistan rivalry. Though Pakistani officials had publicly indicated support for the Indian leg of the pipeline as a 'win-win proposition', prior to its cancellation, it is unclear whether Pakistan would in fact have permitted the pipeline to be extended to India.[56] Moreover, skepticism about the prospects for Indo-Pakistani energy co-operation can be reinforced by Pakistan's reluctance to co-operate with a number of Indo-Iranian energy interdependence schemes in recent years. Though India and Iran have discussed a range of means of delivery; overland or under water pipelines, overland

56. Dadwal, Shebonti Roy (1997). "India's Energy Situation: Crisis in the Making", *Strategic Analysis*. New Delhi: IDSA. June.

train in Pakistan territory or territorial waters or usual LNG transports; yet there is both skepticism and apprehension affecting policy making in this regard.

According to some analysts,[57] perhaps the most frustrating and certainly the oddest geopolitical impediments for India, which would appear a natural economic relationship, is the case of neighbouring Bangladesh. For one of the world's poorest country—Bangladesh—its substantial proven gas reserves (around 11 trillion cu.ft.) could have become a source of economic prosperity, had these resources been marketed in the immediate vast Indian energy market. But a host of self-imposed obstacles have not only stifled the exploration and production of Bangladeshi gas, despite strong initiatives from major multinational firms like, Shell, Unocal, Occidental and Halliburton;[58] but also any initiatives to export to India. Moreover, there are supposed to be apprehensions in the Bangladeshi policy-making circles that economic integration with India would disadvantage its domestic industry, and more broadly, increased Indian domination. Therefore one analyst has rightly observed, "Why the Bangladeshis are reluctant to sell gas to India is one of the great mysteries."[59]

It can be mentioned that in recent years there are some positive developments regarding the source of diversification of import sources. Though these endeavours are marginal in comparison to attempts by China to secure oil imports from abroad, yet these give respite and encouragement for the future.

India is taking a 'calculated risk' to venture into countries where multinational angels fear to tread. ONGC Videsh Limited, the only firm permitted to pursue overseas exploration projects, has gone into strife-torn Sudan, outcast Libya, and explosive Iraq to secure that extra energy. The strategy was to tie up with countries, which required less investment, but were oil-rich, since safe havens like Saudi Arabia, Kuwait and the UAE were already cornered by the MNCs. That strategy is reflected in the country's *Hydrocarbon Vision 2025*, a report prepared by a Group of Ministers chaired by then Finance Minister Yashwant

57. *EIA*, "India-Country Survey", online at *http://www.eia.doe.gov*.
58. *EIA* (1999). "South Asia Regional Overview". US: Department of Energy. April.
59. *The Hindu*, 13th October, 1999.

Sinha. In the medium term, it said, the focus should be to build strong relations in focus countries with high attractiveness like Russia, Iraq, Iran and North African countries.

No wonder then that India's gambles—some of which are now paying off—include Sudan, Libya, Syria, Iraq, Myanmar and now Angola, where OVL plans to acquire Shell's 50 per cent equity in a large discovered field. On the radar is Nigeria and Azerbaijan (see Figure 4.3).

Figure 4.3

India's Energy Diplomacy

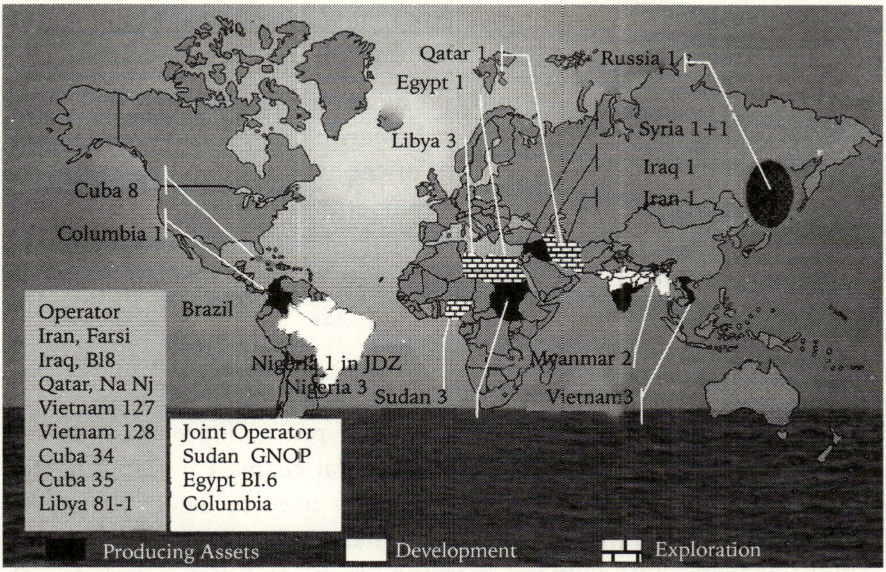

Source: ONGC Videsh Ltd. as of 24th July 2007.

The oil diplomacy is also using another tool suggested by the Group of Ministers: leveraging India's 'Buyer Power' to obtain quality exploration and production projects abroad. Last year, it managed to arm-twist Iran into yielding highly prospective oil fields in return for

India's purchase of five million tonnes of liquefied natural gas (LNG). Tehran even agreed to give OVL and its Indian partner's equity in the South Pars field to provide gas for conversion to LNG. Indian Oil Corporation, which has established deep relations with Middle-East exporters because of its annual term purchases of crude oil, has been able to get its foot in Saudi Arabia's exploration programme.

The security concern has also translated into diversifying the crude purchase points. India currently sources 67 per cent of its crude imports from the Middle East but the strategy is to reduce the country's dependence on the forever troubled region. A government strategy paper suggests that refineries switch over to low sulphur crude oil from Nigeria and net imports from the North Sea, Venezuela, West Africa, and the Far East, etc. In the last few years, India has tied up with new sources like Brunei, Libya, Nigeria and Yemen and efforts are on to build new contracts with Venezuela and Angola.

However, the ground reality is different as per analysts. India cannot afford to lower its dependence on the Gulf region as the domestic as well as global realities of the world oil and gas industry has transformed dramatically with competition spiralling to hurricane proportions. Being fiscally and technologically deficient, these efforts to shy away from the Gulf regions and diversifying imports from other parts of the world is really a Herculean task.

Mutual Vulnerabilities of India and GCC Countries

As discussed above, oil security was of prime importance for the oil importing countries before the structural changes initiated in the global oil industry. Oil producing countries used to detect the terms for the oil consuming countries at that time. The oil importing countries were quite vulnerable to the whims and caprices of the oil suppliers. The extent of their vulnerability could be seen in the wake of the world energy crises of 1974. The price shocks of 1974 led to usurious rates of inflation from an already high rate of 8 per cent in the world's major industrialised countries to double-digit levels. Economic growth in the industrialised countries slumped from an average annual rate of 4.9 per cent in 1965-1973 to 2.7 per cent in 1973-1979. Similar effects occurred after the second price shocks.

Price shocks caused more domestic resources to be traded for each unit of energy, with a loss in consumer purchasing power. The 1974 oil price shock meant a transfer of about 2 per cent of GDP from the developed countries to the oil-exporting countries.

But due to the structural changes, as discussed above, the oil consuming countries, especially the developed countries became capable of facing any supply disruptions owing to their improved technology and some legislation, oil security for them became somehow less relevant. And the oil exporting countries, which until that time were the superiors, became conscious about oil security, due to their significant loss of oil revenue which accounted for their overall affluence over the years. Their situation further worsened due to their loss of market coupled with lower oil prices and environmental regulations around the globe. These factors made them strive for survival and imposed lots of socioeconomic hardships on them. The Gulf Cooperation Council (GCC) oil exporting countries therefore became vulnerable and are in desperate search for stable outlets for their energy exports.

Unlike the developed oil consuming countries, the developing oil consuming countries are not secured in the wake of any eventual supply disruptions, because of their insatiable appetite for oil imports to augment economic development. The developing oil consuming countries especially those in the Asian region, which accounted for the major proportion of global oil demand during the decade of the 1990s, are likely to be vulnerable in the wake of any supply disruptions. India, an emerging vibrant economy, with its present degree of dependence on the Gulf and future dependence on the Gulf for vital energy imports, is therefore quite vulnerable in the wake of any possible supply disruption in the future.

Given the fact that, the oil supply pattern for the world's three major oil consuming regions—North America, Europe, and Asia—shows that major increases in oil supplies may be expected both within and near American and European markets, as noted earlier, the dependency of these, markets is not so intense in comparison to that of the Asian region. On the other hand, underlying the fact that domestic and regional oil/gas supplies are not sufficient to match the demand in the future and possible greater dependence on oil/gas imports from the Gulf, signifies the vulnerabilities of India and other Asian countries to supply disruptions. From the perspective of the GCC oil and gas exporting countries, on the other hand, India and the rest of Asia appear as promising future markets. If assuring oil supply and price security will be important for India, the security of demand and price will be equally important for the GCC countries. Moreover, underlying GCC countries' search for market stability is their concern for stable flow of energy export revenues, which render them anxious to protect their earning capacity, in order to defray their mounting government expenditures. Thus, such stability cannot be established without the effective cooperation of their major customers—the oil importers like India and other Asia. This implies that the rising dependence of the GCC countries on India and other Asian countries will increase their economic vulnerabilities owing to any cyclical disruptions in the growth rate of energy demand—the effects of 1998 Asian Financial Crisis on the GCC countries is notable here. This can be substantiated from the trends of mutual dependence of Middle East and Asia from the demand as well as supply aspects.

There are also other issues like the price of crude exports from the Middle East to the Asian market in comparison to other markets is high, given the fact that the Asian region is and will remain the stable outlet for oil exports from the Gulf region. This will in fact create apprehensions in the Asian importing countries in general and India in particular to seek imports from other regions. Figure 4.4 shows the Asian oil premium.

Thus, in the global energy regime, the oil producing/exporting and oil consuming/importing countries are mutually vulnerable and the interdependence is gaining strength day by day, which also emphasises the degree of their future vulnerabilities to any possible demand as well as supply disruptions. It will therefore be important for India and the GCC countries to strategically modify the energy sector interdependence framework, to minimise the cost of interdependence and increase the benefits of interdependence, in order to ensure the energy security of both. This calls for pragmatic policies from both to hedge against the apprehensions of energy security. The possible and

Figure 4.4

Asian Premium: Average Price Differentials for Arab Light Crude (fob), between Asia and EU, US

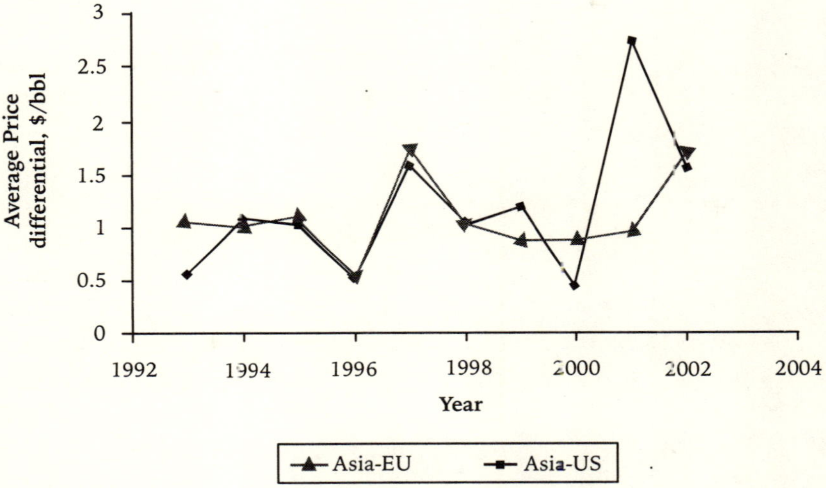

Source: Calculated from Platts Data, 2005.

most appropriate way in this perspective would be to augment mutually beneficial economic relations, given that both share a traditionally long illustrious coprosperity framework of interaction.

5

The Interdependence Framework

A Catalyst to Augment Economic Relations

As discussed in the previous chapters, the energy fundamentals of both India as a potential vibrating consumer and the GCC countries as producers are in the process of evolution towards a framework of interdependence due to their sheer strategic positioning in the present global oil and gas regime. Besides there are renewed apprehensions regarding energy security from the perspective of demand security for the GCC countries and supply security for India. These factors are compelling them to address the issues of vulnerabilities of energy security through a broad-based interaction in the form of mutual economic relations basically premised on the 'newer realities of energy interdependence' in order to hedge against the concerns and to strengthen their position in the world oil and gas regime in the coming years. The present chapter seeks to analyse these issues and implications thereof. The chapter starts by highlighting the sustained economic relations between India and the GCC countries over the years as a background and then focuses on the prospective areas and means of broader economic relations evolving around the hydrocarbon interdependence between India and GCC countries, as enunciated in the present global oil and gas regime. The unfolding opportunities in the liberalisation phase in both the regions will be minutely identified to delineate the future pattern of economic interaction between India and the GCC countries.

Economic Relations between India and GCC Countries: An Overview

The Gulf region with its geo-strategic location is important to India from the economic and security viewpoints. Centuries-old interaction between India and the region and the region's centrality in the Islamic world makes the Gulf also, politically important. India enjoys traditionally cordial relations and cooperation with the GCC countries. India's old, historical ties with GCC states, coupled with increasing imports of oil and gas, growing trade and investment opportunities, and presence of 3.5 million Indian workers in the region, are of vital interest to India. India's economic linkages with the GCC have increased steadily during the 1970s, 80s and 90s, especially due to the growth in oil imports. These continue to make steady progress to date.

Patterns of Trade between India and GCC

The GCC countries are important trading partners for India, and bilateral trade has witnessed impressive growth in recent years. During the last five years, India's total trade with the GCC countries has risen nearly three-fold, from US $7 billion in 2000 to US $19.3 billion in the year 2005 (Figure 5.1). Rise in both exports to and imports from the GCC countries have underlined the buoyancy in India's overall trade with the block.

Figure 5.1

India's Trade with GCC: Various Indicators

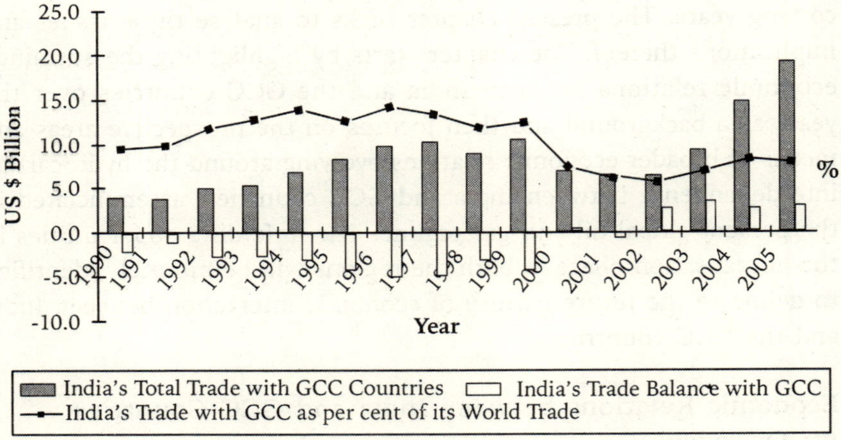

Source : Calculated from Direction of Trade Statistics (DOTS) CD-ROM, IMF, 2006.

India's exports to the GCC have risen from US $3.73 billion in the year 2000 to US $11.22 billion in the year 2005. After a marginal decline in the year 2001, India's exports to the region witnessed a robust growth thereafter, with an annual average growth rate of 35.3 per cent during 2002-2005. As a result, the share of GCC countries in India's total exports has increased from 8.75 per cent in 2000 to 11.21 per cent in 2005, indicating an increase of 89 per cent. Among the GCC countries, the UAE is the leading market for India's exports, accounting for as much as three-fourths of India's total exports to the bloc in the year 2005, followed by Saudi Arabia, Kuwait, Oman, Bahrain and Qatar. Due to the dominant share of the UAE, India's exports to the GCC have been in line with the trend in exports to that country (Figure 5.2). The GCC countries are also major destinations for India's project exports. This can be assessed from the fact that the GCC as a block accounted for as much as 42.5 per cent (Rs. 85.34 billion) of the total value of contracts secured by Indian project exporters during the period 2000-01 to 2004-05 (Rs. 200.8 billion).[1]

Figure 5.2

India's Exports to GCC Countries, 2004-05 (Per cent Share)

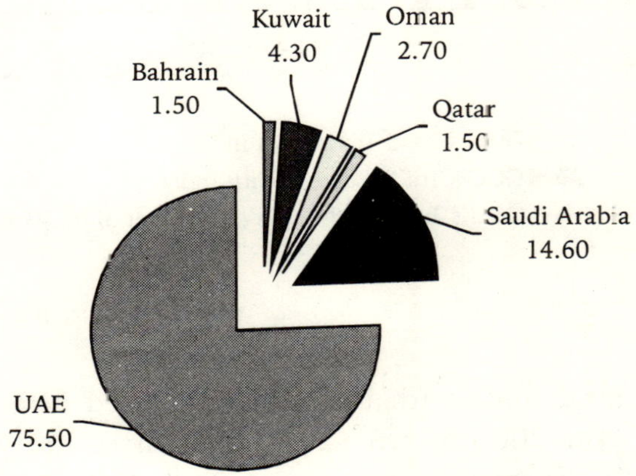

Source : Calculated from Export-Import Database, DCICIS, 2005-2006 .

1. EXIM Bank (2006). "GCC Countries: A Study of India's Trade and Investment Potential", *Occasional Paper* No. 110.

India's total imports from the GCC have also witnessed an increase from US $3.68 billion in the year 2000 to US $8.13 billion in the year 2005. Excluding Petroleum, Oil & Lubricants-related imports from the total figures, show that India's imports from the GCC have increased from US $1.67 billion in 2000 to US $6.92 billion in 2005, underlined by the sharp increase of imports from the UAE, Saudi Arabia and Qatar for the same period. The UAE is again the leading import source, accounting for 66.3 per cent of India's total imports from the block in the year 2005, followed by Saudi Arabia, Qatar, Kuwait, Bahrain and Oman.

Though for the GCC, India is not so important a trading partner, yet the recent years have witnessed some impressive trends (Figure 5.3).

Figure 5.3

GCC's Trade with India: Various Indicators

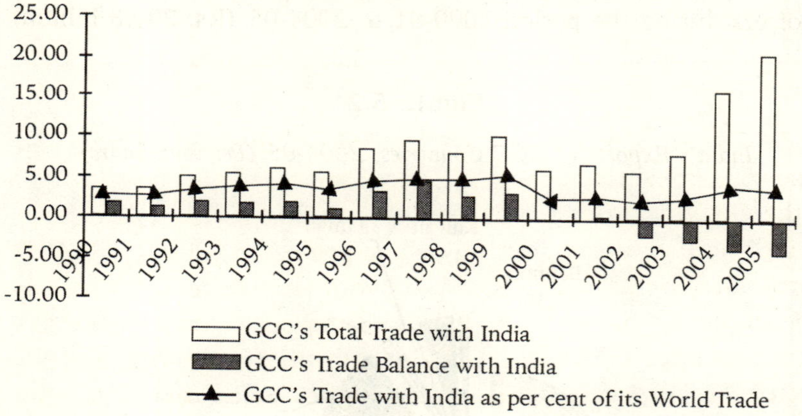

Source : Calculated from Direction of Trade Statistics (DOTS) CD-ROM, IMF, 2006.

The GCC's total trade with India has increased from US $6.08 billion in the year 2000 to US $20.41 billion in the year 2005. Importantly, GCC countries total imports from India has increased phenomenally from US $3.29 billion in the year 2000 to US $12.30 billion in the year 2005, whereas exports to India has registered a moderate increase from US $3.02 billion to US $8.11 billion, during the same period. Moreover, India's share in the GCC's world exports and imports has registered moderate growth during the same period. This implies the enormous scope for increasing India's share in the GCC's trading profile. Table 5.1 below shows the relative mutual importance of India and GCC in each other's trade profile.

Table 5.1

India and GCC: Relative Mutual Importance in Trade Profile

Indicators/Year	*2000*	*2001*	*2002*	*2003*	*2004*	*2005*
India's Exports to GCC as % of India's World Exports	8.75	6.71	9.18	10.68	11.70	11.21
India's Imports from GCC as % of India's World Imports	6.43	6.25	3.12	3.93	6.00	5.83
GCC's Exports to India as % of GCC's World Exports	1.8	2.17	1.18	1.41	2.39	2.35
GCC's Imports from India as % of GCC's World Imports	4.09	3.51	3.73	4.38	6.38	6.16

Source : Calculated from Direction of Trade Statistics (DOTS) CD-ROM, IMF, 2006.

Indo-Gulf economic ties have remained confined to oil, spices and manpower. As the trend shows, the economic relations between India and the GCC countries which developed during the oil boom period remained limited in composition despite growth in volume. The GCC countries transacted more extensively with the Western market. But as the decline in oil revenue has forced these countries to diversify their economies by developing the non-oil sector and building capacities to process oil to realise higher value added to their products, India with a market of 100 billion becomes relevant for them. It is not merely energy consumption, but the heavy demand for oil-based products like petrochemicals and fertilisers that provided the basis for a more asserted beneficial economic relationship between the two.[2]

The Gulf region gained prominence in India's foreign trade particularly after the trade policy liberalisation which began in 1991.

2. Pant, Girijesh (1999). "The Changing Gulf Market and India: Trends and Prospects", in A.K. Pasha (ed.), *Perspectives on India and Gulf States*. New Delhi: Détente Publishers. pp.112-126.

Trade policy reforms have provided an export friendly free trading environment conducive to accelerated export performance with simplified procedures. In order to promote trade interest India has granted Mutual Most Favoured Nation (MFN) status to the Gulf countries. India's principal exports commodities to this region are tea, spices, fruits, vegetables, tobacco, oil cakes, chemicals, drugs and pharmaceuticals, engineering goods, electronic engineering goods, electrical goods, textiles, etc. India's trade with the GCC countries is conducted against payments in free foreign exchange.[3] India's trade and economic relations with the GCC countries is kept under regular review through bilateral Joint Commissions. India has such institutional arrangements with all GCC countries.[4]

Importantly, the 1990s witnessed a large migration of workers from India to the GCC countries and consequent sustained flow of remittances from these countries. As per one recent study,[5] labour migration from India to the Middle East picked up momentum since 1992. Also, in recent years a clear shift towards workers with higher skills is noticed in the outflow of Indian labour primarily to the Middle East.

Recent Initiatives

India and the six-member Cooperation Council for the Arab States of the Gulf (GCC) share a strong and rapidly growing trade and economic relationship. Further strengthening and deepening of this relationship is a major priority for both, with governments committed to sustaining the impressive trade and economic performance achieved in recent years. The signing of the Framework Agreement of Economic Cooperation between India and the member states of the GCC in New Delhi on 25th August 2004 and the consequent first round of negotiations on March 21-22, 2006 was a reaffirmation of this commitment.

The Framework is a broad-based and forward-looking document, which has set a clear agenda for the bilateral trade and economic

---

3. Ibid, p.108.
4. Ibid.
5. Majumdar, Manab (2003). "Symposium on Movement of Natural Persons", 19th March, Tokyo. For FICCI, New Delhi.

relationship over the coming years. It covers a wide range of activities aimed at improving commercial and policy linkages, and delivering improvements to the overall business environment to both countries' mutual benefit. As part of the Framework, India and the GCC countries agreed to undertake possible negotiation of a bilateral free trade agreement (FTA).

The Framework Agreement enhances the strength of this commercial relationship. It reaffirms each country's commitment to the ongoing development of trade and investment, including within the context of the WTO and strengthens bilateral economic cooperation and dialogue. It provides that India and the GCC will, through all-round economic and trade cooperation, "achieve balanced and comprehensive trade and investment facilitation and liberalisation."

The Framework also provides for a wide range of specific steps to strengthen the trade and economic relationship, including:

- Enhancing the exchange of information on foreign trade.
- Encouraging business communications particularly between the institutions and organisations concerned with foreign trade.
- Giving attention to training and technology transfer.
- Appropriate arrangements for capital flows between them, setting up joint investment projects and facilitating corporate investments in various fields of economy, trade and industry.
- Encourage the exchange of visits of representatives, delegations and economic, commercial and technical missions between them and organising temporary exhibitions and providing necessary facilities and assistance with a view to furthering economic cooperation.
- A Joint Committee for Economic Cooperation shall be formed under this Agreement. This Committee shall convene alternatively in the countries of the two Parties on mutually agreed periodicity. The level of participation in the Committee will be specified in advance. Functions of the Committee shall be:
    1. Following up implementation of the provisions of this Agreement and other bilateral agreements or protocols made between the two Parties based on this Agreement.

2. Handling any difficulties or disputes that might arise from interpretation/implementation of the provisions of this Agreement.
3. Adopting recommendations for enhancing economic, commercial, technical and investment cooperation between the two contracting parties, and fostering their economic relations and increasing the volume of trade between them.
4. The Joint Committee is authorised to set up any sub-committees or specialised working teams, at its discretion and when deemed necessary. The Committee shall designate the duties and functions of such sub-committees and working teams, provided that the said sub-committees and working teams shall submit their reports and recommendations to the Joint Committee.

The joint FTA negotiation injects a new dynamism into consideration of the liberalisation of trade in goods between India and the GCC. In committing to this negotiation, India and the GCC recognise that multilateral trade negotiations are the most effective mechanism to achieve trade liberalisation and thereby to promote national and regional economic development. Each country does, however, also recognise, through their existing bilateral free trade negotiations with other selected trading partners, the potential for WTO consistent free trade agreements to deliver benefits at a more rapid pace. Such agreements can, in turn, support and reinforce multilateral liberalisation in the WTO. Furthermore, both recognise that free trade agreement negotiations involving products across all sectors serve more broadly as instruments for demonstrating closer relations, and so enhancing mutual interests. The implications of a possible FTA between India and GCC need to be considered in this broader context, as well as in terms of its direct effects on trade in goods.

India's Economic Relations with Individual GCC Countries

Bahrain

Bahrain and India have enjoyed strong economic and trade relations spanning several centuries. Since the oil boom of the early

70s these relations received a new impetus. Relative prosperity and higher standard of living boosted global imports of goods and services, including from India. The Bahrain Government's policy of industrial diversification also played its role in enhancing economic cooperation between the two countries. In addition, new job opportunities attracted a large number of Indian expatriates to the Island.

Bahrain accounted for 1.5 per cent of India's exports to the GCC region in 2004-05. Exports to the country have risen consistently from US $75.9 million in 2001-02 to US $141.9 million in 2004-05. Imports from Bahrain also occupy a small percentage of 1.6 per cent in India's total imports from the region, with imports having declined from US $134.5 million in 2001-02 to US $74.7 million in 2003-04, before rising to US $112.7 million in 2004-05. Major items of export to Bahrain have been presented in Table 5.2.

Table 5.2

India's Major Export Items to Bahrain

(US $ Million)

Commodity	*2000-01*	*2001-02*	*2002-03*	*2003-04*	*2004-05*
Cotton Yarn Fabrics Made-ups, etc.	23.5	18.7	26.1	22.1	23.6
Aluminium Other than Products	0.01	—	—	4.8	14.8
Machinery & Instruments	4.6	3.5	4.6	7.5	14.3
Manufacture of Metals	3.5	3.9	4.1	5.8	10.2
Paper/Wood Products	2.4	2.0	2.5	3.0	5.7
Transport Equipment	1.0	0.8	2.0	1.4	5.2
Fresh Vegetables	2.1	2.5	4.6	6.2	4.7
RMG Cotton incl. Accessories	3.8	4.6	7.2	8.3	4.6
Manmade Yarn Fabrics Made-ups	2.9	3.8	4.7	3.1	3.9
Primary & Semi-Finished Iron & Steel	0.8	1.4	2.9	3.0	3.4

Source : DGCIS, Ministry of Commerce and Industry (MoCI).

While cotton yarn and fabrics remain the largest exports to the country, recent trends have witnessed stagnation in exports. On the other hand, items including aluminium other than products, machinery and instruments and manufactures of metals have registered increase. India's import profile from Bahrain is dominated by metalliferous ores and metal scrap, and non-ferrous ores. Inorganic chemicals are also an important import item (Table 5.3).

Table 5.3

India's Major Import Items from Bahrain

(US $ Million)

Commodity	*2000-01*	*2001-02*	*2002-03*	*2003-04*	*2004-05*
Metalliferous Ores & Metal Scrap	16.9	20.0	19.9	22.4	25.7
Non-Ferrous Metals	19.7	19.8	11.9	20.0	23.3
Inorganic Chemicals	6.2	15.5	9.5	2.3	11.6
Pulp & Waste Paper	1.0	0.8	1.5	2.2	2.8
Sulphur & Unroasted Iron Pyrites	0.7	2.7	1.1	4.1	1.3
Crude Fertiliser	—	—	—	—	0.7
Manufactures of Metals	0.1	0.7	0.1	0.1	0.5
Transport Equipment	0.2	0.01	0.01	2.0	0.5
Cotton Yarn Fabrics	-	0.1	0.02	0.6	0.4
Non-Electrical Machinery	0.2	0.1	0.01	0.2	0.2

Source: DGCIS, Ministry of Commerce and Industry (MoCI)

India and Bahrain signed an economic and technical cooperation agreement in April 1981, during the visit of the Amir to New Delhi. Instruments of Ratification were exchanged in 1983.[6] The first meeting of the Indo-Bahrain Joint Economic and Technical Committee was held in New Delhi in 1986 and the second in Bahrain in 1991. The third session was held in New Delhi on 11-12 November 1998. The two sides identified a number of areas of cooperation including economic, commercial, educational, training and cultural.

There are good prospects for export of Indian products, particularly agricultural products, sanitary fixtures, drugs and pharmaceuticals, plywood, ceramic tiles, power generation and transmission equipment, light engineering goods, leather products, textiles and related products. Information Technology is the new emerging field of India's exports.

6. For details see, *http://www.meadev.nic.in*.

Kuwait

India and Kuwait continue to enjoy traditional friendly relations. Geographical proximity, historical trade links, cultural affinities and presence of a large number of Indian expatriates in Kuwait have all continued to sustain and nurture the longstanding relationship over the years. India was a natural trading partner and a destination for higher learning. Until 1961, the Indian rupee was legal tender in Kuwait.

The presence of a huge Indian workforce in Kuwait has ensured close cultural interaction and bond between the two countries. The two countries continue to build on long established commercial relations. This friendship found a new impetus with the discovery of oil in Kuwait as it is exporting oil and other petrochemical products to India while numerous commodities are imported from India. In fact, India was perhaps the first country to establish trade links with Kuwait centuries ago.[7]

Though India was the first country to establish trade links with Kuwait centuries ago, but with the inflow of goods from other parts of the world, it lost its leading position. In 1989, a joint trade committee met in Kuwait to evolve ways and means of diversifying and augmenting trade. However, the Kuwaitis were not so receptive about the Indian efforts due to low competitiveness in terms of quality of Indian goods in comparison to goods from other parts of the world. Mr. Abdur Rahim, the Director of Foreign Trade in the Kuwaiti Ministry of Commerce at that time remarked that,

> Although India produces high-quality goods, they are unable to face competition from other foreign goods due to their unimpressive finishing and packaging.[8]

But in the mid-1990s, Indo-Kuwaiti trade registered marked improvement, despite keen competition from countries in Southeast Asia, Europe, US and Japan, each persisting to secure a share in an open market condition. During 1988-89, the country's total exports to Kuwait amounted to Rs. 1.54 billion—an increase of Rs. 0.49 billion

---

7. Khan, Jawed Ahmad (1999). *India and West Asia: Emerging Markets in the Liberalisation Era*. New Delhi: Sage Publications. p.95.

8. Ibid.

over the figure for 1987-88. Its corresponding import bill touched Rs. 5.03 billion, an increase of Rs. 0.2 billion over the previous financial year. Trade between the two countries also started to pick up after the disruption caused by the Iraqi invasion, but the balance of trade was in favour of Kuwait because of India's oil imports. In 1991-1992 Indian exports to Kuwait were of the order of Rs. 0.74 billion and imports were of the order of Rs. 3.64 billion. India was the third largest trading partner of Kuwait in the year 1999.[9]

India's exports to Kuwait have increased consistently; from US $207 million in 2000-01 to US $405 million in 2004-05, with a share of 4.3 per cent of India's total exports to the GCC region (Table 5.4). While *basmati* rice and RMG cotton have remained traditional export items, sharp rise in the exports of other items such as glassware, primary and semi-finished iron and steel, petroleum products have resulted in recent years.

Table 5.4

India's Major Export Items from Kuwait

(US $ Million)

Commodity	*2000-01*	*2001-02*	*2002-03*	*2003-04*	*2004-05*
Basmati Rice	49.8	41.3	35.8	30.0	52.0
Glass/Glassware/Ceramics	13.6	6.6	10.7	19.3	36.3
RMG Cotton incl. Accessories	17.1	20.1	22.5	41.5	34.3
Primary & Semi-Finished Iron & Steel	2.2	0.9	6.4	9.9	30.2
Petroleum & Crude Products	0.02	0.1	22.3	18.3	22.1
Manmade Yarn Fabrics Made-ups	10.7	14.4	12.9	20.6	19.8
Machinery & Instruments	7.5	9.6	9.6	17.1	18.9
Meat & Preparations	5.8	4.1	6.5	13.9	18.5
Manufactures of Metals	6.8	11.1	12.3	15.3	17.7
Oil Meals	7.1	6.4	6.2	8.0	11.7

Source : DGCIS, Ministry of Commerce and Industry (MoCI).

Two items such as organic chemicals and metalliferous ores and metal scrap are the dominant items in India's imports from Kuwait. Imports of these two items have increased considerably recently (Table 5.5).

9. *http://www.ikcc.org/objectives.htm*

Table 5.5

India's Major Import Items from Kuwait

(US $ Million)

Commodity	*2000-01*	*2001-02*	*2002-03*	*2003-04*	*2004-05*
Organic Chemicals	4.7	0.03	8.7	36.5	85.8
Metalliferous Ores & Metal Scrap	13.8	18.0	20.6	33.0	50.4
Sulphur & Unroasted Iron Pyrites	11.7	8.6	6.2	8.2	11.8
Artificial Resins, Plastic Materials	4.5	4.0	5.5	5.0	6.1
Inorganic Chemicals	26.4	4.2	15.5	8.9	5.6
Electronic Goods	0.04	0.01	0.7	0.1	1.5
Other Textile Yarn, Fabrics, Made-ups	0.1	0.3	0.1	0.4	1.3
Pulp & Waste Paper	0.5	0.5	0.7	0.7	1.1
Wool Raw	0.2	0.2	0.3	0.5	0.8
Iron & Steel	0.1	0.02	0.1	0.2	0.7

Source : DGCIS, Ministry of Commerce and Industry (MoCI).

It is to be noted that a new dimension was added to the Indo-Kuwait relationship in the post-Gulf War period when Indian companies played a major role in the restoration of war-ravaged Kuwait in record time. India's economic liberalisation policy has opened new avenues to foreign investors. Kuwait has responded positively to the liberalisation policy, which has borne fruit in the form of joint ventures between the two friendly states. To give a fillip to the traditional Indo-Kuwait relations, the India-Kuwait Chamber of Commerce (IKCC) was formally inaugurated on 8th December 2003 in the Commission Hall of the FICCI (Federation of Indian Chamber of Commerce and Industries). The India-Kuwait Chamber of Commerce (IKCC) is a registered establishment incorporating members from both India and Kuwait with the avowed objectives:[10]

- to facilitate the expansion of business relationships between India and Kuwait;
- to guide the Indian and Kuwaiti businessmen towards new business opportunities through market research and dissemination of business commercial and regulatory information in India and Kuwait; and

10. *http://www.ikcc.org/objectives.htm*

- to analyse the economic and political policy announcements in India and Kuwait through regular reports to help the trade, and to sponsor scholarships, grants, awards in recognition of excellence in the fields of trade, culture and education.

Oman

Exchanges between India and Oman go back to centuries. Until the Omani Renaissance that commenced with Sultan Qaboos taking over the reins of the country, Oman almost entirely depended on India to meet its basic necessities. Such extensive commercial interaction helped greatly in laying the foundation for the development of a multi-dimensional relationship between the two countries, in modern times. Oman has, of late, taken a conscious decision to make India its main economic partner in its drive towards industrialisation and diversification of the Omani economy, taking into account the size of the Indian market, and India's industrial capabilities.

Mindful of India's large market and its industrial and technological capabilities, Oman sees India as a major economic partner. The current economic imperatives have made Oman increasingly look towards India for sourcing both goods and technology. The two countries have already concluded Agreements on Avoidance of Double Taxation and Promotion and Protection of Bilateral Investments, which provide the requisite legal framework for facilitating trade and investment flows. Several local business houses that have had traditional links with India and are keen to explore mutually beneficial opportunities for trade and investment. The presence of a large number of Indians in senior positions in the private sector is a helpful factor in generating awareness of Indian capabilities.

In 2002, India was the 8th largest source for Omani imports (about 3.5 per cent). Major items of Indian exports include textiles and garments, machinery and equipment, electrical and electronic items, chemicals, iron and steel products in addition to traditional items like tea, coffee, spices, rice and meat products. The bilateral trade figures for the last five years have been as follows as depicted in Tables 5.6 and 5.7.

Table 5.6

India's Major Export Items to Oman

(US $ Million)

Commodity	*2000-01*	*2001-02*	*2002-03*	*2003-04*	*2004-05*
Machinery & Instruments	14.1	19.6	30.5	69.0	45.0
Manufactures of Metals	16.4	17.9	16.8	16.0	31.3
Non-Ferrous Metals	0.3	0.6	1.7	8.4	29.7
Manmade Yarn Fabrics Made-ups	10.4	12.3	15.8	14.7	11.8
Meat & Preparations	9.6	9.0	11.5	13.0	11.3
Electronic Goods	4.1	3.6	9.1	7.8	8.1
Poultry Products	2.5	3.9	5.4	7.4	7.8
Plastic & Linoleum Products	4.7	4.6	5.0	5.3	7.6
Transport Equipment	1.8	3.1	2.7	5.4	7.4
Wheat	6.0	7.5	0.03	16.5	7.0

Source : DGCIS, Ministry of Commerce and Industry (MoCI).

Table 5.7

India's Major Import Items from Oman

(US $ Million)

Commodity	*2000-01*	*2001-02*	*2002-03*	*2003-04*	*2004-05*
Metaliferrous Ores & Metal Scrap	0.6	0.9	1.7	1.7	6.2
Non-Metallic Mineral Manufactures	0.1	1.5	2.5	3.8	3.8
Non-Ferrous Metals	-	-	1.9	6.6	3.4
Iron & Steel	-	-	-	0.3	1.2
Artificial Resins, Plastic Materials	0.4	0.5	1.0	0.8	0.8
Dying & Colouring Materials	0.1	0.2	0.3	0.5	0.7
Fruits & Nuts	1.6	2.4	1.5	2.0	0.7
Transport Equipment	0.1	0.02	0.3	31.6	0.5
Pulp & Waste Paper	0.2	0.2	0.3	0.4	0.5
Electrical Machinery	0.2	0.1	0.6	0.9	0.3

Source : DGCIS, Ministry of Commerce and Industry (MoCI).

Qatar

India's traditional and historical friendship with Qatar has over the years matured into a strong relationship, which makes both the sides reliable economic partners having shared interests in trade and commerce, economic and technical cooperation and energy security. From the economic standpoint, there is a growing synergy between India and Qatar in the hydrocarbons and other industrial sectors.[11] Indian private sector companies are getting more and more involved in industrial and civil construction and consultancy projects in Qatar.

The economic framework for bilateral cooperation is well in place. The Avoidance of Double Taxation Agreement (DTAA) and Bilateral Investment Promotion and Protection (BIPA), which were signed during the visit of Qatari Emir His Highness Sheikh Hamad Bin Khalifa al-Thani to India in April 1999, have since been ratified and are in force. The first meeting of the Joint Business Council (JBC), launched between the Qatar Chamber of Commerce and Industry (QCCI) and the Federation of Indian Chambers of Commerce (FICCI) is scheduled to take place in October 2001. The other Memoranda of Understanding (MoUs) signed by QCCI with the Confederation of Indian Industry (CII) and the National Small Industries Corporation (NSIC) are under different stages of implementation.

In the year 2000, India was the 5th largest destination of Qatar's exports, behind Japan, Singapore, South Korea and Thailand and the 10th most in terms of value of Qatar's imports. According to the Economic Statistics Indicators released by Qatar's Planning Council, India's exports to Qatar during the first half of 2000 crossed QR 190.92 million, while its imports from Qatar during the corresponding period reached QR 280.55 million. India is the topmost supplier of Qatar for ready-made garments, tea and vegetables. India also has a significant share in Qatar's import market for rice (23.98 per cent), marble (11.74 per cent), gold and precious metals (10 per cent), bus tyres (7.42 per cent), beauty products (6.43 per cent) and textiles and ceramics (each over 5 per cent). During 1999, India's exports to Qatar stood at QR 238.52 million while its imports from Qatar stood at QR 567.74 million.

Indo-Qatar bilateral trade increased has considerably in the recent years. Inorganic chemicals, organic chemicals, artificial resins and plastic materials, and sulphur and unroasted pyrites were the top five commodities of India's import from Qatar. Machinery and

---

11. Sayeed, Ausaf, "India-Qatar: Synergy in the Oil & Gas Sectors", *http://www.indianembassy.gov*

instruments, RMG cotton, cotton yarn, fabrics and made-ups, paper and wood products and glass, glassware and ceramics were the top five commodities exported by India to Qatar. Tables 5.8 and 5.9 shows India's major items of Exports to and imports from Qatar for the period 2000-01 to 2004-05.

Table 5.8

India's Major Export Items to Qatar

(US $ Million)

Commodity	*2000-01*	*2001-02*	*2002-03*	*2003-04*	*2004-05*
Glass/Glassware/Ceramics	1.5	4.0	5.1	9.2	20.6
Machinery & Instruments	5.0	5.0	12.0	22.3	15.4
Manufactures of Metals	3.7	4.8	8.3	9.0	14.2
Transport Equipment	1.4	1.6	19.4	22.0	12.8
Primary & Semi-Finished Iron & Steel	0.9	0.8	1.4	2.1	9.7
Electronic Goods	0.6	0.8	1.0	0.8	5.6
Rubber Manufactured Products	1.5	2.1	2.9	3.1	5.0
Processed Minerals	0.8	1.2	1.4	3.6	4.6
Meat & Preparations	0.9	1.1	2.3	3.2	4.3
Plastic & Linoleum Products	1.4	2.6	1.9	3.3	3.3

Source : DGCIS, Ministry of Commerce and Industry (MoCI).

Table 5.9

India's Major Import Items from Kuwait

(US $ Million)

Commodity	*2000-01*	*2001-02*	*2002-03*	*2003-04*	*2004-05*
Organic Chemicals	18.2	31.9	60.8		124.2
Inorganic Chemicals	39.4	35.7	35.4	78.4	69.4
Fertiliser Manufactured	—	—	—	67.3	35.9
Artificial Resins, Plastic Materials	10.6	12.6	7.7	—	19.7
Sulphur & Unroasted Iron Pyrites	8.6	4.1	8.9	12.1	11.5
Metalliferous Ores & Metal Scrap	—	0.1	0.04	8.1	5.5
Pulp & Waste Paper	0.03	0.01	0.1	2.4	0.3
Non-Electrical Machinery	0.4	0.1	0.01	—	0.3
Electrical Machinery	—	—	—	—	0.3
Dying & Colouring Materials	0.01	—	—	0.3	0.1

Source : DGCIS, Ministry of Commerce and Industry (MoCI).

Significantly, this increase in exports is not limited to just traditional areas of exports like agricultural products, but extends to diverse areas like project goods, machinery and instruments, ready-made garments, bulk drugs and pharmaceuticals and ores and minerals.

Saudi Arabia

India and Saudi Arabia are old business partners: their trade relations go back centuries. Today, the bilateral business ties are being steadily expanded and further strengthened by continuous interaction and cooperation, including regular exchange of business delegations. Besides being a major trade partner, India sees the Kingdom as an important economic partner for investments, joint ventures, transfer of technology projects and joint projects in third countries.

Institutional framework for improving trade and economic relations in the form of Joint Commission for economic, trade, scientific, technical and cultural cooperation (JCM) between India and the Kingdom was established in 1981. A meeting of the Indo-Saudi Joint Business Council was held in 1997 in New Delhi and FICCI has proposed to hold the next session in Riyadh soon. A Bilateral Investment Protection and Promotion Agreement (BIPPA) has been finalised between the two countries in June 2001 and are expected to be formally signed soon. This will provide an institutional mechanism to protect and further enhance economic interaction between the two countries.

Saudi Arabia is India's second largest trading partner in the GCC region, having a share of 14.6 per cent in the year, 2004-05. Main Indian exports to Saudi Arabia are *basmati*/non-*basmati* rice, manmade yarn, fabrics, made-ups, RMG cotton yarn, primary and semi-finished iron and steel, chemicals, plastic and linoleum products, machinery and instruments (Table 5.10).

India's major imports from Saudi Arabia are organic and inorganic chemicals, artificial resins and plastic materials (Table 5.11).

India and Saudi Arabia have cherished a long-term vibrant economic relationship through impressive trade and investment programmes in their respective economies and there are future potentials to be strategically exploited for mutual benefits. India has to focus more and

Table 5.10

India's Major Export Items to Saudi Arabia

(US $ Million)

Commodity	*2000-01*	*2001-02*	*2002-03*	*2003-04*	*2004-05*
Basmati Rice	240.9	222.8	218.0	233.0	349.6
RMG Cotton incl. Accessories	73.3	80.2	89.5	115.5	100.7
Manmade Yarn Fabrics Made-ups	43.0	48.9	72.7	106.1	99.1
Non-Basmati Rice	46.2	39.2	9.5	36.7	67.3
Manufactures of Metals	38.0	47.7	43.5	57.2	62.5
Non-Ferrous Metals	13.9	38.7	42.4	27.0	61.8
Machinery & Instruments	27.9	34.1	44.7	58.8	60.1
Plastic & Linoleum Products	18.1	26.0	27.2	27.9	48.6
Meat & Preparations	7.1	0.2	0.9	12.1	39.1
Transport Equipment	5.7	4.6	6.5	16.5	31.9
RMG Manmade Fibres	26.4	22.6	24.4	29.0	31.1

Source : DGCIS, Ministry of Commerce and Industry (MoCI).

Table 5.11

India's Major Import Items from Saudi Arabia

(US $ Million)

Commodity	*2000-01*	*2001-02*	*2002-03*	*2003-04*	*2004-05*
Organic Chemicals	128.4	122.2	117.5	202.7	364.3
Inorganic Chemicals	115.0	42.1	47.6	49.0	90.0
Artificial Resins, Plastic Materials	28.8	41.3	48.7	53.6	67.3
Metalliferous Ores & Metal Scrap	10.3	23.3	22.3	30.6	54.9
Leather	5.3	11.8	13.1	20.5	30.8
Gold & Silver	5.2	12.7	17.0	15.9	29.5
Fertiliser Manufactured	3.4	1.9	1.7	-	15.2
Pulp & Waste Paper	10.6	6.0	9.4	10.9	12.6
Sulphur & Unroasted Iron Pyrites	20.0	9.3	6.7	9.4	10.2
Manufactures of Metals	0.6	0.2	0.2	0.5	6.3

Source : DGCIS, Ministry of Commerce and Industry (MoCI).

more on value added industrial products and services. Saudi Arabia today is moving steadily towards a free market economy with gradual decontrolling of many important sectors of the economy. Structural changes are being effected to ensure a smooth transition in the economy keeping in view the changing international economic environment.

UAE

Trading links between India and UAE have existed since long. Growing Indo-UAE economic and commercial relations over the years has contributed to the stability and strength of a rapidly diversifying and deepening bilateral relationship with both sides striving to further strengthen these ties.[12]

The UAE is of crucial significance for India's foreign trade as the second largest destination for India's exports after the United States. During the last fiscal (2004-05), India's exports to the UAE accounted for 9 per cent of India's total exports. In the GCC region, the UAE is India's largest market accounting for a whopping share of 75.5 per cent of India's total exports to the region in the year 2004-05. Over the last five fiscal years, both India's exports to and imports from the UAE have registered phenomenal growth. Gems and jewellery are the largest item in India's export basket to the UAE, followed by plastic and linoleum products, petroleum products, RMG cotton, manmade yarn, manufactures of metal, etc. (Table 5.12).

The UAE is among the 4th largest source of India's imports, after China, USA and Switzerland, with a share of 4.3 per cent of India's total imports during the last fiscal. Two items *viz.*, pearls, precious and semi-precious stones, and gold and silver dominate India's import basket from the UAE (Table 5.13).

As the above analysis shows, India and the GCC countries strive to realise huge untapped potentialities and embark on a path of renewed assertive economic cooperation premised on the hydrocarbon interdependence. The major factor behind this renewed cooperation has been and will be the interdependence between India and the GCC countries due to their strategic positioning in the global oil and gas regime.

---

12. *http://www.indembassyuae.org/text2.htm*

Table 5.12

India's Major Export Items to UAE

(US $ Million)

Commodity	*2000-01*	*2001-02*	*2002-03*	*2003-04*	*2004-05*
Gems & Jewellery	440.7	544.0	663.6	1377.2	2500.1
Plastic & Linoleum Products	66.6	73.0	75.7	257.6	786.1
Petroleum Products	30.1	5.7	399.4	332.4	500.8
Manmade Yarn Fabrics Madeups	166.5	215.0	274.2	337.6	395.4
RMG Cotton incl. Accessories	373.7	254.7	296.4	449.8	330.2
Manufactures of Metals	177.1	179.1	204.5	293.7	322.5
Machinery & Instruments	109.4	105.2	141.4	242.9	238.6
Primary & Semi-Finished Iron & Steel	50.3	48.0	74.8	96.3	133.2
Non-Ferrous Metals	3.2	10.2	40.9	75.0	129.1
Cotton Yarn Fabrics	111.0	77.1	93.1	89.1	107.2

Source: DGCIS, Ministry of Commerce and Industry (MoCI)

Table 5.13

India's Major Import Items from UAE

(US $ Million)

Commodity	*2000-01*	*2001-02*	*2002-03*	*2003-04*	*2004-05*
Pearls Precious & Semi-Precious Stones	194.0	248.6	386.6	650.7	1904.4
Gold & Silver	42.0	239.3	189.5	820.0	1742.8
Metaliferrous Ores & Metal Scrap	59.7	81.7	83.9	126.2	186.9
Transport Equipment	6.8	10.4	5.8	51.6	110.6
Artificial Resins, Plastic Materials	6.7	9.0	26.8	32.0	41.6
Non-Electrical Machinery	8.4	17.8	23.6	27.0	38.1
Fertiliser Manufactured	6.7	3.3	3.1	3.6	35.3
Non-Ferrous Metals	9.4	15.2	14.6	18.4	31.7
Vegetable Oil (Edible)	1.0	0.4	0	2.4	29.7
Sulphur & Unroasted Iron Pyrites	24.0	16.1	20.4	9.9	27.1

Source : DGCIS, Ministry of Commerce and Industry (MoCI).

Besides there are other recent developments having been contingent to augment and reassert economic ties between India and the GCC countries. The Iraq War and the resultant anti-West sentiment in the Gulf region have worked to the advantage of India. The country is playing host to Gulf investment like never before. Besides, trade between India and the Gulf at $10 billion during 2002-03 compared to $8 billion during 2001-02 has also shown remarkable growth. In the words of Saleh Mohd Al Ghamdi, ambassador of Saudi Arabia in New Delhi,

> The governments in the Middle East had realised that they should have better economic relations with India. Recently a group of 22 businessmen from Saudi Arabia was here to explore opportunities in various sectors, especially information technology (IT); IT enabled services, pharmaceuticals and higher and technical education. The idea was to establish better trade relations between the two countries. The Saudi businessmen are looking for investment opportunities in India, simply because India is an important country in the global economy. It is the fourth largest economy in the world.[13]

Mr. Kamaluddin Ahmed, Indian Ambassador to the Kingdom of Saudi Arabia, echoing the similar sentiments, said that,

> Saudi Arabian businessmen were increasingly becoming aware of the rich opportunities for investment in India, where their capital, coupled with locally available state-of-the-art technologies, unmatched human resources/expertise, large and expanding market, skilled labour, etc can bring in rich rewards.[14]

Besides the burgeoning merchandise trade, the GCC region has also become the major destination for India's project exports. The importance of the GCC countries in India's project exports sector can be assessed from the fact that the region accounted for 42.5 per cent of the total value of contracts secured by Indian project exporters during the period 2000-01 to 2004-05. The value of contracts secured by Indian companies in the region have risen from Rs. 9.34 billion in 2000-01 to Rs. 21.98 billion in the year 2004-05. During the current fiscal (April to January 2005-06), India's project exports to the GCC region rose sharply to Rs. 43.48 billion. Table 5.14 presents the trend.

---

13. Siddiqui, Huma (2004). "Anti-West Feelings Have Gulf Companies Turning To India", *The Financial Express*. January 22.

14. Ibid.

Table 5.14

Project Exports to GCC Countries

(Value in Rs. Crore)

Category	*2000-01*		*2001-02*		*2002-03*		*2003-04*		*2004-05*		*2005-06 (Apr-Jan)*	
	No	*Value*	*No*	*Value*	*No*	*Value*	*No*	*Value*	*No*	*Value*	*No*	*Value*
Civil Construction	1	52.3	1	62.6	6	708.5	5	800.1	6	1246.0	3	248.2
Consultancy Services	9	177.2	5	117.9	8	10.0	6	39.3	6	106.2	6	19.2
Turnkey Projects	7	704.1	7	1394.2	10	1141.2	11	1132.9	7	845.8	7	4081.1
Total	17	933.6	13	1574.7	24	1859.7	22	1972.4	19	2197.9	16	4348.5

Source : EXIM India, 2006.

In the GCC region, the UAE is the leading destination for India's project exports accounting for 32.2 per cent of the total value of all contracts secured during the period 2000-01 to 2004-05, followed by Oman (26.2 per cent), Saudi Arabia (19.2 per cent), Qatar (16.4 per cent, Kuwait (5.1 per cent) and Bahrain (0.9 per cent) (Figure 5.4).

Figure 5.4

Country Shares in India's Total Project Exports to GCC (in Per cent)

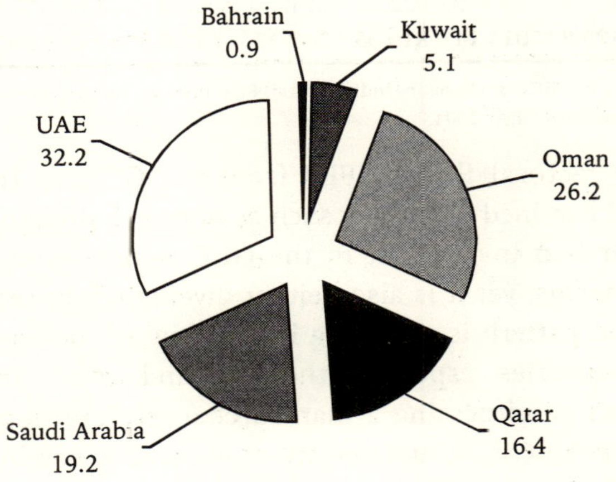

Source : Calculated from EXIM Bank Data, 2006.

Bilateral Investment Flows between India and the GCC

The bilateral FDI flows between India and the GCC are meagre at the current stage. The share of the GCC in India's total FDI inflows during 1991-2004 stood at 0.01 only. However, as the trends show there is lot of scope for future growth in the movement of bilateral FDI between India and the GCC (Table 5.15) due to two prime reasons. One relates to the low volume and the other relates to the volatility. Policy measures need to be set in place to address these issues. Recently, among GCC countries, Saudi Arabia and the UAE have emerged as the major investors in India followed by Oman, Kuwait and Qatar.

Table 5.15

FDI Flows to India from GCC

(Rs. Million)

Country	*1991-1999*	*2000*	*2001*	*2002*	*2003*	*2004*	*1991-2004*	*Per cent of Total GCC*
Bahrain	1867.67	165.95	11.16	20	176.2	148.22	2389.2	6.49
Kuwait	5843.6	7.33	149.45	9.2	1.7	0	6011.28	16.34
Oman	5787.14	37.64	32.8	222	46.37	367.8	6493.75	17.65
Qatar	315.3	4300	0	0	7.2	0	4622.5	12.57
KSA	8118.77	2.32	0.5	14.54	40.54	0.96	8177.63	22.23
UAE	6493.33	500.9	622.14	491.73	405.79	563.65	9077.54	24.68
Total GCC	**28425.9**	**5014.14**	**816.05**	**757.47**	**677.8**	**1080.63**	**36771.9**	**0.01***

Note : * Implies for GCC's share in India's total FDI inflows for the period 1991-2004.
Source : *Annual Newsletter*, SIA, 2004.

Moreover, sectoral flow of FDI from the GCC to India is not diversified and confined to sectors such as port and shipping, fertiliser, etc. Though Indian investment in the GCC is not so impressive in sheer volume terms, yet it is also neither diversified. In recent years a clearly different pattern is emerging in the flow of Indian investment to the GCC countries, especially the UAE and others and also the sectoral pattern is witnessing a marked change. Traditionally Indian investments in the GCC countries are more or less confined to joint venture projects undertaken by Indian companies or in investment in trading activities. However, with the global reach and expansion of the

Indian IT sector, Indian companies have also made inroads to the GCC countries in the form of establishing manufacturing units in the urban free zones of the GCC countries such as in the UAE. Recent times have witnessed Indian companies identifying Outward Direct Investment (ODI) in a number of countries, including those of the GCC. In terms of sectoral distribution the preferred area of investment by Indian companies is found to be in the field of information technology, more specifically IT and software services including training and human resource development. In addition a number of Indian pharmaceutical companies have also been investing abroad. Table 5.16 shows the trends of India's approved ODIs in the GCC countries from the period 1996–2004-05.

Table 5.16

India's Approved ODI in GCC

(US $ Million)

Country	*1996-00*	*2000-01*	*2001-02*	*2002-03*	*2003-04*	*2000-04*
Bahrain	8.56	1.30	1.50	1.16	—	3.96
Kuwait	11.81	—	—	0.04	0.21	0.25
Oman	139.80	64.92	0.16	0.35	1.51	66.94
Qatar	—	—	—	—	0.32	0.32
KSA	16.92	1.83	0.06	0.12	3.27	5.28
UAE	87.21	11.27	11.76	12.60	32.07	67.7
GCC	264.30	79.32	13.48	14.27	37.38	144.45
India's Total Approved	**3138.63**	**1377.14**	**3028.27**	**1472.22**	**1451.0**	**7328.63**
GCC Share in India's Total	**8.42**	**5.75**	**0.44**	**0.96**	**2.57**	**1.97**

Source : Ministry of Finance (2004). "Indian Direct Investment in JVs/WOs Abroad", GoI, August 26.

During the period 2001-2005, around 133 joint ventures (JV) and 259 wholly owned subsidiaries (WOS) were approved in the region. The major areas include software development services, engineering services, tourism, ready-made garments, chemical products, agriculture and allied activities, etc. In this context, two points are worth highlighting. Firstly, Indian ODI in the GCC is very small and more importantly it has declined in recent times. Second, only one country (*viz.*, the UAE) accounts for most of the Indian ODI directed towards the GCC. These dimensions need policy-attention while aiming at investment cooperation between India and the GCC. Table 5.17 shows country-wise JVs and WOS approved by India in the GCC region for the period 2001-05.

Table 5.17

Indian JVs and WOS Approved in GCC Countries

(No. of Approvals)

Country	*2001*	*2002*	*2003*	*2004*	*2005*	*Total*
Bahrain	2 (-)	1 (2)	- (-)	- (1)	- (1)	3 (4)
Kuwait	- (-)	- (-)	3 (-)	6 (5)	2 (-)	11 (5)
Oman	1 (-)	2 (-)	1(13)	2 (2)	6 (-)	12 (15)
Qatar	- (-)	- (-)	2 (-)	1 (-)	- (-)	3 (-)
Saudi Arabia	- (-)	1 (-)	2 (-)	1 (-)	- (-)	4 (-)
UAE	9 (18)	12 (26)	23 (43)	27 (51)	29 (97)	100 (235)
Total	**12 (18)**	**16 (28)**	**31 (56)**	**37 (59)**	**37 (98)**	**133 (259)**

Note : Figures in parentheses denoted the number of approved Indian WOS in GCC.
– means no approval.

Source : India Investment Centre and Reserve Bank of India.

Thus, there are tremendous potentials to be exploited through pragmatic policies not only in the oil and gas sector but also in other most promising areas as outlined above. The most promising area in this regard will be the knowledge sector where India has global leverage and the Gulf countries are striving on establishing such to achieve broad-based human resource development to absorb their mass educated unemployed youth.

Energy Interdependence: The Synergy between Energy and Knowledge

As discussed before, the most significant aspect of interdependence between India and the GCC countries is the respective areas of deficit such as the energy requirements of India and the GCC countries thrive to establish a knowledge society to address their internal vulnerabilities. Thus, the synergy between energy and knowledge will act as an impetus for both the GCC countries and India due to their global leverage in these areas to usher in a newer assertive framework of close economic relations in the coming years.

Building Knowledge Society: Major Policy Thrust by the GCC Countries

The Gulf States depend heavily on rents from the exploitation of state-owned petroleum reserves to fund their development efforts and generous welfare policies. Over the years they have gone through far-reaching social and economic transformation while maintaining social stability.

The oil boom of the previous era provided the impetus to the GCC states to build up infrastructure catering to the needs of the changing times. The states generally depended upon the expatriate labour force for such purposes as the domestic workforce were either reluctant or semi-skilled in comparison to the expatriates. There is wide ranging debate on this issue especially among analysts and experts of this region. While some argue that the faulty human resource development policies of the states are responsible for this, others argue that the oil boom is the major factor as it evolved welfare states in these countries or what is called *Baksish States*—the premise is that it is the responsibility of the states to take care of all the needs of their citizens.

However with the oil revenues dwindling in the years, the policy makers in these countries realised the heavy burden of such institutional arrangements and the pernicious impact of such policies for the long-term sustenance of the regimes in these states. Simultaneously, the countries of the GCC experienced voluminous population growth and consequent large pool of workforce. The major problem facing the GCC countries is perhaps how to absorb the large pool of domestic workforce in their respective economies overwhelmingly occupied by expatriate labour force. The result is growing discontent among the idle workforce, which has severe implications besides the immediate threat to the ruling regimes in these countries. In short, the challenge is the transition from rentier economy to knowledge economy in the GCC countries. Thus, despite ample reserves, new development challenges over coming decades will test their ability to reconcile traditional institutions with the requirements of a modern economy in an increasingly competitive global environment.

In such a scenario, like all other sectors where the GCC countries have initiated structural programmes, they are also devising ways to build a knowledge society—the key to be integrated with the global economy. The importance of building a knowledge society in the Gulf has been aptly delineated by the second *Arab Human Development Report* (AHDR), 2003:

> Deficient knowledge capabilities represent a formidable impediment for the Gulf countries in their attempts to face the challenges of the 21st century. These countries cannot make any tangible progress in the long term without acquiring the knowledge and technological capabilities that are indispensable for prosperity in the new millennium. Indeed the absence of these prerequisites could well invite unforeseen disasters. Ingraining and embedding knowledge in Gulf societies is the crux of any attempt to resolve the human development crisis in this region. Knowledge is one of the key instruments of human development, be it in instituting good governance, guaranteeing good health, producing the ingredients of material and moral welfare, or promoting economic growth. As such knowledge is a vital factor of modern production and an essential determinant of productivity and competitive capacity.[15]

One of the main features of the production pattern prevailing in the Gulf countries, which influences knowledge acquisition, is the high dependence on the depletion of raw materials, chiefly oil, and reliance on external rents. This rentier economic pattern entices societies to import expertise from outside because this is a quick and easy resort that however ends up weakening local demand for knowledge and forfeiting opportunities to produce it locally and employ it effectively in economic activity. A large part of Gulf countries' economic activity is concentrated on primary commodities, as in agriculture, which remains largely traditional, and in industries specialising in the production of consumer goods, which depend heavily on production licenses obtained from foreign companies. At the same time, the share of the capital goods industry and of industries embodying higher technology continues to shrink. Demand for industrial products is negatively influenced by the small size of Gulf markets, the weak competitiveness of Gulf economies and the absence

15. UNDP (2003). *Arab Human Development Report (AHDR)*. p.VI.

of transparency and accountability, which encourages overlap, and sometimes collusion, between political and business elites. Lack of competition reduces productivity and therefore demand for knowledge in economic activity. Instead, competitive advantage and the ability to maximise profits derive from favouritism in power structures, manifested in money and politics. Resistance to opening up to the outside world by the Gulf economies due to their old perceived notion of 'Resource Nationalism' in the heydays of the oil boom period and their lack of exposure to foreign competition coupled with at times excessive protection to local products through import substitution policies, have also slowed the advancement of productivity and the employment of knowledge to that end.

Demand for knowledge has been weakened not only by faltering economic growth and productivity in the Gulf countries during the last quarter-century but also by the over-concentration of wealth in a few hands. Although some economies of the world have succeeded in the past in achieving economic growth while their income and wealth distribution patterns were skewed, this occurred in a different global context, characterised by a large number of closed economies throughout the world. The opening up of capital markets promoted by globalisation reduces the chances of local growth through concentration. The vast amount of Gulf capital invested in industrialised countries and, therefore, denied to this region, is strong evidence that, in human development terms, it is not the possession of money and wealth that matters but how productively such wealth is invested.

Therefore, it has been argued that recovery of economic growth in the GCC countries and its main driver-increased productivity through diversifying their narrow depleting-resource based economies—are the two prerequisites for the advancement of knowledge in order to achieve overall human resource development.[16] Therefore, there is a perceived urgency for the development of a knowledge society in the Gulf, as this is the key policy framework to be integrated with the present global economy for their sustenance. Thus in such a backdrop, it can be visualised that there are tremendous opportunities for major

16. Ibid.

players in the global knowledge economy like India to penetrate into the vast unexploited knowledge sector of the GCC countries.

India a Global Leader in knowledge Industry: Role to Play in the GCC Countries' Knowledge Society

The question whether the 21st century could be India's arises because the Industrial Revolution which moulded global economic power structures for over two centuries is now drawing to a close, and a new revolution is beginning, built around information technology. Speaking about global economic power structures, with the United States of America occupying the 'core' and maintaining its hegemony for many centuries, India's potential to emerge as a leader in the knowledge industry is threatening the United States of America's un-relinquished position.

How has this situation arisen? All revolutions throw up new leaders. The agricultural revolution threw up civilisational leaders like India, Egypt and China. The Industrial Revolution threw up at least two: Britain and the United States of America. The logic is the same as it was during the Industrial Revolution. Wherever there was coal, sooner or later, coal mines came up. In any economy the trend has always been that industry goes to the raw material and not *vice versa*. In the global economy resourcing is also a global function. The chief cause of the success of the InfoTech industry in India has been its ability to deliver low-cost, high-quality raw material.

There are three inter-locking driving forces that shaped the knowledge economy. The first is the globalisation of products that cater to the global market. This combined with knowledge intensity and the third most important force, connectivity, which drives and shapes the new economy in the process of globalisation. Thus, globalisation provided an opportunity to India to emerge as a leader in the software industry.

It can be noted that India has traditionally fought automation due to pro-labour policies followed by successive governments. The information technology industry received its initial boost in 1986 when the government reduced duties on imported computer components. The engine behind the growth of the information technology industry in India has been software exports. This industry has been growing at an annual rate of 30 per cent since 1998. There are no signs of abatement in that growth rate. There is an abundance of software programmers and skilled management personnel in India and this would attract more international companies to form tie-ups. The customer base for hardware is split equally between the government and the private sector firms. The customer base transcends the type of industry.

Computers in India have a longer life period compared to developed countries. Due to the low cost of maintenance and high cost of new hardware, Indians tend to use computers for many years. The crucial advantage for India is the ability to leapfrog over many intermediate technologies and use the latest. The high cost of hardware forces programmers to develop cost-effective and efficient programmes that gets the best out of machines.

The information technology industry in India has been recording an annual average growth rate of 25 per cent, since July 1991. Large platform usage in India is restricted to big firms in the public sector and the private sector. The hardware market in India was estimated at $1 billion in 1994. Sale of PCs was just 1,80,000 which is a mere 1 per cent of the total sales in the world. This figure is expected to touch the 1 million mark by the end of this century. Approximately 6,00,000 PCs are in use all over the country with nearly 20 per cent of them connected in LANs. While PCs still dominate the hardware market, LAN server sales are growing at a fantastic rate. The growth rate in 1993-94 in the LAN server segment was a whopping 152 per cent. India's computer companies have formed strategic alliance with major foreign players to meet the changing demand of Indian consumers.

The Indian strength in hardware is in design and integration of computers rather than manufacture of components. India's traditional strength has always been software because of the abundant availability of cheap and talented programmers. The software industry in India generated more than $600 million, most of it in exports in 1993 and its growth over the last 8 years has been more than 30 per cent annually. National Association of Software and Services Companies (NASSCOM) has estimated that revenues from IT software and services yielded around Rs. 60,000 crores, almost 2.4 per cent of India's GDP in 2002-03. Close to 80 per cent of this—Rs. 47,500 crores-was accounted for by exports. Much of this growth was driven by the Information Technology Enabled Services (ITES) sector, which alone grew at over 65 per cent, upping revenues from Rs. 71 billion in 2001-02 to Rs. 117 billion in 2002-03.[17] In the information technology industry, software exports and offshore services are the biggest area of export from India. Clearly India's advantage lies in its vast resource of technically skilled computer personnel. A recent World Bank report showed that India's software exports could touch $10 billion by the end of 2005.[18] The biggest consumer of India's exported software is the United States followed by Western Europe where Germany is the most important market. The biggest advantage for India is that it could offer a wide spectrum of software services ranging from clerical support and data processing to sophisticated software systems. The most important point worth mentioning is that recent years have witnessed a spurt in the software trade of India with Gulf countries.[19] In short, India's strengths in the information technology area are:-

- Availability of unlimited pool of cheap and talented software personnel.
- Presence of the biggest English speaking population after the United States.
- Availability of western educated management personnel.
- Lack of regulation in the software industry.
- Burgeoning middle class of nearly 150 million consumers and
- No baggage of outdated software technology.

Looking at India, keeping the evolution of this new economy in perspective, the advantage for India lies in generating a high quality of knowledge resources at the lowest possible cost. The American and the European countries, because of a high level of automation, have a high

---

17. The Frontline (2004). "Meeting the Challenge", *The Frontline*. March 12. Chennai. pp.55-56.
18. Nayar, Vineet (2000). "The Virtual Asset", *Business World* (Special Millennium Issue), January 17.
19. In fact, besides remittances by the Gulf expatriates, software exports to the Gulf constitute a major component in India's record foreign exchange reserves in the current financial year 2003-04.

ingredient cost, thereby affecting their position in the knowledge-ware business. The cost per person to generate knowledge-ware in India continues to be one of the lowest in the world. Hence with respect to the cost and the quality of raw material, the knowledge economy will be in the hands of low-cost economies such as China, India and Malaysia amongst others.[20]

Here are other reasons why India is an emerging leader among the winners in the global Knowledge society:

(a) Industries that will define most of this century—information technology, telecommunications—are areas where India and Indians have shown a surprising amount of skill and creativity. Software exports now account for eight per cent of our total exports, a little over one per cent of the global market, and are still booming. Meanwhile India is increasingly coming to be identified with software—in the same sense as Japan was once identified with consumer electronics or Germany with engineering.

(b) As jobs become more and more fungible across borders, India's large base of skilled manpower is finally going to be an advantage. The expected earnings from IT-related services in 2008 is $17 billion, and that is more than half of India's total exports today.

(c) The explosion of Indian enterprise has happened in the closing years of the 20th century; middle-class India has woken up to the entrepreneurial dream and the new, mind ware-related businesses that they are starting are not as dependent on the efficiency of the government as the older businesses are. It has been aptly remarked by Lester Thurow,

> Each of the leading industries of the twenty first century depends on brain capacity. Any one of them may be installed anywhere in the planet. Where they will end up going depends on who has the brain capacity to take advantage of them. In the coming century, the comparative advantage of nations (India) will be entirely a human creation.[21]

---

20. Joseph, Tony (2000). "The Turning Point", *Business World* (Special Millennium Issue). January 17. p.8.

21. Ibid.

Thus, it can be contended that India is a leading player in the present global knowledge sector. There are various opportunities and consistent policy perspectives to reap the benefits of the booming sector to strengthen India's economic prowess. In this scenario India has the strategic leverage to penetrate into the emerging knowledge markets of the GCC countries, still at an evolving stage. This assertion has been recently confirmed by the Economic and Social Commission for Western Asia (ESCWA) of the United Nations in the World Summit on the Information Society (WSIS) held at Beirut, 4th to 6th February March 2003.[22]

Role to be Played by India in the Gulf Knowledge Society

Given the traditional trading affinity of India with the GCC countries and the vast potentials of economic engagement between the two in the globalised environment, India's prospective role in the emerging Gulf knowledge society can be identified as follows:

- *Hard Infrastructure*: This denotes hardware, telecommunications, networks, databases, telephones services, personal computers, mainframe and supercomputers, etc. In a nutshell, this constitutes the foundation over which all other components rest.
- *Soft Infrastructure*: Also referred to as the policy and regulatory environment; this includes laws, regulations, intellectual property, cyber laws, electronic signature, etc. The ICT environment cannot function harmoniously without this safety net.
- *Talent Base*: This is related to skill development and human resources within the technology sphere. This is concerned with: (1) efforts attracting a pool of talents from the region; (2) development of nationals within the local community; and, (3) instituting information technology training in the professional educational sector.
- Help in setting up service sectors such as the BPO (Business Process Outsourcing) as India has a global advantage. This sector

22. For details see UN/ESCWA (2003). "Information Knowledge Society: The Case of UAE", Western Asia Preparatory Conference for the World Summit on the Information Society (WSIS). Beirut. February 4-6.

is the main ingredient in providing highly sophisticated jobs in India. This may be useful for GCC countries to emulate the Indian model to employ their surging workforce. In fact as per press reports Iran is presently pursuing the strategies to initiate BPO sectors in their domestic economy.

- India's successful experience in e-commerce and e-governance can be also helpful for the GCC countries.

Thus, India has a larger role to play in the knowledge economy of the GCC countries in the coming years. It is here worth mentioning that in recent years there are some interactions between India and the GCC countries in the perspective of the information knowledge society which can be summarised as follows:

- Several well-known Indian IT companies participated in the three-day event organised by the Indian Business Council, Dubai, in collaboration with the Consulate General of India and NASSCOM in March 1999.
- Indian firms such as Wipro, Tata Consultancy Services, Pentafour, Aptech, Congruent Software, DSQ Software, Online Solutions and Orient Information Technology are presently active in some GCC countries.
- Four masters of computer applications courses in the Arabic script started in Madras, Aligarh, Hyderabad and Delhi, where students from the GCC countries will be offered education.

However, there are concerns regarding India's policy front to garner efforts to exploit the potentialities. This has happened due to the present global economic landscape and the emergence of China, in particular, its assertive and astute economic diplomacy in the Gulf region. As one analyst[23] has remarked that, "Is India losing the Gulf to China?". He further asserted that:

> India is in the danger of becoming a big loser in the Persian Gulf if it does not quickly respond to the economic changes taking place in the region. India's concerns in the Gulf have had a rather narrow mercantile focus on oil purchases, labour exports and remittances from expatriates. But as the Gulf States move towards regional

23. Raja Mohan, C. (2003). "Is India Losing the Gulf to China", *The Hindu*. February 13.

> economic integration and seek to globalise, India could easily squander the many natural advantages it has in the region. While the Gulf States are looking towards greater economic cooperation with India, which they see as a big future market, New Delhi may not be doing enough to tap the new opportunities that are opening up in the Gulf.
>
> If India is dozing at the wheel, China is rapidly raising its economic presence in the Gulf. Chinese consumer goods are already flooding the markets. For Chinese business, the rich Gulf area is a new and important destination. China, with its more open economic environment is also drawing huge investments from the region. With deepening economic links to the region, it is inevitable that Beijing's political influence in the Gulf will begin to grow. The slow pace of India's reforms and an unwillingness to devote political energies to exploit economic possibilities in the Gulf are giving a relatively free hand to China which could emerge as a future player in an area of vital concern to India.
>
> Cultural affinities and historic relations make the Persian Gulf a natural economic partner for India. If India continues to dither, it could well find China outflanking it in the region.[24]

Therefore, the need of the hour is to take pragmatic policy decisions in order to harness the opportunities and potentialities as India has high stakes other than the economic involved in this strategic region. It can be mentioned that there are some positive developments in this regard in recent years. This can be substantiated from the first ever industries ministers' meeting was held between India and the GCC countries in February 2004 at Mumbai, jointly organised by the CII, and the Ministry of External Affairs.[25]

Moreover, from the strategic point of view, India and the GCC share the desire for political stability and security in the region. The common political and security concerns of India and the GCC translate into efforts for peace, security and stability in the Gulf region and South Asia. The emerging common security perceptions create further opportunities for the GCC-India cooperation in the future. The GCC states are going through important changes and transformation; the

24. Ibid.

25. *The Economic Times*, February 19, 2004.

process of understanding and integration is coming of age. Along with it the areas for cooperation are also widening beyond investments, trade and commerce and sharing and development of human resources to security. This envisages jointly preparing to meet emerging domestic and regional challenges, foremost being the common threat from terrorism and extremism.

Thus as evident from the developments, Indo-GCC economic ties premised on the narrow oil-gas, worker remittances, is poised to swell and diversify in the coming years. This will be the ideal framework to hedge the vulnerabilities of both in the global oil and gas regime in the wake of any future supply as well as demand disruptions.

6

Competition-Interdependence Dilemma in Asia

Implications for India's Gulf Strategy

It is well recognised now that there are several key obstacles in realising India's quest for stable, secure and sustainable energy supplies at relatively stable prices. Apart from domestic structural rigidities reflected in the oil and gas sector and adhocist policy implementation, the most onerous challenges exist at the external front. India is sandwiched in a complex geopolitical matrix that restrains its external policy manoeuvrability to access foreign energy sources in a convenient manner. Therefore, policy re-energising is the need of the hour. This chapter after briefly overviewing the challenges plaguing India's energy security strategy, focuses on a detailed analysis of the energy security strategy of the major Asian countries and their implications for India's strategy towards the GCC region.

While there are key obstacles in realising India's quest for securing energy, these vary in kind and in degree from one energy source to another, and they are essentially two-fold in nature, *viz.*, at the domestic level, the slow pace of sectoral reforms, internal problems of political/bureaucratic inertia and entrenched resistance to outward looking liberalised trade and investment policies, and at the external level, the built-in constraints of complex geopolitics and ensuing keen competition from other regional importers. The various key issues and challenges pertaining to India's energy sector (all sub-sectors) are briefly mentioned in the Box 6.1.

Though, the visible onerous challenges in the hydrocarbon sector are multifaceted, they can be broadly grouped under three heads, such as supply risk, market risk and technical risk. The various factors underlying India's quest for energy security in the past and also in the coming years can be identified as, accessibility and affordability of adequate oil and gas supplies in a domestic resource deficit and globally constrained market amidst escalating oil prices, lack of Demand Management Practices (DMPs), irrational Pricing Regime and multiple distortionary duty regime, slow pace of reforms and inadequate restructuring and clash of interests among decision making bodies, barriers to entry for private (both domestic and foreign) players and outdated legal mandates, regulatory deficits leading to sectoral malfunctioning and improper governance, maladministration of product subsidies, negative environmental spillovers due to low-gradation of products. bearing huge opportunity costs, inadequate domestic infrastructure and lack of investment to meet the sectoral demand, technological incapability to adopt advanced sectoral practices, and complex geopolitical vortex to access overseas resources.

Box 6.1

India's Energy Sector: Major Issues and Challenges

Hydro
- Well below potential
- Long gestation period
- Implementation constraints—rehabilitation, Environmental clearances

Coal
- High emissions
- Low efficiency
- Low calorific value and high ash content
- Concentration in Eastern and South Eastern region

Nuclear
- Below potential
- Security of supply
- Implementation constraints—uranium availability, financing, international treaties

Renewables
- Huge potential available
- Gap between technical horizon and commercial horizon
- Lack of investment and major players
- Must for rural security
- R&D needed

Contd...

...Contd...

Oil & Natural Gas	• Vulnerable to disruptions • Security of supply—supply risk • High price volatility—market risk • Technical risks • Rising import bill and impact on GDP • Regulatory deficits • Access to pipeline gas • Leverage over LNG suppliers • Huge infrastructure needs • Distorted duty and pricing regime, subsidies, inefficiency and sectoral rigidities • Geopolitical bottlenecks complicating accessing oil and gas from abroad • Keen competition from other major importers like China in almost all producing regions • No substantive energy deals with major producers such as the Gulf region

Source: Author's own assessment.

The Indian energy sector is overwhelmingly dominated by the central public sector organisations. Through the public sector functioning and development, a lot has been achieved and simultaneously inefficiencies and distorted policy parameters have enabled structural rigidities that are plaguing the performance of the energy sector. The hydrocarbon sector is no exception, though the refining sector is scarcely presented by private players after the deregulation. The controlled pricing regimes, distortionary duty structure, over presence of political consideration in decision making have resulted in sectoral inflexibilities hindering fair competition and integrated development of the sector. In fact, the lack of synergy in reforms across all energy sub-sectors has exacerbated the inflexibility in India's energy policy space.

Moreover, lack of expertise and technical ability, financial constraints and inadequate policy decisions have compounded the problem. India's oil refining and oil recovery capabilities and overall energy technology is inadequate to meet the challenges of recent changes in the global energy sector. Though some public and private sector entities like ONGC Videsh Ltd. and Reliance Industries Ltd.

have recently entered into technological alliances with foreign partners, a lot is to be done to overcome these hurdles. The meagre equity levels and financial strength of Indian oil and gas companies has affected their international presence. High interest rates in India relative to other countries have acted as a liability for the Indian oil and gas companies to compete for equity oil abroad. Moreover, generating loans in the international market for oil and gas sector operations has not been successful due to India's lower position in world financial markets' country ranking. In addition, neither Indian banks nor the Indian government have provisions of special incentives in the form of soft loans or aids for equity oil projects.

Regardless of the limited efficacy of sectoral reforms, India's hopes of diversifying supply as a means of enhancing energy security have been—and will continue to be—constrained by its political geography for the foreseeable future. India's geopolitical realities in regard to oil and gas resources are in many respects, the reverse of many other Asian countries.[1] For example, Japan has spent tens of billions of dollars over the past three decades searching for oil fields in the Middle East or pursuing oil and gas schemes with Russia in an effort to diversify supplies. More recently, as we have seen, China has also purchased oil fields from Sudan to Central Asia and entertained the idea of constructing massive pipelines that have little economic rational in the hope of diversifying supplies in the name of geopolitics and energy security. India is constantly being outpaced by China in these endeavours. But for India, the opposite is true: energy projects that have a compelling economic logic are stifled by the geopolitical realities of South, Central and West Asia. This can be best substantiated from the recent developments concerning the proposed pipelines, such as Iran-Pakistan-India (IPI), Myanmar-Bangladesh-India (MBI) and Turkmenistan-Afghanistan-Pakistan-India (TAPI).

Theoretical Approach to Energy Security Strategy

Though there is no particular theoretical approach to energy security as such, yet the vast array of literature on this field and

1. Manning, Robert A. (2000). *The Asian Energy Factor: Myths and Dilemmas of Energy, Security, and the Pacific Future*. New York: Council on Foreign Relations.

approaches and strategies of most of the energy consuming and importing countries make a viable reference addressing the issue theoretically. One of the important strategies or policy perspective is based on the experience of the European Union (EU) which can be incorporated while attempting a theoretical approach in the context of India. On the basis of the above theoretical underpinnings, the Energy Security Strategy Quadrant Model (ESSQM) can be constructed, which embodies the matrices of domestic social, political, economic and strategic variables along with their external spillovers to analyse a country's energy security strategy.

Figure 6.1

The Energy Security Strategy Quadrant Model (ESSQM)

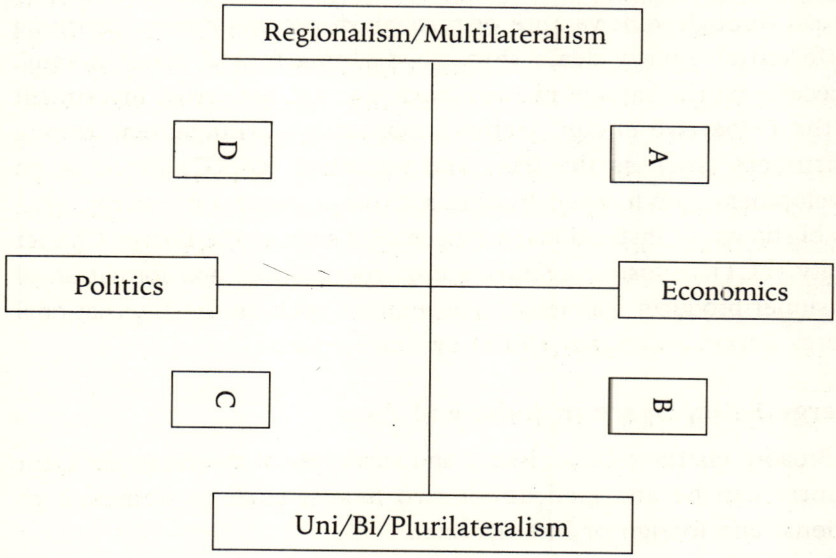

The above model reveals the various alternative policy variables influencing the internal as well as external dimension of a country's energy security strategy. At the national level, countries generally, devise and adopt policies keeping in view certain objectives as determined by the domestic resource constraints such as optimum utilisation of available domestic sources of energy by diversifying the domestic energy portfolio, without compromising economic efficiency and competitiveness and environmental imperatives, energy efficiency and most competitive production process, so that the country can compete and sustain itself in the globalised economy, exploration and production of indigenous renewables keeping in view the discrepancy between the technical and economic horizon of these energy sources, and judicious energy mix confirming the economy's production pattern, etc.

The international or foreign energy strategy of a country involves adoption of different techniques and conventional foreign policy instruments to a country's energy cause in surplus regions or countries at various levels, unilateral, bilateral, plurilateral, sub-regional, regional, or multilateral levels. This envisages various strategies such as: acquiring equity energy resources (oil or gas) abroad through joint venture or through direct investment; clinching preferential energy deals through diplomatic and other means, especially on the basis of bilateral trade and aid, etc.; cross investment in the respective energy sectors; cooperative arrangement among consumers (such as the IEA) and suppliers (OPEC) focusing on development, production, trading and other aspects of energy, etc.; establishment of institutional arrangements such as the Energy Charter Treaty (ECT) to foster regional energy cooperation, and formation of consumer-producer framework cooperation such as the International Energy Forum Secretariat (IEFS) by Saudi Arabia.

Energy Policy Space in India and Asia

Broadly, energy security issues and strategies of an energy deficient country can be analysed under two heads, such as domestic or national and foreign or international.

The domestic or national strategies focus on the various institutional, technical, economic, social, political, and security aspects of the energy scenario within the country concerned and formulation of suitable policy accordingly, specific to a particular energy source or in an integrated manner to ensure security of energy supplies. The international or foreign energy strategy of a deficient country on the other hand incorporates conventional foreign policy instruments along with other techniques such as 'economic or resource diplomacy' to secure its energy security overseas to address the domestic resource constraints. On the basis of the above theoretical background, the succeeding section attempts to assess India's and Asia's current energy security strategy scenario.

At the domestic level, India's current energy security strategy involves, reforms and restructuring to allow entry of more players and development of competitive market environment, intensification of exploration efforts and achievement of 100 per cent coverage to enhance domestic availability through the five phases of the New Exploration Licensing Policies (NELP), exploitation of untapped potential of alternate fuels in the sector, approval for setting up of strategic crude oil storage, aspiring to be the regional hub in oil refining and products trade in the region and framing policies in this regard, partially raising retail prices of mass consumption products like petrol and diesel, subsidising oil marketing companies, removing the road cess, etc. diversifying oil and gas import portfolio geographically, and devising an Integrated Energy Policy. At the global level India's current strategies include acquiring overseas equity oil and gas, consistently pursuing policies and advocacy to be successfully integrated with the world energy market and trying to participate in multilateral cooperative frameworks, etc. However, the most significant aspect of India's external energy strategy can be witnessed at the regional level. India's actions at the regional level include, working on diplomatic channels to secure equity oil and gas deals in countries and regions, where India has maintained good relations over the years, striving for establishing regional cooperative arrangements for pursuing energy security initiatives—holding round-table conferences of consumers and producers as well, acquiring observer status in the Energy Charter Treaty, incorporating energy sector cooperation in all bilateral economic pacts with both consuming and producing countries, campaigning for an Asian energy market by establishing an Asian marker for crude imports from the Dubai market (to take care of the Asian Premium), started exporting refinery equipment and also products to the GCC countries in 2003-04 and working on cross investment proposals with oil and gas exporting countries in all possible regions, from the Gulf, Africa, Russia, Central Asia, East Asia, South Asia, Latin America, and North America.

In fact, there are similarities between India's strategies and the strategies adopted by other major Asian consumers like China, Japan and Korea, though there are differences in the degree of involvement and success. In the recent past, China has emerged as the most proactive strategist not only in the regional context but also at the global level to secure its energy requirement across the globe through multidimensional approaches. This in a way has restricted the policy flexibility by other major Asian players including India in strategising their external energy security strategy.

Currently, Asian oil and gas sector is under strict regulations and controls according to policies that put much weight on stable import sources and the supply structure is characterised by high dependence on the Gulf, basically exhibiting the features of a sellers' market. There is also the lack of a regional marker crude which obstructs the development of integrated trade of flexible and fluid materials including crude oil and products and gas in the region. Major players in the regional oil and gas sector (the national companies as well as the respective governments) aim for stable supplies making the regional market less competitive in comparison to other regions of the world. The concerns of energy security particularly with respect to oil and natural gas has resulted in nationalistic oil security policies and zero-sum strategies, which may risk the disruptive impact on the global oil market in the event of a booming demand scenario in the near to the medium term scenario. Moreover, such competitive posturing has in fact inflated asset prices and E&P costs in areas which could have warranted lower prices in the true competitive market scenario.[2]

However, with the growing perception of energy security amidst developments in the global oil and gas market, energy policy space in the countries of the region has marked a change and insisted on implementation of various defensive tactics, albeit at the national levels. The contours of energy policy space in Asia can be overviewed in the light of recent developments and policy implementation in various countries. Box 6.2 summarises the latest developments.

---

2. The competitive bidding for oil companies in Kazakhstan by China and India and the conflict between Japan and China in the Trans-Siberian pipelines are two cases of such aggressive posturing for energy deals.

Box 6.2

Recent Developments in Energy Security Policies in Asia

Type of Activity	*Countries Involved*	*Status*
Import Portfolio Diversification	All	Rising trend of oil imports from Africa, Sakhalin, Siberia, and Caspian sea.
Equity Oil & Gas Assets Overseas	Japan, Korea, China, India	China's tremendous success
Cross border pipelines	Japan, ASEAN, China, India, Korea	Formative stage marred by overriding politics
Oil stockpiling system	China, and India	China has already started, India is yet to start.
Allowing capital investment in domestic downstream from oil producing countries, Gulf	ASEAN-Philippines, Korea, Japan, China, and India	Gaining momentum
Strategic partnership through crisscross investment proposals with oil exporters	China, Japan and India	China-Saudi Arabia, Japan and India in other Gulf countries
Cooperation and dialogue among major consumers and producers in the region	Indian initiative	Successful
Regional oil market development	Japan and India	Only in discussion, no concrete steps

Source: Compiled from various sources.

Looking at the developments, it is quite evident that, there are clear indications of policies pursued by Asian countries at the individual country level or at least bi/tri-lateral level and not at the multilateral level. Though individual efforts by the countries at the national level increases energy security to an extent both at the domestic and regional level, yet in the event of exclusivity, such policies may lead to confrontation and a factor that may create suspicion and worsen the region's energy security. Moreover, the issues pertaining to the oil and gas sector in particular are beyond the ability of individual countries to ensure security. In such a background, the importance of regional cooperation for energy security becomes imminent and pertinent. In other words, energy security issues should not be viewed as a special issue at the individual country level rather in the context of a broader economic integration issue at the regional level in Asia. Nevertheless the pattern of energy cooperation in Asia, especially at the sub-regional level points out the potentials and necessity of transforming such initiatives through proper linkage and institution building at the pan-regional level to secure Asia's energy future. The absence of collective effort in a win-win proposition for regional energy cooperation points to the complex geopolitical context in which India has to carve a niche for its energy future. A brief analysis on the status of energy cooperation in Asia would substantiate the ground reality and implications for India's strategy towards the Gulf region.

Energy Cooperation in Asia: Current Trends and Patterns

Though there is intense public discourse about the importance of energy cooperation in Asia, yet the current form and pattern of cooperation is overwhelmingly confined to either bilateral or plurilateral attempts at sub-regional level. Moreover, the concerns of impending energy security and the potential complementarities have resulted in a series of overlapping and competing proposals for energy cooperation in Asia. Such proposals of energy cooperation at sub-regional level in Asia can be briefly analysed as Box 6.3.

Box 6.3

Sub-Regional Energy Cooperation in Asia: Trends and Patterns

Countries/Region	*Trends and Patterns of Cooperation*	*Remarks*
South Asia	SAARC Energy Cooperation, SAARC Energy Centre, Studies for the development of 'energy chain'	Preliminary stage, contentious issues remain such as pricing, opening trade, political difference, etc.
	BIMSTEC Energy Cooperation, headed by Myanmar: Development of regional hydrocarbon and hydropower, energy infrastructure (natural gas), energy information centre and energy trading network between members	Formative stage, no real forward march
	India-Bhutan Hydro-Electricity Cooperation	Most successful example of cooperation

Contd...

	India-Sri Lanka-Bhutan-Nepal Petro Product and crude trading	Successful, but no concrete infrastructure
	Proposed Gas Pipelines: Iran-Pakistan-India, Myanmar-Bangladesh-India, Turkmenistan-Afghanistan-Pakistan-India, India-Nepal oil pipeline	Hostage to political, economic, security difficulties and extra regional power influence. However, IPI is making steady progress, though there are serious issues to be managed.
	SAARC-ASEAN Cooperation in the Energy Sector	SAARC-ASEAN cooperation recently developed between the two Secretariats recommended the proposal of visit by the Experts from the SAARC region to relevant ASEAN institutions coordinated by the ASEAN Secretariat-Dhaka Summit
	South Asia Regional Energy Coalition (SAREC) supported by USAID and American Chambers of Commerce and Business	Ambitious plans and started some country specific and sector specific studies, but progress is little in physical terms.
ASEAN	ASEAN Petroleum Security Agreement, APSA, 1986: Emergency oil sharing	Less specific on how it is activated and it never got activated.
	Future Import Expansion and proposed review of APSA	Currently under way
	Large-scale infrastructure plan covering the whole ASEAN region: TAGP, TAPG	Preliminary stage
APEC	Joint Oil Data Initiative (JODI): Joint initiative to improve oil data transparency—APEC, IEA, EU, OLADE, OPEC and UN.	Way forward.
	Sea lane security: EWG to review the activities of implemented by APEC Transportation Working Group and the International Maritime organisation.	
	Real Time Emergency Information Sharing: EWG to work together	

Contd...

	to identify contacts to share information and establish a system of sharing information. Oil supply emergency response: EWG to implement a feasibility study of joint stockpiling by net oil importing economies of APEC Non-petroleum and long-term concerns: EWG to consider broader issues to enhance energy security.	
ASEAN+3	ASEAN+3 Energy Ministers' Meeting, IEF, OSAKA Hiranuma Initiative was agreed upon: emergency network, oil stockpiling, Asian premium, expansion of natural gas in energy mix Forums were established to study each agenda. Energy ministers Meeting, Manila, June 2004 ASEAN+3 Energy Partnership was agreed upon	Dialogue and under discussion
EC-ASEAN Energy Facility (EAEF)	A Programme of cooperation between the European Communities (EC) and the Association of Southeast Asian Nations (ASEAN) to facilitate partnerships between ASEAN and European organisations in developing specific joint projects in the energy sector. The objectives are: 1) to increase the security of energy supply of ASEAN countries and indirectly of Europe; 2) to increase economic cooperation between European Union and ASEAN countries; 3) to improve environment of local and global levels; and 4) to facilitate the implementation of the ASEAN Plan of Action for Energy Cooperation 1999-2004, and subsequently its continuation for 2004-2009. EAEF was launched in March 2002 with duration of five years until February 2007. Four different categories of projects called "facility" are available. This includes: market awareness; institutional frameworks; feasibility	A best case of inter-regional energy cooperation in a multilateral framework.

Contd...

	studies and demonstration projects. Consistent with the ASEAN Plan of Action for Energy Cooperation, the Programme focuses on electricity interconnection, gas pipeline interconnection, clean coal technology, energy efficiency, and renewable energy.	
Northeast Asia	Asia-pacific energy community, Japan centred multilateral energy cooperation plan proposed by 32 Japanese companies: 42,500 km pipeline extending from Yakutsk to Dampier in northwestern Australia, connecting China, Korea, Japan, Taiwan and six ASEAN countries	No headway
	The Vostok plan, promoted by Russia to develop and utilise Sakha and Sakhalin Gas for export to South Korea and Japan to North Korea	Never started
	The Energy Silk Route Project: Turkmenistan-China-Japan natural gas pipeline	Under discussion
	The Irkutsk Region Gas Project: Pipeline routes from Russia to China and South Korea through Mongolia	No headway
	Angarsk Pipeline Project: Pipeline routes from the eastern Siberia oilfield of Angarsk to China and Japan	Diplomatic and economic rivalry between China and Japan over the routes
Others	Pan-Asian Continental Oil Bridge: Chinese strategy in the 1990s to link Japan with the Middle East under Chinese control	Never started
	Council for Security Cooperation in the Asia Pacific, (CSCAP)	Not much advance
	Shanghai Cooperation Organisation (SCO)	Started discussion
	The Japan America China Conference	Not much headway
	Tumen River Area development Programme	Ongoing, slow pace
	Dialogue between major consumers and producers of the broader Asian region, initiated by India with support from other major consumers	Ongoing dialogue and discussion, awareness and concern about various issues—positive developments

Source: Compiled from various sources.

As evident there are several plans and proposals of energy cooperation in the Asian region at the sub-regional level and the approach of the players has been more bilateral and plurilateral and less multilateral. The several projects and proposals such as cross-border pipelines, integrated oil market, stockpiling, data collection and information sharing, etc. are in a way though positive steps in a good direction, yet they have failed to see the light of day due to inherent political, economic, technical and security considerations.

Moreover, a bilateral and competitive approach to energy security has some negative economic and political underpinnings that can be detrimental to the security of not only individual countries in the region but also the region as a whole. So the prudent way to approach regional cooperation for energy security is to focus on a multilateral approach in a pan-Asian perspective. The obvious advantages of a pan-Asian approach in regional cooperation for energy security are multifaceted: bilateral and competitive approach will lead to underdevelopment of regional resources, over-investment, duplication of infrastructure and possibility of unfavourable prices by the supplying countries, etc. in a multilateral approach, regional cross-border trade, investment, infrastructure development, transit fee, demand allocation, secured flow of the fuels will be facilitated as it involves multi-countries and multi-stakeholders, it will aptly contribute to regional development by creating new institutions that will complement existing bilateral institutions, and the multilateral approach will lead to the development of an integrated area facilitating operations from developing to dispensing across the energy value chain.

Therefore, it becomes important to reorient the strategies towards fruitful energy cooperation. It is pragmatic and prudent to focus on urgent issues such as those in the oil and gas sector, as there are clear indications of rising imports in the coming years. Moreover, the effort should be to cater to viable and feasible projects at the sub-regional level that can be further extended beyond the sub-region. However, it should be carefully designed so as to take care of the scale and cost aspects so as not to conflict with other sub-regional projects. In such a background, therefore, a pan-Asian multilateral approach becomes essential while devising strategies at the sub-regional level. Moreover, institution building and proper legal framework are necessary, which requires reforms and restructuring not only at the individual country level but also on the proper alignment of the sectoral fundamentals of all countries. Moreover, in such a background and realities, it is prudent to focus on a staged or step-by-step manner. In other words, efforts should be put first towards sub-regional energy cooperation in the region that can be calibrated into a full-fledged Asian energy community at a later stage. However, caution is to be followed while delineating the norms and patterns of sub-regional energy cooperation that may not override the interests of other sub-regions or countries.

Rationale for Pan-regional Energy Cooperation in Asia

A comparison of the several national energy structures of surplus and deficiency in Asia suggests a significant asymmetry of substantial economic opportunities and liabilities. This makes the case for regional cooperation insidious to take care of the energy security imperatives as well as augment regional economic integration in Asia. As mentioned earlier, the oil and gas sector fundamentals in Asia exhibit the existence of sectoral comparative advantages which can be seen from the qualitative comparison of production characteristics, which in fact, is the cornerstone of regional cooperation (Table 6.1).

Table 6.1

Qualitative Comparison of Production Characteristics of Asian Countries

	Oil & Gas	*Coal & Minerals*	*Labour*	*Capital*	*Technology*	*Managerial Expertise*
Japan	VP	S	S	VR	VR	VR
China	R	VR	VR	VP	S	S
India*	**S**	**R**	**VR**	**VP**	**S**	**S**
South Korea	A	S	S	VR	R	R
North Korea	A	R	R	VP	VP	VP
Taiwan	S	S	S	R	R	R
Russia	VR	VR	VP	VP	S	S
Central Asia*	R	R	S	VP	VP	VP
Persian Gulf*	VR	S	VP	S	R	S

Note: VR = Very Rich; R = Rich; S = Short; VP = Very Poor; A = Absent; * = Own assessment.

Source: Paik, Keun Wook (1995). *Gas and Oil in Northeast Asia*. London: Royal Institute of International Affairs. p.274.

Moreover, as discussed before, the issues pertaining to the oil and gas sector need urgent attention and active participation of all countries. This can be addressed only through a multilateral approach. The strategy should be to synergise the complementarities from common risk sharing and benefit in a win-win manner. For example, Japan and Korea, two IEA members have the technology, capital and expertise in the oil and gas sector, while countries like China, India, Indonesia, and Vietnam lack capital and technology to develop their resources. So it becomes imperative to pool the resources (physical, technical, financial, etc.) of the countries to a common framework for co-prosperity and the common benefit of all.

There is significant scope for advancing regional economic development by increasing energy access and supply and improving energy security, reliability and quality of life in the region. There are numerous potential spillovers from more open regional energy trade, investment and infrastructure regimes that can augment economic integration in the region. This can act as a fundamental part of regional resource management and broader regional integration. This can supplement better accessibility to global investment and technology flows in the region. The major benefits of energy cooperation can be harnessed by exploiting complementarities and comparative advantages in regional energy endowments, experiences, technology developments, resource development costs and integration of complementary demand profiles. Regional integrated market offer enhanced opportunities from the economies of scale and comparative advantage at the global level. Cooperation also helps in accessing diverse import sources and faster outcomes for energy security. The bottom line of regional cooperation is to reduce costs of supply for all participants from the win-win opportunities.

Asia-Gulf Energy Linkage: Implications for India's Strategy

As outlined in previous chapters, the dominant and seemingly inexorable trend of the present regime is the growing energy interdependence between Asia and the Gulf region. These trends have emerged since the 1990s and are currently being intensified. The result is that major Asian consumers especially Japan and China are diligently cultivating energy ties to the Gulf energy producers in general and Saudi Arabia in particular; that underscores a profound awareness of the limits of Indian involvement in the Gulf energy domain.

The burgeoning Asia-Gulf energy ties have become permanent structural features of the new global energy regime. As the current oil market is now shaped more by transport costs albeit less by political relationships, the result has been a largely bifurcated global market, with oil flows from the Middle East gravitating to Asia; while oil supplies from the western hemisphere (Mexico, Venezuela, Colombia, Canada), and the Atlantic Basin (North Sea, West Africa) have to a large degree, displaced Gulf oil in the US market.[3] The central consequence of the Middle East-Asia oil link that has begun to unfold is a complex set of interlocking economic ad financial relationships, a deepening commercial network weaving the two regions together: Asians investing in upstream oil and gas sectors in the Middle East; while OPEC Middle East exporters invest in downstream Asian activities.[4] This has been aptly remarked by the then OPEC Secretary General in his speech,

> Asian investors, traders, operators and others are active in the energy sectors of the Gulf. On the other hand, Middle East companies and individuals have significant interests in the downstream energy industry in Asia.[5]

Thus, the emerging Asia-Gulf energy interdependence points to the complex web of geoeconomics and geopolitics, in which India will face daunting challenges in order to delineate a concrete energy linkage with the Gulf countries. India's energy security imperatives, as pointed out earlier, envisage a clear dependence on the Gulf region and therefore in the changed structure of the global oil and gas regime, India has to devise pragmatic and astute diplomacy to fructify its energy linkages with the GCC region. Given the fact that, in the absence of a collective regional cooperative framework in Asia, India

---

3. Manning, Robert (2004). "The Asian Energy Market: A New Geopolitics", in ECSSR (ed.), *Asian Energy Markets: Dynamics and Trends*. ECSSR.
4. The recently concluded successful crisscross investment and technology transfer deal between China and Saudi Arabia is the best example of the link.
5. Rilwanu Lukman's speech in John Calabrese (ed.) "Gulf-Asia Energy Security". Washington: Middle East Institute. 1998.

should devise an appropriate external energy strategy imbibing a balance between foreign policy and economic diplomacy; and a renewed strategy towards the vital region of the Gulf. This calls for a judicious mix of aggressive bilateralism and a regional cooperative framework.

7

Conclusion

Towards an Asian Energy Charter

The global oil and gas regime has undergone structural shifts and basic transformations over the years, repositioning the major players—both consumers and producers, reshaping the geopolitics of energy, and redefining the patterns of trade, pricing, etc. Most importantly, one aspect that has become evident throughout the transition is that although the Gulf Region did experience erosion of power in the global regime, yet it retains its strategic salience. In the coming times they are likely to regain the loss of status, though it might not be of the same quantum. The other most important significant change is the strategic positioning of Asian countries in general and India in particular in the global energy map as the most vibrant consumers of imported energy especially oil and gas. The factor behind this transition is attributed to the definitive shift of global economic hotspot and the growth induced structural changes in the major emerging Asian economies, like India; clearly pointing to a regional shift in the global energy regime.

The Asian region in general and India has taken centre stage in the global oil and gas demand pattern. With the global economic strength centering on this region, the centre of gravity of energy consumption has shifted to this region at the beginning of the 1990s, when the region overtook both Western Europe and North America's oil consumption. The emerging trends discernible in the region during recent years reveals that the region is poised to overtake the whole of America (including Mexico) in the foreseeable future by the year 2030 to become the world's largest consumer of crude oil.

The real growth of oil and gas demand in India started with the rapid economic growth rate in the 1990s as a result of economic reforms and liberalisation policies pursued by the government. Paralleling impressive growth rates, the demand for every form of energy in general and oil and gas in particular surged up. Though India's energy mix was heavily biased towards coal due to its abundance, but gradually, it became oil reliant premised on the pattern of economic growth and production process. It does not mean that oil and gas was substantially available domestically rather it was the cheaper imports of oil, as other sources of domestic energy such as electricity and specifically coal was not optimally used. The meagre domestic as well as regional oil and gas sources have resulted in increasing volumes of oil imports from the Gulf region. The strong oil demand growth in India encouraged refining capacity expansion. By the mid-1990s, India built new and additional refineries. However, currently India has excess refining capacity and since 2003, has been exporting petroleum products. Amid such emerging supply-demand gap, India relied heavily on oil imports. The oil demand surges combined with refining sector boom sent India's oil demand soaring and resulted in voluminous crude imports, particularly from the Gulf region. Because growth of domestic oil production plateaued over the years and because India is situated far from the non-Gulf producing area and because Indian refineries are technically designed to process Nigerian and Gulf crude, consequently the dependence on the Gulf region rose considerably, despite the fact that, Indian and Asian bound oil cargoes have been more costly than those shipped to Europe and the US (The differential widened to around $3 per barrel in the year 2000). However, with the entry of private players such as the state-of-the-art grassroot refinery of Reliance Industries Ltd, including others, a wide variety of crudes from several countries can be processed in India.

However, sensing the strategic importance of the hydrocarbon sector in the overall economic set up and the underlying heavy import dependence, the Government of India started reforming the petroleum sector, albeit slowly. The pace of reforms, though, was slow initially, yet has resulted in some desired achievements. Most importantly among the achievements are the discoveries of major oil and gas fields in recent years by private as well as public sector joint ventures facilitated through the NELP, securing equity oil abroad through joint ventures in an attempt to diversify import sources from the Gulf, equalising prices of petroleum products on import parity, managing subsidies, etc.

Despite such policy measures taken by the GoI to be secure on the vital energy front by diversifying the import sources of oil and gas, yet the present and future trends of oil and gas consumption concretely envisage that the dependence on the Gulf is likely to remain and even increase in the near future. So given the nature of the Gulf region as politically volatile and vulnerable, there are apprehensions regarding India's perennial quest for energy security.

The supply side transformation witnessed in the global regime over the years is that the Gulf countries are constantly facing threats regarding their survival and stability. The threats are from both demand as well as supply side of the global oil game. On the demand side, the threats are the byproducts of the measures that were undertaken by the industrialised and major oil importing countries in reaction to the two oil shocks of the 1970s. They include successful price-induced energy conservation measures—implemented through fiscal policies and technological innovations and an increase in the pace of oil discovery and production outside OPEC spurred by the high prices of 1973-74—through tax incentives and technological breakthroughs. Among other developments that slowed down the re-establishment of the Gulf as the dominant force in the world oil market are the relatively low economic performance of the industrialised oil importers (which reduced oil demand) and moves away from oil towards other energy sources especially natural gas. This has in fact created a supply structure 'away from the Gulf syndrome' in the global oil regime. These factors would not have represented a problem were it not for the risk of 'oil obsolescence' for OPEC producers, holding huge reserves; less Gulf oil will be needed as more conservation and energy efficiency measures are put in place; as alternative sources of energy developed and as new non-OPEC sources are brought on line to increase world supply.

It is apparent that OPEC and Gulf countries in particular have contributed to their marginalisation and also their past policies of defending prices at all costs (through their role as residual producers) have encouraged other non-OPEC producers to expand their exploration programmes, to develop technology to extract oil and gas in domestic and remote areas that were inaccessible a few years ago and to increase the productivity and longevity of existing oil wells. This has resulted in substantial non-OPEC supply in the world oil market. In fact, OPEC's residual role in the world oil market has resulted in the present 'production-at-will mentality' that prevails in the non-OPEC countries and in a declining OPEC share of world oil output that has recently begun to recover from the lows of the 1980s, owing to the Asian region's in general and India and China's heavy dependence on this region.

Besides the aforesaid external factors, several internal developments within the Gulf region also threaten to undermine the dominance of Gulf in the global oil regime. Just the Gulf countries experience challenges externally due to increased competition from non-OPEC supply, an increasing domestic consumption of energy, resulting in drain of oil revenue earnings. The ever-expanding government expenditures to maintain welfarism combined with the lowest oil prices in the 1990s and consequent lower oil revenues have made matters worse for the Gulf countries. This has further been exacerbated by their low financial strength to augment investment in the oil and gas sector to penetrate into new emerging consuming destinations and thereby secure market share lost during the 1980s.

However the trends of world oil and gas reserves, production, and exports reveal that there is every likelihood of Gulf countries' re-establishment in the global oil and gas regime. As analysed in the study, the non-OPEC reserves, production and supply are highly fluctuating and in fact organically related to market prices and investment movements. Gulf countries holding nearly 65 per cent of the world's oil reserves having more than 100 years of R/P ratio are the ultimate source of global oil and gas supply in the coming years. Given the fact that the centre of incremental world oil and gas consumption is Asia in general and India in particular, there is tremendous scope for the GCC countries for their re-establishment in the regime due to the region's strategic location and geographical proximity to these emerging markets.

Thus, as evident there are complementarities between India and the GCC countries in the present global oil regime which place them strategically in the global energy scenario—India as an emerging vibrant consumer and importer of oil and gas and the GCC countries as the dominant suppliers and exporters of oil and gas. A pattern of interdependence in the oil and gas sector can also be witnessed between India and the GCC countries. There are also other aspects of such interdependence, but the oil and gas factor is the most fundamental one. Another argument for a potentially brighter future for the GCC states emphasises the fact that the world economy has changed in a fundamental way in recent years and that only a thorough understanding of the new emerging markets will lead to successful competition in the world oil and gas trade. The new patterns point to the Gulf's greater trading affinity with India than other countries of the Asian region. However, care should be taken not to assume that the GCC countries would reap all the benefits that an increase in oil and gas demand of India will generate. Given the region's past experience with hostilities and inherent instabilities, India will seek diversification of its import sources. Yet due to numerous constraints such as geopolitical, bilateral and financial besides others, the diversification attempts will not be adequate enough to bridge the gap between demand and supply. This can be substantiated from the continuing interaction—both upstream as well as downstream—between India and the GCC countries premised on hydrocarbon interdependence in recent years.

There are also clear indications of the Gulf countries' dependence on India and the rest of Asia for a secure stable outlet for their oil and gas exports. The dependence of Gulf countries on the Asian market can be substantiated from the pernicious effects of the Asian currency crisis in 1998, resulting in lower oil demand in these countries and consequent lower world oil prices and lower oil revenues for the oil exporting GCC countries. However, thanks to China and India, the two untouched by the crisis, maintained their steady growth in oil demand and accounted for 3 per cent and 7 per cent (1999) growth in their oil imports from the GCC countries, which somehow stabilised the Gulf prospects. Thus, there is a shift from complementarities to interdependence between oil consumers and producers in recent years, which have made both vulnerable to the bottlenecks and periodical rigidities of the global oil and gas regime.

Moreover, given the fact that Asia is going to be the main centre of energy consumption in the near future and importantly the main market of the GCC oil and gas exports, India due to its strategic positioning and refining expertise and strength can be the destination to penetrate into the booming Asian market through locating refineries, which will definitely curtail the transportation costs. Besides there are also tremendous opportunities, especially in the petrochemical and other downstream activities in India that can be beneficial for the GCC countries.

Thus, the oil suppliers and importers have become vulnerable in the present regime due to their skewed interdependence. This is radically different from the earlier eras when the producers and suppliers used to dictate the terms of the trade for the importers. This mutual vulnerability of both the exporters and importers is therefore being regarded as the major indicator of the prospect of the global oil and gas business in the coming years.

The concerns of demand as well as supply disruptions generated from the matrices of the interdependence framework have compelled the producers as well as consumers to seek more assertive vigorous interaction to address the vulnerabilities thereof. The oil suppliers of the GCC are reciprocating interdependent relations with India and other importing countries in the Asian region. This framework of interdependence points to a dissonance between the emergence of the international oil market dominated more than ever by economic forces and domestic economies in the oil exporting countries dominated by political considerations not always in agreement with an optimal allocation of resources. This is therefore a challenge for the GCC oil producing states to adhere and devise prudent policies to accommodate consuming country's wishes and simultaneously initiating efforts for their survival.

This calls for the extension of the framework of interdependence as a catalyst to augment economic relations between India and the GCC to taper off the mutual vulnerabilities of energy security. In recent years, both have focused on such arrangements to augment their economic relation to higher proportions for their mutual benefit, acknowledging the emerging potentials of both in the global oil and gas regime as the background.

In this respect another promising area of interdependence between India and the GCC countries can be visualised in the liberalised economic regimes, especially the knowledge economy. As mentioned earlier, the GCC countries are pursuing such policies that they can establish a knowledge society in order to harness all round human development. Effectively they can absorb the surmounting unemployed workforce in such sectors in their countries where semiskilled jobs are available but the domestic workforce was earlier reluctant to go. India, having global leverage from the knowledge industry perspective is suitably placed to penetrate these booming markets.

Besides the interdependence between India and the GCC countries, there are also concerns regarding the ensuing competition for secured energy sources in the GCC countries by other Asian countries. As analysed before, though the Asian countries are pursuing a strategy to diversify the sources of supply particularly with Central Asian hydrocarbons showing a lot of promise yet trends indicate that the Persian Gulf region is going to be the major hunting ground, hence it is competitive. The recent report from FACTS, *Energy Advisory No. 264: Asia-Pacific Crude Oil Market—An Update,* points out that in 2000, Asia Pacific imported nearly 55 per cent from West Asia.

> Future crude oil import requirements are crucially dependent on the refinery construction in the region over the next 10 years. Based on our survey of the regional refining industries, it is obvious that a few countries are continuing with their plans to expand their refining capacities and upgrading capabilities. By 2010 imports of crude oil from outside the region are projected to be up substantially from 2000. Of the total crude use in 2010, oil from outside the Asia-Pacific region is expected to rise substantially to 70 per cent in 2010. The share of the region's crude imports from the Middle East is expected to increase to 62 per cent in 2010 while crude imported from other parts of the world is forecast to reach 8 per cent. If the Asian countries are building bridges with the Gulf countries, the latter also need the Asian market, thus there is a kind of mutually dependent relationship .[1]

1. FACTS (2002). "Middle East Crudes Will Supply Most of the Rise in Asian Demand", *OPEC Bulletin*, Vol. XLV(4). 28th January.

Taking into account the demand-supply matrix, the Asian players especially China, India and Japan will actively be pursuing their interest in the Gulf market. Whether their search will enhance the intensity to competition and conflict could be an issue of debate.[2] Moreover, while it is naturally important for the individual countries to make efforts to secure their own energy supplies, there is also a possibility that excessive pursuit of the national interest by any single country could damage the energy security of the rest of the region. It is consequently becoming increasingly important for the issue to be treated as one in which all countries in the region have a common stake. One has aptly remarked that the greatest challenge before the Asian energy dependent countries is perhaps the transit route that is the Strait of Hormuz—the potential strategic choke point—that portends future conflict among the major oil importers of the Asian region.[3]

In a changing context where hydrocarbons despite being a strategic commodity are moving to the arena of market to be traded as "just another commodity", the pressure of the market seems to be prevailing in defining the parameter of the emerging regime. One plausible scenario could be:

> Asia's tremendous expansion of energy demand over the next two decades will force key regional powers such as India and China to accept far greater levels of cross-border energy dependency, and this will constitute a new cultural mindset for leaders long accustomed to viewing energy primarily as security vulnerability. As such, we choose as our pinnacle moment the shift from buying natural gas *via* LNG ships to erecting permanent pipelines that create long-term energy interdependencies.[4]

However it will be too simplistic to assume that the market will be the decisive factor. The perceived strategic concern expressed by the

---

2. Pant, Girijesh and Samir Ranjan Pradhan (2004). "Emerging Asian Competition for Gulf Hydrocarbon Resources: Implications for India's Energy Security", Paper presented at the National Seminar on *India's Energy Security*. New Delhi: JNU. February 19-20.

3. Cordesman, Anthony H. (1998). "The Changing Geopolitics of Energy—Part VI: Regional Developments in East Asia, China, and India". Strategic Energy Initiative. Center for Strategic and International Studies. August 12.

4. *Asian Energy Futures Event Report (VI): The There and Then of Asian Energy, 2020*, on the site *http://www.nwc.navy.mil/newrulesets/AEFreport6.htm*

dominant power namely the USA cannot be ignored. There is a school which argues that,

> There is a shift in strategic geography hence new emphasis on the protection of supplies of vital resources, especially oil and natural gas. Whereas Cold War-era divisions were created and alliances formed along ideological lines, economic competition now drives international relations—and competition over access to these vital economic assets has intensified accordingly. Because an interruption in the supply of natural resources would portend severe economic consequences, the major importing countries now consider the protection of this flow a significant national concern. In addition, with global energy consumption rising by an estimated two per cent annually, competition for access to large energy reserves will only grow more intense in the years to come.[5]

Thus, the recipe for avoiding a catastrophe is cooperation and information exchange among countries. Energy security is as much a collective concept as military security. The Institute of Energy Economics, Japan (IEEJ) in a recent presentation has rightly noted that,

> In Asia (and East Asia in particular), achievement of the "three Es" (economic development, energy security, and environmental preservation) can no longer be viewed as a task to be addressed by each country separately; instead, it should be approached through region wide cooperation as a goal of common interest. Similarly, the perspective of region wide optimisation as opposed to pursuit of national interest should take on increasing importance. In this context, Japan would have a critical role to play as a leader in the aspects of technology, infrastructure, economic power, and institutional design. It should regard this role not merely as a variety of assistance to fulfill its obligations as a developed country but also as a huge opportunity for development of business deriving from energy and the environment.[6]

India must take the lead in bringing the important Asian energy consumers into a forum, which could reduce the cost of research, improve energy efficiency and work towards an Asian Energy Charter.

---

5. Michael, T. Klare (2001). "The New Geography of Conflict", *Foreign Affairs*, May/June.
6. IEE (2004). *Asia/World Energy Outlook: Burgeoning Asian Economies and the Changing Energy Supply-Demand Structure*. Japan: IEE. March 10.

Here the example of the Energy Charter, an inter-governmental organisation promoting energy cooperation, is worth mentioning. The Energy Charter Conference is the governing body of the Energy Charter Treaty. The Energy Charter Treaty is a legally binding treaty under public international law uniting 51 European and Central Asian states in the establishment of an energy policy foundation addressing transit of energy, energy investment, energy trade and energy efficiency and environmental policy. The Energy Charter Transit Protocol currently being negotiated by 51 European and Central Asian states, including the member states of the European Union, the Russian Federation, the Commonwealth of Independent States and Japan, is expected to contain public international law provisions encouraging the removal of any obstacles to the execution of cross-border energy swaps. This important energy policy initiative is expected to facilitate secure, efficient, uninterrupted and unimpeded execution of cross-border energy swaps. The 51 states will also take necessary measures to prevent and address illegitimate taking of energy being delivered or redelivered under cross-border energy swaps.[7]

Thus the Asian Energy Charter, if formed, would facilitate transit of gas through third countries and open up international gas trade in Asia. The same forum would help in an oil supply crisis through joint management of strategic reserves and by cooling down the market through exchange of information on stocks, taxation and rationing proposals, etc. In this respect it can also be mentioned that the Asian Energy Charter should include the GCC countries, who are also traditional energy suppliers to India and the whole of Asia. This would be on the lines of the much discussed OPEC's consumer-producer dialogue process, initiated in recent years to address the complexities of the interdependence between producers and consumers.

However, the success of this forum will depend on the participation of India, China and Japan. Neither ASEAN nor APEC includes all of these countries. Could either of these be persuaded to expand its membership? Is it possible to link the research institutes

7. By cross-border energy swap is understood the exchange of energy by two players in two different jurisdictions based on a mutually beneficial sharing of energy price differentials.

and think- tanks in these countries together for collaborative research? It is time we took a good long look at these questions. However, the feasibility of such a forum is possible in the light of a recent development when the ASEAN became an official observer-organisation to the Energy Charter Conference.[8]

Looking at the status of external energy strategies of major Asian countries such as Japan, China and Korea and the fact that there is a move towards exclusive bilateral, or at least plurilateral energy cooperation in the region; India should devise and reorient its external energy strategy. The complex geopolitical matrix of the region and intense competition from the major importers like China in all producing regions in general and the Gulf region in particular, India is left with restricted policy exercise and manoeuvrability. This calls for strategising its external energy policies through a balance between her foreign policy imperatives and economic diplomacy. The more imminent seems to reorient India's overall strategy towards the Gulf region.

However, in a multi-polar world, whose prosperity and security is considerably influenced by such transnational commodities as oil and gas, each group has to tread cautiously if it is not to provoke a drastic reaction from other actors to the detriment of all parties concerned. This applies to various aspects of decision making, such as pricing, trade and investment. Also of significance in this interdependence is the fact that each group is not composed of homogenous members. There are wide disparities in conditions, needs and priorities. This diversity may furthermore facilitate the development of cross group relations and alliances, which has already witnessed the development of relations between the United States and Saudi Arabia—the two major players in the global oil regime during the 1970s and 1980s. In this regard one factor that may act as a hindrance in greater ties between India and the GCC countries can be visualised as the growing and deepening defence and other relations between India and Israel. But given the fact that there are imminent economic compulsions of the changing times will compel both India and the GCC countries to strive for mutually beneficial relations premised on the hydrocarbon

8. *http://www.pipelinedubai.com/press/pr_1329.htm*

interdependence in order to position them securely in the global oil and gas matrix.

Oil, as analysts have put it, has remained a key vector of rivalry or cooperation in transnational relations. Institutions created in response to various challenges posed by the oil and gas sector will have to evolve by adapting their (India as an emerging consumer and the GCC countries as suppliers) functions and operations to the changing realities—if they are to survive and develop. The essence of sustained cooperation is, therefore, adaptability.

Annexures

Annexure 1.1

A Brief History of Major Oil Companies in the Gulf Region

Amoco

1889	:	Standard Oil (Indiana) founded as subsidiary of Standard Oil Trust.
1911	:	Standard Oil of Indiana founded with dissolution of Standard Oil.
1910s	:	Standard Oil of Indiana purchases Pan American Petroleum.
1914	:	Standard Oil of Indiana licenses 'thermal cracking' process for producing gasoline to competing oil companies.
1925	:	Standard Oil of Indiana acquires controlling interest in Pan American Petroleum and Transport Company.
1932	:	Standard Oil of Indiana sells Venezuela operation to Jersey.
1954	:	Pan American and Standard of Indiana merge, new company is called American Oil Company (Amoco).
1957	:	Begins joint venture with Iran independent of Iranian Oil Consortium.
1958	:	Amoco signs agreement with Shah of Iran.
1960s	:	Amoco Egypt Oil Company, Cairo, founded.
1980s	:	Amoco Sharjah Oil Company, Sharjah, UAE, in partnership with UEA, produces natural gas and natural gas liquids in Sharjah.
1990s	:	Amoco Oman Oil Company begins oil and gas exploration programme.
Corporate Office	:	Amoco Corporation, 200 East Randolph Drive, Chicago, IL 60601-7125, Phone: (312) 856-6111, E-mail: *info@amoco.com*.

ARCO

1866	:	Atlantic Petroleum Storage Company founded.
1870	:	Atlantic Petroleum Storage Company establishes Atlantic Refining Company (Atlantic).
1874	:	Atlantic sold to John D. Rockefeller's Standard Oil Trust.
1905	:	Richfield Oil Corporation founded.
1911	:	Standard Oil Trust dissolved under the Sherman Antitrust Act, and Atlantic is spun off as independent company.

1916	:	Sinclair Oil Corporation, founded by Harry F. Sinclair.
1931	:	Richfield goes into receivership and Sinclair merges with Rio Grande Oil and Prairie Pipeline and Prairie Oil and Gas Companies.
1936	:	Richfield Oil Corporation emerges from receivership.
1952	:	Atlantic begins offshore Gulf Coast production.
1963	:	Atlantic purchased the Hondo Oil & Gas Company.
1966	:	Richfield Oil Corporation merges with Atlantic Refining Company, creating Atlantic Richfield Company (ARCO).
1968	:	ARCO partners with Exxon for Alaskan North Slope production.
1969	:	ARCO acquires Sinclair Oil Corporation.
1972	:	ARCO headquarters moves from New York City to Los Angeles.
1977	:	ARCO acquires the Anaconda Company.
1985	:	ARCO divests East Coast marketing and refining operations.
1988	:	Tricentrol acquired by ARCO.
1988	:	ARCO completes merger with Houston based Union Texas Petroleum Holding Inc.
1989	:	ARCO forms a new publicly held company, Lyondell Petrochemical.
1993	:	ARCO's US oil and gas business restructured and divided into four business units—ARCO Permian, ARCO Western Energy, ARCO Long Beach, Inc., and Vastar Resources Inc.
1994	:	Vastar Resources Inc. initiates a public offering of 17 million shares of its common stock.
1996	:	ARCO signs Production Sharing Contract with Sonatrach, the Algerian state oil company, to undertake major Enhanced Oil Recovery project in Algeria's second largest oilfield, Rhourde el Baguel.
1997	:	ARCO and Russia's largest oil company, LUKOIL, sign joint venture agreement to invest in oil and gas projects in Russia and other countries.
1998	:	ARCO subsidiary (Western Midway Co.) and a unit of Mobil Corporation reaches agreement to exchange oil and gas properties in California's San Joaquin Valley and the Gulf of Mexico; The California properties owned by Western Midway go to Mobil, while Mobil oil and gas properties in the Gulf go to Western Midway. Upon completion of the exchange, Western Midway will be sold to Vastar Resources Inc. (82.2 per cent owned by ARCO).
1998	:	ARCO sells majority interest in ARCO Chemical Company and divests its coal assets in the US.
Corporate Office	:	Arco Corporate Headquarters, 515 South Flower Street, Los Angeles, CA 90071, (213) 486-3511.

Ashland Oil

1924	:	Ashland Refining Company of Ashland, Ky., founded as a refining arm of Swiss Oil Company of Lexington.
1930	:	Ashland purchases Tri-State Refining.
1931	:	Acquires Cumberland Pipeline Company's eastern Kentucky pipeline network.
1936	:	Ashland Refining merges with Swiss Oil to form Ashland Oil & Refining Company.
1946	:	Ashland Oil & Refining Company products first sold under the brand name 'Ashland'.
1948	:	Ashland and Allied Oil merge.
1949	:	Ashland and Aetna Oil merge, Ashland acquires Kentucky retail marketing operation Freedom-Valvoline, including Valvoline Motor Oil brand and also acquires Southern Pipe Line Company.
1950	:	Frontier Oil Refining of Buffalo, N.Y., and National Refining of Cleveland, Ohio, joins Ashland.
1956	:	Acquisition of R.J. Brown Company of St. Louis.
1963	:	Ashland acquires United Oil.
1966	:	Ashland acquires Warren Brothers Construction Company.
1967	:	Ashland purchases ADM Chemical Group and forms Ashland.
1969	:	Ashland forms Ashland Petroleum operating division and Arch Mineral.
1970	:	Ashland changes name to Ashland Oil, Inc.
1970	:	Ashland acquires Northwestern Refining of St. Paul, Minn. and the Super America retail marketing chain.
1971	:	Exploration and production activities are consolidated into Ashland Exploration.
1975	:	Construction division is formed, and Ashland Coal is created.
1991	:	Ashland acquires The Permian Corporation and merges with Scurlock Oil Company.
1992	:	Ashland Chemical acquires most of Unocal's chemical distribution business, establishing the IC&S division.
1994	:	Ashland's Valvoline acquires Zerex.
1995	:	Ashland changes company's name to Ashland Inc.
1997	:	Ashland signs agreements with Marathon to combine the refining, marketing and transportation assets of the companies. Ashland acquires 38 per cent of Marathon Ashland Petroleum LLC.
Corporate Office	:	Ashland Inc Headquarters, 1000 Ashland Drive, Russell, KY 41169, (606) 329-3333.

Chevron

1879	:	Pacific Coast Oil Company established.
1900	:	Pacific Coast Oil purchased by Standard Oil, but remains separate operation.
1906	:	Pacific Coast Oil consolidated with other Western US operations of Standard Oil into Standard Oil Company (California).
1911	:	Dissolution of Standard Oil Trust makes Standard Oil of California (Socal) independent.
1926	:	Socal merges with Pacific Oil Company.
1929	:	Socal establishes Bahrain Petroleum Company to hold Bahrain concession.
1932	:	Bahrain Petroleum strikes oil in Bahrain.
1933	:	Socal wins Saudi Arabia concession; Socal establishes California-Arabia Standard Oil Company, Casoc, to hold concession for Saudi Arabia.
1933	:	Socal discovers oil in Saudi Arabia.
1936	:	Texaco joins with Standard Oil of California (later Chevron), to found the Arab-American Oil Company (Aramco).
1936	:	Texaco purchases half interest in Bahrain Petroleum and California-Arabian Standard Oil Company (Calarabian) from Socal.
1936	:	California-Texas Company, Caltex, founded as a joint venture between Socal and Texaco as outlet for future oil production in Bahrain and Saudi Arabia.
1954	:	Consortium of oil companies, including British Petroleum, Exxon, Socony, Texas Oil, Socal, Gulf, Royal Dutch/Shell Group, and CFP form the Iranian Oil Participants Ltd. (IOP) and negotiates agreement with the Iranian government for oil production in Iran.
1961	:	Socal buys Standard of Kentucky.
1974	:	Bahraini government acquires 60 per cent interest in BAPCO.
1980	:	Bahraini government acquires remaining interest in BAPCO.
1984	:	Socal buys Gulf Corporation and after restructuring changes name to Chevron Corporation.
1993	:	Chevron undertakes a joint venture with the government of the Republic of Kazakhstan forming a new company named TengizChevroil.
1993	:	Pennzoil Company assimilates Chevron.
Corporate Office	:	Chevron Corporation, 575 Market Street, San Francisco, CA 94105-2856, 415-894-7700.

Conoco

1875	:	Continental Oil and Transportation Company founded.
1885	:	Continental Oil and Transportation Company reincorporated as Continental within the Standard Oil Trust.
1913	:	Continental Oil reincorporated after breakup of Standard Oil Trust.
1917	:	Marland Oil Company founded.
1929	:	Continental Oil Company merged with portions of Rocky Mountain (a former component of Standard Oil) and Marland.
Mid-1950s	:	Continental joins partnership with Marathon and Amerada, called Oasis Group.
1981	:	Conoco becomes a wholly owned subsidiary of by E.I. Du Pont de Nemours & Company.
1981	:	Conoco reorganised as Continental Group.
Corporate Office	:	Conoco Center, 600 North Dairy Ashford, Houston, TX 77079, P.O. Box 2197, Houston, TX, ZIP Code 77252, Phone: (281) 293-1000, Telex: 775347, Fax: (281) 293-1440.

Exxon

1882	:	Standard Oil of New Jersey formed by Standard Oil Trust.
1888	:	Standard Oil of New Jersey establishes Anglo-American Oil Co. (predecessor of Esso Petroleum Co.) to market oil in the British Isles.
1899	:	Standard Oil of New Jersey becomes a holding company for Standard Oil Interests, a subsidiary of Standard Oil.
1898	:	Standard Oil of New Jersey gains control of Imperial Oil Limited of Canada.
1928	:	Standard Oil of New Jersey acquires interest in Turkish (now Iraq). Petroleum Co.
1911	:	Standard Oil of New Jersey (Jersey) becomes independent with the dissolution of the Standard Oil Trust.
1911	:	Humble Oil Company formed.
1919	:	Jersey acquires majority ownership of Humble Oil.
1930	:	Anglo-American acquired by Jersey.
1933	:	Socony-Vacuum and Standard of New Jersey merge their Far East facilities and interests into a 50-50 venture called Standard-Vacuum Oil Co., or Stanvac.
1947	:	Jersey affiliate, Imperial, strikes oil in Canada.
1947	:	Anglo-Iranian, Jersey and Socony sign 20-year contract with Iran.
1948	:	Jersey (30 per cent) and Socony-Vacuum (10 per cent) join Socal (30 per cent) and Texaco (30 per cent) in Aramco venture.
1954	:	Consortium of oil companies, including British Petroleum, Exxon, Socony, Texas Oil, Socal, Gulf, Royal Dutch/Shell Group, and CFP form the Iranian Oil Participants Ltd. (IOP) and negotiate agreement with Iranian government and for oil production in Iran.

1959	:	Jersey buys remainder of Humble Oil.
1959	:	Jersey strikes oil in Libya.
1960	:	Jersey begins to market gasoline under the brand name Esso.
1960	:	Jersey purchases Monterey Oil.
1961	:	Jersey buys Honolulu Oil.
1962	:	Assets of Stanvac split between Jersey and Socony Mobil.
1972	:	Jersey changes name to Exxon.
1972	:	Iraq nationalises Iraq Petroleum Company, of which Exxon is 12 per cent owner.
1972	:	Saudi Arabia, Abu Dhabi, Kuwait and Qatar acquire 25 per cent interest in Exxon's production operations (in country), with right to increase stake to 51 per cent by 1982.
1980	:	Exxon buys Colony Oil Shale Project.
1981	:	Exxon sells Esso Standard Libya to Libyan government.
1982	:	Exxon ends Colony Oil Shale Project.
1985	:	Exxon acquires 48 per cent of Hunt Oil Company's production sharing agreement in North Yemen.
1998	:	Exxon and Mobil announce plans for merger.
Corporate Office	:	5959 Las Colinas Blvd, Irving, TX 75039-2298, Phone: 972-444-1000, Fax: 972-444-1882.

Getty

1928	:	Pacific Western Oil Corporation incorporated as a holding company for Edward L. Doherty and family which subsequently came under the control of J. Paul Getty.
1930s	:	Rocky Mountain division of Pacific Western, a Getty subsidiary, begins oil exploration in Saudi Arabia.
1933	:	Pacific Western wins Saudi Arabia concession.
1949	:	Getty's Western Pacific Oil Corporation signs concession for Saudi half of the Neutral Zone with Saudi government.
1956	:	All of J. Paul Getty's oil holdings organised under Getty Oil.
1953	:	Getty acquires Tidewater Oil.
1984	:	Texaco acquires Getty.

Gulf Oil

1901	:	Guffey Oil founded.
1901	:	Gulf Refining Company founded.
1907	:	William Mellon reorganises Guffey Oil and Gulf Refining under name of Gulf Oil Corporation.
1922	:	Gulf Oil Corporation forms Eastern Gulf Oil Company.
1928	:	Gulf joins the Turkish Petroleum Company.

1929	:	Gulf buys Paragon Refining Company.
1934	:	Gulf sells its share of the Iraq Petroleum Company to Socal.
1934	:	Anglo-Iranian and Gulf Oil Corporation establish Kuwait Oil Company as a 50-50 joint venture to compete for Kuwait concession (which they obtain); subsequent agreement establishes British control of KOC.
1954	:	Consortium of oil companies, including British Petroleum, Exxon, Socony, Texas Oil, Socal, Gulf, Royal Dutch/Shell Group, and CFP form the Iranian Oil Participants Ltd. (IOP) and negotiate agreement with Iranian government and for oil production in Iran.
1955	:	Acquires Warren Petroleum.
1971	:	Gulf purchases 10 per cent in Syncrude Canada Limited.
1984	:	Chevron buys Gulf.

Marathon

1887	:	Ohio Oil Company founded.
1889	:	Ohio Oil Company purchased by J.D. Rockefeller subsequently consolidated into the Standard Oil Trust.
1905	:	Marathon headquarters moved to Findlay, Ohio.
1911	:	Standard Oil Company of Ohio (Sohio) separated from Rockefeller's 'Standard Trust'.
Mid-1950s	:	Sohio joins partnership with Continental and Amerada, called Oasis Group.
1962	:	Ohio Oil Company renamed the Marathon Oil Company.
1962	:	Marathon buys Plymouth Oil.
1982	:	Marathon becomes a wholly owned subsidiary of United States Steel Corporation, which has since become USX Corporation.
1991	:	USX issues separate shares of common stock to reflect the performance of its two major businesses (steel and oil) and reinstates Marathon's symbol (MRO) on major stock exchanges.
1990	:	Marathon Oil Company headquarters moved to Houston.
1997	:	Ashland signs agreements with Marathon to combine the refining, marketing and transportation assets of the companies; Marathon Ashland Petroleum LLC formed Ashland acquires 38 per cent of Marathon Ashland Petroleum LLC.

Mesa Petroleum

1956	:	After resigning as a geologist with Phillips Petroleum Co., T. Boone Pickens forms development and production company called Petroleum Exploration.
1959	:	Altair Oil and Gas is established to conduct oil and gas exploration in Canada

1964	:	Petroleum Exploration Inc., and Altair merge to form Mesa Petroleum Co.
1967	:	Mesa Petroleum Co. shares began trading on the American Stock Exchange.
1969	:	In hostile takeover, Pickens merges larger Hugoton into Mesa.
1979	:	Mesa sells holdings in Canada and the North Sea to reduce debt and buy additional Hugoton reserves; Mesa also creates the Mesa Royalty Trust.
1983	:	Mesa forms the Gulf Investors Group (GIG).
1984	:	Mesa repurchases nearly 90 per cent of the GIG units in a $500 million public tender offer.
1985	:	The Mesa Petroleum Company changes its name to the Mesa Limited Partnership.
1986	:	Mesa purchases Pioneer Corporation.
1988	:	Mesa partnership acquires gas reserves from Tenneco Inc.
1991	:	Mesa Limited Partnership changes name to MESA Inc.

Mobil

1866	:	The Vacuum Oil Co. incorporated.
1879	:	Standard Oil Co., headed by John D. Rockefeller, purchases a three-quarter interest in Vacuum.
1870	:	Rockefeller and four partners organise Standard Oil Company in Ohio.
1882	:	Rockefeller organises his various oil holdings into the Standard Oil Trust, with headquarters in New York.
1882	:	Standard Oil of New York formed.
1911	:	Standard Oil Company of New York (Socony) founded with dissolution of Standard Oil.
1918	:	Socony purchases a 45 per cent interest in Magnolia Petroleum Co.
1926	:	Socony purchases the properties of General Petroleum Corp. of California.
1929	:	Vacuum acquires the Lubrite Refining Co., a refining and marketing company based in St. Louis.
1930	:	Socony acquires White Eagle Oil & Refining Co.
1930	:	Vacuum acquires Wadhams Oil Corp., and the White Star Refining Co.
1931	:	Socony acquires all the assets of Vacuum Oil Co. and changes its name to Socony-Vacuum Corp.
1933	:	Socony-Vacuum and Standard of New Jersey merge their Far East facilities and interests into a 50-50 venture called Standard-Vacuum Oil Co., or Stanvac.
1934	:	Socony-Vacuum Corp. changes its name to Socony-Vacuum Oil Co., Inc.

1947	:	Anglo-Iranian, Jersey and Socony sign 20-year contract with Iran.
1948	:	Jersey (30 per cent) and Socony-Vacuum (10 per cent) join Socal (30 per cent) and Texaco (30 per cent) in Aramco venture.
1954	:	Consortium of oil companies, including British Petroleum, Exxon, Socony, Texaco and Socal, Gulf, Royal Dutch/Shell Group, and CFP form the Iranian Oil Participants Ltd. (IOP) and negotiate agreement with Iranian government and for oil production in Iran.
1955	:	Socony-Vacuum changes name to Socony Mobil Oil Company.
1959	:	Magnolia Petroleum and General Petroleum merged with other domestic subsidiaries into Socony Mobil Oil Company; two major operating divisions created within the company: Mobil Oil Co. for the US and Canada, and Mobil International Oil Co. for the rest of the world (except the areas in which Stanvac had interests).
1960	:	Mobil Chemical Co. formed.
1960	:	Mobil Petroleum Co. Inc. formed to oversee Socony Mobil's 50 per cent interest in Stanvac.
1962	:	Assets of Stanvac split between Jersey and Socony Mobil.
1966	:	Socony Mobil Oil Co. changes name to Mobil Oil Corporation. Mobil Oil Co. becomes the North American Division; Mobil International becomes the International Division, with coordinating responsibility for Mobil Petroleum Co. Inc.
1971	:	Mobil enters joint venture with the Iranian Oil Company.
1972	:	Mobil's 11.875 per cent stake in the Iraq Petroleum Company is nationalised.
1975	:	Mobil increases its share of Aramco from 10 per cent to 15 per cent.
1976	:	Mobil completes acquisition of Marcor, the holding company for Montgomery Ward Department Stores.
1976	:	Mobil Corporation formed as a holding company.
1979	:	Mobil sells 51 per cent of its Turkish refinery to Turkish Petroleum.
1984	:	Mobil acquires 100 per cent of Superior Oil.
1985	:	Yanbu Petrochemical Company (Yanpet), a joint venture petrochemicals complex at Yanbu, Saudi Arabia plant begins operation; Mobil and Saudi Basic Industries Corporation (SABIC) are 50-50 partners in Yanpet.
1996	:	The Qatargas project, in which Mobil has a 10 per cent interest, comes on line producing first LNG from Qatar.
1996	:	Mobil commissions two new plants in Yemen and Syria.
1997	:	Second Qatargas liquefaction train completed.
1998	:	Exxon and Mobil announce plans for merger.
Corporate Office	:	3225 Gallows Rd., Fairfax, VA 22037-0001, Phone: 703-846-3000, Fax: 703-846-4669.

Occidental Petroleum

1910	:	Cities Service Company formed.
1920	:	Occidental Petroleum founded.
1953	:	Cities Service Company obtains Dhofar province concession in Oman.
1956	:	Armand Hammer buys Occidental Petroleum.
1965	:	Cities Service Company begins marketing products under the brand name "CITGO".
1965	:	Occidental wins oil concession in Libya.
1983	:	Occidental acquires Cities Service Company.
1983	:	Occidental reorganized Cities' assets and sells newly formed "CITGO Petroleum Corporation" to Southland Corporation.
1980s	:	Libya nationalises 51 per cent of Occidental's operation in Libya.
1986	:	Occidental acquired the Midcon Corporation.
1994	:	Occidental Petroleum Corp. completes acquisition of Placid Oil Co., which was founded in 1936 by H.L. Hunt.
1995	:	Occidental purchases 19 per cent stake in Clark US.
1998	:	Occidental and Royal Dutch/Shell, Anglo-Dutch oil group complete a $1 bn global asset swap.
1998	:	Occidental sells Occidental Netherlands Inc. unit to TransCanada Pipelines Ltd.
Corporate Office	:	Corporate Headquarters, Occidental Petroleum Corporation, 10889 Wilshire Boulevard, Los Angeles, California 90024-4201, (310) 208-8800.

Pennzoil

1889	:	South Penn Oil Company organised as a unit of Standard Oil Company.
1916	:	Name "Pennzoil" trademarked by Pennsylvania Refining Company, a predecessor to Pennzoil.
1954	:	Bill Liedtke, John Overby, and George Bush form Zapata Offshore Oil Company.
1963	:	Pennzoil Company is formed through consolidation of South Penn Oil Company, Stetco Petroleum Corporation and Zapata Offshore Oil Company.
1965	:	Pennzoil Company acquires United Gas Corporation.
1993	:	Pennzoil Company assimilates Chevron.
1994	:	Pennzoil Company signs oil development deal with Qatar.
1995	:	Pennzoil Company agrees to concession agreement with Egypt for the Gulf of Suez.
1998	:	Pennzoil-Quaker State Company was formed with the merger of Pennzoil and Quaker State.

1998	:	Simultaneous with the Pennzoil-Quaker State merger, the Pennzoil Company's marketing, manufacturing and fast oil change businesses (Pennzoil Products Group) is spun off and renamed the PennzEnergy Company.
Corporate Office	:	Pennzoil, 700 Milam, Houston, TX 77002, (713) 546-4000.

Phillips Petroleum Company

1905	:	Phillips brothers begin oil exploration.
1917	:	Phillips Petroleum Company founded by Frank Phillips.
1922	:	Phillips forms the predecessor to what today is GPM Gas Corp.
1925	:	Research and Development Group formed.
1969	:	Phillips' Kenai LNG Plant begins operation.
1985	:	Phillips successfully fends off hostile takeover attempts.
1992	:	GPM Gas Corporation formed.
Corporate Office	:	411 S. Keeler Ave., Bartlesville, OK 74004, Phone: 918-661-6600, Fax: 918-661-6279.

Shell

1833	:	Marcus Samuel starts import-export business in London.
1890	:	Royal Dutch Company launched.
1892	:	Marcus commissions the first special oil tanker and delivers 4,000 tonnes of Russian kerosene to Singapore and Bangkok.
1897	:	Samuel's company begins to operate under the name Shell Transport and Trading Company, Limited.
1903	:	Shell and Dutch company, N.V. Koninklijke Nederlandsche Maatschappij tot Explotatie van Petroleumbronnen in Nederlandsch-Indië form the Asiatic Petroleum Company.
1903	:	Royal Dutch and Shell group begins joint marketing campaign under name "British Dutch".
1906-1914	:	British Dutch Group acquires producing interests in: Romania (1906); Russia (1910); Egypt (1911); Venezuela (1913) and Trinidad (1914).
1907	:	Royal Dutch/Shell partnership is extended worldwide, with the creation of the Royal Dutch/Shell Group of Companies.
1912	:	Trading in the US starts after the acquisition of the American Gasoline Company, an American marketing company.
1912	:	Turkish Petroleum Company founded with 50 per cent ownership by Turkish National Bank, 25 per cent Deutsche Bank, 25 per cent Royal Dutch/Shell.
1915	:	Formation of the Shell Company in California.
1918	:	Royal Dutch/Shell buys Mexican Eagle.
1922	:	Shell Union Oil Corporation (later Shell Oil Company) formed to consolidate Shell interests in the US with those of the Union Oil Company of Delaware.

1937	:	Shell, Total, and Partex form the consortium Petroleum Development (Oman and Dhofar) later, Petroleum Development Oman.
1945-55	:	Exploratory drilling in Tunisia, Algeria, Nigeria, Trinidad and offshore in British Borneo; production from the Iraq Petroleum Company increases dramatically.
1949	:	In 1949 Royal Dutch shortens its corporate title to the name "Shell".
1954	:	Consortium of oil companies, including British Petroleum, Exxon, Socony, Texas Oil, Socal, Gulf, Royal Dutch/Shell Group, and CFP form the Iranian Oil Participants Ltd. (IOP) and negotiate agreements with the Iranian government for oil production in Iran.
1956	:	Shell discovers oil in the Sahara.
1959	:	Joint Shell/Esso exploration company called N.V. Nederlandse Aardolie Maatschappij (NAM) discovers gas fields in Groningen in the Netherlands.
1974	:	Omani government claims 25 per cent interest in Petroleum Development Oman.
1975	:	Omani government raises its interest in Petroleum Development Oman to 60 per cent.
1979	:	Shell acquires Belridge Oil.
1984	:	Shell buys minority interest (30 per cent) in Shell Oil US.
Mid-1980s	:	Royal Dutch/Shell buys the remaining 31 per cent of Shell Oil USA (the remainder that it did not yet own).
1998	:	Shell Oil Co. Texaco Inc. and Saudi Aramco initiate joint venture combining their eastern US. refining and marketing assets under the name Motiva Enterprises LLC, paralleling a joint venture launched by Shell and Texaco under the name Equilon Enterprises LLC for their Midwest, Southwest and West Coast downstream assets; Shell to own 35 per cent of Houston-based Motiva, while Texaco and Aramco will each own 32.5 per cent.
1998	:	Occidental and Royal Dutch/Shell, Anglo-Dutch oil group complete a $1 bn global asset swap.
Corporate Office	:	Shell Oil, One Shell Plaza, Houston, TX 77002, Phone: 713-241-6161, Fax: 713-241-4044; Royal Dutch/Shell Group, 2596 HR The Hague, The Netherlands, Phone: +31-70-377-3395, Fax: +31-70-377-4848.

Sun Company Inc.

1886	:	Robert Pew founds the Sun Oil Company.
1901	:	New Jersey Oil and Gas incorporated.
1968	:	Sun buys Sunray (DX).
1971	:	Sun Oil Company reorganised and renamed Sun Company Incorporated.
Corporate Office	:	Ten Penn Center 1801 Market Street, Philadelphia Pa 191031699, Phone: +215-977-3000.

Texaco

1897	:	Joe Cullinan founds Texas Fuel Company.
1903	:	Joe Cullinan and Arnold Schlaet found The Texas Oil Company in Beaumont, Texas.
1906	:	Texas Oil Company registers the trademark name, 'Texaco'.
1930s	:	Texas Oil Company joins with Standard Oil of California (later Chevron), to found the Arab-American Oil Company (Aramco).
1936	:	Texas Oil Company purchases half interest in Bahrain Petroleum and California-Arabian Standard Oil Company (Calarabian) from Socal.
1936	:	Texas Oil Company joins with Standard Oil of California (later Chevron), to found the Arab-American Oil Company (Aramco).
1936	:	California-Texas company, Caltex, founded as a joint venture between Socal and Texas Oil Company as outlet for future oil production in Bahrain and Saudi Arabia.
1954	:	Consortium of oil companies, including British Petroleum, Exxon, Socony, Texas Oil, Socal, Gulf, Royal Dutch/Shell Group, and CFP form the Iranian Oil Participants Ltd. (IOP) and negotiate agreements with the Iranian government for oil production in Iran.
1956	:	Texas Oil Company acquires Regent Oil, a British company.
1959	:	Texas Oil Company purchases the Paragon group of companies.
1959	:	Texas Oil Company adopts the name Texaco for all of its businesses.
1962	:	Texaco acquires the White Fuel Corporation.
1964	:	Purchases Superior Oil Company, Venezuela.
1984	:	Texaco acquires Getty Oil Company.
1988	:	Texaco Forms Star Enterprise, a 50-50 joint venture with Saudi Refining Inc., to refine, distribute and market Texaco-branded products in the Eastern US.
1995	:	Texaco and Norsk Hydro formed a joint venture, Hydro Texaco, to market petroleum products throughout Scandinavia.
1998	:	Texaco acquires Monterey Resources, a California based independent oil and gas producer.
1998	:	Texaco and Shell Oil form downstream alliance in the Western US.
1998	:	Shell Oil Co., Texaco Inc. and Saudi Aramco initiate joint venture combining their eastern US. refining and marketing assets under the name Motiva Enterprises LLC, paralleling a joint venture launched by Shell and Texaco under the name Equilon Enterprises LLC for their Midwest, Southwest and West Coast downstream assets; Shell to own 35 per cent of Houston-based Motiva, while Texaco and Aramco will each own 32.5 per cent.
Corporate Office	:	Texaco Inc., 2000 Westchester Ave., White Plains, NY 10650, 9140 253-4000.

Union Oil (Unocal)

1890	:	Union Oil formed in California by merger of Hardison & Stewart Oil Company, the Sespe Oil Company, and the Torrey Canyon Oil Company.
1917	:	Union purchases Pinal-Dome Oil Company.
1922	:	Shell buys 25 per cent of Union Oil of California.
1922	:	Shell Union Oil Corporation formed to consolidate Shell interests in the US with those of the Union Oil Company of Delaware.
1965	:	Union acquires Pure Oil.
1983	:	Union Oil changes name to Unocal.
1992	:	Ashland Chemical acquires most of Unocal's chemical distribution business, establishing the IC&S Division.
Corporate Office	:	2141 Rosecrans Ave., Ste. 4000, El Segundo, CA 90245, Phone: +310-726-7600, Fax: +310-726-7817.

British Petroleum (Anglo-Persian Oil)

1886	:	Burmah Oil founded in Scotland.
1901	:	Shah of Iran signs concession agreement with William D'Arcy.
1904	:	Burmah Oil signs agreement to supply oil to British Admiralty.
1905	:	Burmah Oil and D'Arcy Oil merged into Concession Syndicate
1908	:	Oil struck in commercial quantities in Iran.
1909	:	Anglo-Persian Oil formed and Burmah Oil buys majority (97 per cent) of shares in initial public offering.
1914	:	British government becomes the majority stockholder in Anglo-Persian Oil.
1918	:	Anglo-Persian Oil purchases British Petroleum from British Government, which in turn had seized the company from Deutsche Bank during World War I.
1932	:	The Shah cancels Anglo-Persian concession.
1933	:	Anglo-Persian wins back Iran concession.
1934	:	Anglo-Iranian and Gulf Oil Corporation establish Kuwait Oil Company as a 50-50 joint venture to compete for Kuwait concession (which they obtain); subsequent agreement establishes British control of KOC.
1935	:	Anglo-Persian renamed Anglo-Iranian Oil Company Ltd.
1947	:	Anglo-Iranian, Jersey and Socony sign 20-year contract with Iran.
1951	:	Mossadegh nationalises Anglo-Iranian assets in Iran and founds the National Iranian Oil Company (NIOC) to administer nationalised assets.
1954	:	Anglo-Iranian renamed British Petroleum, previously the name of one of its subsidiaries.

1954	:	Consortium of oil companies, including British Petroleum, Exxon, Socony, Texas Oil, Socal, Gulf, Royal Dutch/Shell Group, and CFP form the Iranian Oil Participants Ltd. (IOP) and negotiate agreements with Iranian government for oil production in Iran.
1962	:	British Petroleum begins commercial development in Abu Dhabi.
1966	:	British Petroleum begins commercial development in Libya.
1969	:	British Petroleum signs agreement with the Standard Oil Company of Ohio, which became effective in January 1970; according to the agreement Standard takes over BP's leases in Alaska; in return, BP acquires 25 per cent of Standard's equity, a stake that would rise to a majority holding in 1978.
1970	:	BP sells 33 per cent of El Bunduq oilfield to a Japanese consortium in exchange for access to Japanese markets.
1972	:	BP sells 33 per cent of Abu Dhabi Main Areas Ltd. to a Japanese oil company.
Mid-1980s	:	BP buys 53 per cent of Sohio, Sohio becomes BP's American arm, eventually buying all of the outstanding stock.
1987	:	British government sells its stock in BP.
1987	:	British Petroleum acquires remaining stock of Sohio as well as British company Britoil.
1987	:	Sohio merged with other BP interests to form BP America.
1988	:	Kuwait Investment Office (KIO) holding of BP stock reaches 21.6 per cent.
1989	:	British government forces reduction in KIO holding to 9.9 per cent of BP stock.
1998	:	BP announces merger with Amoco, new company will operate under the name BP Amoco Plc.
Corporate Office	:	Britannic House, One Finsbury Circus, London EC2M 7BA, UK, Phone: +44-171-496-4000, Fax: +44-171-496-4630.

Elf Aquitaine

1941	:	Société Nationale des Pétroles d'Aquitaine (SNPA) incorporated at the initiative of the French government.
1966	:	French government merges gas and oil interests into Enterprise de Recherches et d'Activities Petrolieres (ERAP), giving ERAP majority ownership of SNPA.
1974	:	ERAP begins onshore and offshore exploration in Iran.
1976	:	ERAP is reorganised and increases share of SNPA ownership to 70 per cent.
1976	:	ERAP changes name to Société Nationale Elf Aquitaine, known as Elf Aquitaine Group.
Corporate Office	:	Elf Aquitaine, Inc. 444 Madison Avenue - 20th floor, New York - NY 10022, USA, **Phone:** +1 212 922 30 04, **Fax:** +1 212 922 30 74.

Ente Nazionale Idrocarburi (ENI)

1953	:	Enrico Mattei founds Ente Nazionale Idrocarburi (ENI) as a conglomeration of 36 subsidiaries including AGIP, with government sanction.
1956	:	Signs 50-50 oil cooperation deal with National Iranian Oil Company.
1970-75	:	Founds Agip (Qatar) Ltd.
1980s	:	Libya gains control of 50 per cent of ENI Libya.
1981	:	Enoxy, a joint ENI occidental petrochemical and mining venture founded.
1985	:	ENI wins contract to construct pipeline in Iraq.
1986	:	ENI wins portion of a pipeline contact for Yemen.
1992	:	ENI transformed into the Joint Stock Company traded on Italian and New York Stock Exchanges.
Corporate Office	:	Piazzale Enrico Mattei 1, 00144 Rome, Italy, Phone: +39-0-6-59-822-624, Fax: +39-0-6-59-002-141.

Iraq Petroleum Company

1912	:	Turkish Petroleum Company is founded with 50 per cent ownership by the Turkish National Bank, 25 per cent Deutsche Bank, 25 per cent Royal Dutch/Shell.
1914	:	Turkish Petroleum Company reorganised, with Anglo-Persian holding 50 per cent, Deutsche Bank and Shell each holding 25 per cent.
1914	:	Ottoman Grand Vizier promises Mesopotamian concession to Turkish Petroleum Company, but final concession agreement is not signed.
1922	:	CFP joins the Turkish Petroleum Company.
1925	:	Turkish Petroleum Company gains oil concessions in Iraq.
1928	:	Gulf joins the Turkish Petroleum Company.
1928	:	Royal Dutch/Shell, Anglo-Persian, CFP, Exxon, Mobil, Atlantic Richfield, Gulf Oil Corporation, Standard Oil of Indiana (Amoco), and Participations and Explorations Corp., establish a joint venture called the Near East Development Company; The Near East Development Company signs "Red Lines Agreement" binding participating companies to cooperate with the Turkish Petroleum Company in any ventures in Turkey, the Levant, Iraq and Arabian Peninsula (Atlantic, Gulf, and Standard eventually sell their shares to other participants).
1929	:	Turkish Petroleum changes its name to Iraq Petroleum Company.
1932	:	Mosul Petroleum Company formed to hold northern portion of IPC's Iraq concession.
1938	:	Basrah Petroleum Company formed to hold southern portion of IPC's Iraq concession.
1939	:	IPC establishes Abu Dhabi Petroleum Company Ltd. (ADPC) to hold Abu Dhabi concession.
1939	:	British government seizes IPC shares held by CFP.
1966	:	Iraq revokes portions of the IPC concession and nationalises these concessions.

1972 : Iraq nationalises remaining IPC concessions.

1973 : Iraq nationalises assets of foreign assets in Basrah Petroleum Company.

National Iranian Oil Company

1951 : Iran nationalises National Iranian Oil Company.

1954 : Consortium of oil companies, including British Petroleum, Jersey, Socony, Texaco and Socal, Gulf, Royal Dutch/Shell Group, Iricon Agency Ltd. Richfield Oil Corp. Signal Oil and Gas, Aminoil, Sohio, Getty, Atlantic Oil, Tidewater Oil, San Jacinto Petroleum Corp., and CFP form the Iranian Oil Participants Ltd. (IOP). IOP then negotiates agreement with the Iranian government for oil production in Iran.

1973 : Oil Services Company of Iran (OSCO) formed by NIOC to takeover operations of IOP.

1957 : National Iranian Oil Company signs deal with ENI for oil production.

1971 : Mobil enters joint venture with National Iranian Oil Company.

1990 : National Iranian Oil Company signs agreement to import about 200,000 barrels a day of gas oil and kerosene from Bahrain, Qatar and Abu Dhabi refineries ending embargoes established during the Iran-Iraq War.

Kuwait National Petroleum Company

1934 : Anglo-Iranian and Gulf Oil Corporation establish Kuwait Oil Company as a 50:50 joint venture to compete for the Kuwait concession (which they obtain); subsequent agreement establishes British control of KOC.

1934 : Sheikh Ahmed grants 75-year concession to KOC.

1951 : KOC oil concession extended for additional 17 years.

1960 : Kuwait National Petroleum Company established as a shareholder company owned by the government and the private sector.

1968 : KNPC commissions Shuaiba Refinery, the world's first all hydrogen refinery.

1974 : Kuwaiti government acquires 60 ownership of KOC.

1975 : KNPC becomes a fully state-owned company.

1980 : Kuwait Petroleum Corporation created, KNPC becomes fully owned by KPC; KNPC takes charge of the three oil refineries; Mina Al-Ahmadi, Mina Abdulla and Shuaiba, in addition to the LPG plant in Mina Al-Ahmadi.

1981 : Kuwait Oil Company purchases the Santa Fe International Corp. of California.

Corporate Offices : Head Office, P.O. Box 70 Safat, 13001 Safat – Kuwait, Phone: Buildings 1 & 2: (+965) 2420121/2425553, Emad Center: (+965) 2436333, Behbehani Building: (+965) 2449401, Fax: (+965) 2433839.

Saudi Aramco

1933	:	King Abdul Aziz Bin Abdul Rahman Al-Saud signs agreement authorising Standard Oil of California (Socal) to explore for oil in what is now the Eastern Province of the Kingdom.
1933	:	Saudi government signed a concession agreement with the Standard Oil Company of California, predecessor of today's Chevron.
1938	:	Commercial oil production begins in Saudi Arabia.
1944	:	Calarabian a joint venture of Socal and Texaco changes name to Arabian American Oil Company (Aramco).
1948	:	Jersey and Socony-Vacuum join Socal and Texaco in Aramco venture.
1949	:	Saudi Arabia builds Tapline through northern Saudi Arabia, Syria, Jordan and Lebanon to the Mediterranean.
1973	:	Saudi Arabian Government begins purchasing Aramco's assets from its shareholders, Socal (later Chevron), Texaco, Exxon and Socony-Vacuum (Mobil).
1975	:	Aramco initiates work to design, build and operate twin industrial cities at Jubail on the Gulf and Yanbu on the Red Sea.
1980	:	Saudi Government acquires 100 per cent of Aramco's shares, although Aramco partners continue to operate and manage Saudi Arabia's oilfields.
1985	:	Yanbu Petrochemical Company (Yanpet), a joint venture petrochemicals complex at Yanbu, Saudi Arabia plant begins operation; Mobil and Saudi Basic Industries Corporation (SABIC) are 50:50 partners in Yanpet.
1988	:	Royal decree establishes the Saudi Arabian Oil Company (Saudi Aramco) to takeover the management and operations of Saudi Arabia's oil and gas fields from Aramco.
1988	:	Saudi Aramco forms a joint venture with Texaco called Star Enterprise; under the agreement, a Saudi Aramco subsidiary acquires a 50 per cent share in Star's three refineries in the United States.
1991	:	Saudi Aramco acquires a 35 per cent interest in Sangyong Oil Refining Company, South Korea's third-largest refiner and leading lubricant manufacturer.
1993	:	Royal decree merges all of the Kingdom's state-owned refining, product-distribution and marketing operations, as well as the Government's half-interest in three joint-venture refineries into Saudi Aramco.
1994	:	Saudi Aramco enters joint venture with the Philippine National Oil Company (PNOC) purchasing a 40 per cent stake in Petron Corp.
1996	:	Saudi Aramco acquires a 50 per cent interest in Motor Oil Hellas and Avin Oil, the refining and distribution affiliates of Greece's Vardinoyannis Group.
1998	:	Shell Oil Co., Texaco Inc. and Saudi Aramco initiate joint venture combining their eastern US refining and marketing assets under the name Motiva Enterprises LLC, paralleling a joint venture launched by

		Shell and Texaco under the name Equilon Enterprises LLC for their Midwest, Southwest and West Coast downstream assets; Shell to own 35 per cent of Houston-based Motiva, while Texaco and Aramco will each own 32.5 per cent.
Corporate Office	:	P.O. Box 5000, Dhahran 31311, Saudi Arabia, Phone: +966-3-875-4915, Fax: +966-3-873-8490.

Total Oil (CFP)

1924	:	Foundation of the French Compagnie Francaise des Pétroles (CFP), which assumes French shares of Turkish Petroleum Company.
1927	:	Discovery of the first oilfield near Kirkuk in Iraq.
1954/5	:	Creation and registration of the trademark Total, and foundation of the first companies marketing Total products.
1954	:	Consortium of oil companies, including British Petroleum, Exxon, Socony, Texas Oil, Socal, Gulf, Royal Dutch/Shell Group, and CFP form the Iranian Oil Participants Ltd. (IOP) and negotiate agreement with the Iranian government for oil production in Iran.
1956	:	Discovery of the Hassi Messaoud oilfield and Hassi R'Mel gas field, in the Algerian Sahara.
1960	:	CFP absorbs the OFP (Omnium Francaise des Pétroles) group.
1970	:	French Petroleum Company of Canada founded. The company is renamed Total Petroleum (North America) later that year.
1973	:	First listing of CFP shares on the London Stock Exchange.
1978	:	CFP signs an agreement with Abu Dhabi covering development of the Upper Zakum field and production of butane and propane as well as the condensates associated with the oil produced by ADPC (GASCO).
1980	:	Total acquires Vickers Petroleum Corp., expanding Total's presence in the United States.
1985	:	CFP changes company name from CFP to Total CFP.
1985	:	Total CFP acquires all United States hydrocarbon assets of Lear Petroleum Partners.
1987	:	Total CFP acquires hydrocarbon assets held by TIPCO in the United States as well as those of Francarep Italia, and divests of all refining assets and most of the Group's marketing interests in Italy.
1988	:	Total CFP acquires CSX OIL & GAS in the United States.
1991	:	Total CFP changes company name to Total.
1991	:	Reduction of the French government's direct shareholding in Total from 31.7 per cent to 5.4 per cent.
1995	:	Total signs agreements for establishing the Yemen Gas liquefaction project and a development contract for the Iranian offshore fields Sirri A and E.
1996	:	Divestment by the French State of a further 4 per cent of Total's capital, reducing the government's stake to 0.97 per cent; Total signs a production-sharing agreement for development of Algeria's Tin Fouyé Tabankort field.

1998 : Total announces details of its development plans for Iran's giant South Pars gas field in coordination with the National Iranian Oil Co.

Corporate Office : TOTAL 24, Cours Michelet, 92069 Paris La Défense Cedex, France, Phone: +33 (0)1-41-35-40-00 (Switchboard), Fax: +33 (0)1-41-35-28-27.

American Independent Oil Company (Aminoil)

1947 : Consortium of Phillips, Ashland, Signal Oil and Gas, J.S. Abercrombie, Sunray Mid-Continent Oil Co., Globe Oil and Refining Co., and Pauley Petroleum Inc. formed to bid on Neutral Zone concession; Consortium is named American Independent Oil Company (Aminoil).

1948 : Aminoil wins Neutral Zone concession from Kuwait.

1970 : Aminoil acquired by R.J. Reynolds Industries Inc.

Eastern and General Syndicate

1919 : Major Frank Holmes establishes Eastern and General Syndicate.

1925 : Eastern and General Syndicate wins al-Hasa Concession.

1925 : Eastern and General Syndicate awarded oil concession in Bahrain.

Standard Oil Company

1870 : John D. Rockefeller and Henry Flagler found Standard Oil.

1882 : Rockefeller organises his various oil holdings into the Standard Oil Trust, with headquarters in New York.

1886 : Standard Oil founds Natural Gas Trust.

1901 : Standard establishes regional affiliate, Republic Oil.

1907 : Standard establishes Standard Oil of California.

1911 : Standard dissolved under court order, creating Standard Oil of New Jersey (Exxon), Standard Oil of New York (Mobil), Standard Oil California (Chevron), Standard Oil of Ohio (Sohio, arm of BP), Standard Oil of Indiana (Amoco), Continental Oil (Conoco), Atlantic (ARCO).

Major Oil Companies Operating in the Gulf Region (By Country)

Bahrain

State Companies

The Bahrain National Oil Company (BANOCO), wholly owned by the Bahrain Government, and is the holding company for the Bahrain Petroleum Company (BAPCO).

Joint Ventures

Bahrain National Gas Co. (BANAGAS) is owned 75 per cent by the government of Bahrain, 12.5 per cent by Caltex, and 12.5 per cent by the Arab Petroleum Investment Corp.

Bahrain Aviation Fuelling Co. (BAFCO) is the aviation refuelling service at Bahrain International Airport. It is owned by BANOCO, 60 per cent; Caltex 27 per cent; BP, 13 per cent.

Original Concession Holders

Bahrain Petroleum Co. Ltd., an equal partnership of Texas Oil Co. and Socal, also offshore concession granted to Continental Oil Co.

Continental Oil Co. of Bahrain, Continental Oil Co., Pure Oil Middle East Inc. (Union Oil of California).

Major Foreign Oil Company Involvement

Harken Oil of Grand Prairie, Texas, who is backed in part by Bass Enterprise Production Company of Fort Worth, Texas Harvard University, a major shareholder in Harken through an affiliate, and George W. Bush.

Iran

State Companies

National Iranian Oil Company (NIOC)—oil and gas exploration and production, refining and oil transportation; National Iranian Gas Company (NIGC)—manages gathering, treatment, processing, transmission, distribution, and exports of gas and gas liquids; National Petrochemical Company (NPC)—handles petrochemical production, distribution, and exports.

Original Concession Holders

Anglo-Persian Oil Company, replaced in 1954 by *Iranian Oil Participants Limited*, a joint venture of British Petroleum, Jersey, Socony, Texaco and Socal, Gulf, Royal Dutch/Shell Group, Iricon Agency Ltd., Richfield Oil Corp., Signal Oil and Gas, Aminoil, Sohio, Getty, Atlantic Oil, Tidewater Oil, San Jacinto Petroleum Corp., and CFP.

Iran Pan American Oil Co., American International Oil Co. (Standard Oil of Indiana).

Iranian Offshore Petroleum Co., Tidewater Oil, Superior Oil, Sunray DX, Cities Service, Kerr-McGee, Atlantic Richfield, Skelly Oil.

Lavan Petroleum Co., Atlantic Richfield, Murphy Oil, Sun Oil Co., Union Oil of California.

Major Foreign Oil Company Involvement

Gazprom

Petronas

Shell

Total

Recent Developments
(Concluded at least with negotiations):

Elf Aquitaine
Japex, the state-owned Japanese Exploration and Production Co.
Petro-Canada
Ultramar (Canada)

The US Treasury has allowed two American companies (Chevron, Coastal) to import Iranian crude.

Iraq

State Companies

The Oil Ministry oversees the nationalised oil industry through the Iraq National Oil Company (INOC). Autonomous companies under INOC include: State Company for Oil Projects (SCOP)—design and engineering of upstream and downstream projects; Oil Exploration Company (OEC)—exploration; Northern Oil Company (NOC) and Southern Oil Company (SOC)—upstream activities in northern/central and southern Iraq, respectively; State Organization for Oil Marketing (SOMO)—crude oil sales and OPEC relations; Iraqi Oil Tankers Company (IOTC).

Original Concession Holders

Iraq Petroleum Company (Mosul Oil Company and Basrah Oil Company), Royal Dutch/Shell, Anglo-Persian, CFP, Exxon, Mobil, Atlantic Richfield, Gulf Oil Corporation, Standard Oil of Indiana (Amoco), and Participations and Explorations Corp., under auspices of the Near East Development Company.

Recent Developments

US previously operating in Iraq includes Haliburton, Howe-Baker Engineering Inc., Mobil Oil, and Pullman-Kellogg.

Iraq's State Oil Marketing Organization (SOMO),—pending UN approval—is in discussions with: US companies Coastal Corp., Phoenix, Chevron Corp. and Mobil Corp.

Iraq has current contracts with Coastal, Russian Sidanco and France's Total SA.

The *Oil Daily* reports that Shell, BP, Chevron, and Coastal are among the companies interested in buying Iraqi crude.

Kuwait

State Companies

Subsidiaries of Kuwait Petroleum Corp. include: Kuwait Oil Co. (KOC), Kuwait National Petroleum Co., Petrochemical Industries Co. (PIC), Kuwait Oil Tanker Co., Kuwait Foreign Petroleum Exploration Co. (KUFPEC), and Kuwait Petroleum International (KPI, London).

Original Concession Holders

Kuwait Oil Co. Ltd., subsidiary of BO (Kuwait) Ltd., and Gulf Kuwait Co., Kuwait Shell Development Co. Ltd., owned by Royal Dutch/Shell Group.

For Kuwaiti portion of Neutral Zone

Offshore: *Arabian Oil Company Limited*, Japan Petroleum Trading Co. Ltd.

Onshore: *American Independent Oil Co.*, joint venture of Phillips Petroleum, Signal Oil and Gas, Ashland, J.S. Abercrombie, Sunray Mid-Continent Oil Co., Globe Oil and Refining Co., and Pauley Petroleum Inc.

Major Foreign Oil Company Involvement

British Petroleum Co. Plc

Chevron

Getty Oil Co.

Gulf Oil

Japan's Arabian Oil Co. (AOC)

Mobil Corp.

Royal Dutch/Shell,

Shell International Petroleum Co. Ltd.

Texaco

Total

Oman

State Companies

Petroleum Development Oman Ltd. (PDO) controls all oil resources. Oman Oil Company (OOC) is the overseas investment arm of the Ministry of Petroleum, until recently headquartered in Houston and headed by John Deuss.

Joint Ventures

Petroleum Development Oman Ltd. (PDO) controls all oil resources. PDO is a partnership between the Omani government (60 per cent), Shell Petroleum Co. Ltd. (34 per cent), Total CFP (4 per cent), and Partex (Oman) Corp. (2 per cent).

CXO Ltd. is a joint venture of Oman Oil Co. Ltd. and Caltex.

Original Concession Holders

Petroleum Development (Oman) Ltd., Shell Group, CFP, Participations and Explorations Corp., and John W. Mecom.

Mecom-Pure-Conoco, John W. Mecom, Pure Oil, Continental Oil.

Major Foreign Oil Company Involvement

There are two American concessionaires: Occidental/Gulf and Amoco. Ashland Oil manages Oman's sole refinery, and US firms lift Oman's crude.

Qatar

State Companies

The Qatar General Petroleum Corporation (QGPC).

Joint Ventures

QGPC owns 65 per cent of Qatar Liquefied Gas Co. (Qatargas) the rest of the interest is divided among France's Total SA. (10 per cent), Mobil Qatar Gas Inc. (10 per cent), Mitsui & Co. Ltd. (7.5 per cent), and Marubeni Corp. (7.5 per cent).

Qatargas Upstream, partners are Total, 20 per cent, Mobil 10 per cent, and Mitsui and Marubeni, 2.5 each.

QGPC holds 66.5 per cent of Ras Laffan LNG Co. (RasGas); Mobil 26.5 ; the Japanese companies Itochu Corp. and Nissho Iwai, respectively, 4 per cent and 3 per cent.

Qatar Vinyl Co. (25.5 per cent QGPC, 31.9 per cent QAPCO, 29.7 per cent Norsk Hydro, and 12.9 per cent Elf Atochem).

Qatar Fuel Additives Co. (50 per cent QGPC, 20 per cent Chinese Petroleum Corp., 15 per cent Lee Chang Yung Chemical Industry Corp., and 15 per cent International Octane Ltd.)

Original Concession Holders

Continental Oil Co. of Qatar, Continental Oil Co., Pure Oil Middle East Inc. (Union Oil of California).

Anglo Saxon Petroleum Company, Shell.

Major Foreign Oil Company Invoivement

ARCO Qatar Inc., (as operator for a consortium of Germany's Wintershall A.G. and Preussag A.G., British Gas Co., and Gulfstream Resources Canada Ltd. of Calgary)

Chevron Over-seas Petroleum (Qatar) Ltd. and its partner Magyar Olaj Gazi (MOL), the Hungarian Oil & Gas Co. Ltd.

Elf Petroleum Qatar.

Enron

Maersk Oil Qatar Co.

Marubeni

Methanex Corp. (Vancouver)

Mitsui

Mobil Oil Qatar

Mobil, MOL

Occidental Petroleum of Qatar Ltd.

Pennzoil Qatar Oil Co.

Phillips Petroleum Co.

Royal Dutch Shell

Wintershall

Saudi Arabia

State Companies

Saudi Aramco

SAMAREC

Petromin

Petromin Lubricating Oil Refining Co. (Luberef), (Mobil Oil Corp. holds a minority interest in this company).

Petromin Lubricating Oil Co.,

Saudi Arabian Basic Industries (SABIC)

Original Concession Holders

Arabian American Oil Company, Socal, Texas Oil, Jersey, Socony-Vacuum.

For Saudi portion of Neutral Zone: Getty Oil Co., Japan Petroleum Trading Co.

Joint Ventures

Star Enterprise (US)—Saudi Refining Inc. (50 per cent), Texaco (50 per cent);

Ssangyong Oil Refining Co. (S. Korea)—Saudi Aramco (35 per cent), Ssangyong (65 per cent); Luberef—Mobil (30 per cent) and Petrolube—Mobil (29 per cent).

Samref, an export fuels company—Mobil is a 50 per cent shareholder.

Subsidiaries: Aramco Services Co. (Houston), Aramco Overseas Co. (Netherlands), Saudi Petroleum International Inc. (New York), Saudi Petroleum Overseas Ltd. (London/Tokyo).

Major Foreign Oil Company Involvement

Mobil

Shell

UAE

State Companies

Abu Dhabi National Oil Company (ADNOC) has controlling interest in 21 domestic oil and natural gas companies.

Joint Ventures

Abu Dhabi Co. for Onshore Oil Operations (ADCO) is held by ADNOC (60 per cent) and a consortium comprising British Petroleum (BP) (9.5 per cent), Shell (9.5 per cent), Total (9.5 per cent), Exxon (4.75 per cent), Mobil (4.75 per cent), and Partex (2 per cent).

Abu Dhabi Marine Operating Company (ADMA-OPCO) is held by ADNOC (60 per cent) and a consortium comprising BP (14.7 per cent), Total (13.3 per cent), and Japan's Jodco (12 per cent).

Zakum Development Company (ZADCO) is operated by ADNOC (88 per cent) and a consortium (12 per cent) comprising BP, Jodco, and Total.

Original Concession Holders

Union Oil Co., venture of Union Oil Co. and Southern Natural Gas Co.

Abu Dhabi Marine Areas Ltd., BP, CFP, Continental.

Dubai Marine Areas Ltd., Continental Oil, BP, CFP, Deutche Erdol AG, Sun Oil Co.

Phillips-AGIP-Aminoil, joint venture of Phillips, AGIP, and Aminoil

Major Foreign Oil Company Involvement

BP

Caltex Petroleum Corp.

Mitsui & Co. Ltd.

Parrex

Pennzoil

Shell Gas BV

Total

Source: Thompson, Eric V. "Petroleum Archives Project", Arabian Peninsula and Gulf Studies Program, University of Virginia.

Annexure 1.2

Organisation of India's Energy Sector

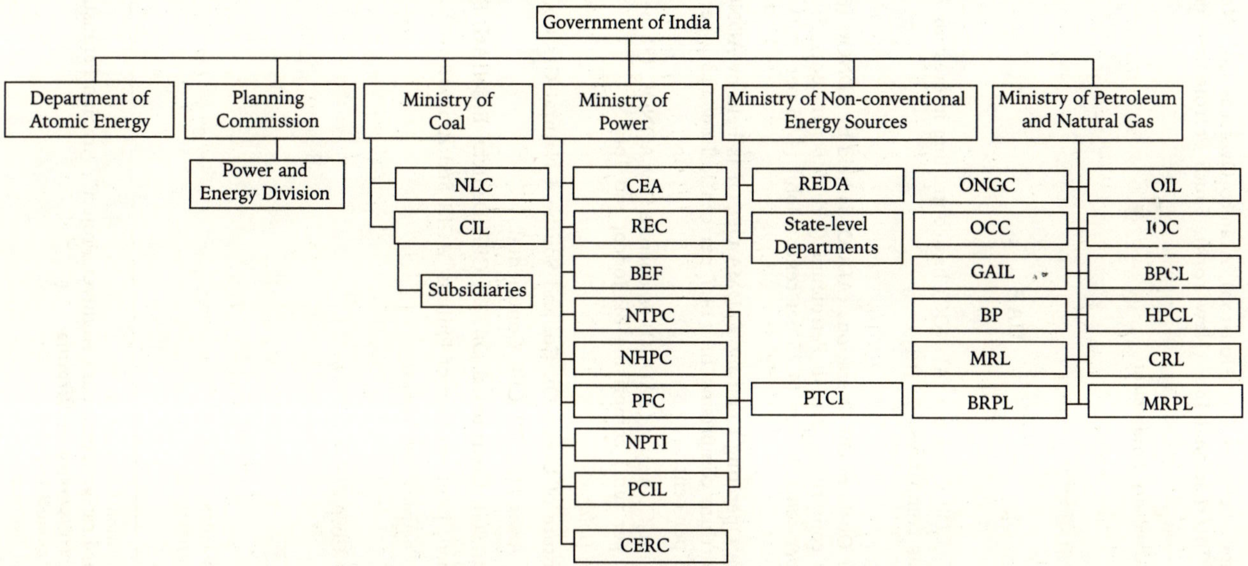

BPCL: Bharat Petroleum Corporation Ltd.
BEF: Bureau of Energy Efficiency
BRPL: Bongoigaon Refinery and Petrochemicals Ltd.
CEA: Central Electricity Authority
CERC: Central Electricity Regulatory Commission
CIL: Coal India Limited
CRL: Cochin Refineries Ltd.
DAE: Department of Atomic Energy
GAIL: Gas Authority of India Ltd.
HPCL: Hindustan Petroleum Corporation Ltd.
IOC: Indian Oil Corporation Ltd.
IREDA: India Renewable Energy Development Agency
IBP: Indo-Burmo Petroleum Company Ltd.
MRL: Madras Refineries Ltd.
MRPL: Mangalore Refinery and Petrochemicals Ltd.
MINES: Ministry of Non-conventional Energy Sources
NHPC: National Hydro-electric Power Corporation
NLC: Neyveli Lignite Corporation
NPTI: National Power Training Institute
NTPC: National Thermal Power Corporation
OCC: Oil Coordination Committee
OIL: Oil India Limited
ONGC: Oil and Natural Gas Corporation
PCIL: Powergrid Corporation of India Ltd.
PFC: Power Finance Corporation
PTCI: Power Trading Corporation of India Ltd.
REC: Rural Electrification Corporation

Annexure 1.3

Categorisation of Sedimentary Basins

*Category**	*Basin*	*Basinal Area (Sq.Km.)*		*Total*
		Onland	*Offshore*	
Up to 200m ISOBATH				
I	Cambay	51,000	2,500	53,000
	Assam Shelf	56,000	—	56,000
	Bombay Offshore	—	116,000	116,000
	Krishna Godavari	28,000	24,000	52,000
	Cauvery	25,000	30,000	55,000
	Assam-Arakan Fold Belt	60,000	—	60,000
	Rajasthan	126,000	—	126,000
	Sub Total	**346,000**	**172,500**	**518,500**
II	Kutch	35,000	13,000	48,000
	Andaman-Nicobar	6,000	41,000	47,000
	Sub Total	**41,000**	**54,000**	**95,000**
III	Himalayan Foreland	30,000	—	30,000
	Ganga	186,000	—	186,000
	Vindhyan	162,000	—	162,000
	Saurashtra	52,000	28,000	80,000
	Kerala-Konkan-Lakshadweep	—	94,000	94,000
	Mahanadi	55,000	14,000	69,000
	Bengal	57,000	32,000	89,000
	Sub Total	**542,000**	**168,000**	**710,000**
IV	Karewa	3,700	—	3,700
	Spiti-Zanskar	22,000	—	22,000
	Satpura-South Rewa-Damodar	46,000	—	46,000
	Narmada	17,000	—	17,000
	Deccan Syneclise	273,000	—	273,000
	Bhima-Kaladgi	8,500	—	8,500
	Cuddapah	39,000	—	39,000
	Pranhita-Godavari	15,000	—	15,000
	Bastar	5,000	—	5,000
	Chhattisgarh	32,000	—	32,000
	Sub Total	**461,200**	—	**461,200**
Total		**1,390,200**	**394,500**	**1,784,700**
	Deep Waters (Kori-Comorin 85° E Narcodam)	—	—	1,350,000
Grand Total		—	—	**3,134,700**

Notes: * Categorisation based on the prospectivity of the basin as presently known. The four recognised categories are basins which have:

I. Established commercial production.

II. Know accumulation of hydrocarbons but no commercial production as yet.

III. Indicated hydrocarbon shows that are considered geologically prospective.

IV. Uncertain potential which may be prospective by analogy with similar basins in the world. This categorisation will necessarily change with the results of further exploration.

Source: DGH, MoPNG, Govt. of India.

Annexure 1.4

Investment Opportunities in the Petroleum Sector

Under the new investment policy for different sectors announced in July 1991 for facilitating the inflow of foreign capital and to encourage entrepreneurs to invest in India, a number of policy initiatives have been taken by the Government of India, such as:

- Equity participation in commercial and industrial ventures has been freed from all restrictions and foreign companies can now invest up to 100 per cent of equity in different activities in the petroleum sector.
- Rupee convertibility on the current account.
- Deregulation and delicensing of various petroleum products in the country.
- Gradual decontrol of pricing and distribution.
- Freedom to form JVCs for the development of infrastructure and for marketing and refining activities.
- The procedure for obtaining industrial licenses has been greatly simplified. For obtaining industrial license, applications are to be submitted to the Secretariat for Industrial Approvals (SIA), Department of Industrial Policy & Promotion, Ministry of Commerce & Industry, Udyog Bhavan, and New Delhi-110011.
- Approvals will normally be available within six to eight weeks of filing the application. Empowered committees have been constituted to accord various approvals under a fast time-bound schedule.
- Under the New Industrial Policy, proposals for foreign investment need not necessarily be accompanied by foreign technology agreements.

All such proposals, including those proposing investments by NRIs or for 100 per cent export oriented units, are considered for approval by the Foreign Investment Promotion Board (FIPB). In case of composite proposals, i.e., proposals seeking other industrial approvals like industrial licenses, technical collaboration, etc. alongside approval for foreign investment, the FIPB provides composite clearance.

Pricing

The country has traditionally operated under an Administered Pricing Mechanism for petroleum products. This system is based on the retention price concept under which the oil refineries, oil marketing companies and the pipelines are compensated for operating costs and are assured a return of 12 per cent post-tax on net worth. Under this concept, a fixed level of profitability for the oil companies is ensured subject to their achieving their specified capacity utilisation. Upstream companies, namely ONGC, OIL and GAIL, are also under retention price concept and are assured a fixed return.

The administered pricing policy of petroleum products ensures that products used by the vulnerable sections of the society, like kerosene, or products used as feedstock for production of fertiliser, like naphtha, may be sold at subsidised prices.

Gradually, the Government of India is moving away from the administered pricing regime to market-determined, tariff-based pricing. Free imports are permitted for almost all petroleum products except petrol and diesel. Free imports are permitted for almost all petroleum products except petrol and diesel. Free marketing of imported kerosene, LPG and lubricants by private parties is permitted. It is contemplated that in a phased manner, all administered price products will be taken out of the administered pricing regime and the system will be replaced by a progressive tariff regime in order to provide a level playing field for new investments in a free and competitive market.

The Exim Policy

Imports

Importation of all petroleum products is permitted under the Open General Licensing Scheme, except for the following:

- Crude Oil
- Motor Spirit
- Diesel
- ATF
- FO
- Bitumen
- Imports permitted under freely tradable Special Import Licenses.

Exports

Exports of the following products are canalised through Indian Oil Corporation Ltd.

- ATF
- Bitumen

- Crude Oil
- Diesel
- Kerosene
- LPG
- Motor Spirit
- Naphtha
- Raw Petroleum Coke

All other products can be freely exported.

Map 1

New Significant Discoveries of Oil and Gas in India

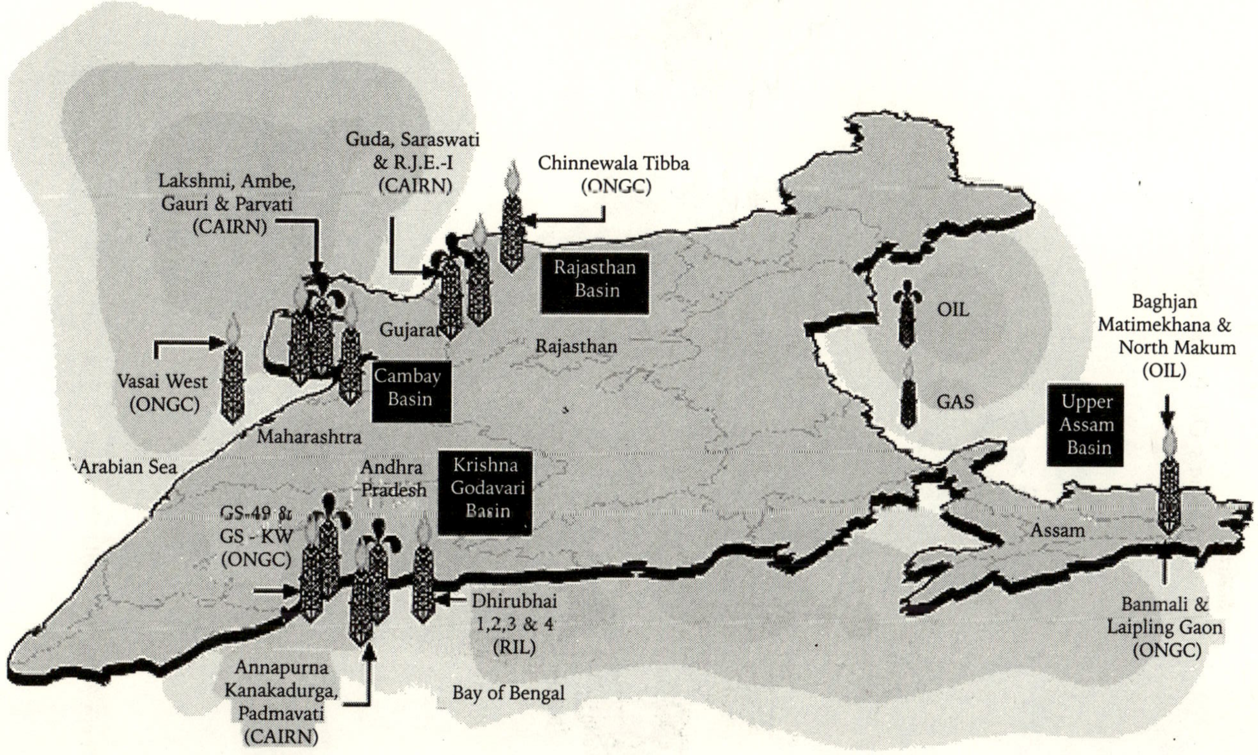

Source: Indian Express 25th Jan 2004.

Map 2

India's Oil Product Pipelines

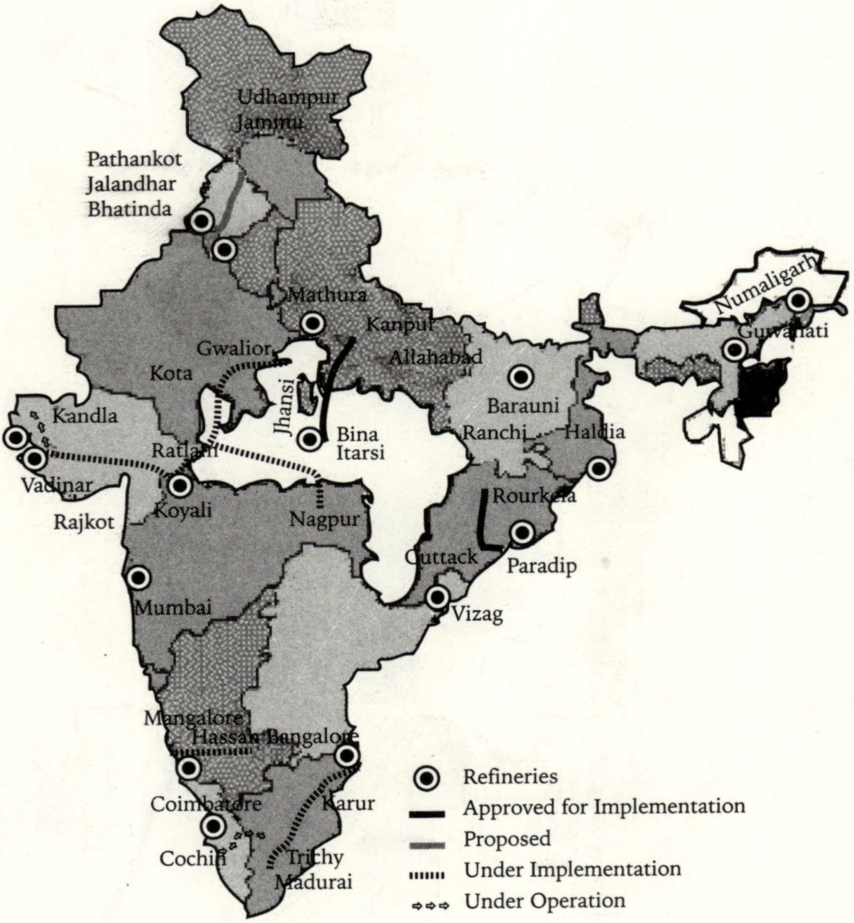

Source: TERI, New Delhi, 2003.

Map 3

Blocks Awarded under NELP I II III IV

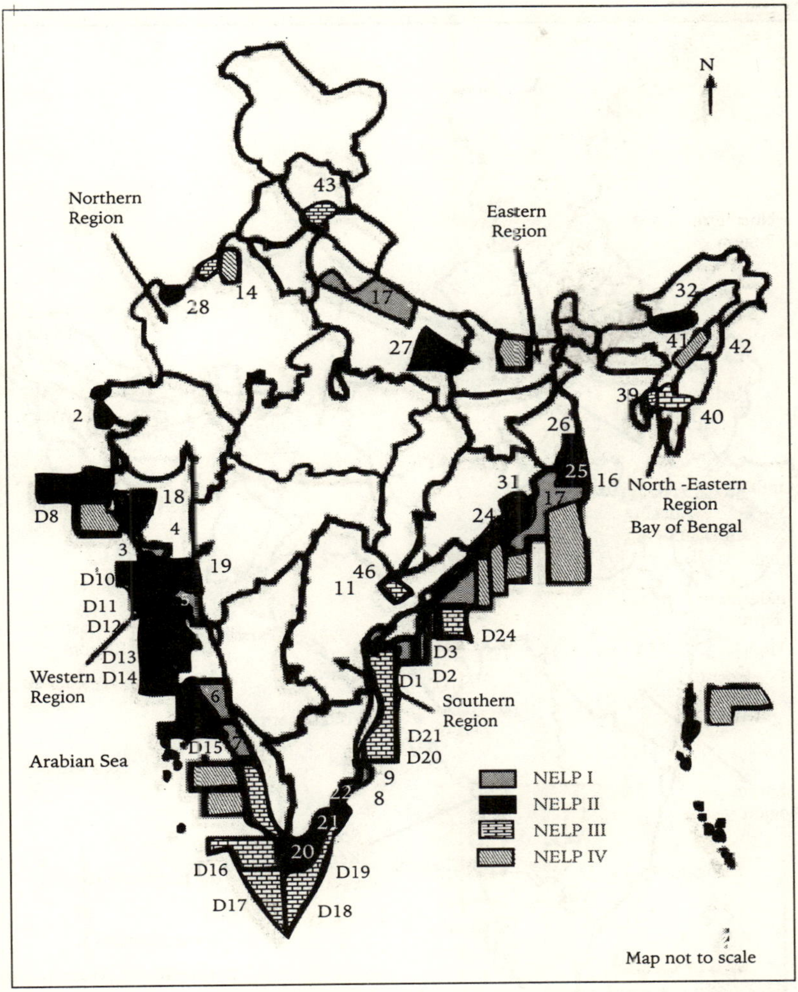

Source: DGH 2004.

Map 4

Crude Pipelines Existing and Proposed

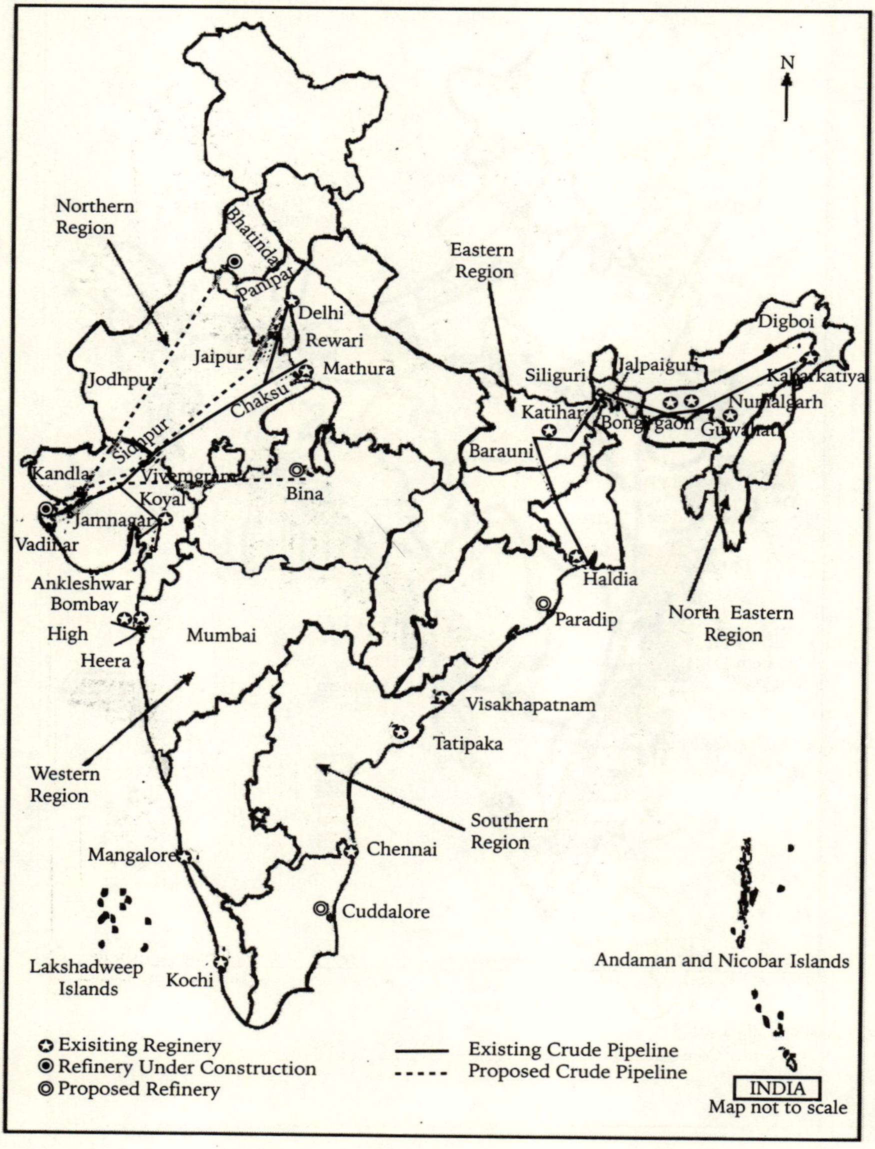

Map 5

Product Pipeline: Existing and Proposed

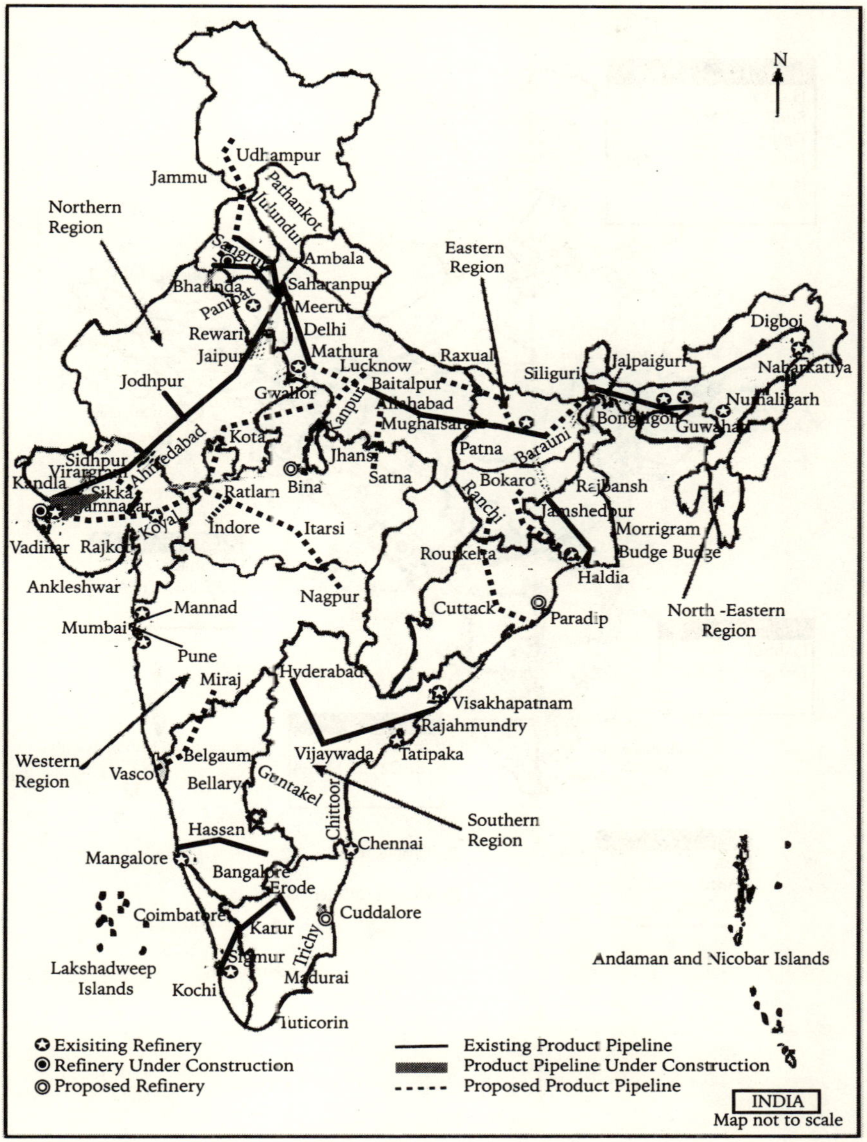

Map 6

Prominent LNG Terminals, Proposed Gas Import Pipelines and National Gas Grid

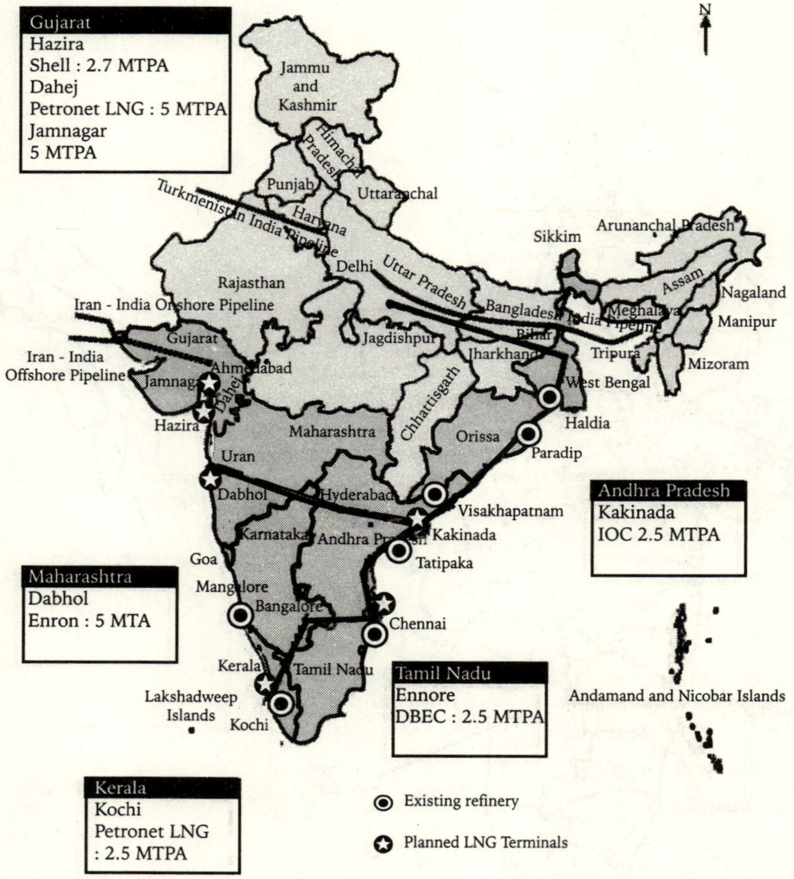

Map 7

HBJ Transmission System

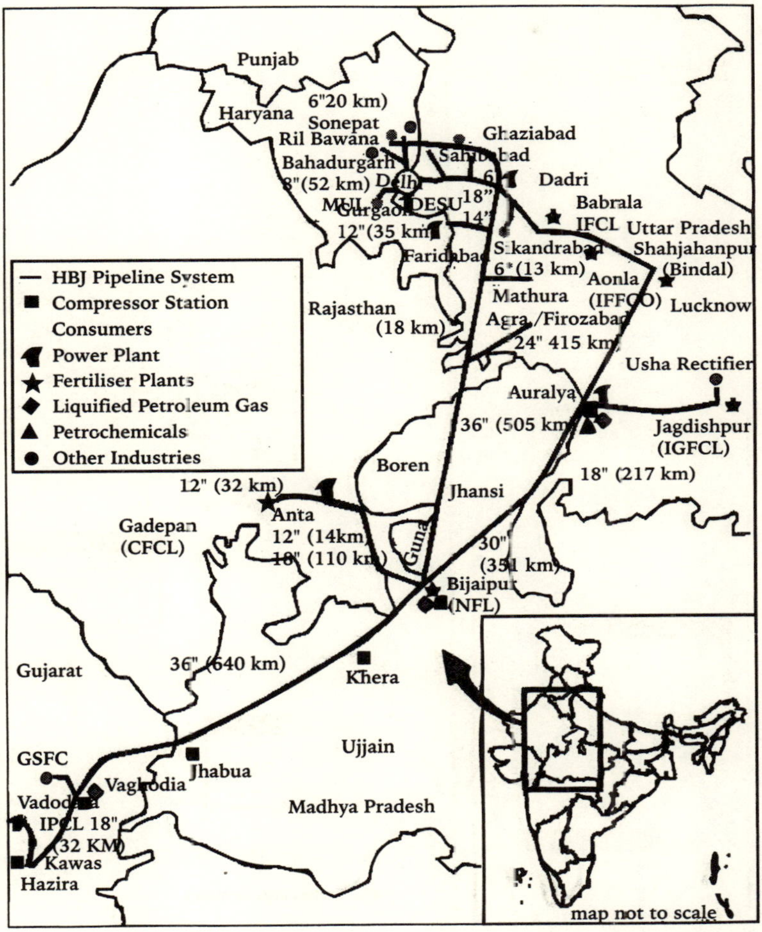

References

Primary Sources

Government of India (1996). *Restructuring Group Report.* New Delhi.

(2001). *Handbook on Indian Petroleum and Natural Gas Industry and Investment Scenario 2001.* New Delhi: India Book Centre.

International Monetary Fund (various years). *Direction of Trade Statistics Yearbook,1998-2003.* Washington DC.

———. *International Financial Statistics, 1998-2003.* Washington DC.

International Trade Centre (1995). *International Procurement of Crude Oil and Petroleum Products,* Guide No. 24, UNCTAD/WTC Import Management.

Ministry of Commerce (various years). *Annual Reports 1991-92–2001-2002.* New Delhi: Government of India.

Ministry of Finance (various years). *Annual Reports 2001-02–2002-03.* New Delhi: Government of India.

Ministry of Petroleum and Natural Gas (MoPNG), *Annual Report 1990-91–2002-2003.* New Delhi: Government of India.

———. (2000). *Hydrocarbon Vision 2025.* New Delhi.

Planning Commission (1998). *Ninth Five Year Plan Documents.* New Delhi: Government of India.

TERI (2002-03). *Indian Oil and Gas Conference (3rd & 4th) Papers.* New Delhi.

United Nations (various years). *Annual Yearbook of World Energy,* UN, (issues up to 1995). Paris.

Reports

Al-Harthy, Khalifa Bin (2002). "Oman's Foreign Policy and Relations with India", *GSP Guest Lecture Series,* GSP 2000. GSP, CWAAS, SIS, JNU. New Delhi.

Commercial and Economic Report for Qatar for the Month of March, 2001. http://www.trade-india.com

EIA (various years). *International Energy Outlook 2000 and 2001.* Washington DC: US Department of Energy.

———. (1999). *South Asia Regional Overview.* Washington DC: US Department of Energy.April.

El-Beblawi, Hazem (1983). "The Oil Decade: An Appraisal in Perspective", *The IBK Papers Series* No. 10. Kuwait: The Industrial Bank of Kuwait K.S.C. September, p.42.

FICCI-IDSA (2001). *India's Energy Security and Managing Oil Shock.* New Delhi: FICCI-IDSA. November.

GAO (1983). *Oil Supply Disruptions: Their Price and Economic Effects.* Washington DC.

ICRIER (1983). *Colloquium on Gulf Oil Exporting Countries and India: Trade and Investments.* New Delhi: Indian Council for Research on International Economic Relations.

IEA (1998). *Caspian Oil and Gas.* Paris: IEA/OECD.

———. (1999). *Monthly Oil Market Report,* January.

———. (1999). *Energy Policies of IEA Countries*. Paris: IEA/OECD.

———. (1995). *Middle East Oil and Gas*. Paris: IEA.

———. (2000). *Natural Gas Information 2000*. Paris: IEA/OECD.

———. (1995). *Oil Supply Security: The Emergency Response Potential of IEA Countries*. Paris: IEA/OECD.

———. (2001). "Safeguarding Energy Supply Security", in *Towards a Sustainable Energy*. Paris: IEA/OECD.

———. (2001). *Towards a Sustainable Energy Future*. Paris: IEA/OECD.

———. *World Energy Outlook 2002*. Paris: IEA/OECD.

———. (1996). *Asia Gas Study*. Paris: IEA.

MacDougall, Michael, and Peter T. Linder (1992). *Long Term Outlook for World Gas Trade: 1990-2015*. Calgary, Canada: Canadian Research Institute.

Mitra, A. (1990). *Oil and Natural Gas Explorations in India: Acceleration of Output and Private Sector Participation—A Package of Recommendations*. New Delhi: Business India Policy Unit.

Pant, Girijesh (2002). "India's Energy Security: The Gulf Factor", *GSP Occasional Paper Series*, GSP 2002/2. GSP, CWAAS, SIS, JNU. New Delhi.

Petroleum Economist (1995). "India: It's Energy Potential", *Petroleum Economist*. London.

Porter, Edward D. (1999). *Non-OPEC Supply and World Petroleum Markets: Past Forecasts, Recent Experience and Future Prospects*. Washington DC: American Petroleum Institute.

Tata Energy Research Institute (TERI) (various years). *TERI Energy Data and Directory Year Book 1998-99 to 2001-02*. New Delhi.

———. (2002). *Defining an Integrated Energy Strategy for India: A Document for Debate, Discussion and Action*. New Delhi.

———. (1999). *India's Energy Security*. New Delhi.

———. (2001). "Roadmap to Deregulation of the Indian Petroleum Industry", in *Reforms in Energy Sector*. New Delhi.

———. (2001). *TERI Directions, Innovations, and Strategies for Harnessing Action (DISHA)*. New Delhi.

United Nations (UN) (2001). *World Energy Assessment and the Challenge of Sustainability*. Paris.

———. (1999). *World Population Prospects: The 1998 Revision*.

World Bank (1993). *The East Asian Miracle: Economic Growth and Public Policy*. Oxford: Oxford University Press (OUP).

———. (1992). *World Development Report 1991*. Oxford: Oxford University Press (OUP).

Secondary Sources

Books

Abidi, A.H.H. (ed.) (1989). *Indo-Gulf Economic Relations: Patterns, Prospects and Policies*. New Delhi: Intellectual Publishers.

Adelman, M.A. (1993). *Economics of Petroleum Supply*. Cambridge, MA: MIT Press.

———. (1995). *The Genie Out of the Bottle: World Oil Since 1970*. Cambridge, MA: MIT Press.

Ahrari, Mohd. E. (1986). *OPEC: The Falling Giant*. The University Press of Kentucky.

Al-Chalabi, F.G. (1980). *OPEC and the International Oil Industry: A Changing Structure*. Oxford: Oxford University Press (OUP).

Al-Otaiba, Mana Saeed (1975). *OPEC and the Petroleum Industry*. London: Croom Helm.

Amuzegar, Jahangir (1999). *Managing the Oil Wealth: OPEC's Windfalls and Pitfalls*. New York: I.B. Tauris Publishers.

Bernad, P.D. (1998). *Asian Energy Chartbook: Checking the Pulse of the Asian Oil Industry*. New York: Goldman Sachs & Co.

Bhatia, R. (1986). *Energy Demand Management Policies in India.* Manila: Asian Development Bank. December.

Blair, John (1976). *The Control of Oil.* New York: Pantheon Books.

Bohi, Douglas R. and W. David Montgomery (1982). *Oil Prices, Energy Security and Import Policy.* Washington: Resources for the Future Inc.

Bradley, P.G. (1985). *The History of Global Energy Demand in the Perspective of Oil Trade.* MIT Centre for Energy Policy Research.

Chambers, Ann (1999). *Natural Gas and Electric Power in Non-Technical Language.* Tulsa, Oklahoma. : Penwell Pub. Co.

Cremer, Jacques and Djavad Salehi-Isfahani (eds.) (1991). *Models of the Oil Market.* Switzerland: Harwood Publishers.

Cyrus, Bina (1985). *The Economics of the Oil Crisis.* New York: Merlin Press Ltd.

Dadwal, Shebonti Roy (2003). *Rethinking Energy Security in India.* New Delhi: Knowledge World.

Dasgupta, B. (1971). *Oil Industry in India: Some Economic Aspects.* London: Frank Cass.

Datt, Ruddar and K.P.M. Sundaram (2001). *Indian Economy.* new Delhi: S. Chand & Company.

Deese, David A. and Joseph S. Nye (1981). *Energy and Security.* Cambridge: Ballinger Publishing Company.

Duncan, Raymond W. *et al.* (2002). *World Politics in the 21st Century.* New York: Longman.

Economic Intelligence Unit (EIU) (1983). *OPEC and the World Oil Outlook: Rebound of the Exporters?.* London.

Economides, Michael (2000). *The Color of Oil: The History, the Money and the Politics of the World's Biggest Business.* Texas: Round Oak Publishing Company, Inc.

ECSSR (ed.) (2000). *Caspian Energy Resources: Implications for the Arab Gulf.* UAE: ECSSR.

———. (2001). *The Future of Natural Gas in the World Energy Market.* Abu Dhabi, UAE: ECSSR.

El Azhary, M.S. (ed.) (1984). *The Impact of Oil Revenues on Arab Gulf Development.* Croom Helm: University of Exeter.

El Mallakh, Ragei (ed.) (1981). *OPEC: Twenty Years and Beyond.* New York: West View Press, Inc.

El-Beblawi, Hazem (1983). "The Oil Decade: An Appraisal in Perspective", *The IBK Papers,* Series No. 10. Kuwait: The Industrial Bank of Kuwait K.S.C.. September.

Ferrier, R.W. and A. Fursenko (eds.) (1989). *Oil in the World Economy.* New York and London: Routledge.

Field, Michael (1975). *A Hundread Million Dollars a Day.* London: Sidgwick and Jackson.

Gilbar, Gad G. (1997). *The Middle East Oil Decade and Beyond.* London: Frank Cass.

Hartshorn, J.E. (1993). *Oil Trade: Politics and Prospects.* Cambridge: Cambridge University Press.

Harvey, D. (1989). *The Condition of Post Modernity,* Blackwell, Oxford, p.241.

Heal, Geoffrey and Graciela Chichilnisky (1991). *Oil and the International Economy.* Oxford: Clarendon Press.

Henderson, P.D. (1975). *India: The Energy Sector.* New York: Oxford University Press for the World Bank.

Hogan, W.W. (1992). *Oil Market Adjustments and the New World Order.* Cambridge, Massachusetts, USA: Centre for Business and Government, John F. Kennedy School of Government, Harvard University.

Hoopes, Stephanie M. (1997). *Oil Privatization, Public Choice and International Forces.* London: Macmillan Press Ltd.

Horsenell, Paul and Robert Mabro (1993). *Oil Markets and Prices: The Brent Market and the Formation of World Oil Prices.* Oxford: Oxford University Press.

Horsnell, Paul (1997). *Oil in Asia: Markets, Trading, Refining, and Deregulation.* Oxford: OUP for Oxford Institute for Energy Studies.

Jasjit Singh (ed.) (2001). *Oil and Gas in India's Security.* New Delhi: Knowledge World and Institute for Defence Studies and Analysis (IDSA).

Jeremy, Russel (1983). *Geopolitics of Natural Gas.* Cambridge: Ballinger Publishing Company.

Jones, R.J.B. (1995). *Globalisation and Interdependence in the International Economy.* London: Pinter.

Joshi, Vijay and I.M.D. Little (1996). *India's Economic Reforms, 1991-2001.* New Delhi: OUP.

Katouzian, Homa (1981). *The Political Economy of Modern Iran.* NY and London: NY University Press.

Kent, Marian (1976). *Oil and Empire, British Policy and Mesopotamian Oil 1900-1920.* London: Macmillan Press.

Khan, Jawed Ahmad (1999). *India and West Asia: Emerging Markets in the Liberalization Era.* New Delhi: Sage Publications.

Lall, Sanjaya (1996). *Learning from the Asian Tigers, Studies in Technology and Industrial Policy* Basingstoke and Laos: Macmillan Press.

Levy, Walton J. (1982). *Oil Strategy and Politics, 1941-1981.* London: West View Press.

Luciani, Giacomo (1984). *The Oil Companies and the Arab World.* London: Croom Helm.

Mabro, R. (1998). *Oil Price Crisis of 1998.* Oxford: Oxford Institute for Energy Studies.

Manning, Robert A. (2000). *The Asian Energy Factor: Myths and Dilemmas of Energy, Security and the Pacific Future.* New York: Council on Foreign Relations.

Manoharan, S. (1974). *The Oil Crisis-End of an Era.* New Delhi: S. Chand Publishers Pvt. Ltd.

Marcus, A.A. (1992). *Controversial Issues in Energy Policy*, Vol. 2. New York: Sage Publications Inc.

Marcus, Alfred Allen (1992). *Controversial Issues in Energy Policy.* New York: Sage Publications Inc.

Mc Veigh, J.C. and J.G. Mordue (eds.) (1999). *Energy Demand and Planning,* Report No. 31, E&SPON, for the Watt Committee on Energy, NY and London.

Mehetre, M.G. (1990). *Energy Crisis in India.* Allahabad: Chugh Publications.

Mehta, Balraj (1974). *India and the World Oil Crisis.* New Delhi: Sterling Publishers Private Ltd.

Mikdashi, Zuhayr (1966). *A Financial Analysis of Middle East Oil Concessions, 1901-1965.* New York: Praeger Publishers.

———. (1972). *The Community of Oil Exporting Countries.* New York: : Cornell University Press and Itchaca Press.

———. (1986). *Transnational Oil: Issues, Policies and Perspectives.* London: St. Martin's Press.

Mitchell, J.V. (2002). *Renewing Energy Security.* London: The Royal Institute of International Affairs, Sustainable Development Programme. July.

Mitchell, John *et al.* (1996). *The New Geopolitics of Energy,* The Royal Institute of International Affairs, London.

Nazli, Choucri (1981). *International Energy Futures: Petroleum Prices, Power and Payments.* London: MIT Press.

Niblock, Tim and Rodney Wilson (eds.) (1999). *The Political Economy of the Middle East,* Vol. I, Economic Development. Cheltenham: Edward Elgar Publishing Ltd..

Noreng, Oystein (1978). *Oil Politics in the 1980s: Patterns of International Cooperation.* USA: McGraw Hill Book Company.

Norouha, L. (1989). *Oil Exploration and Development in India 1974-75–1986-87.* New Delhi: TERI.

Nye, Joseph S. Jr. (2000). *Understanding International Conflicts: An Introduction to Theory and History,* 3rd Edition. New York: Longman.

Odell, P.R. (1986). *Oil and World Power,* 8th Edition. Harmondsworth: Penguin.

Oweiss, Ibrahim M. (2000). *The Arab Gulf Economies.* UAE: ECSSR.

Owen, Roger and Sevket Pamuck (1998). *A History of Middle East Economies in the Twentieth Century.* London: I.B. Tauris Publishers.

Pachauri, R.K. (1985). *The Political Economy of Global Energy.* New Delhi: OUP.

Pant, Girijesh (1996). *The Arab Gulf Economies*. New Delhi: Haranand Publishers.

Pasha, A.K. (ed.) (1999). *Perspectives on India and Gulf States*. New Delhi: Détente Publishers.

Pees, S.T. (ed.) (1989). *History of the Petroleum Symposium Guidebook*. Titusville: American Association of Petroleum Geologists.

Penrose, Edith T. (1968). *The Large International Firm in Developing Countries: The International Petroleum Industry*. London: Allen and Unwin.

Penrose, Edith (1971). *The Growth of Firms, Middle East Oil and Other Essays*. London: Frank Cass & Co. Ltd.

Peterson, J.E. (1983). *The Politics of Middle East Oil*. Washington DC: Middle East Institute.

Rachkov, Boris (1967). *Oil Nationalism and Imperialism*. New Delhi: People's Publishing House.

Randell, Stephen J. (1976). *United States Foreign Oil Policy, 1919-1948*. Kingston and Montreal: McGill–Queen's University Press.

Rouhani, Fuad (1971). *A History of OPEC*. New York: Prager Publishers.

Rybczynski, T.M. (1976). *The Economics of the Oil Crisis*. London: Macmillan.

Sepro, Joan E. and Jeffry A Hart (1997). *The Politics of International Relations*, 5th Edition. New York: St. Martin's Press.

Shaffer, Ed (ed.) (1983). *The United States and the Control of World Oil*. New York: St. Martin's Press.

Shafik, Nemat (ed.) (1998). *Economic Challenges Facing the Middle Eastern and North African Countries: Alternative Futures*. London: Macmillan Press Ltd.

———. (ed.) (1998). *Prospects for Middle Eastern and North African Economies: From to Boom to Bust and Back?*. London: Macmillan Press Ltd., for Economic Research Forum for the Arab Countries.

Shojai, Siamack (ed.) (1995). *The New Global Oil Market: Understanding Energy Issues in the World Economy*. London: Praeger.

Shukri, Ghanem (1988). *OPEC: The Rise and Fall of an Exclusive Club*. London: KPI.

Sick, Gary G. and Lawrence G. Potter (eds.) (1997). *The Persian Gulf at the Millennium: Essays in Politics, Economy, Security and Religion*. London: Macmillan Press Ltd.

Smith, V.K. (1981). *Scarcity and Growth Reconsidered*. Baltimore, MD: John Hopkins University Press.

Tippe, Bob (1993). *Where's the Shortage?-A Non-Technical Guide to Petroleum Economics*. Oaklahoma: Penwell Books.

Tussing, A. and Bob Tippe (1995). *The Natural Gas Industry: Evolution, Structure and Economics*. Oaklahoma: Penwell Publishing Company.

Visvanath, S.N. (1990). *A Hundred Years of Oil: A Narrative Account of the Search for Oil in India*. New Delhi: Vikas Publishing House.

Wilkins, Mira (1970). *The Emergence of Multinational Enterprise: American Business Abroad From The Colonial Era to 1914*. Cambridge Mass: Harvard University Press.

Yergin, Daniel (1991). *The Prize: The Epic Quest for Oil, Money and Power*. New York: Simon & Schuster.

Articles

AFP (Agence France-Presse) (1998). "Gulf States can not Afford to Finance Another War", *Jordan Times*, February 16, p.10.

Acharya, K.K. *et al*. (1998). "Challenges in Deregulated Scenario", in *Hydro-Carbon Technology*, Centre for High Technology, August.

Aissaoui, Ali (2002). "Gas-Exporting Countries: Towards Cartelization", *MEES*, Vol. 45(32): D1-D3, August 12.

Al-Nasseri, HE Obaid Bin Saif (1999). "OPEC's Role in the Asia-Pacific Oil Supply in the Aftermath of the Economic Crisis", *OPEC Bulletin*, October, pp.4-6.

Al-Ajmi, Fahed M. (1990). "Effects of Socio-Political Events on OPEC's Market Share Stability", *Journal of Energy and Development*, Vol. 15(2): 275-85, Spring.

Amirahmadi, Hooshang (1996). "Oil at the Turn of the 21st Century", *Iranian Journal of International Affairs*, Vol. 8(1): 34-72, Spring.

Azhar, Mohd. (1996). "India and Oil Exporting Countries: Scope for Energy Cooperation", *OPEC Bulletin*, March, pp.4-6.

Bose, B.K. (1999). "Indian Oil Sector Transits into a Demanding Future-A Few Hindsights, Insights and Foresights", *Oil Asia Journal*, January-March, p.6.

Bhattacharya, A. (1997). "Bridging the Energy Gap in Asia: Experience of Strategic Alliances/Joint Ventures in India", *Oil Asia*, April-June-August, pp.10-12.

Bakhtiari, A.M. Samsam (1999). "The Price of Oil", *OPEC Review*, Vol. XXIII(1): 5, March.

Barnett, Steven and Rolando Ossowski (2002). "Operational Aspects of Fiscal Policy in Oil-Producing Countries", *IMF Working Paper* 02/177. Washington: International Monetary Fund.

Bahgat, Gawdat (2001). "The Geopolitics of Natural Gas", *OPEC Review*, September, p.278.

Chaudhury, Kiran Aziz (1989). "The Price of Wealth: Business and State in Labour Remittance and Oil Economics", *International Organization*, Vol. 27: 101-145.

Chhabra, Hari Sharan (1989). "Oil Price War: Over-Production is the Reason of Oil Crisis", *World Focus Monthly Discussion Journal*, Vol. 10(5), May.

Chalabi, Fadhil J. (2000). "Gulf Oil *vs*. The Oil of the Caspian Sea", in ECSSR (ed.), *Caspian Energy Resources: Implications for the Arab Gulf*. Chapter 8. pp.156. ECSSR: UAE.

Chaturvedi, B.K. (2004). "Domestic Resourcing of Energy, Gulf and Future of Global Energy", Paper Presented at the National Seminar *on India's Energy Security*. GSP, JNU. New Delhi. February 19-20.

Cordesman, Anthony H. (1999). "Are Energy Wars Still Possible?". Washington DC: Centre for Strategic and International Studies. February 1.

Dadwal, Shebonti Roy (1997). "India's Energy Situation: Crisis in the Making", *Strategic Analysis*, Vol. 21(6). New Delhi: IDSA. June.

———. (1999). "Energy Security", *Strategic Analysis:* 653-670, July.

David, S.R., "Saving America from the Coming Civil Wars", *Foreign Affairs*, Vol. 78: 103-16.

Ewing, B.T. *et al.* (2002). "Volatility Transmission in the Oil and Natural Gas Market", *Energy Economics*, Vol. 24(2): 525-538, March.

Fasano, Ugo (2001a). "With Limited Oil Resources, Oman Faces Challenges of Economic Diversification, Structural Reforms", *IMF Survey*, July 30, pp.254-57.

———. (2001b). "Sluggish Growth, Declining Oil Resources Prompt Qatar to Diversify Economy Away from Oil", *IMF Survey*, November 26, pp.382-84.

———. (2002a). "With Open Economy and Sound Policies, the U.A.E. Has Turned Oil 'Curse' into a Blessing", *IMF Survey*, October 21, pp.330-32.

———. (2002b). "Testing the Relationship Between Government Spending and Revenue: Evidence from GCC Countries", *IMF Working Paper* 02/201. Washington: International Monetary Fund.

Fasano, Ugo *et al.* (2003). "Monetary Union Among Member Countries of the Gulf Cooperation Council", *IMF Occasional Paper* No. 221. Washington: International Monetary Fund.

Fasano, Ugo and Qing Wang (2001). "Fiscal Expenditure Policy and Non-Oil Economic Growth: Evidence from GCC Countries", *IMF Working Paper* 01/195. Washington: International Monetary Fund.

Fasano, Ugo and Zubair Iqbal (2002). "Common Currency", *Finance & Development*, December, pp.42-45.

Fesharaki, Fereidun (1999). "Energy and the Asian Security Nexus", *Journal of International Affairs*, Vol. 53(1), Fall. New York: Colombia University.

Fesharaki, Fereiudin and Yamaguchi Nancy (1992). "Energy Supply and Demand Outlook in the Asia-Pacific Region", *Link*, 34(50), July 26.

Fesharaki, Fereidun, Allen Clark and Duangjai Intarapravich (1995). *Pacific Energy Outlook: Strategies and Policy Imperatives to 2010*. Hawaii: East-West Centre, Honolulu.

Franssen, Herman (2002). "Arab-US Energy Needs in Perspective", *MEES*, Vol. 45(37): D1-D7, September 16.

Gately, Dermot (1984). "A Ten Year Retrospective: OPEC and the World Oil Market", *Journal of Economic Literature*, Vol. 22(2), pp.11-14.

———. (1995). "Strategies for OPEC's Pricing and Output Decisions", *The Energy Journal*, Vol. 10(3).

Gause, Gregory F. (1997). "The Gulf Conundrum: Economic Change, Population Growth, and Political Stability in the GCC States", *The Washington Quarterly*, Vol. 20(1): 145-65.

Goswami, Rajnish (1998). "India's Oil Needs: Scope for Gulf Suppliers in the Coming Century", *Oil Asia Journal:* 31-39, November-December.

Goyal, Rishi (2003). "Non-Oil Growth, Competitiveness, and the Labor Market", in *United Arab Emirates: Selected Issues and Statistical Appendix*. IMF Country Report.

Gray, Dale (1995). "Reforming the Energy Sector in Transition Economies: Selected Experience and Lessons", *World Bank Discussion Papers*, No. 246. Washington DC.

Hasan, Ashraful (1993). "Geo-Politics of Petroleum and Gulf Security", *Regional Studies*, 11(4): 28-46, Autumn.

IMF (1997). *IMF Financial Statistics*, January.

Jones, Mathew (2000). "Enron and Elf in the Mid-East Venture", *Financial Times*, March 2, on the web, *www.ft.com*.

Kemp, Geoffrey (1998-99). "The Persian Gulf Remains the Strategic Price", *Survival*, Vol. 40(4): 132-49, Winter. International Institute for Strategic Studies, Washington DC.

Krichene, N. (2002). "World Crude Oil and Natural Gas: A Demand and Supply Model", *Energy Economics*, Vol. 24(2): 557-576, March.

Koyama, Ken (1995). "Outlook for Oil Supply and Demand in Asia Pacific Region and Role to be Played by Japan's Oil Industry", *Energy in Japan*, No. 132, March.

———. (1998). "Oil Supply Security in Asian Economies: Growing Oil Imports and Their Response Measure", *Energy in Japan*. Japan: Institute of Energy Economics (IEE). January.

Lichtblau, John H. (1994). "Oil Import and National Security: Is There Still a Connection", *Petroleum Research Foundation*. New York.

Look Japan (1998). "Necessary Interdependence: Building the Asian Energy Infrastructure", *Look Japan*, August.

Lynch, Micheal C. (2001). "Oil Market Structure and Oil Market Behaviour", *Middle East Economic Survey* (MEES), Vol. 43(52): D1–D11, December 25, 2000/44(1), January 1.

Majumdar, Manab (2003). "Symposium on Movement of Natural Persons", March 19. Tokyo. for FICCI, New Delhi.

Manning, Robert A. (2000). "The Asian Energy Predicament". *Survival*, Vol. 42(3), Spring. The International Institute for Strategic Studies.

MEES (1994). "The Investment Requirements for the Development of the Arab Oil and Gas Sector and Related Downstream Activities until the End of the Decade", Arab Petroleum Investment Corporation, presented at the *Fifth Arab Energy Conference*, Cairo, 7-10, May, *MEES*, Vol 45(12), May 27.

———. (2002). "Arab Countries Fail to Capture Proportionate Share of FDI", *MEES*, Vol. 45(11), March 18.

———. (2000). "Deadline Looms for IOCs Gas Proposals", *Middle East Economic Digest (MEED)*, Vol. 44(22): 8, June.

———. (1999). "Reforms Raise the Stakes for Investors", MEED Special Report, *MEED*, January 15, pp.9-13.

———. (1995). "KPC to Set up Indian Oil Refinery", *MEED*, January 27, p.21.

Mitchell, J.V. (1997). *Will Western Europe Face an Energy Shortage?*. Strasbourg: Energy Council of Europe, .

Mohan, C. Raja (1996). "Geopolitics and Energy Security", *Strategic Analysis*, Vol. 19(9): 1269-76. December.

Morse, Edward L. and James Richard (2002). "The Battle for Energy Dominance", *Foreign Affairs:* 16-31, March/April.

Nayar, Vineet (2000). "The Virtual Asset", *Business World* (Special Millennium Issue), January 17.

Neelanjana, Mitra (1992). "Energy Policy Planning in India: Case of Petroleum and Natural Gas", *Economic and Political Weekly*, Vol. 27(35): 192-95, August 29.

Odell, Peter R. (1997). "The Global Oil Industry: The Location of Production-Middle East Domination or Regionalization", *Regional Studies*, Vol. 31(3): 311-322.

Oil Asia Journal (1992). "Economic Liberalisation and the Oil Sector in India", *Oil Asia Journal:* 91-94, October-December.

"Oil, Technology and War in the Next Decade", Crustal Fluids GP/PE/GES 200, *Spring Quarter*, 1995/1996. *http://srb.stanford.edu/nur/classes/otw.html.*

Pant, Girijesh (1987). "Indo-Gulf Economic Relations: A Profile", *International Studies*, Vol. 24(3). New Delhi: Sage Publications.

———. (1999). "The Changing Gulf Market and India: Trends and Prospects", in A.K. Pasha (ed.), *Perspectives on India and Gulf States*, Détente Publishers, New Delhi, pp.112-126.

Petroleum Intelligence Weekly (1998). "Oil Market Intelligence (OMI)", *Petroleum Intelligence Weekly.* London. December.

Raja Mohan, C. (2003). "Is India Loosing the Gulf to China", *The Hindu*, February 13.

Ramcharan, H. (2002). "Oil Production Responses to Price Changes: An Empirical Application of the Competitive Model to OPEC and Non-OPEC Countries", *Energy Economics*, Vol. 24(2): 97-106, March.

Rao, Saudamini (2001). "The Indian Oil and Gas Sector Bracing for Deregulation", *Oil Asia Journal:* 25-54, January-April-June. Mumbai.

Reddy, B.S. and P. Balchandran (2002). "A Sustainable Energy Strategy for India Revisited", *Economic and Political Weekly (EPW)*: 5264-5269, December 28.

Rhodes, Anne (2000). "UAE Offsets Moves Westward", *OGJ*, Vol. 98(36), September 4, p.31.

Robert W. Fisher (1997). "The Future of Energy", *The Futurist*, September-October.

Roy Choudhury, Rahul (1995). "Sea Power and Indian Security", *Brassey's*. London. p.89.

Sadek, Ali T. and Ali A. Bolbol (2001). "Capital Flows, FDI and Technology Spillovers: Evidence from Arab Countries", *World Development Journal*, Vol. 29(12).

Salameh, Mamdouh G. (1997). "The Geopolitics of Oil in the Asia-Pacific Region and its Strategic Implications", *OPEC Review:* 125-130, June.

Sayeed, Ausaf, "India-Qatar: Synergy in the Oil & Gas Sectors". *http://www.indianembassy.gov*

Siddiqui, Huma (2004). "Anti-West Feelings Have Gulf Companies Turning To India", *The Financial Express*, January 22.

Singh, Jasjit, "Geopolitics of Energy and Its Security", in Jasjit Singh (ed.), *Oil and Gas in India's Security.* New Delhi: Knowledge World and Institute for Defence Studies and Analysis (IDSA). p.13.

Srivastava, Leena and R. Goswami (1999). "The Indian Oil Experience: A Case Study", in ECSSR (ed.), *Privatisation and Deregulation in the Gulf Energy Industry.* UAE: ECSSR.

Steevens, Paul (1994). "Middle East Oil", *Middle East Economic Digest (MEED)*, Special Report, January 16, pp.3-8.

———. (1998). "Asia's Insatiable Oil Needs: Implications for the Gulf", *Oil & Gas Journal (OGJ):* 29-36, September 23.

Stevenson, Michael J. and Paul Suddaby (2000). "Middle East Petroleum Sector Offering More Foreign Investment Opportunities", *OGJ Special:* 34-40, February 14.

Tahmassebi, Cyrus H. (1995). "The Changing Structure of World Oil Markets and OPEC's Financial Needs", *OPEC Bulletin*, March.

TERI/FACTS (2003). "Gas Demand". Unpublished Internal Paper, New Delhi: TERI.

The Economist (1994). "Power to the People: A Survey of Energy", *The Economist*, June 18, p.14.

———. (1998). "The Suffering Gulf", *The Economist*, October 24.

———. (2001). "Energy and Geopolitics: Addicted to Oil", *The Economist*, December 13, on the site, *http://webs.wichita.edu*

The Frontline (2004). "Meeting the Challenge", *The Frontline*, Chennai, March 12, pp.55-56.

The Khaleej Times (1998). "The Coming World Oil Crisis", *The Khaleej Times*, June 16.

Weiner, R.J. (1991). "Is the World Oil Market 'One Great Pool'", *The Energy Journal*, Vol. 12(3): 95-108.

Yousefi, M.G. (1995). "The Impact of Oil Export on the Economy of OPEC Countries: An Empirical Investigation", *The Indian Economic Journal*, Vol. 42(3), January-March.

Zanoyan, Vahan (1997). "A Relevant Framework for Understanding the Global Crude Oil Market", in ECSSR (ed.), *Gulf Energy and the World: Challenges and Threats*. Abu Dhabi, UAE: ECSSR.

Newspapers and Journals

Asian Energy News: Energy, Economy and Environment Press Review. Thailand: CEERD, School of Environment Resource and Development, Asian Institute of Technology. Monthly Review.

Energy Policy. United Kingdom: Elsevier Sciences Limited.

International Oil and Gas Finance Review 1999. UK: Euro Money Publications.

Monthly Review of Indian Economy and Foreign Trade Review of India. Mumbai: Centre for Monitoring Indian Economy (CMIE).

Middle East Economic Digest (MEED). UK.

Middle East Economic Survey (MEES). Nicosia, Cyprus.

Middle East International (Monthly). London.

Natural Resource Forum. UN Journal.

Oil and Gas Journal (OGJ). Tulsa, Okalahoma.

Oil Asia. Mumbai.

OPEC Annual Statistical Bulletin (Annual). Vienna: OPEC.

OPEC Bulletin (Bi-Monthly).

OPEC Review (Quarterly Journal). London: Blackwell Publishers for OPEC.

Oxford Energy Forum (Quarterly Journal). Oxford: Oxford Institute for Energy Studies.

Petroleum Economist, London

Strategic Analysis and *Strategic Digest*. New Delhi: Institute for Defence Studies and Analyses.

Tata Energy Data and Directory Yearbook (TEDDY). New Delhi: TERI.

TERI Information Digest on Energy (TIDE) (Monthly).

TERI Newswire (Monthly).

The International Studies . New Delhi: Journal of the School of International Studies, Jawaharlal Nehru University.

The Frontline, Chennai.

The India Today, New Delhi.

The Times of India, New Delhi.

The Hindu, New Delhi.

The Financial Times, New Delhi.

The Indian Express, New Delhi.

The Hindustan Times, New Delhi.

The Economic Times, New Delhi.

World Oil Market Report (Monthly). Paris: IEA.

as in Newpapers Website References

http://www.meadev.nic.in

http://www.hinduonnet.com

http://www.ikcc.org

http://www.eia.doe.gov

http://www.iea.org

http://www.trade-india.com

http://www.indembassyuae.org

http://www.indiaonestop.com

http://www.cgijeddah.com

http://www.gasandoil.com

http://www.oilcrisis.com

http://www.let.leidenuniv.nl

http://www.nasscom.org/

Index

A

Abd al-Aziz Ibn Saud 47
Abu Dhabi National Oil Co. 221, 399
Administered Pricing Mechanism 189, 402
AGIP 51, 55, 390, 399
Ahmed, Kamaluddin 328
al-Thani, Sheikh Hamad Bin Khalifa 322
American 'Majors' 43, 26, 48, 50
American oil history 43
Anglo-Iranian Oil Company 49, 50, 388
Arab Human Development Report 334
Arabian light crude 207
Aramco (Arabian American Oil Company) 44, 45, 48, 216, 217, 238, 239, 378, 379, 383, 386, 387, 393, 393, 398, 399
ASEAN 31, 107, 108, 111, 113, 373, 373
Asia Pacific 72, 88-90, 92, 93, 97, 98, 100, 106, 110, 115, 116, 131, 132, 140, 204, 280, 369
Asian energy community 359
Asian marker 351
Asian Premium 351
Asia's energy future 354
Avoidance of Double Taxation Agreement 322

B

Bilateral Investment Promotion and Protection (BIPA) 322
BP 45, 50, 66, 67, 81, 217
BP Amoco 220, 221
Burma-Shell Refineries Ltd. 151

C

Caltex Oil Refinery 151
Carlsberg-Namotas 153, 155
Chevron 45, 68, 217
Club of Rome 80
CNG 180, 181
commercialisation 66
commodity ambivalent 38
Compagnie Francaise des Petroles 50
Confederation of Indian Industry 322, 342
consortia 44, 80
Consulate General of India 341
Continental Oil Company 42
costs of interdependence 228, 251

D

demand management practices (DMPs) 346
diplomacy, economic or resource 350
Directorate General of Hydrocarbons 164
Dolphin 219, 221
Drake, Colonel Edwin 41
dual economy 117
Dubai market 351

E

Eastern Hemispheres 57
Economic and Social Commission for Western Asia (ESCWA) 340
economy, new 117, 336, 338
Emirates National Oil Co. 222

energy
dependence 251
import dependence 251
intensity of GDP 110
intensive manufacturing 105
interdependence 32, 33, 35, 150-250, 287-289, 299, 307, 332, 360, 361
security 32, 33, 35,114, 116, 122, 128, 251-305, 307, 322, 345, 348-54, 358-61, 365, 368, 370, 371
debate 32, 255, 262, 263, 291
dilemma 116
externality 278
strategy 345, 348, 349, 351, 352
transition 39, 119, 122
Energy Charter Treaty 350, 351
ENI 51, 55, 160, 220
energy security strategy quadrant model (ESSQM) 349
environmental imperative 61
European Union (EU) 132, 349. 372
Exxon 42, 263
ExxonMobil 67, 68, 219, 220, 221

F

'fifty-fifty' agreements 49
Forum of the Gas Exporting Countries 282
four little dragons 104
free on board 188
free rider problem 130
free trade agreement, bilateral 313, 314

G

G7 111
Ghamdi, Saleh Mohd Al 328
Gulf 32, 45, 49, 72, 75, 76, 81, 83, 84, 87, 96, 114, 115, 127, 128, 131, 132, 143, 146, 148, 192, 197, 200, 202-07, 210, 217, 222, 225,-27, 230-33, 236, 237, 239. 248, 251, 254, 256-58, 262, 266, 267, 269,-72, 276, 279, 285-90, 293, 302-04, 307, 308, 311, 312, 328, 332-35, 338, 341, 351, 352, 354, 360-74
Gulf Cooperation Council (GCC) 32-35, 72, 87, 129, 132, 133, 135-48, 266-77, 197, 199, 203-05, 207, 209, 210, 212, 213-17, 221-231, 236, 238, 242, 247-49, 251, 252, 257, 259, 260, 284, 293, 303, 304, 307-15, 318, 324, 326-34, 340-43, 351, 361, 366-74
Gulf knowledge society 340
Gulf War (1990-91) 161, 162, 202, 217, 224, 260, 277, 296, 319
Gulbenkian, Calouste 47
'Mr. Five-Per Cent' 47

H

human resource development 136, 246, 331, 332, 333, 335
hydrocarbon vision 2025, India 126, 179, 186, 300

I

ideal types 84
independent grey cells 80
Indraprastha Gas Ltd. (IGL) 181
India-Kuwait Chamber of Commerce (IKCC) 319
Indian Refinery Limited 151
India's exports to the GCC 309, 315
Indo-Gulf economic ties 311
Indo-Saudi Joint Business Council 324
Indo-Stanvac Petroleum Project 154
Information Technology Enabled Services (ITES) 338
Iran Oil Participants (IOP) 50, 51
Iran-Pakistan-India (IPI) 348, 355
Iraq Petroleum Company 44
interdependence
benefits of 228, 304
economic 228
energy 32, 33, 35, 150-250, 287-289, 299, 307, 332, 360, 361
International Energy Agency (IEA) 39, 82, 112-114, 143, 184, 225, 226, 259, 268, 272, 276, 277, 286, 288, 350, 360
International Energy Forum Secretariat (IEFS) 350

J

Jebel Ali 222
Joint Commission for economic, trade, scientific, technical and cultural cooperation (JCM) 324
joint ventures 33, 116, 189, 192, 195, 221, 232, 239, 240, 319, 324, 331, 364

K

Kissinger, Henry 78, 82
knowledge society, global 339
Kuwait Oil Company 45

L

liquid revolution 37
long-term contacts 63

M

Majlis 49
majors 34, 37, 41-44, 46-51, 54, 55, 56, 62-64, 68, 78-81, 84, 156-58, 193, 220, 233, 236-38
  non-majors 50, 51
  order of the majors 84
Malviya, Keshava Deva 150
market friendly view 104
mesoeconomic reforms 162
Mexico energy debate 40
Mahanagar Gas Ltd. (MGL) 181
Ministry of Petroleum and Natural Gas (MoPNG) 190
Mobil 42, 48, 192, 263
Mossadeq's government 45
mutual dependence 75, 227, 228, 304
Myanmar-Bangladesh-India (MBI) 348

N

NASSCOM 337, 341
National Energy Policy Development 254
National Iranian Oil Company (NIOC) 49, 50, 158
National Small Industries Corporation (NSIC) 322
Near East Development Corporation (NEDC) 43, 47
Nehruvian vision 151
neo-imperialism 54
neoclassical economic view 103
new exploration licensing policy (NELP) 164, 166, 234, 351, 364
non-government organisations 61
North Sea Brent 232

O

OECD 60, 63, 64, 69, 71, 72, 75, 82, 99, 100-03, 112, 143, 211, 267, 269, 286, 287
  non-OECD 71, 102, 278
Oil and Natural Gas Commission (ONGC) 151, 154, 159, 164, 166, 168, 179, 193
oil
  and gas regime, global 34, 37-85, 87, 129, 140, 141, 147, 149, 223, 227, 229, 248, 263, 269, 285, 307, 326, 343, 361, 363, 366-68
  cartel 53, 155, 157, 161, 260
  concessions 39, 40, 43, 49, 160
  crisis, first 58, 87, 200, 268
  glut 84
  industry, integrated 57, 155
  industry restructuring group 190
  intensity of 110
  'new' high-cost 204
  order, new 84
  pool accounts 189
  price spikes 259, 268
  regime, first 59, 73
  regime, second 58, 59, 74, 75,
  regime, third 79
  reserves, proven 201, 212, 220
  shock, reverse 83, 84
  supply disruptions 260, 268, 269
Oil Coordination Committee (OCC) 189, 191
Oil Cost Review Committee 189
Oil India 151, 154, 158
oligopolistic status 56

ONGC Videsh Ltd. 298, 300, 347
OPEC 31, 39, 51, 52, 54-61, 63, 64, 70-85, 87, 96, 129-32, 137, 141, 142, 146, 197, 200-10, 212, 221, 224, 226, 230, 256, 258, 260, 265-68, 270-76, 279, 282-84, 288, 350, 361, 365, 366, 372
  non-OPEC 71, 72, 79, 83, 87, 141, 143, 205, 207, 208, 212, 224, 264-67, 271, 272, 275, 276, 365,
    supplies 83, 207, 226, 366
Outward Direct Investment 331

P

Pan-regional energy cooperation 359
paper market 64, 143
participation principle 56
participation process 55
pipeline-based trade 97
politics of the budget 141
posted prices 52, 54, 58, 59

Q

Qatar Chamber of Commerce and Industry (QCCI) 322
quota principle 130

R

Reading & Bates 153, 155
Red Line Agreement 44
Reliance Industries Ltd. 347
resource nationalism 54, 59, 335
resources implications 105
Rockefeller, J.D 42

S

Sam Reno Peace Conference Agreement 46
Saudi Arabia 45, 47-49, 54, 60, 61, 75, 77, 79, 129, 130, 132, 133, 136-39, 145, 202, 203, 205, 206, 210, 215,-17, 220, 221, 224, 241, 254, 267, 271, 272-76, 289, 290, 300, 302, 309, 310, 324, 325, 328-30, 350, 361, 373
  Saudi policy 275
self-sufficiency imperative 61
sellers' market 61, 353
sensitivity 228, 229, 252, 280
sovereign-hierarchical 85
Standard Oil Company of New Jersey (SONJ) 42, 43, 46-48,
Standard Oil of California (SOCAL) 42, 47, 48,
Standard Oil of Indiana 42
Standard Oil of New York 42
Standard Oil Trust 42
supply complacency 142, 143
swing producer 205, 216
SWOT analysis 34, 149

T

take-or-pay contracts 281, 282
TEESE 182
terror premium 38
TotalFinaElf 219-21
transnational-competitive 85
Truman Doctrine 76
Turkmenistan-Afghanistan-Pakistan-India 348

U

Union Oil of California (Unocal) 193, 299, 300

V

valued stock account (VSA) 188

W

Western Hemispheres 57
wholly owned subsidiaries 331
World Summit the Information Society (WSIS) 340
WTO 40, 313, 314

Z

zero sum 228
  non-zero sum 228